The Catholic Faith

The Catholic Faith

Rev. Robert J. Fox

Our Sunday Visitor, Inc.
Huntington, Indiana 46750

Nihil Obstat:
Rev. James M. Joyce
Censor Librorum

Imprimatur:
✠Paul V. Dudley, D.D.
Bishop of Sioux Falls
November 3, 1983

Excerpts from *The Jerusalem Bible*, copyright © 1966 by Darton, Longman & Todd, Ltd., and Doubleday & Company, Inc., used by permission of the publisher. Excerpts from *Vatican II: The Conciliar and Post Conciliar Documents*, copyright © 1975 by Costello Publishing Company, Inc., and Reverend Austin Flannery, O.P., used by permission of the publisher.

Library of Congress Catalogue No: 83-61889
ISBN 0-87973-614-3

Printed in the United States of America

Topical Table of Contents

Church Still Exists Since Jesus Is God / Oneness in Faith Needed to Convert the World / The Church Is Necessary for Salvation / Membership in the True Church by Desire / Church Is Holy in Founder and Offers Members Holiness / The True Church Must Be Universal / Church Is Apostolic in Its Origin / Heresy of Modernism

Chapter 13: *Divine Liturgy and the Sacraments of the Church* / 177

Public Divine Worship of the Community / Liturgy Renews Faith / Jesus Christ the Priest Is Present in Liturgy / New Covenant Sacrifice Replaces Old Covenant Sacrifice / Liturgy Is an Exercise of the Priesthood of Christ / Function of the Liturgy / The Priest Acts in the Person of Jesus Christ / Sacraments Are the Acts of Christ Extended in Time and Space / Sacraments Give Glory to God and Grace to Man / Sacraments Contain the Power of Christ Which They Signify / Seven Sacraments Have Seven Purposes

Chapter 14: *Baptism and Confirmation* / 186

The Three Indelible Seals of Jesus Christ / Baptism Is Essential for Salvation / Priesthood of the Faithful / Powers of the Baptismal Seal / Indelible Seal for Honor and Glory or for Shame / Radical Change in a Person Who Is Baptized / Baptism Is the Door to the Church / Baptism of Water, Blood and Desire / Baptism Cannot Be Repeated / Confirmation Makes One an Adult Christian / Confirmation Gives Grace to Witness to Christ / Confirmation Gives One a Sense of Mission

Chapter 15: *Confession — Sacrament of Reconciliation* / 195

Guilt Gives One the Natural Desire to Confess / Sacrament of Reconciliation / Seal of the Confessional / Christ's Easter Gift to the Church / Jesus Himself Forgives Sin in the Sacrament of Reconciliation / Confession Is Like a Second Baptism / Absolution Is God's Sign of Forgiveness / Confession Must Be Complete / Sorrow for Sin Is Essential / Firm Intention to Avoid Sin Required / Sacramental Confession Required for Grievous Sin / Sin Is Social / Communal Penance Services / Frequent Confession Desirable

Chapter 16: *Holy Eucharist — Sacrament* / 205

Different Kinds of the Presence of Jesus Christ / Only Species of Bread and Wine Remain After Consecration / Real Presence of Jesus Christ in Holy Eucharist / Transubstantiation / The Sacrament of the Holy Eucharist Continues with the Preservation of the Species / Church Fathers and the Holy Eucharist / The Holy Eucharist Is the Mystery of Faith / Permanent Presence of Eucharistic Jesus / Adoration of "Latria" Due the Holy Eucharist / Visits to the Blessed Sacrament / Body of Christ Is Inseparable from His Divinity / The Whole Christ Is Present Under Either Species and in Each Part / Holy Eucharist Is Primary Sacrament for Growth in Grace / Holy Eucharist Is the Fountain of All Graces / Effects of Holy Communion / Preparation for Holy Communion / Thanksgiving After Reception of Holy Communion

Chapter 17: *The Holy Eucharist as Sacrifice* / 219

First Act of Christ's Soul / The Mass Perpetuates the Sacrifice of the Cross / Jesus Christ Died Physically but Once / Old Covenant Forms of Sacrifice / The Sacrifice of Melchizedek Foreshadowed the Mass / Priesthood of Jesus Christ Is Eternal / Perpetual Sacrifice of the New Covenant / Twofold Consecration Necessary for Sacrifice / Sacrifice of the Mass Is an Unbloody Sacrifice / Sacrifice of the Mass Makes Present the Sacrifice of the Cross / Sacrifice of the Mass Is Offered to God Alone / The Mass Is the Sacrifice of the Church / Mass Is a Gift-Exchange with God the Father / Fruits of the Sacrifice of the Mass / Obligation to Participate in the Sacrifice of the Mass

Introduction

This book, *The Catholic Faith*, grew out of a successful television series of inquiry classes which the author produced before a live audience in Detroit. The series has been appearing on the Eternal Word Network. These classes now have been extended into a more formal presentation by means of this volume, which carefully documents sources.

Teaching aids available with the use of this book are available in the form of an audio-cassette album of 24 lessons, each lesson approximately 33 minutes long, given by the author. The entire album is available for $70 from Marian Media, Box 20, Redfield, SD 57469. Each cassette lesson, delivered in a lively, informal manner to stimulate study, corresponds exactly with each chapter of this book. The album is titled: *Instructions in the Catholic Faith*.

For those who want both sound and picture, the original television classes are available in 26 programs of one-half hour each for both VHS and Beta-Max TV attachments. Again, each televised class corresponds with the chapters of this book, except that there are two additional TV programs. Lesson 9 of the television series reviews previous classes, and the chapter on the Blessed Mother found in this book has two televised classes: one for the doctrines of the Church on Mary and the other for devotions to the Blessed Mother. The TV series is titled: *Sharing the Faith*. The VHS and Beta-Max TV program-classes are suitable for home and classroom use. The entire TV series is available for $700 from Marian Media, Box 20, Redfield, SD 57469.

This volume will prove valuable for students in their last years of high school, for those in the beginning years of college, for adult inquiry classes for non-Catholics seeking a full course of Catholic instructions, and for lifelong Catholics interested in studying the faith in greater depth.

The author, in writing this book, drew heavily from Sacred Scripture, the ecumenical councils of the Church, especially the Second Vatican Council, official pronouncements of the Church since Vatican II, the general and national catechetical directories, Church history, the Fathers of the Church, papal encyclicals, and the dogmas of Catholicism.

The author has more than a quarter of a century of pastoral experience in teaching the faith to all ages. He also has conducted inquiry classes for non-Catholics for 28 years. The result is a clarity of style which makes the teachings of the Church come alive and makes Jesus Christ personal to those who study this book in a prayerful manner.

Those who are not Catholic who use this book are asked to pray daily with an open heart for guidance from the Holy Spirit to lead them to the fullness of true faith and wherever God in His love desires them to be. During the course of instructions they also should attend Mass each Sunday. For that reason, it may be advantageous to look ahead to the chapters devoted to the Holy Eucharist as *Sacrament* and especially as *Sacrifice* so that they may have some appreciation of the meaning of the Divine Liturgy in which, it is hoped, they eventually will be led to participate fully.

If you have little acquaintance with prayer, you would do well to look ahead to the chapter on prayer to aid you in studying the remaining chapter prayerfully. At the same time, all who study this book are alerted to the necessity of order in acquiring knowledge. We say this because the chapters are presented systematically so that one chapter builds on another. As a result, knowledge of preceding chapters usually is required in order to completely absorb the intent of the chapters which follow.

CHAPTER 1

The Existence of God

Does God exist? For modern man, in general, God does not exist. The Catholic Church's Second Vatican Council, a gathering of more than 2,300 Catholic bishops of the world together with and under the authority of the pope, declared that atheism is one of the greatest problems facing mankind today.

Atheism is the denial of a personal God who is entirely distinct from the world He created. "Some people expressly deny the existence of God. Others maintain that man cannot make any assertion whatsoever about Him. Still others admit only such methods of investigation as would make it seem quite meaningless to ask questions about God. Many, trespassing beyond the boundaries of the positive sciences, either contend that everything can be explained by the reasoning process used in such sciences, or, on the contrary, hold that there is no such thing as absolute truth. With others it is their exaggerated idea of man that causes their faith to languish; they are more prone, it would seem, to affirm man than to deny God. Yet others have such a faulty notion of God that when they disown this product of the imagination their denial has no reference to the God of the Gospels. There are also those who never enquire about God; religion never seems to trouble or interest them at all, nor do they see why they should bother about it. Not infrequently atheism is born from a violent protest against the evil in the world, or from the fact that certain human ideals are wrongfully invested with such an absolute character as to be taken for God. Modern civilization itself, though not of its very nature but because it is too engrossed in the concerns of this world, can often make it harder to approach God" (*Church in the Modern World*, I, 19).

In the second chapter of this book we shall see that God created us in His own image and likeness. The mentality of many, however, has been making God over into man's image and likeness. Certainly millions, even billions of people, express belief in a "god." The question is: "What kind of god do they believe in?" Modern man too often concocts a god with whom he is very comfortable, one who makes no demands, one against whom you cannot sin. All that is needed to love this kind of god is self-fulfillment.

People today want to hear assurances such as "You are beautiful" or "You're okay." They do not want to hear about the need for atonement, forgiveness or repentance. They do not want to feel guilty even though there are times when people need to experience guilt. People do not want a god they can offend but a theology which sees no sin, or, at least, which acknowledges only one sin for which we would be accountable — to deny that there is a god. The kind of god they imagine is not the one true God revealed in the Old Testament of the Bible and whose Son became man 2,000 years ago.

People today have been creating a new Gospel. They are committed to a "Christianity" which allows them to interpret God's Word to reaffirm their own position. Even many who call themselves "Christian" come to God's Word already committed to their own ways. Others come to God as if to help Him out.

The Second Vatican Council (1962-1965), which older adults sometimes blame for the problems in the Church today, is only history to the younger generation. Vatican II, however, said basically the same thing we are saying.

"Without doubt those who willfully try to drive God from their heart and to avoid all questions about religion, not following the biddings of their conscience, are not free from blame. But believers themselves often share some responsibility for this situation. For atheism, taken as a whole, is not present in the mind of man from the start. . . . It springs from various causes, among which must be included a critical reaction against religions and, in some places, against the Christian religion in particular. Believers can thus have more than a little to do with the rise of atheism. To the extent that they are careless about their instruction in the faith, or present its teaching falsely, or even fail in their religious, moral or social life, they must be said to conceal rather than to reveal the true nature of God and of religion" (*Church in the Modern World*, I, 19).

"Modern atheism often takes on a systematic form also which, in addition to other causes, so insists on man's desire for autonomy as to object to any dependence on God at all. Those who profess this kind of atheism maintain that freedom consists in this, that man is an end to himself, and the sole maker, with supreme control, of his own history. . . . They claim that this outlook cannot be reconciled with the assertion of a Lord who is author and end of all things or that at least it makes such an affirmation altogether unnecessary. The sense of power which modern technical progress begets in man may encourage this outlook.

"Among the various kinds of present-day atheism, that one should not go unnoticed which looks for man's autonomy through his economic and social emancipation. It holds that religion, of its very nature, thwarts such emancipation by raising man's hopes in a future life, thus both deceiving him and discouraging him from working for a better form of life on earth. That is why those who hold such views, wherever they gain control of the state, violently attack religion, and in order to spread atheism, especially in the education of young people, make use of all the means by which the civil authority can bring pressure to bear on its subjects" (*Church in the Modern World*, I, 20).

These observations bring to mind the question: "Just what kind of image do we have of God?" It is best, therefore, to define what is meant by "God."

God is one absolutely and infinitely perfect spirit who is the creator of everything. God is the Supreme Being. He is everywhere. God is all-powerful. Being infinite in every perfection, God has to an infinite degree every goodness we can name. But there can be only one being who fulfills every attribute perfectly. It is impossible to have two gods who are infinite. That would be a contradiction. Infinite means that which has no bounds or limitations; there is no goodness independent of its own boundless perfection. The First Vatican Council, Session III, Chapter I, said that God is "infinite in intellect and will and in every perfection." In the one true God there is no potentiality. There is no such thing as God in himself "becoming" or on the way to greater perfection. God *is*. His very nature is to exist. In God His existence is identified with His nature or essence. God could not *not* exist. He must exist for He is existence itself. This is what is meant when we say that in God there is no potentiality but only pure actuality. God always was and always will be. God does not change. The infinite, boundless perfection of God, pure act, that is, every perfection, was always realized within himself. God had no beginning and He will have no end.

The First Vatican Council listed God's attributes in the following manner: "The holy, Catholic, apostolic Roman Church believes and professes that there is one true, living God, the Creator and Lord of heaven and earth. He is almighty, eternal beyond measure, incomprehensible, and infinite in intellect, will and in every perfection. Since He is one unique spiritual substance, entirely simple and unchangeable, He must be declared really and essentially distinct from the world, perfectly happy in himself and by His very nature, and inexpressibly exalted over all things that exist or can be conceived other than himself" (Denzinger, 3001).

It is important that we have a clear definition of what we mean by "God." Even heads of Communist states, e.g., Russia, have been heard to use the term "god." It is doubtful, however, that the head of an atheistic government has in mind the "God" defined by the Catholic Church.

Anytime we begin to limit God, we are no longer talking about the one true God, the infinite being who is self-subsistence. God alone must be. All other beings exist only because of the will of God, whose essence and existence coincide.

Listen sometime to the frivolous conversations which take place in the name of religion. Often faith and morality are reduced to mere emotions or feelings. Even those are sometimes based on one's own conveniences or prejudices. People make God out to be for the sake of man, rather than man for the sake of God.

In recent decades, the secular knowledge of mankind has surpassed all of the knowledge which had been accumulated in all previous centuries. This is not to downgrade the wealth of knowledge bestowed upon us by our ancestors. It was they who laid the groundwork making it possible for us to acquire the knowledge we have today. Still, knowledge is increasing at a rapid pace today. And it appears that this trend will continue unless man destroys himself by abusing this knowledge, knowledge which he only discovers and which God possesses by His very nature. Whatever man discovers, no matter how vast in scope it may be, is very limited and but a token and a reflection of the infinite knowledge of God which has existed from all eternity.

Technologically man has advanced and is advancing greatly. Unfortunately, his insights into the supernatural world, into faith and morals, has not kept pace with his technological advancement. An understanding of the Christian faith has remained at the grade-school level for many even though they have advanced through high school and college and into postgraduate studies. With or without any advanced formal education, the average person today is exposed to much secular knowledge, thanks to the modern media which is mostly secular, even anti-Christian.

A grave danger is posed when people increase their secular knowledge but stand still religiously. With only a child's basic knowledge of religion they are not equipped to answer the questions of a world growing more and more atheistic. This need not be so.

All knowledge comes from God. The knowledge which we receive from true faith will never contradict the knowledge which we discover using reason. If it seems to do so, then there is something wrong either with our interpretation of the faith or with our secular knowledge. Chapter 5 will provide basic principles regarding truth to help us better understand subjects introduced in this first chapter.

To the reasonable man there is nothing more certain or more reasonable than this — God exists. (God, that is, as defined by the Church.) In fact, it is most unreasonable to claim that God does not exist. For, if God does not exist, then we are totally without answers to the world about us. The order, the mathematical precision of the universe itself, speaks of an all-powerful intelligent cause. But without God we have no cause. Without God we have no conscious intelligence behind the laws which billions of galaxies seem to obey. An unmoved Mover is a necessity. To hold that all came from nothing of itself or created itself is sheer nonsense and contrary to right reason.

To hold to a Supreme Being with infinite intelligence as the First Cause and Mover of all, however, is reasonable. A First Cause that was uncaused. A First Mover which had no one to first move It (Him) but which always was and always will be is the only reasonable solution possible. Later we shall see that in addition to man's right use of reason concluding that a Supreme God exists, that this God is a loving God who has revealed himself as such to man.

A sample of a direct revelation from God, whose existence is identified with His essence, whose very nature is to exist, is the revelation made to Moses. "And God said to Moses, 'I Am who I Am. This,' he added, 'is what you must say to the sons of Israel: I Am has sent me to you.'"

A principle of causality is that the greater or more perfect does not come from the less perfect. Rather, the imperfect comes from the more perfect. This is self-evident and is known by common sense.

The famous theologian, Father Reginald Garrigou-Lagrange, O.P., put it this way: "The greater does not proceed from the less, the more perfect from the less perfect, but contrariwise; but men, who contingently exist, have being, life, intelligence, morality, and sometimes holiness; therefore there must be a First Cause which possesses, by reason of itself and eternally, these perfections of existence, life, intelligence, and holiness. Otherwise, the greater would come from the less, as the proponents of absolute evolutionism are obliged to admit, and it is by recourse to this method of absurdity that God's existence is proved who is absolutely perfect and distinct from the world" (*One God*, p. 138).

Long ago Parmenides said: "Nothing is made from nothing." This means that without a cause, nothing could come into being. If the more perfect or greater were to come from the less perfect this would mean that the greater degree of being would be without a cause.

The principal perfections in the world are existence, life and intelligence. These are found in human beings. But human beings certainly are not the cause of other beings such as horses, dogs or cats. They are dependent because they are born and they die.

The conclusion is that there must be an eternally existing being, life and intelligence. Furthermore, there is an eternally self-existing being, life and intelligence. This being has the cause within itself and we call this being God.

It is the nature of the intellect to seek truth. To apply the principles summarized above will lead one to recognize the truth of the First Cause of everything, the First Mover who is totally independent and upon whom everything else depends and takes its original cause for coming into existence.

There are other great religions in the world besides Christianity but none has the credibility consistent with right reason which Christianity has, and none, we shall discover, has a founder who was put to death and rose from the dead, save Jesus Christ with whom Christianity is identified.

The Moslem or Islamic religion is a mixture of paganism, Christianity and Judaism. Mohammed claimed he received his new religion in a vision, but research shows his real sources. As a merchant, he learned something of the Old Testament of the Bible as well as the teachings of Jesus Christ from the New Testament. He combined his paganism with Judaism and Christianity. Mohammed wrote his doctrines on leaves, stones and leather. These were rewritten after his death and put into one volume known as the Koran.

When Mohammed died, a friend and disciple named Omar ran from his tent, sword in hand, and shouted: "I will kill any man who says the prophet is dead." But Mohammed was never seen alive again. Jesus Christ, on the other hand, as we shall see in Chapter 3, rose from the dead and was seen for 40 days by hundreds of people at a time.

All the founders of man-made religions, such as Confucius, Buddha and Mohammed, died. In our study of the Catholic Faith, however, we shall see that Jesus Christ lives yet today in heaven and in the world through His Church.

So, we could use reason, as we do, to prove the existence of one God, but we could not use the same reasoning process to prove the existence of three persons in one God. We know, however, from divine revelation, given to us by Jesus Christ, that in the one God there is a Blessed Trinity. God the Father is the first person of the Blessed Trinity. God the Son is the second person, and God the Holy Spirit is the third person of the Blessed Trinity.

All three persons in God, Father, Son and Holy Spirit, are equal. All three are infinite and eternal. It is impossible to demonstrate the intrinsic possibility of the Trinity. At the same time, once it is revealed that there are three equal persons in one God, it is not contrary to reason to accept the Blessed Trinity. There is no contradiction implied in this mystery of the Blessed Trinity.

Neither can we deny the possibility of the Blessed Trinity. As stated, it cannot be known as evidently possible without faith in divine revelation.

St. Thomas Aquinas stated: "We can make use of philosophy in sacred doctrine . . . by defending the faith against those who attack it, either by showing that their statements are false or that they are not convincing" (*In Boetium, De Trinitate*, q.2, a.3).

Each of the three persons in the Blessed Trinity is God. They are one and the same God because they have the same nature and spiritual substance. God the Father is especially known to us as the creator of heaven and earth and all things. God the Son is especially known as the Savior, or Redeemer, of the world. The Holy Spirit is known as the Consoler and the Sanctifier. Each is a distinct person with the same divine nature.

That there are three persons in one God is a mystery of faith. A mystery of faith is a divinely revealed truth whose possibility cannot be rationally conceived before it is revealed by God and, after it is revealed, the inner essence of the mystery cannot be fully understood by the mind of man. By divine revelation, we know that God the Father generates the Son eternally; the Son is eternally begotten of the Father and together, the Father and the Son breathe forth the Holy Spirit. By an eternal procession, the Holy Spirit has His divine nature from the first two persons of the Blessed Trinity.

Christians believe in the mystery of the Blessed Trinity because it was revealed by God, who expects man to accept it on the authority of the one true God. When we believe, we make an act of faith. Faith is believing what God has made known to us. Faith is not the result of understanding something as the fruit of our own reason. Faith is accepting the word of another because of the authority of the one speaking. It is called divine faith, rather than human faith, when the one believed is God. A later chapter on baptism will explain how the act of divine faith is the assent of the mind to what God has revealed. An act of supernatural faith requires a special grace from God. Reason can reflect further on what God has revealed and thereby come to a deeper understanding of what God has revealed. Theology is defined as faith seeking understanding. As already mentioned, however, there are some truths of faith which can never be understood since they are beyond human comprehension, although they are not contrary to reason.

A study of the Catholic Faith, if done correctly, will bring us to a personal relationship with Almighty God. God does not wish to be a distant God. He wants to be close to us — indeed, to dwell within us as in a temple. The infinite God about whom we have been speaking in this first chapter — existence itself who said "I Am who I Am"; the same one true God who is everywhere; who can do all things; who knows all things; sees all things, even our most secret thoughts, words and actions; who in His infinite spirit is without body, but has understanding and free will; the God

17

who never changes; who is just and at the same time merciful; the God who is love itself — is the one true God who has adopted us as His children (as Chapter 7 will explain) making us His own adopted sons and daughters, sharing His divine life with us, and who destined us to spend eternity with Him in our true home which is heaven, while we are but on pilgrimage on this planet earth.

The God of heaven and earth, this one true God, desires that each one of us respond to Him in a personal way. Our knowing and loving response to Him will be expressed by keeping His commandments and in daily prayer. Prayer is our voluntary response to the awareness of God's presence. In Chapter 22 we shall learn that this prayerful response may take the form of acknowledging His greatness and our total dependence on Him. We call this adoration. Prayer also may take the form of gratitude for His benefits. We call this thanksgiving. Our prayers may express sorrow for sins committed and beg God's forgiveness. Such prayers are called prayers of expiation or reparation. Our prayer might simply express our love for God who is all good, or it may ask God for the natural and spiritual things we need.

If our faith is to develop we must pray. It is important to pray every day. Those who have little concept of prayer may need to study Chapter 22 before continuing their study of the chapters which immediately follow. The study of the Catholic faith must not be simply an intellectual pursuit but a prayerful pursuit in union with God. Prayer is necessary to develop a personal relationship with Almighty God.

Sincere Catholics know about the requirement to worship God in His way through the Sacrifice of the Mass at least every Sunday, the Lord's Day. Those who are using this text, who are not Catholic, but who are investigating the Catholic faith, would do well to participate in the Holy Mass every Sunday. Those who are studying the Catholic faith with a view to eventually attaining full membership in the Catholic Church should specially consider it important to participate in the Sacrifice of the Mass every Sunday. As Catholics they will be expected to participate each Sunday not only because it is a privilege but because it is a serious obligation in faith. Only Catholics may receive the sacraments of the Church. Those seeking membership, however, though they cannot receive the sacraments, should practice the Catholic faith to the best of their ability as they come to know it. In that way their initiation into the Catholic faith will be gradual.

While future chapters are dedicated to the meaning of the Sacrifice of the Mass, i.e., to the Holy Eucharist as sacrifice and sacrament, a brief explanation of the meaning of the Mass is given in the conclusion to this first chapter for the sake of those participating in Mass each week who

18

have not had an opportunity to study the Holy Sacrifice of the Mass.

The Mass is the sacrifice of the Eucharist and is the central act of worship in the Catholic Church. The Mass cannot be understood apart from the sacrifice of the Cross on Calvary. On Mount Calvary, on Good Friday afternoon, Jesus Christ, the second person of the Blessed Trinity, namely, God the Son, who became man, died on the Cross for the salvation of the world. Jesus freely laid down His life for the salvation of the world, offering himself to God the Father in order to make infinite and perfect reparation for the sins of all.

Never had mankind been able to offer to God adoration which was perfectly pleasing to Him. Man was powerless of himself, before the coming of Jesus Christ, to atone for his own sins and to offer to God the Father a perfectly pleasing gift. Many sacrifices were offered by mankind in Old Testament times, that is, before the coming of Jesus Christ, but none of these sarifices were powerful enough to take away sins. Only the blood of the Cross could do that. God himself had determined that.

When Jesus Christ died on the Cross, offering himself in sacrifice for all men, God received for the first time from man adoration which was perfect and of infinite value. It was perfect and it had an infinite value because the man offering the gift, the man making the sacrifice, was both God and man.

At the Last Supper, the night before He died, Jesus Christ gave to His Church, in the persons of the apostles, the power to change bread and wine into His own body and blood which could be adored and received. Jesus Christ also made it possible for His apostles and their successors, the bishops and priests today, in celebrating the Holy Eucharist or Mass, to perpetuate the selfsame sacrifice which He offered at the Last Supper in a sacramental manner and which He offered in a bloody manner Good Friday afternoon on the Cross.

Jesus gave His first priests the power to do the same as He had done at the Last Supper. The Last Supper was the first Mass ever offered. The Last Supper was already a sacrifice. Mount Calvary was the scene of the perfect sacrifice on Good Friday afternoon, when Christ died for the redemption of the world. The Mass today is a sacrifice, the selfsame sacrifice as that of Calvary's Cross. There are not three different sacrifices, the Last Supper, Calvary and Mass. There is one and the same sacrifice in all three. The only difference is the time and the manner of the offering. The Sacrifice of the Mass today represents what Jesus did in sacramental form at the Last Supper and what He did physically on the first Good Friday. The representation is not merely symbolic. Jesus becomes really present in His humanity at Mass, but He no longer dies a physical death. He no longer experiences the pain of the Cross. Nonetheless, Jesus offers himself through the power of His acts in the Sacrament of the Holy Eucharist. At Mass, Jesus acts as the same eternal high priest as really and truly as He did on Mount Calvary. Only now, at the Sacrifice of the Mass, you are there. You participate. You, too, offer to God the Father, the infinitely pleasing sacrifice of Jesus Christ on the Cross. Only the priest at the altar, however, has the power to produce the victim of the sacrifice.

Mass, then, is not simply the reading of Sacred Scripture, or listening to the Word of God in a sermon, and the receiving of Holy Communion. It is all of that, but it is more. The same Jesus Christ who offered himself once in a bloody manner on the altar of the Cross, is present and offers himself now in an unbloody manner.

For those who are not Catholic, for those who have not yet come to the fullness of the Catholic faith, the paragraphs above (summarizing all too briefly the faith of the Catholic Church in the mystery of the Holy Eucharist, the Mass) will be challenging and will seem impossible. You are reminded that a mystery of faith is something we cannot fully understand but we know that it is true because God has revealed it. You cannot come to the fullness of faith on your own power. You will need a special gift of God. You will need to receive from God the gift of supernatural faith in order to believe. You are reminded that although something seems impossible to man, yet, to the God about whom we have been speaking "all things are possible."

We must put no limitations on the infinitely good God. He who made the billions of galaxies out of nothing and set them in motion, in the order of His universe, cries out to modern man, and even to the scientist who is humble and hears His voice: "I Am who I Am," "I exist," "I love you." "I love you so much that I sent My Son to your world to die on the Cross for you so that you could spend eternity with Me in perfect happiness in heaven."

There are many things about the Catholic faith which can be explained. There also are many mysteries which God has revealed in His Son which cannot be fully explained or understood. They must simply, in humility, be believed. The Sacrifice of the Mass is one of these divine mysteries. Touching so briefly on the subject of the Mass so early in our study of the Catholic faith, will, it is to be hoped, give you a foretaste of the greatness, the loveliness, the power and the glory of what God has done for us and what He has revealed to us.

Because the study which lies before you is so great and because it involves your eternal destiny, it is important for you to develop a personal relationship with God in daily prayer.

Perhaps at this time you can do no more than pray, "I do have faith. Help the little faith I have!" (Mark 9:24). In fact, you may only be able to pray the second half of that short prayer, "Help the little faith I have." Even that, if prayed sincerely and humbly, will be acceptable to God.

One thing is certain. No one will come to the fullness of true faith by simply reasoning his or her way there. Study and reason may dispose one if it is done humbly, but, ultimately, God must touch the human heart. God must infuse into the human soul divine faith.

By study and humble prayer each one of us can come to pray in all sincerity: "I believe, Lord. . . . Lord, increase my faith."

DISCUSSION QUESTIONS

1. What conditions make for a spirit of atheism among people?

The spirit of atheism can stem from many causes including a faulty notion of the reality of the God of the Gospels. It may come from a protest against evil in the world. Also the spirit of materialism, being engrossed in worldly concerns, causes atheism.

2. How can believers be a cause of atheism?

Christians can contribute to the spirit of atheism by not being well instructed in their faith; by presenting teachings falsely or poorly; by not living sincerely the Christian faith.

3. How would you describe or define God?

Strictly speaking, God, who is a supreme being, infinite or unlimited, cannot be defined in human terms. God is living, the creator, the beginning and end. He is almighty, eternal, incomprehensible, infinite in intellect and power. He is but one and is distinct from the world He created.

4. Would it be possible to have two true Gods?

There cannot be two supreme beings. To be infinite means to have no potentiality but only pure actuality. This means more than that God has no limitations. God has within himself the fullness of all perfection, whether it be knowledge or power or being. God is "infinite in intellect and will and in every perfection" (First Vatican Council, Session III, Chapter I). It is a contradiction to suppose that there could be more than one infinite being we call God.

5. How do some try to change the image of God?

God made man in His own image and likeness. Some mentally reduce God to man's image and likeness. These people do not understand or have faith in a God who is an infinite being.

6. Explain: "Man's moral and religious knowledge has not kept pace with his advancements in technology."

Man's knowledge, as well as his technology, has increased by leaps and bounds in recent decades. His understanding of religion, both in faith and morals, however, is lagging. Scientific advancements could be used to further the cause of true religion and to help man to better comprehend the all-good God, but man has become secularized. He has made himself, rather than God, the creator, the center of all. Yet, man merely discovers what God has created and the laws which He has established in the universe.

7. Is it reasonable to accept faith in the existence of God?

Not to believe in the existence of God is unreasonable. The only reasonable explanation for the world in which we live is an infinite creator who always was and always will be. Without an infinite First Cause, we would suppose unintelligent things were the cause of themselves and that the greater came from the less.

8. Explain briefly how the existence of God can be proven by reasoning from a First Mover as the ultimate cause of things?

Using the sound reasoning of St. Thomas Aquinas we can say: We observe things moving. Whatever moves is moved by another. There cannot be an infinite number of moved movers. Therefore, there must be a First Mover which is unmoved. It is contrary to right reason to suppose that things came from unintelligent forms of life or that they came or were created by no one.

9. Why is the Christian faith the most credible of all faiths?

The Christian religion is the most credible because it alone has a founder who said He was God as well as man and then proved it by dying and rising again.

10. How do we know that there are three persons in one God?

We know by faith that there are three divine persons in one Godhead because God himself revealed it in Jesus Christ.

11. Since there is only one God, what is the difference in the three persons in one God?

There is one divine nature in God but three distinct persons. Creation is especially attributed to God the Father; salvation and redemption is especially attributed to God the Son become man; sanctification and consolation especially to the Holy Spirit. God the Father is not the Son but generates the Son eternally; the Son is eternally begotten. The Holy Spirit has His divine nature by eternal procession from the Father and the Son. The three persons are coequal, coeternal and consubstantial.

12. What is meant by a Mystery of Faith?

A Mystery of Faith is a divinely revealed truth which cannot be concluded from reason alone. After it is revealed, it cannot be fully understood by man's mind. We believe a Mystery of Faith because God has revealed it.

13. What is the supernatural Gift of Faith?

By the supernatural Gift of Faith is meant a special gift from God, empowering man to believe what has been revealed by God.

14. Can faith and reason ever be in contradiction?

True faith and right reason can never be in contradiction because both have as their ultimate source, God himself. If they appear to be in contradiction then something is wrong either with the reasoning process or with one's understanding of the faith.

15. Why is participation in the Sacrifice of the Mass important for those taking instructions for reception into the Catholic Church?

The Sacrifice of the Mass is central to Catholic Faith and to the practice of religion. Those who take instructions with a view to seeking membership in the Catholic Church should consider regular attendance at Sunday Mass as important to their gradual admittance into the Catholic Faith as they do their official Catholic instructions.

16. Explain briefly the meaning of the Sacrifice of the Mass.

The Sacrifice of the Mass is the perpetuation of the Sacrifice of the Cross. The adoration given God the Father is infinite in value for it is Jesus Christ, true God and true man, who is the chief priest or offerer of every Holy Mass in the unity of the Holy Spirit. The sacrifice offered God in the Mass is the same sacrifice offered on Mount Calvary on the first Good Friday.

CHAPTER 2

Nature and Creation of Man

St. Thomas Aquinas said that every human being begins to reflect on his own being when he reaches the age of reason, or soon thereafter. That is why every person, even outside the Christian world, has a chance to save his soul.

There are certain basic questions of life which have come into man's intellect from the beginning. Who am I? Where did I come from? How did I get here? Why am I here? Where am I going? These are questions for which every reasoning person must find answers.

Man has always put forward, and will continue to put forward, many views about himself, views which, at times, are contradictory. There are two extremes. Man may set himself up as the absolute measure of things, or he may debase himself to the animal level, which brings despair.

For those who have faith in divine revelation, as we shall explain in Chapter 4, the answers to the basic questions of life have been given in Genesis, the first book of the Bible.

Sacred Scripture teaches that man was created in the image of God (Wisdom 2:23), as able to know and to love his Creator, and as set by Him over all earthly creatures (Genesis 1:26) that he might rule them, and make use of them, while glorifying God (see Ecclesiasticus 17:3-10). "Ah, what is man that you should spare a thought for him, the son of man that you should care for him? Yet you have made him little less than a god, you have crowned him with glory and splendor, made him lord over the work of your hands, set all things under his feet" (Psalm 8:4-6).

"But God did not create man a solitary being. From the beginning 'male and female he created them' (Gen. 1:27). This partnership of man and woman constitutes the first form of communion between persons. For by his innermost nature man is a social being; and if he does not enter into relations with others he can neither live nor develop his gifts.

"So God, as we read again in the Bible, saw 'all he had made, and indeed it was very good' (Gen. 1:31)" (*Church in the Modern World*, I, 12).

Vatican II said: "Man, though made of body and soul, is a unity. Through his very bodily condition he sums up in himself the elements of the material world. Through him they are thus brought to their highest perfection and can raise their voice in praise freely given to the creator (Dan. 3:57-90). For this reason man may not despise his bodily life. Rather, he is obliged to regard his body as good and to hold it in honor since God has created it and will raise it up on the last day. Nevertheless, man has been wounded by sin. He finds by experience that his body is in revolt. His very dignity, therefore, requires that he should glorify God in his body (Cf. 1 Cor. 6:13-20), and not allow it to serve the evil inclinations of his heart.

"Man is not deceived when he regards himself as superior to bodily things and as more than just a speck of nature or a nameless unit in the city of man. For by his power to know himself in the depths of his being he rises above the whole universe of mere objects. When he is drawn to think about his real self he turns to those deep recesses of his being where God who probes the heart (Cf. 1 Kg. 16:7, Jer. 17:10) awaits him, and where he himself decides his own destiny in the sight of God. So when he recognizes in himself a spiritual and immortal soul, he is not being led astray by false imaginings that are due to merely physical or social causes. On the contrary, he grasps what is profoundly true in this matter" (*Church in the Modern World*, I, 14).

"Man, as sharing in the light of the divine mind, rightly affirms that by his intellect he surpasses the world of mere things" (*Church in the Modern World*, I, 15).

In brief, man is a living substance, composed of a material body which dies and a spiritual soul which is immortal. Man is a creature made by God in His own image and likeness, to praise, to reverence and to serve God in this life and, thereby, attain eternal life in God after the death of the body. Philosophically, we would say, man is a rational animal and, collectively, is the human species, or the human race.

Man is not simply the highest creature in the animal kingdom. Man, being made in the image and likeness of God, has an immortal soul. In relationship to the rest of the material world, man is a superior creature. At the same time, man is a fallen creature.

The immortal soul of man is spiritual. The spiritual element in man is imperishable. The soul is immaterial and, therefore, will never be discovered by a surgeon's scalpel. The brain is simply the material part of man through which the soul operates. The soul, being spiritual, has the characteristic of simplicity, that is, the soul has no parts. There is no such thing as the soul having parts outside parts. The soul is whole and entire in every part of the living body. It is possible for the soul to live apart from the body and that, in fact, happens after the death of the body. The soul cannot die.

The soul animates the body. The soul is an immaterial substance which is naturally ordained toward a body. Separated from the body it is an incomplete substance because a human person is ordained to be composed of both a body and a soul. After death, the soul separated from the body is still aware of God and its own existence while it awaits the resurrection of the body, as we shall learn later of souls which have entered eternal life.

The soul of each human person was individually created by God. The soul was infused into the body at the moment of conception. The soul is created for the body it will inform. The soul is not the total human nature because a human person is composed of both body and soul.

In philosophy, animals and plants are said to have souls because they have life. Animal and plant souls, however, are perishable and the use of the term "soul" in relation to both simply refers to the life of these things. The rational soul of man contains all the powers of the "souls" of the plant and animal kingdoms inasmuch as the soul of man also contains sensitive and vegetable functions.

The highest faculties of the human soul are intellect and free will. The intellect is the power by which the soul acquires knowlege in a non-material way. True, knowledge begins with the senses, but the faculty of thinking is essentially higher than the senses. One knows with the intellect and is able to do abstract reasoning. Intellect is possessed by human beings, disembodied souls, and the good angels, as well as the fallen, or demonic, angels.

The human will is that power of the soul which tends toward a good and shies away from that which is judged to be an evil by the intellect. It is a rational appetite with the functions to intend, choose, desire, hope, consent, hate, love and enjoy. God created man with a free will, which means the power to determine and to act of itself, that is, without any outside force. Irrational beings respond to a stimulus, act on instinct or are conditioned by sensory objects. Because man has a free will, however, he can love God freely. He also is free to reject God's love and, therefore, to reject salvation.

Catholics may *not* believe in the evolution of the soul. Evolution is a theory which holds that something was or is in a state of necessary development. *Materialistic* evolution assumes that there has always existed uncreated matter and that there emerged from this matter all plants, animals and human beings through a natural evolutionary process. This is contrary to Christian revelation.

Theistic evolution is not incompatible with Christianity provided it postulates an evolution of the body under the guidance of Divine Providence, with the human soul created separately and individually.

Man as man could not evolve because man is a creature of God composed of both body and soul. Man as man did not evolve from lower forms of life.

St. Luke says of our most remote ancestors that Seth was of Adam, who was of God (Luke 3:38).

Biology texts and teachers in some schools teach about the evolution of man as though it were fact.

Such an approach is most unscientific because evolution is only a theory, not a proven fact. Those who teach evolution as a certain science go beyond what is experimentally known. They are not teaching sound science but a religion of their own.

The Catholic Church does not condemn the theory of evolution. It does require, however, that those who are influenced by it, if they are to be sincere believing Catholics, must hold that the human soul did not evolve. The soul was created separately and immediately by God. *IF* evolution took place, God was responsible. Since man is composed of both soul and body and since the soul did not evolve, we must conclude that man as man did not evolve.

Genesis does not contradict the theory of evolution. The Genesis account contains much that is in harmony with the theories of evolution. God, in Genesis, took man from the earth. "Yahweh God fashioned man of dust from the soil. Then he breathed into his nostrils a breath of life, and thus man became a living being" (Genesis 2:7). Note: Indications are that God first formed a body before breathing life or creating a soul. *IF* a body evolved, it was not a man until God created and infused an immortal soul into that body.

In addition to the two conditions named upon which Catholics may hold to the theory of evolution, namely, that the soul was created immediately by God, and that God caused the body to evolve, there is still another condition. Catholics must hold to the unity of the human race. Polygenism is out.

Polygenism is the doctrine or belief that, evolution being an established fact, all human beings came from two or more ancestral types, not from one human set of parents, namely Adam and Eve. This position is contrary to the official teaching of the Catholic Church. Pope Pius XII in his encylical letter to the world in 1950, *Humani Generis*, declared: "It is unintelligible how such an opinion can be squared with what the sources of revealed truth and the documents of the magisterium of the Church teach on original sin, which proceeds from sin actually committed by an individual Adam, and which, passed on to all by way of generation, is in everyone as his own."

The Church teaches then that Adam and Eve were historical people.

27

Adam was not simply a generic term for many ancestors. "Original sin is the result of a sin committed, in actual historical fact, by an individual man named Adam. . . ." (*Humani Generis*, 1950)

Exactly when the human race began in Adam and Eve, our first parents, is lost in antiquity. The earth itself is probably at least four and a half billion years old and, according to scientists, man could have been on earth as long as two million years ago. Whenever man got here, it is Catholic faith that God created man in His own image and likeness with an immortal soul. Modern scientists more and more are moving toward the position that there is insufficient evidence to substantiate the theory of evolution.

God created man in a state of original justice. Adam and Eve were created in grace (Chapter 7) with certain preternatural gifts. Adam was a perfect man in the natural sense. Preternatural gifts refer to favors granted by God above and beyond the powers of the nature which receives them although they are not contrary to created nature. These gifts, which were given to our first parents, perfected human nature without destroying it or carrying it beyond the limits of created nature. Adam and Eve, therefore, possessed the gifts of infused knowledge, an absence of concupiscence and bodily immortality.

Our first parents did not make stupid mistakes such as running through the forest and stumbling over a log. They had complete control over the passions of the body and they could not have misused the appetites of the flesh in any manner. Had Adam never sinned, he never would have had to die but, after a time of trial on earth, he would have been taken, body and soul, directly to heaven. Had Adam not sinned, the state of original justice would have been passed on to all his descendants.

While Adam, through repentance, personally regained forgiveness, neither he nor his descendants ever recovered the state of original justice.

The sin which Adam committed is called Original Sin. The sin of Adam was personal and grave. Adam freely committed it. It seriously affected human nature. The gravity of the sin is seen in the serious consequences imposed by the command of God and in its effect on the entire human race. Adam's progeny was deprived of supernatural life and the preternatural gifts which it would have possessed upon entering the world, had Adam not sinned.

Adam and Eve were put on trial in the Garden of Eden. They were expelled after they disobeyed God (Genesis 3:23). Eden is a word used in Scripture to suggest an ideal place to live (Isaiah 51:3; Ezekiel 31:9).

The Genesis account makes no mention of a particular kind of fruit tree. What is mentioned is the "tree of the knowledge of good and evil" (Genesis 2:9). Adam, created in original justice, had known only good. He had never experienced evil until he disobeyed God. Then, the intellect of man was darkened and his will was weakened. Only after the loss of grace did Adam and Eve become ashamed of their nakedness. Then they saw the need for clothes. Before that they beheld everything as good because God had created everything to be good and to be in proper balance, including Adam in his state of original justice. Once our first parents fell, however, they knew evil and the body's perfect harmony no longer existed.

Adam's sin was essentially that of pride. The devil had tempted Adam with the words: "God knows in fact that on the day you eat it [the fruit of the tree] . . . you will be like gods, knowing good and evil" (Genesis 3:5). The wisdom our first parents sought to gain in disobedience brought only shame, unhappiness, suffering and the eventual death of the body in this world, and the loss of eternal life with God in heaven.

When pride is carried to the point where one is unwilling to acknowledge his dependence upon God and refuses to submit his will to God or to lawful authority, it is a grave sin. This certainly was the case with Adam and Eve. One of the results of Original Sin is pride of life, that is, the desire of human beings to do their own will even when it contradicts the will of God. It urges one to self-worship or self-deification, which is at the root of all sin. Again, this was the trap into which our first parents fell at the urging of Satan.

All men are part of the fallen human race as a consequence of the sin of Adam. Since Adam was the head of the human race and fell, all mankind fell in him. We all bear the consequences of Original Sin. While we, too, may be returned to that grace in which our first parents were created, nonetheless, we still bear other weaknesses due to Original Sin. As members of the fallen human race we are inclined toward evil: pride, avarice, lust, envy, gluttony, anger and sloth.

Man was promised a Redeemer immediately after the fall. Not all hope was lost. While the gates of heaven were closed by Original Sin, yet, God made the promise of One who would come to crush the forces of evil.

"Then, Yahweh God said to the serpent: 'Because you have done this, be accursed beyond all cattle, all wild beasts. You shall crawl on your belly and eat dust every day of your life. I will make you enemies of each other; you and the woman, your offspring and her offspring. It will crush your head and you will strike its heel' " (Genesis 3:14-15).

Pope Paul VI, at the close of the Year of Faith, June 29, 1968, proclaimed "The Credo of the People of God" to offer the Christian world, after the Second Vatican Council, a profession of the principal articles of the Catholic faith. In it he stated:

"We believe that in Adam all have sinned, which means that the original offense committed by him caused human nature, common to all men,

29

to fall to a state in which it bears the consequences of that offense, and which is not the state in which it was at first in our first parents, established as they were in holiness and justice, and in which man knew neither evil nor death. It is human nature so fallen, stripped of the grace that clothed it, injured in its own natural powers and subjected to the domination of death, that is transmitted to all men, and it is in this sense that every man is born in sin. We, therefore, hold, with the Council of Trent, that original sin is transmitted with human nature, 'not by imitation, but by propagation' and that it is thus 'in each of us as his own.' ''

God created the world out of nothing. Having created the world, the crowning act of His creation was man. The Fourth Lateran and the First Vatican councils of the Catholic Church presented it as an article of faith that God alone created the world. This is stated in all the Christian creeds, the basis being divine revelation found in the whole of Sacred Scripture from the first book of the Bible, Genesis, to the final chapter, Revelation, written by St. John.

Some have tried to read the Bible with a modern scientific mind, expecting to find in the Scriptures a scientific explanation of how God created the world. The two creation accounts in Genesis seem in conflict with modern scientific knowledge. What is often forgotten is that the Bible is not a book of science. It is a book of religion. The Bible does not pretend to teach science and we should not expect it to do so. Had the Bible spoken according to the technicalities of modern knowledge of science constantly developing it would have been, for the most part, unintelligible to men of past centuries.

The author of Genesis merely wished to teach that Almighty God was the cause of all, the creator of the universe. The world was described as man saw it at that time. The world of the Hebrews is depicted in the Bible with God's heavenly seat resting above the superior waters which appear to exist above the firmament, or sky, which resembles an overturned bowl supported by columns. There are floodgates, or openings, in its vault where the waters above the firmament may fall upon the earth in the form of rain or snow. The land is a platform which rests on columns and this known earth is surrounded by waters, the oceans. The inferior waters lie underneath the columns. In the depths of the earth is Sheol, the home of the dead, called the nether world. The prescientific concept of the universe also was held by the Hebrews' pagan neighbors. It is simply the way the world appeared to man who had not had sufficient time to collect knowledge of the earth on which he lived. The stars, the moon, the sun moved across the sky, just under the waters above the firmament.

While descriptions of the world in the Bible are, at times, unscientific, the Bible does not tell us how the heavens go but how to go to heaven.

It did not bother the poetic Hebrew mind that a description of the creation of the world could have God creating light the first day while not creating the sun and the moon until the fourth day in the seven-day account of creation as explained in Genesis 1. The purpose of the author is not to examine the world scientifically but simply to explain that God, in fact, did create all out of nothing. It is much like an artist who prepares the canvas for painting. In painting a landscape there is no need to follow a scientific procedure. So, the author of Genesis, after explaining different aspects of God's creation, decorates the sky with sun, moon, stars and birds.

One who ridicules the Genesis account of creation as utterly unscientific may demonstrate his knowledge of science but he also demonstrates his ignorance of religion and of the real message to be found in Sacred Scripture about the creation of the world.

The two creation accounts in Genesis contrast the pagan mythologies of the Babylonians, the Egyptians and the Phoenicians. God's chosen people, the Hebrews, were warned not to be contaminated with the false beliefs of these pagans around them. The Babylonians had their "Enuma Elish" account which described the struggle between chaos and the gods. All the pagan accounts depict many gods. The Babylonians worshiped the sun and the moon. The Egyptians adored beasts and birds.

The Jews knew well the various pagan accounts of creation which consisted of good gods and bad gods in struggle and of the world having been made of the substance of a slain bad god, etc. We study, then, the contrast with the singular and unique account given in Genesis. Here there is only *One God*. That God is supreme. The one true God makes everything out of nothing, not out of something, not out of a slain god or anything else. Being all-powerful, the one true God simply says: "Let there be . . . ." and so it is.

The sun and the moon are not worshiped but are simply objects of creation by the one God. These things are at the service of man, and man has dominion over the beasts and the birds, which pagan neighbors adored. The lesson is most powerful and implicit and easily recognized by the Hebrews.

In one of the popular pagan accounts, man is presented as an afterthought. After the world is made of the slain god there is something left over out of which man is made. The world, including man being made of a slain bad god, would imply that the world and man were evil. But Genesis, inspired by the Holy Spirit, as we shall see is true of all of Scripture (Chapter 4), presents each aspect of God's creation as "good." Man is the crowning act of God's creation, made in God's own image and likeness, and all the rest was created to prepare a home for man. Finally, when man is created, God saw not simply that it was good, as was the case in the description of the other days of creation, but "very good." "God saw all he had made, and indeed it was very good" (Genesis 1:31).

The author of Genesis was a literary genius, especially when we consider that he had to teach true religion in contrast to the popular pagan mythologies. The author weaves the account of creation around the number "seven." "Seven" in biblical language already means goodness, perfection. The author, as it were, plays the concept of goodness in creation to death, in contrast to pagan mythologies. Not only does the Genesis account keep repeating after each act of God's creation that God saw that it was good but he wraps the total account around the symbolical number of goodness.

The intention in Genesis then is not to teach the element of time, namely, seven days in the creation of the world. Some have attempted to explain each day as symbolic of a period of time — each day standing, perhaps, for thousands, even millions of years. When that approach is used, however, it is still an attempt to make the Bible present scientific explanations. The seven-day account is simply a literary vehicle to teach people true religion most effectively. Basic questions of life are answered at the same time in the early chapters of Genesis.

In conclusion, it should be said that God did not create man because He was lonely. To consider God as lonely is to consider Him as imperfect. Rather, God created the world and man in it to manifest and to share His power and glory. It is the nature of goodness to diffuse itself, and the all-good God created a good world and created man in goodness to share His happiness. Sharing God's happiness requires a creature with intellect and will, one which can know and love as God knows and loves. In order for that creature to have such powers, God created man in His own image and likeness.

Man thus embodies both the spiritual world and the material world, being partly matter, partly spiritual. In time God will become one with man, one with all His creation. That is the subject of our next chapter.

DISCUSSION QUESTIONS

1. What are the basic questions of life which occur to every person after he reaches the age of reason?

The basic questions of life which occur to every person upon reaching the age of reason are: Who am I? Where did I come from? How did I get here? Why am I here?

2. What power does man have which places him above the whole universe of mere objects?

Man has the powers of intellect and free will which place him above the world of mere things.

3. How is man supernatural in relation to the material world?

In relationship to the rest of the material world, man is supernatural in the sense that, possessed of an immortal soul with intellect and free will, he can know and desire and he will live forever. The soul of man can never die.

4. Explain what is meant by the soul of man.

The soul of man is immaterial. It is a spirit that will never die. Its highest faculties are intellect and free will.

5. Why have surgeons never been able to discover man's soul in exploring every part of the human body?

Surgeons will never discover man's soul with a scalpel because the soul is a spirit which cannot be seen. The soul is an immaterial substance existing in every part of the human body, whole and entire, without one part being in one place and another part being in another place.

6. Explain: The soul separated from the body does not make up a complete human person, yet it is aware of its own existence.

The soul animates the human body and is an incomplete substance because a human person is ordained to be composed of a body and a soul united. The soul operates after death, knowing and loving, but it is still ordered to be joined to a human body.

7. When does each human body receive its soul?

The human soul is created and infused into the body at the moment of conception.

8. Describe the power of each of the two faculties of the soul.

The intellect is the faculty of the soul whereby one knows in a nonmaterial way, that is, it is not mere sense knowledge or feelings. It gives a human person the power to reason abstractly. The human will is the power of the soul to desire what is good, to love or to hate.

9. What are the two types of evolutionary theory and which theory is condemned by the Catholic Church?

Materialistic evolution assumes that matter has always existed, that it was not created and that from it all things came. This may not be believed by sincere Christians. **Theistic** evolution is not incompatible with Christianity provided it holds that if evolution of the body took place it was under divine power while the immaterial and immortal soul of man was separately, individually and immediately created.

10. Explain why man as man could not evolve.

Man as man could not evolve because the very meaning of man is that he is a creature composed of both body and soul. The soul could not evolve, because it is spiritual and immediately and individually created by God. An evolving body without a soul is not a man.

11. Why is the teaching of evolution as a fact unscientific?

It is unscientific to teach evolution as a fact because it has not been proven to be true. In other words, it is only a theory.

12. Name the three conditions under which it is possible to accept the theory of evolution of the human body.

The evolution of the body may be believed by Catholics under these three conditions:

a. The soul was created immediately by God and did not evolve.

b. The evolution of the body, if it took place, was the result of divine power.

c. There is a unity to the human race. All descended from a common set of parents.

13. What were the special gifts God gave to our first parents when He first created them?

The special gifts God gave our first parents were: they were created in grace, in a state of original justice and with preternatural gifts. Our first parents, Adam and Eve, possessed the gifts of infused knowledge, the absence of concupiscence and bodily immortality.

14. What were the effects of original sin, which we all have inherited?

The effects of original sin which all have inherited are the loss of grace, the loss of the preternatural gifts and the loss of the right to heaven. The intellect of man was darkened and his will weakened.

15. Essentially, what kind of sin did Adam and Eve commit? Explain.

Essentially, Adam and Eve committed the sin of pride. True, they disobeyed God by eating from the tree of the knowledge of good and evil, but they did so because they gave in to the temptation of the devil who told them: "God knows well that the moment you eat of it you will be like gods who know what is good and what is bad." The wisdom our first parents sought to gain in disobedience brought only shame, unhappiness, suffering in this world, eventual death of the body and the loss of eternal life with God in heaven.

16. Why is it ridiculous to accuse Genesis of being unscientific in its seven-day account of the creation of the world?

The Genesis account of creation is no attempt to explain the creation of the world from the viewpoint of science but of religion, namely, that God made all out of nothing and made it good, with man being the crowning act of His creation of the world.

17. Explain how the Genesis seven-day account of creation contrasted with the pagan mythologies.

The Genesis account of creation contrasted with the pagan mythologies which were contrary to the revelation that God made all things out of nothing and that He made them good. Also, in Genesis, man made to God's image and likeness is ordered to adore one true God, not many gods.

CHAPTER 3

Jesus Christ: Who Is He?

What is Christianity? What does it mean to be a Christian? Ask that question and you may receive such answers as: "To be a Christian means to be loving and kind, to be charitable." Ask: "What more?" And the answer may come: "Christianity refers to those who believe in God . . . A Christian is one who believes in the one true God." There are Jews and Moslems, however, who believe in one God, creator of heaven and earth, but who have never been baptized and are not Christians because they do not believe that Jesus Christ is God, the second person of the Blessed Trinity, the Word of God made flesh.

A true Christian is one who has been baptized and who professes and believes in the essentials of the Christian faith which, in summary, are expressed in the *Apostles' Creed* (see Chapter 24). A Christian, then, is one who not only believes in the one true God, the infinite Supreme Being, creator of heaven and earth, but he is one who believes that there are three divine persons in the one Godhead and that the second person, namely the Son of the Father, became man through the overshadowing of the Virgin Mary by the Holy Spirit. The Christian believes that Jesus Christ, God made man, died on the cross for the redemption of all men, rose from the dead and ascended into heaven "and there at God's right hand he stands and pleads for us" (Romans 8:34). "It follows, then, that his power to save is utterly certain, since he is living for ever to intercede for all who come to God through him"(Hebrews 7:25). In short, to be a Christian we must believe that Jesus Christ is the Son of God, Savior, true God and true man.

A question may present itself. How many are truly Christian who wear the label "Christian"? "When Jesus came to the region of Caesarea Philippi, he put this question to his disciples, 'Who do people say the Son of Man is?' And they said, 'Some say he is John the Baptist, some Elijah, and others Jeremiah or one of the prophets.' 'But you,' he said, 'who do you say I am?' Then Simon Peter spoke up, 'You are the Christ,' he said, 'the Son of the living God!' Jesus replied, 'Simon, son of Jonah, you are a happy man! Because it was not flesh and blood that revealed this to you but my Father in heaven' " (Matthew 16:13-17).

Jesus accepted Peter's profession of faith that He as Messiah was also "the Son of the living God." At the same time, He told him that his faith in the Son of the living God made man was not due to any natural intellectual conclusion. It was due to the gift of faith bestowed upon Peter by the first person of the Blessed Trinity, the Father, who had sent His Son as man into this world. Jesus asked the crucial question of His disciples who, as the first bishops and priests, the chief teachers of the faith after His ascension and the descent of the Holy Spirit on Pentecost, must confirm the people in the faith that Jesus Christ is true God, true man, the Savior of the world. Peter would be the head of the college of bishops, the apostles, and when he answered for the Twelve that Jesus is "the Son of the living God," Jesus continued His respone with: "So now I say to you: You are Peter and on this rock I will build my Church . . ." (Matthew 16:18). You have just declared, Peter, who I am. Now I will declare who you are. You are the rock, the visible head of my Church and through your declarations of faith "the gates of the underworld can never hold out against it."

In Chapter 8, "The Nature of the Church," we shall better understand in faith how and why Jesus could never permit His Church to be destroyed, because the Church is identified with Jesus Christ and who He is.

Just as the apostles had to answer the question of Christ, "Who do you say I am?" so must each one of us. Our eternal salvation depends upon our acceptance from the Father of the revelation of who He is.

Jesus explained many things privately to His disciples (Mark 4:34). One day, toward evening, Jesus and the disciples crossed over to the other side of the sea. A storm came up "and the waves were breaking into the boat so that it was almost swamped. But he was in the stern, his head on the cushion, asleep. They woke him and said to him: 'Master, do you not care? We are going down! And he woke up and rebuked the wind and said to the sea, 'Quiet now! Be calm!' And the wind dropped, and all was calm again. Then he said to them, 'Why are you so frightened? How is it that you have no faith?' They were filled with awe and said to one another, 'Who can this be? Even the wind and the sea obey him' " (Mark 4:37-41). Later (Mark 8:29), Peter arrives at the answer as already recorded above from Matthew 16. After that experience at sea when they kept asking one another "Who can this be. . . ?" they were to experience such things as Jesus feeding 5,000 men (not counting women and children) with five loaves of bread and two fish (Mark 6:38) and when all had eaten they gathered 12 baskets of leftovers, as well as the miracle of all the sick who touched Him suddenly getting well (Mark 6:56).

A second time Jesus fed 4,000 with seven loaves of bread and had seven wicker baskets of leftovers (Mark 8:8). After that, Jesus arrived in

Bethsaida with His disciples where some people brought Him a blind man and begged Him to touch him (Mark 8:22). Jesus put spittle on the man's eyes and laid his hands on him two times and the blind man could see.

After the multiplication of the loaves of bread on two different occasions with the minds of even the disciples completely closed to the meaning of the events (Mark 6:52) Jesus had to say after the second multiplication: "Are you still without perception?" (Mark 8:21). Finally, Peter's heart and mind are opened to profess: "You are the Christ!" or as Matthew records more completely: "You are the Christ, . . . the Son of the living God" (Matthew 16:16).

Sacred Scripture, God's recorded Word, mentions ". . . Peter, filled with the Holy Spirit, addressed them about 'Jesus Christ the Nazarene, the one you crucified, whom God raised from the dead'; . . . 'For of all the names in the world given to men, this is the only one by which we can be saved.' " (Acts 4:8-12). People ask about the millions in the world who have not had Jesus Christ preached to them, and who do not believe in Jesus as "son of the living God" made man. Are all these people going to hell?

The answer is that not all will be lost. What is certain is this: For men "in the whole world" to get to heaven it can be only through Jesus Christ. They cannot be saved by a Buddha, a Confucius or a Mohammed. There is no such thing as Christians having Jesus Christ for their savior while those of the faith of Buddhism, Hinduism, Islamism (Muslims) or even Judaism, which does not accept Jesus Christ as the messiah, having other saviors.

The 21st and latest ecumenical council of the Catholic Church, the Second Vatican Council (1962-1965) issued a *Declaration on the Relation of the Church to Non-Christian Religions* saying: "The Catholic Church rejects nothing of what is true and holy in these religions. She has a high regard for the manner of life and conduct, the precepts and doctrines which, although differing in many ways from her own teaching, nevertheless often reflect a ray of that truth which enlightens all men. Yet she proclaims and is in duty bound to proclaim without fail, Christ who is the way, the truth and the life (Jn. 14:6). In him, in whom God reconciled all things to himself (2 Cor. 5:18-19), men find the fullness of their religious life" (2).

The same ecumenical council continued: "The Church, therefore, urges her sons to enter with prudence and charity into discussion and collaboration with members of other religions. Let Christians, while witnessing to their own faith and way of life, acknowledge, preserve and encourage the spiritual and moral truths found among non-Christians, also their social life and culture."

"The Church has also a high regard for the Muslims. They worship God who is one, living and subsistent, merciful and almighty, the Creator of heaven and earth, who has also spoken to men. They strive to submit themselves without reserve to the hidden decrees of God, just as Abraham submitted himself to God's plan, to whose faith Muslims eagerly link their own. Although not acknowledging him as God, they worship Jesus as a prophet, his virgin Mother they also honor, and even at times devoutly invoke. Further, they await the day of judgment and the reward of God following the resurrection of the dead. For this reason they highly esteem an upright life and worship God, especially by way of prayer, alms-deeds and fasting"(3).

The same council quoted the Apostle Paul in Sacred Scripture saying that the Jews remain very dear to God for the sake of the patriarchs since God does not take back the gifts He bestowed or the choice He made.

Still, the Church proclaims that Jesus Christ is the Way, the Truth and the Life (John 14:6). No one can be saved except through Jesus Christ. Just how is Jesus Christ going to be the one essential Savior for those who have not in this life professed faith in Jesus we do not know. There is the possibility that Almighty God will send an Angel of Light to the individual soul at the moment of death, at the moment of the separation of body and soul, and reveal that Jesus Christ is Son of God, Savior. At that moment, each individual who did not have the faith in Jesus Christ as "Son of the living God" preached to him or her, will have the opportunity to accept or reject Jesus Christ. We do know that no one will be condemned except through his own fault. No one can innocently lose his soul. Our duty is to preach and profess Jesus Christ. The scandal of divisions among Christians has prevented much of the world from realizing that God the Father sent Jesus. Christians thus have a serious obligation to work for oneness. "Father, may they be one in us, as you are in me, and I am in you; so that the world may believe it was you who sent me" (John 17:21).

Jesus Christ, the eternal Son of the living God, made flesh by the Holy Spirit overshadowing the ever-virgin Mary (Luke 1:35), is the Son of God, son of Mary. That makes Jesus Christ true God, true man. The God-Man has two natures — one divine, which is eternal; the other, a human nature created in time. So pivotal was the coming of Jesus Christ as God-Man, Savior, to this world that we mark all time as so many years before Christ (B.C.) or so many years after His coming, in the year of the Lord, Anno Domini (A.D.). It is in Christ and "through his blood we gain our freedom, the forgiveness of our sins. Such is the richness of the grace which he has showered on us in all wisdom and insight. He has let us know the mystery of his purpose, the hidden plan he so kindly made in Christ from the beginning to act upon when the times had run their course to the end: that he

38

would bring everything together under Christ, as head, everything in the heavens and everything on earth" (Ephesians 1:7-10).

The first person of the Most Blessed Trinity did not become man. The third person of the Most Blessed Trinity did not become man. It was, rather, the second person of the Most Blessed Trinity who became man. Sacred Scripture refers to the Son of God, the second person, as the Word become man in this way: "In the beginning was the Word; the Word was with God and the Word was God. . . . The Word was made flesh, he lived among us, and we saw his glory, the glory that is his as the only Son of the Father, full of grace and truth" (John 1:1-14).

As already noted in an earlier chapter, God the Father, God the Son (the Word) and God the Holy Spirit are all equal to each other. They are three distinct persons in one God. Yet, Jesus Christ said, "The Father and I are one" (John 10:30). Jesus thus indicated that He had one divine nature with the Father. "Everything has been entrusted to me by my Father; and no one knows who the Son is except the Father, and who the Father is except the Son and those to whom the Son chooses to reveal him" (Luke 10:22). When Jesus announced that He was leaving this world, and that the Father would send the Paraclete, the Holy Spirit, in His name (John 14:26), He added: ". . . the Father is greater than I" (John 14:28). By this Jesus did not mean that the divine nature of the Father was greater than the divine nature of Jesus, for they are one in their divine nature; rather, Jesus is speaking as the Word Incarnate and as one going to the Father by glorification of His humanity. The Word as Son was equal to the Father. The Word made flesh, as man, was less than the Father. In short, Jesus is saying: The divine nature of the Father with which my divine nature is one is greater than my human nature, which human nature the Father does not possess. Jesus' leaving was to be by His passion and death for the redemption of the world, something willed by the Father and with which the Son joined His will as one, however difficult it was for His human will to carry out. The human will of Jesus was in conformity with the divine will. Jesus prepared the apostles beforehand so that their faith would not fail with the shock of events, especially the scandal of the Cross.

Jesus constantly spoke of the Father. "I am the Way, the Truth and the Life. No one can come to the Father except through me. If you really know me, you know my Father too. From this moment you know him and have seen him" (John 14:6-7). Even after those strong words Philip said to Jesus: "Lord, let us see the Father and then we shall be satisfied." "Have I been with you all this time, Philip," said Jesus to him, "and you still do not know me? To have seen me is to have seen the Father, so how can you say, 'Let us see the Father'? You must believe me when I say that

I am in the Father and the Father is in me. . . . Believe it on the evidence of this work, if for no other reason" (John 14:8-11).

When led before the Sanhedrin, and put on trial, Jesus was asked by the high priest: "Are you the Christ," he said, "the Son of the Blessed One?" (Mark 14:61). "I am," said Jesus. He was condemned to death for making himself equal to God.

In the early centuries of the Church men asked: "Who is Jesus Christ?" Some came to the wrong conclusions. Consequently, the Church had to clearly define terms in explaining just who Jesus Christ is. A term commonly used to explain that in Jesus Christ there is a union of the human and divine natures in one divine person is *hypostatic union*. Hypostasis means *one substance*. At the Council of Chalcedon, A.D. 451, the Church declared that the human and divine natures of Jesus Christ are joined "in one person and one hypostasis, meaning in one substance." A century later at the fifth general council at Constantinople, A.D. 533, the phrase "hypostatic union" was adopted to express that in Jesus are two perfect natures, divine and human. This means that the eternal divine person, the Word, the Son of God, takes to the very infinite spiritual substance of himself a human nature. The Incarnate Son of God is, therefore, an individual, complete substance. Contrary to the position of Arius (Arianism), the union of the two natures is real. It is not merely the indwelling of God in a man, as Nestorius (Nestorianism) said, because every Christian in the state of sanctifying grace, as we shall see in Chapter 7, has God dwelling in him.

We must not think of the soul of Jesus as being uncreated and as the eternal Son of God indwelling a body. The body and soul of Jesus are hypostatically united (fusing of divine and human substance) to the person of the Son. The soul of Jesus was created as was the body created which was taken from the body of Mary. The divine nature of the Son was hypostatically joined to the human nature of Jesus, which means that the uncreated person of the Son was united with His created body and soul.

✷   The person of Jesus, as eternal Son of God, was not created. The Human nature of Jesus was created, as is the human nature of every one of us. Jesus is the one essential mediator between God and man, between heaven and earth. A mediator is one who bridges, who joins together, like a ladder or stairway, in the case of Christ, reaching from earth to heaven. Only, once one embraces the mediator, Jesus Christ, he already has the goal, which is God the Father, in the unity of the Holy Spirit. To have one of the three divine persons is to have the other two because God cannot be divided.

Jesus as mediator means that He is the one who reconciled God and the human race. This is based on the teaching of the Apostle St. Paul:

40

"There is only one God, and there is only one mediator between God and mankind, himself a man, Christ Jesus, who sacrificed himself as a ransom for them all" (1 Timothy 2:5-6). The sin of Adam, the first head of the human race, was of infinite malice, not that mere man could do anything of infinite value, but the One against whom Adam had sinned was infinite. The justice of God, therefore, required satisfaction corresponding to the gravity of the sin, which was infinite in its evil. Therefore, the satisfaction to be made must be of infinite value to satisfy the justice of an infinite God. Yet, the satisfaction or reparation must be made by a man because a man had committed the sin. The only answer for reconciling God with humanity was a mediator who was both God and man. God the Father in His infinite love and mercy sent His own Son, Jesus Christ, into the world to reconcile divinity and humanity. "Yes, God loved the world so much that he gave his only Son, so that everyone who believes in him may not be lost but may have eternal life" (John 3:16). The Son so loved us that He laid down His life for our salvation.

God the Father in His mercy and love, then, provided the answer to satisfy the divine justice in order to reopen the gates of heaven closed by the sin of our first parents. A Buddha, a Confucius, a Mohammed could never offer the infinite satisfaction needed to reconcile, mediate between, God and man. There is a unity to the human race. All men fell in Adam. A savior was needed for all men. The one true God of the universe becoming a brother to man was the answer. "Now before we came of age we were as slaves to the elemental principles of this world, but when the appointed time came, God sent his Son born of a woman, born a subject of the Law, to redeem the subjects of the Law and to enable us to be adopted as sons" (Galatians 4:3-5).

The various people of the world, different tribes and cultures, had their gods. But, of all the people of the earth to whom the one true God, Yahweh (Jehovah), revealed himself it was to the Hebrew people. When Yahweh promised Moses that He would feed Moses' people, He concluded by saying: "Then you will learn that I, Yahweh, am your God" (Exodus 16:13). For fear of misusing God's name, God's people, rather than pronounce His name, substituted the title "Adonai," meaning "the Lord." The Old Testament had other titles for God as well — El or Elohim or El Shaddai."Old Testament times" refers to the time from the origin of the human race until the coming of Jesus Christ. Old Testament also refers to primitive patriarchal and prophetic revelation. It means the Old Covenant which Yahweh, the one true God, had with the Israelites, the people He singled out as His very own people whom He would protect and form — preparing them for the coming of the Savior promised to Adam and Eve in the garden after the fall (Genesis 3:15). The Old Testament has reference to the collection of books of the Bible which the Church believes to be divinely inspired and which are not of the New Testament, as noted in Chapter 4 on "Divine Revelation."

All the prophecies made about the Messiah to come, many made hundreds of years before His coming, were perfectly fulfilled in Jesus Christ. Yahweh-God sent the credentials of the promised Savior in advance. Jesus was born of a virgin-mother, which we will explain in Chapter 10 and which is known through the creeds of the Church and through Sacred Scripture. Each of the two natures in Jesus Christ, human and divine, has its own will and its own manner of operation. In Jesus Christ His divinity does not swallow up His humanity and His humanity does not diminish His divinity.

The name "Jesus Christ" is special because it refers to the Son of God made man. To simply say, "Jesus is God," is not to express fully who He is. For example, if the question is asked, "Did Jesus Christ exist 2,100 years ago?" the answer is "No," because when the word "God" is used correctly it refers to the one absolutely and infinitely perfect Spirit who is the creator of all and in whose Godhead there are three distinct persons, Father, Son and Holy Spirit. The name Jesus Christ, however, refers only to the Son of God made man. Jesus Christ did not exist as man 2,100 years ago but only since the time of the Incarnation, that is, when Mary said: "I am the handmaid of the Lord . . . let what you have said be done to me" (Luke 1:38).

This God-Man, Jesus Christ, is to be worshiped with one single kind of worship, the absolute worship called *latria*. This highest form of adoration is due to God alone for His supreme excellence. Absolute latria is given only to God, as the Blessed Trinity, or to one of the three Divine Persons, to Christ as God-Man, to the Sacred Heart of Jesus and to His real presence in the Holy Eucharist (Chapter 18). Because the eternal Son of the living God is hypostatically united with the humanity of Jesus Christ, Catholics worship the Sacred Heart of Jesus, the Precious Blood of Jesus Christ, the Holy Face and His five wounds. In reality, the entire body of Jesus Christ is adored. Singling out the Sacred Heart or the Most Precious Blood of Jesus is a subjective response of the faithful to the objective fact of Christ's love, divine and human, symbolized in His physical heart, while the Precious Blood is seen as an integral part of His human nature united with the second person of the Blessed Trinity and which was shed for the redemption of the world.

The human soul of Jesus Christ possessed the *immediate* vision of the Most Blessed Trinity, seeing the divine essence of God even as He is. This beatific vision existed from the first moment of the creation of His human soul and continued without interruption throughout His entire

42

earthly life. The Holy Office of the Vatican declared in 1918 that the contrary could not be taught. Pope Pius XII in his encyclical on the Church as the Mystical Body (*Mystici Corporis*, 1943) declared: "That knowledge which is called vision He possesses in such fullness that in breath and clarity it far exceeds the Beatific Vision of all the saints in heaven. . . . In virtue of the Beatific Vision which He enjoyed from the time when He was conceived in the womb of the Mother of God, He has forever and continuously had present to Him all the members of His Mystical Body (the Church) and embraced them with His saving love."

Unfortunately, some have thought and taught that Jesus Christ had human ignorance, even error, and only gradually discovered who He is. Such has never been the official position of the Catholic Church. Jesus could acquire experiential human knowledge, which means that whereas God the Divine Person of the Son knew all things, yet, as man, His human intellect and will and senses were exposed to things in a human way. The humanity of Jesus became hungry, tired and even angry, as when He made a whip of cords and drove the merchants from their business in the temple (John 2:14-17). What the Son always knew as God He now experienced in a human way.

The God-Man Jesus Christ was absolutely free of all sin, original as well as personal sin. "For it is not as if we had a high priest who was incapable of feeling our weaknesses with us; but we have one who has been tempted in every way that we are, though he is without sin. Let us be confident, then, in approaching the throne of grace, that we shall have mercy from him and find grace when we are in need of help" (Hebrews 4:15-16).

The eternal Son of the living God became man in order to effect the redemption of mankind. Humanity was held captive by being enslaved in sin. Satan had overcome man by inducing him to sin. The human race was held captive as to a debt of punishment, and divine justice required sufficient payment. The passion and death of Jesus Christ was the price or ransom required for freeing humanity from such obligations. Jesus Christ rendered satisfaction by the shedding of His Precious Blood. ". . . To feed the Church of God, which he bought with his own blood" (Acts 20:28). It was by His Most Precious Blood shed on the Cross that Jesus Christ redeemed the world.

When Jesus Christ hung dying on the wood of the Cross, just before giving up His soul, He said: "It is accomplished" (John 19:30). In the original language it needed only one word to express that His life was finished. Jesus had now fulfilled everything which had been prophesied about Him. All was fulfilled that was promised under the Old Covenant from the time of Adam and Eve being driven from the garden when the words containing the precious promise had been made: "I will make you enemies of each other: you and the woman, your offspring and her offspring. It will crush your head and you will strike its heel" (Genesis 3:15). It is sometimes translated "she" shall crush, but the original language refers to the offspring of the woman crushing the serpent's head. We learn in the New Testament that the woman is Mary and the offspring to crush the serpent's head is Jesus Christ. Jesus, by His death, was now about to crush the head of the serpent. "It is accomplished," Jesus calls out from the Cross.

Everything, every little detail from the offering of turtledoves in the temple, every historic foretelling from Abraham who offered his son in sacrifice, to Jonah in the whale's belly foretold Jesus would be in the earth for three days. The prophecy of David that the Messiah would enter Jerusalem on a beast of burden in humility; the prophecy of David that He should be betrayed by one of His own; the prophecy of Zechariah that He would be sold for 30 pieces of silver and that this price should be used to buy a field of blood; the prophecy of Isaiah that He would be treated in a barbarous manner, scourged, crucified between two criminals as Isaiah had foretold and that He would pray for His enemies.

David had prophesied as well, that they would give him vinegar to drink and divide His garments; that He would be a prophet like Moses, a priest like Melchizedek and a lamb to be slain, a scapegoat driven out of the city, wiser than Solomon, more kingly than David. For anyone who seriously studies the Old Testament prophecies it should be obvious that Jesus Christ was the one both Abraham and Moses had looked to in prophecy. He had come and fulfilled everything. His credentials were all in order and so Jesus Christ cried out: "It is accomplished," and then, "Father, into your hands I commit my spirit. With these words he breathed his last."

If it had ended there, men might well not accept Him as being the "Son of the living God," the Son of God the Father, and that He was conceived in the Virgin Mary by the overshadowing of the Holy Spirit, having no natural human father involved in His conception. If it had ended with Jesus being taken down from the Cross and laid in the tomb, there would be insufficient cause to put our faith in our eternal salvation in the carpenter of Nazareth. ". . . If Christ has not been raised, then our preaching is useless and your believing it is useless . . . and if Christ has not been raised, you are still in your sins. And what is more serious, all who have died in Christ have perished. If our hope in Christ has been for this life only, we are the most unfortunate of all people. But Christ has in fact been raised from the dead, the first fruits of all who have fallen asleep. Death came through one man and in the same way the resurrection of the dead has come through one man. Just as all men die in Adam,

44

so all men will be brought to life in Christ. . . ." (1 Corinthians 15:14, 17-22).

The resurrection of Jesus Christ from the dead, as He himself had foretold would happen, is the supreme proof that Jesus Christ is the God-Man, Redeemer of all men. While Jesus performed many miracles it might have been argued by some that they were tricks of magic and that people were deceived. But no man could be put to death, lose so much blood, have a spear pass through his heart, and three days later come back to life. Also, no mere man could have arranged his life and all the events surrounding it to fulfill in every little detail the prophecies made hundreds of years before his birth.

Even non-Christian writers of antiquity have described the belief of Christians in the Christ who was put to death and seen again and whom they believed to be God made man. The Jewish historian Josephus wrote of Christ in this manner. Pliny, the governor of Bithynia, sent a report to the Emperor Trajan telling how Christians "honor Christ, their God."

Jesus[1] is the name of our Lord and is the Latin form of the Greek, *Iesous*, in Hebrew *Jeshua* or *Joshua*, which means "Yahweh is salvation." In short, Jesus means Savior. Jesus is the name through which God the Father is to be invoked. Christ refers to the messianic role of our Lord by which He fulfilled all the ancient prophecies. Literally, the word Christ means "anointed" from the Greek *christos*.

Christianity refers to the teachings and the moral practices which Jesus Christ communicated, and the spiritual lives He encouraged His followers to take up by walking in His footsteps. Those who have faith in Jesus Christ as the Second Person of the Most Blessed Trinity, the eternal Son of God become man in order to redeem the world, accept the teachings of Jesus as the Word of God and strive to live the life He taught in their worship and human conduct of daily living.

Jesus Christ worked many miracles when He was on earth proving that He is, indeed, the Word of God made flesh. Even after His resurrection and ascension back into heaven, the apostles worked miracles in the name of Jesus (Acts 3:6).

Jesus is not merely a great man in whom God dwelled. Jesus is true God and true man. He is the God-Man and the only one who can save us

---

[1]The New Testament abounds in names and titles of Christ. To list but a few: "Alpha and Omega" (Revelation 1:8; 22:13); "Bread of Life" (John 6:35); "Christ the Lord" (Luke 2:12); "Greater Covenant" (Hebrews 7:22); "Head of the Church" (Colossians 1:18); "Holy One of God" (Mark 1:25); "King of kings" (Revelation 17:14; 1 Timothy 6:15); "Lamb of God" (John 1:29, 36); "Light of the world" (John 8:12); "Messiah" (John 1:41; 4:25-26); "Mediator" (1 Timothy 2:5); "Passover" (1 Corinthians 5:7); "Eternal Priest" (Hebrews 5:6).

from our sins if we but put our faith in Him and live according to His teachings. Because Jesus is both God and man we may adore His body and soul. In fact, we have an obligation to do so. At the same time, we adore the entire Blessed Trinity through Jesus Christ because only though His human nature can we go to God. To embrace the humanity of Jesus is to embrace the Godhead and to be at one with God.

The greatest miracle of Jesus, which gives us cause for faith is His resurrection from the dead on the third day after His death and burial. The resurrection of Jesus is a basic truth of Christianity, expressed in all the creeds and in all the rules of faith from the first century. Jesus rose from the dead through His own power. When Scripture says that Jesus Christ was raised by God or by the Father (Acts 2:24; Galatians 1:2), this does not mean that Jesus did not rise up by His own power, but, rather, refers to His humanity. Jesus, as the Word of God, is one with the Father and the Holy Spirit and, thus, the Godhead was the principal cause of the resurrection of Jesus from the dead.

The bodily resurrection of Jesus Christ from the dead is central to the Christian faith. While forms of rationalism have tried to explain away the resurrection, it is contrary to authentic Christianity. Jesus ate after He rose from the dead to prove to the apostles that the body they beheld was not a ghost but the same physical body they had walked with, talked with, and lived with for three years as He taught them and the same body which they had seen crucified until dead.

The risen body of Jesus was in a state of glory, as we see in the Gospels and the Acts of the Apostles. He could appear and disappear, and come through closed doors, no longer restricted by the limitations of space and time. Yet, as proof that this was the same Jesus they knew, Jesus had in His body the marks of the crucifixion (John 20:27).

Sacred Scripture and all the creeds of the Church affirm that Jesus ascended into heaven after His resurrection. Jesus ascended in body and soul by His own power. The ascension was the final elevation of the human nature of Jesus Christ into the divine glory. In heaven, as God equal to the Father and to the Holy Spirit, and still in possession of His human nature, Jesus makes intercession for us (Romans 8:34). By becoming man, the eternal Son of God became our brother. Now we need have no fear of approaching God because Jesus is God, one with us in all things but sin. As the eternal high priest at one with the Father and the Holy Spirit in His divine nature, this Jesus in His human nature pleads for us, bearing in His body for all eternity at the throne of God the glorified wound marks in His hands, feet and side — signs of our redemption. Beholding the God-Man Jesus Christ, the Father can see that His justice has been completely satisfied by the supreme sacrifice of the Cross so that in and through Jesus Christ God's love and mercy flow forth to all men.

WHO IS JESUS CHRIST?

JESUS CHRIST IS SON OF GOD, SAVIOR.

DISCUSSION QUESTIONS

1. What is a Christian?
A true Christian is one who has been baptized, who believes that there is one God, and that Jesus Christ is true God and true man who redeemed all men by his death on the Cross after which Jesus rose from the dead and ascended into heaven.

2. What enabled Peter to make his profession of faith?
Peter was able to make his profession of faith that Jesus was the Messiah, "the Son of the living God," because he was given the gift of divine faith by God the Father.

3. What did Jesus do to bring the Apostles to faith in who He is?
Jesus worked miracles to bring His Apostles to faith in Him.

4. Will all non-Christians go to hell?
No, but those who are not lost must in some way be saved through Jesus Christ. It is possible that God could send an Angel of Light at the moment of their death to reveal to them that Jesus Christ is Lord, God and Savior and they could accept Him or reject Him. Having lived sincerely in life, sincerely seeking truth, men are disposed to accept true faith.

5. What is the official position of the Catholic Church regarding non-Christian religions?
The Catholic Church rejects nothing which is true and holy in other religions, which often reflect a ray of that truth which enlightens all men. Often, other religions have arrived at least at some of the truth, either through the use of natural reason, since faith and reason do not contradict each other, or through acceptance of part of the divine revelation once given to God's people, the Jews.

6. Could non-Christian religions have personal saviors other than Jesus Christ?
There is no savior other than Jesus Christ. He is the one, sole, universal savior.

7. Was the soul of Jesus created? Did He have a divine will or a human will?
The soul of Jesus was created and had a human intellect and a human will. The person of Jesus which is divine also had a divine intellect and a divine will.

8. Jesus said: "Whoever has seen me has seen the Father. . . . I am in the Father and the Father is in me" (John 14). Is the person of the Father, therefore, the same as the person of Jesus? Explain.

47

The person of Jesus is the Second Person of the Holy Trinity and is distinct from God the Father who is the First Person of the Holy Trinity, and the Holy Spirit who is the Third Person. Jesus is one with God the Father because He shares the same divine nature as God the Father. Jesus said: " Everything has been given over to me by my Father" (Luke 10:22).

9. Why was Jesus condemned to death?

Jesus was condemned to death for making himself equal to Yahweh, that is, God the Father.

10. What is meant by the Hypostatic Union?

Hypostatic Union refers to the union of the human and divine natures in the one divine person of Jesus Christ. The expression comes from the word "hypostasis" which means one substance. There is no mere indwelling of God in a man. Rather Jesus Christ is true God and true man.

11. What in Jesus Christ was created and what was not created?

The soul of Jesus was created in time as was His body. His person was not created but is eternal. The person, namely the Second Person of the Blessed Trinity, the Son, was hypostatically united to the body and soul of Jesus Christ.

12. What is a mediator? How is Jesus Christ the Mediator?

A mediator is one who bridges or joins together. Jesus Christ is the one essential mediator between God and mankind, being both God and man.

13. Why cannot a Buddha or a Mohammed reconcile men with God?

Buddha or Mohammed are not mediators who reconcile God and man for they, too, were men born in sin who were in need of redemption.

14. Is Jesus Christ less than God because of His humanity?

The divinity of Jesus Christ does not swallow or destroy His humanity nor does the humanity of Jesus Christ make Him less God. Jesus is true God and true man.

15. Is the name "Jesus Christ" interchangeable with the word "God"?

The name "Jesus Christ" refers to the Second Person of the Blessed Trinity become man and, therefore, our savior. The word "God" as Godhead is not restricted to any one of the three divine persons. It refers rather to the divine essence or nature, with emphasis on God's total transcendence of creation. God means the one absolutely and infinitely perfect spirit who always was and always will be. The very nature of God is to be three persons in one divine nature.

16. What kind of adoration is due Jesus Christ?

The adoration known as latria is due Jesus Christ. Latria is the highest form of adoration which is due God alone for His supreme excellence.

17. Why is it proper to adore the Sacred Heart of Jesus, His Holy Face or His Precious Blood?

The Sacred Heart or the Holy Face or the Precious Blood of Jesus Christ is adored because the entire body and soul of Jesus Christ is hypostatically united to the Son of God, and Jesus Christ deserves the absolute adoration of latria.

18. When did the created soul of Jesus Christ first have the beatific vision of the Most Blessed Trinity?

The created soul of Jesus Christ possessed *immediate* vision of the Most Blessed Trinity in its divine essence from the first moment when His human soul was created. Pope Pius XII stated this explicitly in his encyclical to the world, *Mystici Corporis* (1943).

19. Did Jesus always know who He is? Explain Jesus' growth in experiential knowledge.

Jesus Christ always knew that He was the eternal Son of God made man. His person was the infinite, divine Second Person of the Most Blessed Trinity. To say that Jesus only gradually discovered who He is has been condemned by the Church. Jesus grew in experiential human knowledge. As man, Jesus who was true God and true man experienced things in a human way — hunger, tiredness, etc. His divine intellect knew all things. His human intellect experienced things and He could grow in human experiential knowledge which He already possessed in His divine intellect in a perfect way.

20. Why is the resurrection of Jesus central to our faith in His being the eternal Son of the living God?

The resurrection of Jesus Christ from the dead is crucial to our faith that He is the eternal Son of God made man. "If Christ has not been raised then our preaching is useless and your believing it is useless" (1 Corinthians 15:14). The resurrection of Jesus Christ from the dead is the ultimate proof that He is, indeed, the Son of God.

CHAPTER 4

Divine Revelation

There are two forms of revelation whereby God makes His existence and His will known to the human race. God makes himself known to us in our world of space and time; He speaks to us through the natural world of creation. That is called *natural* revelation. Man using his reason in studying the world comes to knowledge which God wishes to communicate to him. In the Old Testament those who have ". . . not known God and who, from the good things that are seen, have not been able to discover Him-who-is, or, by studying his works, have failed to recognize the Artificer" (Wisdom 13:1) are said to be "naturally stupid." "Ever since God created the world his everlasting power and deity — however invisible — have been there for the mind to see in the things he has made. That is why such people are without excuse. . . ." (Romans 1:20)

Supernatural revelation is a grace from God whereby God speaks to mankind. There are two levels of supernatural revelation. Before the coming of Jesus Christ, God spoke indirectly through the prophets whom He inspired to tell others what God, Yahweh, had told them. In the person of Jesus Christ, God spoke to the human race directly. When Jesus came He spoke as a man to other members of the human race of which the Son of God had made himself one. "At various times in the past and in various different ways, God spoke to our ancestors through the prophets; but in our own time, the last days, he has spoken to us through his Son, the Son that he has appointed to inherit everything and through whom he made everything there is. He is the radiant light of God's glory and the perfect copy of his nature, sustaining the universe by his powerful command. . ." (Hebrews 1:1-3)

Human reason unaided by direct revelation from God cannot discover everything which God wants us to know. There are different levels of intelligence in men and many of them, busy with the need to earn a living, would not have or would not take the time to discover what God wishes to communicate to them in nature. God, in His love and mercy, has broken into our time, and through His Son become man has revealed His Word so that we could know clearly the mind and the will of God.

The Bible is a collection of books accepted by the Christian churches as the true, inspired record of the revelations which God has made to mankind. The Bible is divided into the Old Testament, containing the supernatural revelation given by God before the coming of Jesus Christ, and the New Testament, which contains revelation, God's Word, with the coming of Jesus Christ. The word "testament" means "covenant," since God was under a former covenant, or contract, with mankind before the coming of Jesus Christ and a new covenant with the coming of Jesus Christ.

In the Old Testament, God made an agreement (covenant) with Israel in which He promised protection to the Chosen People, the Israelites, in return for their loyalty. ". . . If you obey my voice and hold fast to my covenant, you of all the nations shall be my very own. . . (Exodus 19:8). And the covenant was sealed.

Years later, Jeremiah prophesied that a new covenant would be offered. Yahweh promised, ". . . I will plant my Law, writing it on their hearts" (Jeremiah 31:33). The prophet Ezekiel foresaw that God would "make a covenant of peace with them, an eternal covenant. . ." (Ezekiel 37:26). Isaiah foretold the universal character of the covenant to come "so that my salvation may reach to the ends of the earth" (Isaiah 49:6).

When Jesus came, He spoke of the new covenant sealed in His Precious Blood. The Apostle Paul, speaking of the institution of the Holy Eucharist to the Corinthians, quoted Christ's words: "This cup is the new covenant in my blood. Whenever you drink it, do this as a memorial of me" (1 Corinthians 11:25). The new covenant of God made with mankind in Jesus Christ, as will more clearly be noted in the chapters on the Holy Eucharist, is restruck every time the Holy Sacrifice of the Mass is offered. Our keeping the new covenant in Christ will lead us to eternal life, heaven.

Most Christians will agree that the Bible is the record of God's Word to us. How do we know that the Bible is God's Word? How do we know that it is the divinely inspired Word of God? By what authority?

Some may think the Bible always existed. Perhaps, some will even have the simplistic view that God's giant hand reached down from the clouds of heaven and He said: "Take and read." And that on the spine of the book it may read: "Catholic Edition" or "King James Edition" or "Standard Revised Edition" or some other edition.

Did Jesus leave the world a Bible? Did He give us the New Testament in book form as the foundation of our faith? Jesus Christ is the Word (Revelation 19:13), the Word of God made flesh (John 1:14). Jesus Christ is the Word (John 1:1), the "only Son of the Father" (John 1:14) come into the world. Jesus himself is the new, "the Greater Covenant" (Hebrews 7:22).

Jesus Christ, as the Word made flesh, lived upon this earth approximately 33 years. He was the Word become our brother and he spoke to mankind *directly*. When He ascended into heaven, did He leave us a book? As a matter of fact, Jesus never wrote a line of the Bible himself.

Did the Christians of the very first centuries have a Bible as we have it today? No. What are the true sources then of God's direct revelation to us, whereby we can know with the certainty of faith, that what we hold is, in fact, the inspired Word of God? Even if we accept the Bible as God's own divine Word, written by men under divine inspiration, the fact is that none of the originally written texts, which were the only inspired texts, exist today. They turned to dust long ago. Divine inspiration does not mean that the copiers of Sacred Scripture were inspired nor was it promised that they would be free of error in recording from earlier texts. The copying of earlier texts has been going on for centuries.

This leads us back to an earlier question. By what authority do we accept Sacred Scripture as the divinely inspired Word of God? Did Jesus give the world a book or a Church? Which came first, the Bible or the Church? These are questions we cannot brush aside.

What our questions really amount to is this: To know what is true faith, which is more important, the Bible or the Church? Is it more important to follow the Bible or the Church? Our answer is: the Church. As a matter of fact, one should not separate the Bible from the Church. The Bible is not the sole rule of faith. To make the Bible the sole rule of faith amounts to putting our confidence in paper, ink and cardboard as we commonly preserve the *record* of God's revelation today. We cannot look to the written Word of God apart from God himself and from His Church to whom He entrusted His Word.

We need the authority of the Church. Without the authority of the Church we would not have the Bible nor would we have an official interpreter to tell us what the Bible means. Speaking especially of the New Testament record of Sacred Scripture, the Church came before the Bible as we have it today. Jesus gave us the Church. The Church gave us the Bible. The Church was in existence years before the last portion of the Bible was written. St. John's Gospel was written around the year A.D. 100, and scholars consider Ephesus as the place of its composition. So, Jesus had ascended into heaven and the Holy Spirit had descended upon the Church on Pentecost Sunday years before the last part of the New Testament was written.

Jesus did not leave the world a book but a Church. Jesus did not say to the apostles to "write"; instead He told them to "teach." He told them that full authority had been given to Him by the Father, both in heaven and on earth. "Go, therefore, make disciples of all nations. . ." (Matthew 28:19). Some of the apostles eventually engaged in some writing to help them teach, but not all of the apostles wrote parts of the Bible. In fact, much of the New Testament was not written by the original 12 apostles. And St. Paul, whose writings under divine inspiration make up the greater portion of the New Testament, persecuted the early Christians. He was not converted to Christianity until some time after Jesus had ascended into heaven.

If you were able to go back and visit the Christians of the first century, or even of the second and third, and speak to them of the Bible as we have it today, they would not understand what you were talking about. They did not have a Bible, that is, the recorded Word of God, as we have today

The Church established by Jesus Christ began to be persecuted by Jewish authorities almost immediately after Jesus' death. The apostles went forth to the pagans of the Roman Empire and struggled with idolatry and immorality. No book of the New Testament existed when the Church was founded, although it already was divinely constituted into a hierarchical order with bishops (the apostles), presbyters (priests), deacons and baptized members of the Church. The divinely instituted sacramental system of the Church was operating and all the fundamentals of the Church as we have it today were functioning without the existence of a single New Testament book.

Ancient Judaism had its living oral traditions and its written law, or Bible. Now, with the coming of Christianity, judged to be the fulfillment of what the Old Testament merely promised, it, too, was to have through the designs of Almighty God, divinely inspired literature. Christianity could have spread with only living oral traditions, and it did at first. But men wrote under the inspiration of the Holy Spirit, describing the infancy, public ministry and saving death of Jesus Christ, and the establishment of the infant Church in the Roman Empire.

The new Sacred Scriptures began with the writing of the first Gospel by the Apostle Matthew and were completed with the writing of the Book of the Apocalypse (Revelation) written by St. John the Apostle at the end of the first century.

The Catholic Church has always taught that the Bible possesses a divine dignity, not only because of its contents, but because the Holy Spirit was present in its writing. God is the primary author of the Bible. The men He used to compose it are considered secondary authors. Pope Leo XIII, in the encyclical, *Providentissimus Deus* (1893), explained the Catholic tradition:

"For, by supernatural power, He so moved and impelled them to write — He was so present to them — that the things which He ordered, and those only, they first rightly understood, then willed faithfully to

53

write down, and finally expressed in apt words and with infallible truth. Otherwise, it could not be said that He was the Author of the entire Scripture."

The men, the secondary authors of the Bible, did not lose their personality in writing God's Word. Their human characteristics, their personality and style shine through in their individual writings. Through inspiration, however, God influenced their minds, wills and memories, their executive faculties, in such a way that God is the principal author of the entire Bible.

The Catholic Church has no dogmatic or definite pronouncements binding in faith as to the secondary authorship of any of the 72 books of the Old and New Testaments. Sometimes the sacred writer is known, sometimes not. What the Church presents as certain to our faith is that God is the primary author.

The inerrancy of the Bible has been the position of every papal encyclical on the Bible and also of the Second Vatican Council (1962-1965).

"For all the books which the Church receives as sacred and canonical are written wholly and entirely, with all their parts, at the dictation of the Holy Spirit; and so far is it from being possible that any error can coexist with inspiration, that inspiration not only is essentially incompatible with error, but excludes and rejects it as absolutely and necessarily as it is impossible that God himself, the Supreme Truth, can utter that which is not true" (Providentissimus Deus).

The *Canon* of Sacred Scripture refers to the catalogue of inspired writings by which the Church has used her God-given authority to identify the contents of both the Old and New Testaments. The origin of the Canon is traced back to Moses, who was ordered by God to write down his experiences and the laws. Gradually there developed an accumulation of scrolls comprising the sacred literature of the Hebrews.

From the fifth to the second century B.C., the time from Ezra and Nehemiah to the time of Jesus ben Sirach, the only document which refers to the collection of sacred books is the Septuagint. The Septuagint was a translation of the divinely inspired Hebrew scriptures into Greek. This translation was done in the third and second centuries B.C. and was made by Jews residing at Alexandria in Egypt. The Septuagint contained all the books that are in Catholic Bibles today and it was the Septuagint which Jesus Christ quoted when He referred to the Scriptures. Both direct and indirect references to the Greek Septuagint are frequent in the New Testament.

By the time of our Lord, the original Hebrew writings had already perished. Copyists are not guaranteed inerrancy in making their copies of the Scriptures in the New Testament, nor were they in the Old Testament.

Jewish Rabbis, about the second century after Christ, determined to obtain a correct official Hebrew text, used the Greek Septuagint translation to check discrepancies which they felt had crept into their texts from copyists. The fact that copyists are not guaranteed inerrancy, points to the need for the living Church, guided by the Holy Spirit, which has received authority from Christ. In accepting the authority of the Church in telling us what is the Canon of Scripture and how to interpret the Bible, we are accepting the authority of Christ who gave to His Church the same authority He had received from God the Father (Matthew 28:18-20).

The Canon as we have it today was accepted by the Council of Hippo (393), and its decisions were confirmed by the two councils of Carthage in 397 and 419 and were sent to Rome for approval. This determined the exact Canon as we have it today. The same Canon has been repeated by popes and councils throughout the centuries. The Council of Trent, on April 8, 1546, formally and dogmatically canonized these books consisting of 45 of the Old Testament and 27 of the New Testament. The decision of the Council of Trent means the list of the Canon cannot be disputed. The Canon of divinely inspired writings is officially declared by the Church to be accepted by the faithful. Without such authority of the Church, given it by Jesus Christ, we would remain in darkness, having no way of knowing which writings were authentically inspired and which were spurious. False writings, which some claimed were divinely inspired, circulated in the Christian world from the first century. The Church's God-given authority was essential in distinguishing spurious writings from authentically inspired writings.

That the Bible is divinely inspired does not mean that each individual who reads the Bible is promised to be free from error in interpreting God's Word. The Bible is a Church book, written by Church men, under the inspiration of the Holy Spirit, for the Church's use. The Holy Spirit who inspired the secondary authors in the writing of the Scriptures is the very same Holy Spirit, the Spirit of Truth, who guides the Church today in interpreting the Bible. If the Holy Spirit infallibly guided each one who reads the Bible, we would all interpret it as one.

A group of men did not sit down one day and decide to write the Bible. The various secondary authors did not necessarily even realize that they were inspired because God used them as instrumental causes. The entire Bible was written over the course of centuries; yet, it may rightfully be considered one book, the Book of Books, because of its divine character and its unified central theme running from beginning to end, namely, the history of God's love for mankind from the promise of salvation at the dawn of creation through its fulfillment in Jesus Christ to the early history of the Church which the Bible itself contains (Acts of the Apostles).

The Catholic Church from its beginning, as founded by Jesus Christ, has accepted the Septuagint, the Greek version of the Old Testament (250-100 B.C.), which was read by the Jews in their synagogues of the Hellenistic and Roman world. This Septuagint version consists of 45 books rather than the 38 books of the Talmudic Canon accepted and read by Jews in their Palestinian synagogues which excludes the seven deuterocanonical books and several other passages: the books of Baruch, Judith, Tobias, Wisdom, Ecclesiasticus (Sirach), First and Second Maccabees, and passages of Daniel (3:24-90 and 13:1-14) and Esther (10:4-16 and 24).

Some Protestant denominations have excluded from their Old Testament Bibles the seven deuterocanonical books and the deuterocanonical passages, a policy followed by the British Bible societies. This accounts for the so-called Catholic Bible having more books than the Protestant versions.

In 1947 there was found a collection of manuscripts and numerous fragments of ancient scriptural texts at the site of the ancient Qumran community, located close to the Dead Sea in Palestine. The dry desert had kept its secret of scriptural writings for 2,000 years. Then a Bedouin, looking for a lost goat, threw a stone into the opening of a cave and heard the clatter of something breaking. He ran away, afraid that the cave was inhabited by spirits. The next day the Arab shepherd, Mohammed Edib, returned with his cousin. They entered the cave and found eight jars, some with their lids still on. They took the jars outside hoping to find gold inside. They were disappointed when they found only bundles of leather with columns of writing which they were unable to read.

One day the shepherd took his find to a Syrian Christian named Khalil Kando and sold them to him. Kando took four of the scrolls to his Metropolitan (or Archbishop) who lived in Jerusalem. The Metropolitan recognized the four scrolls as ancient Hebrew writing and immediately bought them. In 1949 he took them to the United States where they were purchased by Professor Yigael Yadin for $250,000 who brought them back to Israel. Eleazar Sukenik, Yadin's father, had already brought the other three scrolls from Bethlehem.

The shepherds became aware of the high price placed on the scrolls and started searching all over the western region of the Dead Sea. More than 900 pieces of scroll were found in more than 30 caves. The largest quantity of manuscripts was found in Cave IV, discovered by the Bedouin in 1952, only 100 yards from the ruins of Qumran. Qumran refers to the ruins of an ancient Jewish religious community, consisting of huts, tents and caves near the community's center. The main building was 120 feet long by 90 feet wide and constructed of large roughly dressed stones. The community ruins are believed to have belonged to the ascetic Essenes.

The Essenes, who are believed to be the writers of the Dead Sea scrolls, were members of a religious sect who, detesting corruption, retired to the desert where they led a life of prayer, study, meditation, poverty and charity. The ancient historian, Josephus, wrote that the Essenes were "communists to perfection." By 68 B.C. the Essenes had all been murdered by Titus' soldiers on their way to crush the Jewish revolt in Jerusalem. The Essenes obviously hurriedly hid their most valuable possessions, the Sacred Scriptures, in the caves around their settlement and in inaccessible caves high up the side of the nearby cliffs as the Roman legions approached.

The discovery of these ancient biblical texts was the find of the century, and of great value to biblical scholars. The most famous scroll is the Isaiah scroll which is one foot wide and 24 feet long. The study of the scrolls has enabled scholars to make comparisons with more recent copies of Scripture and to appreciate the carefulness of copyists through the centuries. All seven parts, omitted in some Protestant versions of the Bible, were found in remnants among the scrolls. Conservative scholarship holds that the Dead Sea scrolls were composed between 170 B.C. and A.D. 68. These Old Testament writings, including commentaries on Scripture, rules for monastic living, etc., give clues to the meaning of the Christian faith.

Vatican Council II said:

"God graciously arranged that the things He had once revealed for the salvation of all peoples should remain in their entirety, throughout the ages, and be transmitted to all generations.

"Therefore, Christ the Lord, in whom the entire revelation of the most high God is summed up (cf. 2 Corinthians 1:20; 3:16; 4:6), commanded the apostles to preach the Gospel. . . . This was faithfully done; it was done by the apostles who handed on, by the spoken word of their preaching, by the example they gave, by the institutions they established, what they themselves had received. . . .

"In order that the full and living Gospel might always be preserved in the Church, the apostles left bishops as their successors. They gave them 'their own position of teaching authority.' This sacred Tradition, then, and the sacred Scripture of both Testaments are like a mirror, in which the Church, during its pilgrim journey here on earth, contemplates God, from whom she receives everything. . ." (*Dogmatic Constitution on Divine Revelation*, II,7).

"Thus, the apostolic preaching, which is expressed in a special way in the inspired books, was to be preserved in a continuous line of succession until the end of time. Hence, the apostles, in handing on what they themselves had received, warn the faithful to maintain the traditions which they have learned either by word of mouth or by letter (cf. 2 Thessalonians 2:15), and they warn them to fight hard for the faith that had been handed to them once and for all (cf. Jude 3). What was handed on by the apostles comprises everything that serves to make the People of God live their lives in holiness and increase their faith. In this way the Church, in her doctrine, life, and worship, perpetuates and transmits to every generation all that she herself is, all that she believes.

"The Tradition that comes from the apostles makes progress in the Church, with the help of the Holy Spirit. . . . There is a growth in insight into the realities and words that are being passed on. This comes about in various ways. It comes through the contemplation and study of believers who ponder these things in their hearts (cf. Luke 2:19; 51). . ." (*Dogmatic Constitution on Divine Revelations,* II, 8).

"Sacred Tradition and sacred Scripture, then, are bound closely together, and communicate one with the other. For both of them, flowing out from the same divine wellspring, come together in some fashion to form one thing, and move towards the same goal. Sacred Scripture is the speech of God as it is put down in writing under the breath of the Holy Spirit. And Tradition transmits in its entirety the Word of God which has been entrusted to the apostles by Christ the Lord and the Holy Spirit. It transmits it to the successors of the apostles so that, enlightened by the Spirit of truth, they may faithfully preserve, expound and spread it abroad by their preaching. Thus it comes about that the Church does not draw her certainty about all revealed truths from the holy Scriptures alone. Hence, both Scripture and Tradition must be accepted and honored with equal feelings of devotion and reverence. . ." (*Dogmatic Constitution on Divine Revelation,* II,9).

In the Bible (2 Thessalonians 2:15) we read about the apostles warning the faithful to maintain the *traditions* which they learned either by word of mouth or by letter. God, then, is the one wellspring or source of direct divine revelation and it comes to us both in the written word (Scriptures) and in oral traditions. For the *entirety* of God's Word we need both Scripture and Tradition and for these two we need the Church.

St. John ends his Gospel: "There were many other things that Jesus did; if all were written down, the world itself, I suppose, would not hold all the books that would have to be written" (John 21:25).

Sometimes people speak of "ongoing revelation." The Catholic Church, however, teaches that public divine revelation ended with the death of the last apostle. While our understanding of what God has already revealed may develop, that is, become fuller and deeper, God will not add to the *deposit of faith* found in Scripture and Tradition. Vatican

58

II said: "The Christian economy, therefore, since it is the new and definite covenant, will never pass away; and no new public revelation is to be expected before the glorious manifestation of our Lord, Jesus Christ (cf. 1 Timothy 6:14 and Titus 2:13)" (*Dogmatic Constitution on Divine Revelation*, I, 4).

The Church is the guardian of Sacred Scripture and the official interpreter of what the sacred writings mean. That is why it is dangerous for an individual to interpret the Bible, especially if he believes that he is divinely guided. The Church, of course, encourages its members to read the Bible prayerfully and in a spirit of meditation but the faithful, in humility, should realize that they must follow the teachings of the Church regarding interpretations, especially when difficulties arise. Above all, one's own interpretation should never be contrary to what the official Church teaches. Later chapters will explain the promise of Jesus, together with the Father, to send the Holy Spirit, the same Holy Spirit who is the primary author of Sacred Scripture, upon the Church to keep it free from error. Vatican II said that when the Scriptures are read to us in the divine liturgy (the Mass), Jesus Christ is present and speaking to us.

The Bible was written in the ancient languages of Greek and Hebrew. Biblical scholars, therefore, need to know these ancient languages, as well as the culture and the customs of those times, when they interpret the Scriptures. Biblical archeology, i.e., the science of biblical origins, based on the study of the documents, monuments and extensive excavations in biblical lands, all help the scholar to interpret Scripture. The last word, however, is always that of the Church when it comes to an authoritative interpretation. One must beware of "biblicism," which is an extreme preoccupation with the Bible. In practice, this means identifying divine revelation only with the Bible to the exclusion of sacred tradition as a source of revealed truth. The warning against "biblicism" is not intended to downgrade the Bible but to enhance it, because, as already stated, for the *entirety* of the sacred deposit of faith both Scripture and Tradition are needed and the totality of faith requires the teaching authority of the Church.

The Bible must be interpreted in its totality. Texts must not be isolated and interpreted independently. By isolating texts, one could prove almost anything.

If we sincerely desire to ascertain what God wished to communicate to us, since God spoke to us in human ways, we must carefully search out the sacred writers' meaning. To do this, we must study the time and the culture in which the sacred writers lived. We must know contemporary literary forms and realize that the Bible was not written yesterday, that is, in contemporary English. Due attention must be given to the characteristic patterns of each human author's perception, speech and narrative style at the time he wrote.

For those who would attempt to destroy the Gospels of Matthew, Mark, Luke and John, making them only myths or stories used to teach, the official position of the Church is seen in Vatican II's *Dogmatic Constitution on Divine Revelation*, Chapter V, paragraph 19: "Holy Mother Church has firmly and with absolute constancy maintained and continues to maintain, that the four Gospels just named, whose historicity she unhesitatingly affirms, faithfully hand on what Jesus, the Son of God, while he lived among men, really did and taught for their eternal salvation, until the day when he was taken up (cf. Acts 1:1-2). For, after the ascension of the Lord, the apostles handed onto their hearers what he had said and done, but with that fuller understanding which they, instructed by the glorious events of Christ and enlightened by the Spirit of truth (cf. John 14:26; 16:13), now enjoyed (John 2:22; 12-16; cf. 14:26; 16:12-13; 7:39). The sacred authors, in writing the four Gospels, selected certain of the many elements which had been handed on, either orally or already in written form, others they synthesized or explained with an eye to the situation of the churches, while sustaining the form of preaching, but always in such a fashion that they have told us the honest truth about Jesus. . . . Whether they relied on their own memory and recollections or on the testimony of those who 'from the beginning were eyewitnesses and ministers of the Word,' their purpose in writing was that we might know the 'truth' concerning the things of which we have been informed (cf. Luke 1:2-4)."

We should not be disturbed by modern rationalist approaches to the New Testament which seem to explain away its historical character. There are those who present the theory of demythology which claims that the whole language and spirit of the New Testament are mythical in character. These would say that to discover the real facts of Christ's life and teaching, it is necessary to strip the New Testament, especially the Gospels, of its layer of mythology, whereupon they attempt to explain away the miracles and the effects of God's supernatural power in the world.

Modern critics have attempted to hold the position that the infancy narratives about Jesus Christ are not historical. While the infancy narratives do include various types of literary forms, they do *not* represent imaginative, fictitious, decorative events which merely embellish early Christian truths, as some would say. Rather, the history of the infancy of our divine Lord (Luke 1-2; Matthew 1-2) has always been accepted by the Church as true, and the integrity of these chapters cannot be successively destroyed. They all are in the Greek manuscripts.

Those who would attempt to deny the historicity of the infancy narratives are not new in history. Celsus, the precursor of modern rationalists (ca. A.D. 175-180), held that the Incarnation (God become man) was inconceivable. He also rejected all supernatural elements in the Gospels as mere legend or as being fictitious. His objections, however, were satisfactorily answered by the early fathers of the Church.

The confused thinking of some theologians and scholars, who do not speak for the official Church, rejects the supernatural as not being acceptable to the modern mind. If we were to follow their thinking, we would be led to deny the cardinal doctrines of the holy Christian faith, such as the divinity of Jesus Christ and His resurrection. In desupernaturalizing or demythologizing the contents of the Bible, these non-approved authors place the Bible on the same level as uninspired human documents.

The position of the Catholic Church is clear. The Bible is the divinely inspired written Word of God.

We conclude by quoting the words of Pope Pius XII speaking to teachers of Sacred Scripture:

"With special zeal should they apply themselves not only by expounding exclusively these matters which belong to the historical, archeological, philological, and other auxiliary sciences — as, to our regret, is done in certain commentaries — but . . . their exegetical explanation should aim especially at the theological doctrine, avoiding useless discussions and omitting all that is calculated rather to satisfy idle curiosity than promote true learning and solid piety. They should expound what is called the literal meaning and most especially the theological meaning so carefully, explain it so clearly, and implant it so deeply, that in the students there might take place in a certain way what happened to the disciples on the way to Emmaus when, having heard the words of the Master, they exclaimed: 'Was not our heart burning within us while he was speaking on the road and explaining to us the Scriptures?' "

SUMMARY ON DIVINE REVELATION

The Bible is a Church book, written by Churchmen for the Church's use. It was divinely inspired. The men who wrote it, known as secondary authors, while writing in their individual human styles according to their times, nonetheless, were so guided by the Holy Spirit that what they recorded, reflects only divine truth which God wishes us to know and to live by.

Those who study the Bible seriously, prayerfully and in depth, recognize its divine character. God is its primary author. The same Holy Spirit who is the primary author of the Bible is also the one who guides the

Church in officially interpreting the message God wishes to reveal to us through its pages.

The Bible is the living Word of God when it is read and accepted in faith; as Scripture says, God's Word is "sharp as a two-edged sword." The sword of the Spirit is the Word of God. "All scripture is inspired by God and can profitably be used for teaching, for refuting error, for guiding people's lives and teaching them to be holy. This is how the man who is dedicated to God becomes fully equipped and ready for any good work" (2 Timothy 3:16).

The inspiration of the Canon of the Bible is a dogma which must be believed on divine faith, on the authority of God revealing. We have evidence of this divine inspiration from the Bible itself, the witness of the early fathers of the Church and the decrees of the Church authoritatively using the teaching power Jesus bestowed upon the Church in declaring the sacred writings inspired. "At the same time, we must be most careful to remember that the interpretation of scriptural prophecy is never a matter for the individual. Why? Because no prophecy ever came from man's initiative. When men spoke for God it was the Holy Spirit that moved them" (2 Peter 1:20-21).

The Church and the Bible are not in competition with each other. They belong together because the Sacred Scriptures are the written sacred traditions handed down to us from God from days both before Christ and with His holy coming to redeem the world. With God as the primary author of Sacred Scripture, there is an infinite intellect revealed. Consequently, the development of our understanding of the sacred pages will never end.

DISCUSSION QUESTIONS

1. What is natural revelation?

Natural revelation is God speaking to us and our discovering truths about God from the world around us.

2. What is supernatural revelation?

Supernatural revelation is God speaking to mankind, as through the prophets in the Old Testament, before the coming of Jesus Christ, and directly to mankind in Jesus, once He had come into this world.

3. What is the Bible?

The Bible is a collection of books accepted by Christian churches as the authentic inspired record of the revelations made to mankind by God about himself and His holy will for men. It is divided into the Old Testament (Jewish tradition) and the New Testament (Christian tradition).

4. What is the difference between the Old Testament and the New Testament?

The Old Testament is God's Word to man before the coming of the Messiah,

Jesus Christ. The New Testament is the fulfillment in Jesus Christ and His holy Church, of all which the Old Testament looked forward to and promised.

5. Did Jesus write any part of the New Testament?

Jesus Christ did not write even one line of the New Testament himself. Jesus Christ himself, however, "has become our guarantee" of a better covenant (Hebrews 7:22).

6. Does the world today have any of the original pages upon which God's inspired Word was first written?

The original material upon which men wrote the inspired Word of God long ago turned to dust or was destroyed.

7. Have copiers of the biblical texts through the centuries been protected from errors?

No. Copiers of the Bible are not divinely protected from error.

8. By what authority do we accept the Bible as the divinely inspired Word of God?

By the authority of God given to His Church to teach in the name of Jesus Christ the Church has declared certain writings to be inspired.

9. Which came first, the New Testament or the Church?

The Catholic Church existed for years before even one line of the New Testament was written.

10. In discovering what is true faith, which is more important, the Bible or the Church?

The Church is more important than the Bible. Jesus did not give us a book but the Church and to that Church He gave the authority to teach in His name. The two are not in competition.

11. Did Jesus command that the New Testament of the Bible be written?

No. Jesus did not command that the New Testament of the Bible be written.

12. Explain the difference between the primary author and the secondary authors of the Bible.

The primary author of the Bible is God. The instrumental causes or secondary authors were men whom God divinely inspired.

13. Was the New Testament written by all of the original 12 Apostles?

The New Testament was not written by all of the 12 Apostles but by only some of them. Mark and Luke were not of the original 12 Apostles nor was St. Paul, who wrote much of the New Testament.

14. How much of the New Testament had been written by the time the Church was operating with its sacramental system — the pope, bishops, priests, deacons and baptized faithful?

The Church was operating with its sacramental system before one line of the New Testament was written.

15. Could the Church have spread throughout the world without the New Testament?

Absolutely speaking, the New Testament writings were not needed to spread the Christian faith because, in fact, the Church did begin to spread throughout the world before any of the New Testament was written. God willed that the New Testament be written to aid the Church in its teaching.

16. Who was present when the secondary authors (men) wrote the Bible?

The Holy Spirit was present to inspire the secondary authors of the Bible.

17. Has the Church ever dogmatically defined who wrote each book of the Bible?

The Church has never dogmatically defined which men God used to write the Bible. It is of faith, however, that the Bible itself was written under divine inspiration in all of its parts.

18. Is any authorship of the Bible dogmatically defined?

The only authorship of the Bible dogmatically defined is that of the Holy Spirit, the primary author.

19. What is meant by the inerrancy of the Bible?

When we speak of the inerrancy of the Bible we mean that it is without error. This applies to the Bible in its entirety.

20. What does the "Canon of Sacred Scripture" mean?

The Canon of Sacred Scripture means the list of inspired writings of the Old and New Testaments, declared such by the authority of the Church.

21. What is the Septuagint?

The Septuagint is the most important translation of the Hebrew Old Testament into Greek. Jesus quoted the Septuagint, and early Christians used it as a basis for their belief in Jesus as the promised Messiah.

22. Why is the authority of the Church essential so that we may know the Canon?

Without the authority of the Church declaring which canonical or inspired books make up the Bible, we could not be certain in faith as to the authentic list of inspired writings.

23. Is each individual who reads the Bible divinely guided in his or her interpretation?

God has given no promise that each individual reader of the Bible will be divinely guided in interpreting the Bible. Experience, in fact, teaches otherwise because men contradict one another in their interpretations.

24. What is the central theme of the entire Bible?

The central theme of the Bible from the beginning of the Old Testament to the end of the New Testament is God's love for mankind and His desire to bring everyone to salvation.

25. What are the Dead Sea Scrolls and why have they proven valuable?

The Dead Sea Scrolls are a collection of manuscripts and numerous fragments of manuscripts, especially of Old Testament Scripture, which were discovered in the late '40s and early '50s after being hidden for close to 2,000 years in caves near the Dead Sea in the Holy Land. These scrolls are valuable to Scripture scholars because by comparing them to modern texts and translations, which are the result of copies made through the centuries, it is possible to discover discrepancies or errors which copyists might have made. They also throw much light on the meaning of the Christian faith and its development. Being the oldest copies or fragments of Scripture in existence gives them great value.

26. What is Sacred Tradition?
Sacred Tradition is the unwritten Word of God handed down in the Church.

27. Does the Church give its greatest reverence to Sacred Tradition or Sacred Scripture?
The Church gives equal reverence to Sacred Tradition and Sacred Scripture.

28. Do Tradition and Scripture come from different sources?
Tradition and Scripture flow from the one wellspring which is God.

29. Will more be added to the sacred deposit of faith which the Church possessed at the time of the death of the last apostle?
The sacred deposit of faith ended with the death of the last apostle.

30. Who is the official guardian and interpreter of the Bible?
The Catholic Church is the official guardian and interpreter of the Bible.

31. What is needed for the "entirety" of the sacred deposit of faith?
For the entirety of the sacred deposit of faith we need Tradition, the Sacred Scriptures and the authority of the magisterium (the teaching Church).

32. What does the Catholic Church officially say about the historical character of the four Gospels?
The Catholic Church declares that the four Gospels are historical and may not be regarded as legends or myths.

CHAPTER 5

Truth: What Is It?

What is truth? The mind naturally seeks to know the truth. Yet, many people go through life simply accepting what they have always heard. Most are morally good, sincere people who think it would be most improper to question positions held and handed down, sometimes for generations. Today, however, we are witnessing an era of questioning. Almost everything and every position is open to question. This is not necessarily a bad phenomenon if correct reasoning is used. Unfortunately, logical processes for seeking the truth, whereby the mind conforms or is in agreement with things outside itself, either in assenting to what *is* or in denying what is *not*, are not employed. Too often emotions get in the way. The opinions of the majority tend to determine "truth."

What is truth in itself? If a priest asks that question of someone today, he will invariably respond: "I suppose that you are implying that the Catholic Church is the true Church; that you have the true faith and that all others are false." The question "What is truth?" however, is not necessarily a religious question. It can be applied as a test of authentic faith; but let us suppose for the present that the person asking the question is neither a priest nor the representative of any church. A group of people are merely sitting around for an evening of discussion, and to stimulate conversation someone asks: "What is truth?" How would you answer that question?

Try the above experiment with an average group of people who are engaged in informal discussion. Unless you have some very learned people in the group who are educated in Aristotelianism or Platonism, you are likely to receive replies such as: "Truth is when one is sincere; when one sincerely holds a position. . . . Truth is how a person honestly feels about something. . . . Truth is honesty. . . . Truth is an honestly formed opinion on a subject. . . ."

The objection may be raised: "But one can be sincere and still be wrong?" And the reply which quickly follows is: "But it is truth to that person."

The point to be made here is that popular concepts of truth will not stand the test of actual experience for that mind which objectively and logically seeks truth in itself. In fact, popularly held concepts of truth often have led the world into confusion, frustration, disunity and conflict.

When we hold that truth is how a person feels about something, "my opinion," we leave a great deal of room for pride to enter. As a result, men become sorely divided. It is well said that "humility is truth" because one must seek the truth for its own sake. It has been said that "truth hurts." And it does. One sometimes has to swallow pride and admit: "I've been wrong." The human intellect naturally seeks the truth. When humility is possessed as a moral virtue which keeps a person from reaching beyond himself and restrains his unruly desire for personal greatness and recognition, it will lead to an appreciation of absolute truth. The absolute truth, we shall see, is God himself. Truths which we discover in the world are merely reflections of the absolute truth. We should reach beyond ourselves when it means reaching out to truth for its own sake, even though it means admitting that we were wrong. At that moment we become greater because we reject what was wrong, we embrace what is true, and, therefore, we resemble God more closely.

A person may be most sincere and think that he has the truth, but sincerity does not guarantee that what he honestly feels about a subject or thinks to be true will, in fact, prove to be true. Let us demonstrate with a simple example. Teachers sometimes use a telescoping pointer to draw the attention of students to a chart or to some visual aid. Before the pointer is extended it appears to be a ball-point pen. Hold it aloft before a crowd of people and ask: "What am I holding?" Unless it has previous experience of the pointer with its pocket clip, the group will answer: "A pen." Everyone in the group is sincere but they are still wrong. What they think or how they feel about the object which the instructor holds, although sincere, does not give them the objectively true answer. Their minds do not yet conform to the reality of the object which the instructor holds.

We come then to a definition of truth. TRUTH IS CONFORMITY OF THE MIND WITH REALITY.

Keeping this definition in mind, *truth is conformity of the mind with reality*, there are other principles which must follow in recognizing objective truth.

A thing cannot both be and not be at the same time and in the same respect. Place four apples on an empty desk top. Ask 25 men to look at the desk and then tell you how many apples are on that desk. If all 25 individuals are to give the true answer they must agree. They must give the *one* same answer: "Four." If some have faulty vision (for instance, double vision), at the moment they look at the desk, they may in all sincerity say that there are eight apples on the desk. The mind, however, would not be conforming with reality. They would not have the true answer. You may place eight apples on the desk one moment and four apples on the desk another moment but it is impossible to have four apples and eight apples being the sum total of apples on the desk at the same time and in the same respect.

Contradictions cannot be true when you are speaking about the same thing, at the same time and in the same respect. Four apples and eight apples on the desk at the same moment and same respect is a contradiction. It is like asking: "Since God can do all things, can He make a square circle?" It is a contradiction. It makes no sense asking: "Can God do something He cannot do?"

Truth is one. That is the simplest way to explain objective truth as the *conformity of the mind with reality. Truth is one* means simply that contradictions cannot be true — a thing cannot both be and not be at the same time and in the same respect. When one is seeking the truth about something at the same time and in the same respect, only *one* answer is true. How far is the moon from the earth? At different times and in different respects it can vary. At this particular moment, from this particular spot on the earth to another particular spot on the moon, in regard to the shortest distance between the two points, *one* answer is true. It is not a contradiction to speak of the earth as so many miles from the sun in the winter and a different number of miles in the summer, for then one is speaking of a different time and respect. In the conformity of the mind with reality, truth is one. Keeping in mind that "truth is one" when applying this to religion, we will better appreciate our Lord and Savior, Jesus Christ, speaking at the end of His life for the need of oneness in His followers.

Unfortunately, too many use subjectivism in their thinking. Subjectivism is any view of human nature and activity which denies the objective order of reality. Subjectivism can have some very sad, confusing and contradictory effects. It takes three forms:

In *philosophy*, subjectivism claims that a person cannot have direct knowledge or certitude about the world outside the mind. According to this there is no way of knowing the truth.

In *theology*, subjectivism holds that the essence of faith is each individual's own experience, and not the free assent of the mind to what God has revealed. It is dangerous when it determines as "true" what a person holds, gained from knowledge or supposed knowledge arising from one's own immediate awareness and experiences with reality. This leaves room for mistaken judgments.

In *morals*, subjectivism admits of no principles, no absolute norms of conduct, except those created by each individual's own will, which is then the same as one's own independent conscience. The Catholic Church, on the other hand, says that there are *objective absolutes* in determining true morality. These absolutes come from God.

It is possible to have a false conscience. Truth is not essentially what I think or feel but what *God knows*. The modern world likes to take polls and readers like to discover what other people are thinking. Polls, however, do not determine true morality on such matters as abortion, artificial birth control, homosexuality, divorce and remarriage, how many sacraments Jesus instituted for His Church, whether baptism is necessary for salvation, or just what Holy Communion is. Truth is found in what God knows and has revealed and what is in the very nature of things as God created them.

What matters is not the opinion of men when a person desires to know and possess objective truth, objective reality. What matters is to conform one's mind with the ultimate reality, which is God. What is right objectively is in the very nature of things, in the very mind of God. That is where the truth is determined and that is what men must seek. The only three persons you could ever poll and always get the absolutely true answer are God the Father, God the Son and God the Holy Spirit.

In the Christian faith, God the Father sent His Son, who said: "I am the Truth." He, the second person of the Blessed Trinity, sent to this earth by the first person of the Blessed Trinity, promised that the third person of the Blessed Trinity, the Holy Spirit, "the Spirit of truth" (John 16:13), would keep His Church always in the truth. While all cannot be said in this chapter, in the totality of this book, it is our desire to show that when we listen to the Church, we listen to Jesus, who said, "I am the Truth" and "He who hears you hears me." We, as members of the Church, which in a later chapter we will see is the "Body of Christ," are, in reality, the happy recipients of that poll of the three persons in the one God whose divine nature is one and whose knowledge is the truth. This is to say, we accept as true faith what God has revealed and preserves as true through the power of the Holy Spirit.

We have the obligation to accept and to live only by what is truth in reality. We should not live an opinion. We should live the Truth. Jesus said, "I am the Truth" (John 14:6), while His great apostle Paul in his letter to Philemon says, in essence, that "for me to live is Christ." We also are told in the Gospels that men came to Jesus asking Him for His opinion. When they went away, His listeners noted that He spoke with authority. All authority, all truth, is from above. Truth and authority have been given to Jesus Christ. He, in turn, has given them to His Church together with the Holy Spirit to keep it in the truth.

True faith and right reason will never be in conflict. Since all truth comes ultimately from God, whether the subject be a truth men have discovered in mathematics, natural sciences, history, whatever, all truth discovered upon earth is but a reflection of the ultimate truth which is God. God being the source of all truth, religious truth, scientific truth, every truth, can never be in contradiction to himself. If science and religion ever seem to be in contradiction, then something is either wrong with our understanding of science or our understanding of true religion. Truth should never be feared. God is Love and God is Truth. True Love need never be feared.

The devil is the "father of lies" (John 8:44), as Scripture says; he is the spirit of disunity. *Truth is One.* The devil seeks not unity but disunity among mankind. While God is truth, Satan is the opposite.

As we look at the world today, we discover at least 500 different Christian denominations or churches. Sacred Scripture, God's Word, speaks of "one Lord, one faith, one baptism" (Ephesians 4:5).

Jesus founded one Church on the apostles with Peter the Rock as visible head. To His disciples Jesus said: "Anyone who listens to you listens to me; anyone who rejects you rejects me, and those who reject me reject the one who sent me" (Luke 10:16).

It is a scandal to the world that Christians, however sincere, are divided into hundreds of different churches. The need for unity was pointed out strongly and repeatedly by Jesus Christ.

"I have said these things to you while still with you; but the Advocate, the Holy Spirit, whom the Father will send in my name, will teach you everything and remind you of all I have said to you" (John 14:25-26).

"When the Advocate comes, whom I shall send to you from the Father, the Spirit of truth who issues from the Father, he will be my witness. And you too will be witnesses, because you have been with me from the outset" (John 15:26-27).

"I still have many things to say to you but they would be too much for you now. But when the Spirit of truth comes he will lead you to the complete truth, since he will not be speaking as from himself but will say only what he has learned; and he will tell you of the things to come. He will glorify me since all he tells you will be taken from what is mine" (John 16:12-14).

The night before He died (and a man speaks what is closest to his heart when he knows he is about to die), Jesus prayed His great prayer for oneness in His Church, for oneness so essential to true faith. Today, people often ridicule the purity of doctrine saying that doctrines are not important. Doctrines are important because they contain truths about the one whom Christians love and must believe in, in order to be saved. Doctrines help us to know Jesus so that we may develop a personal relation-

70

ship with Him and, thereby, with the Father in the unity of the Holy Spirit. Listen to Jesus' concern for purity in true doctrine:

"Father, the hour has come: glorify your Son so that your Son may glorify you; and, through the power over all mankind that you have given him, let him give eternal life to all those you have entrusted to him. And eternal life is this: to know you, the only true God, and Jesus Christ whom you have sent. . . . They do not belong to the world any more than I belong to the world. Consecrate them in truth; your word is truth. As you sent me into the world, I have sent them into the world, and for their sake I consecrate myself so that they too may be consecrated in truth" (John 17:1-4; 16-19).

Notice that Jesus is praying here not only for the apostles upon whom He built His Church with Peter as its visible head but for believers to the end of time. Jesus continues:

"I pray not only for these, but for those also who through their words will believe in me. May they all be one. Father, may they be one in us, as you are in me and I am in you, so that the world may believe it was you who sent me. I have given them the glory you gave to me, that they may be one as we are one. With me in them and you in me, may they be so completely one that the world will realize that it was you who sent me and that I have loved them as much as you loved me" (John 17:20-23).

How can the world believe that the successors of the apostles speak the truth, that their voice is the voice of Jesus Christ? "Anyone who listens to you listens to me" (Luke 10:16). While missionaries travel to strange lands, and while natives may not be able to explain Aristotelianism or Platonism, yet something instinctive tells them that contradictions cannot be true. Many missionaries contradicting each other are keeping the world from accepting Christ, from recognizing the truth. This is why Jesus, shortly before He died, prayed so intensely: "Father, may they be one in us, as you are in me and I am in you, so that the world may believe it was you who sent me" (John 17:21).

Earlier Jesus had said: "If you make my word your home you will indeed be my disciples, you will learn the truth and the truth will make you free" (John 8:31-32).

The true faith still exists in the world today. Jesus established one Church. ". . . Simon, son of Jonah, you are a happy man! Because it was not flesh and blood that revealed this to you but my Father in heaven. So I now say to you: You are Peter and on this rock I will build my Church. . ." (Matthew 16:17-18). Jesus spoke of one Church, not of many churches. Since truth is one, and Jesus is truth, He could only found one church, not two or many churches contradicting each other (as noted above in the principles for correct thinking). Jesus promised that His one

71

Church would never be destroyed. ". . . And on this rock I will build my Church. And the gates of the underworld can never hold out against it" (John 16:19).

Unless the Church which Jesus established is still in the world today, Jesus Christ was not God because He did not keep His promise. Being God, being truth incarnate, however, He must keep His promise. The Church Jesus founded must continue in the world until the end of time.

". . . All authority in heaven and on earth has been given to me. Go, therefore, make disciples of all the nations; baptize them in the name of the Father and of the Son and of the Holy Spirit, and teach them to observe all the commands I gave you. And know that I am with you always; yes, to the end of time" (Matthew 28:19-20).

Truth is immutable. Truth does not change. A simple example: 2 plus 2 equals 4. Two units added to two more units always has and always will equal four units. That truth will never change. We may express it in different ways. For example, one plus one plus one plus one equals four. Or, three units plus one more unit equals four. But, while the manner of expressing the same truth may change, the reality of the truth itself can never change. If proven mathematical truths and scientific truths cannot change, although our knowledge of such truths may increase without contradicting those established truths, then we must hold the same about religious truths. True faith cannot change. Our understanding of our faith can and should develop. Even as we grow in faith, however, our deeper understanding can never contradict what has always been true in our faith.

Since all truth comes from God and since God in His very nature is immutable, truth in itself cannot change. God is infinite existence. God's very nature is to exist. Being infinite truth, what God has created are simply expressions, images, reflections, of the infinite truth. Scientists discover the secrets of nature; they unfold the laws of nature which, oftentimes, have been hidden for millions of years to the intellect of man, but scientists do not create the truths which they find hidden in nature. They merely *discover* what God has *created* as reflections of himself, the infinite truth.

When Jesus Christ said He was truth itself and that "before Abraham ever was, I am" (John 8:57), His enemies understood that He was saying that He was God. The Jews of that time remembered well that when Moses said to God, ". . . I am to go then, to the sons of Israel and say to them, 'The God of your fathers has sent me to you.' But if they ask what his name is, what am I to tell them?" God replied, "I Am who I Am." This, he added, "is what you must say to the sons of Israel: 'I Am has sent me to you' " (Exodus 3:13-14). "I Am" is the same as saying "I

72

am self-existence. My very nature is to exist. I depend on no one to exist. I am the creator." Jesus was declaring himself to be the infinite truth made flesh equal to God the Father, true God of the fathers of the Israelites. "At this they picked up stones to throw at him; but Jesus hid himself and left the Temple" (John 8:59).

Later, when the Truth Incarnate (Jesus Christ) was brought from Caiaphas to the praetorium, Pilate, who was worried about his own career, came out and said to Jesus: " 'So you are a king then? . . .' 'Yes, I am a king. I was born for this, I came into the world for this: to bear witness to the truth; and all who are on the side of truth listen to my voice' " (John 18:37).

Pilate was standing before the face of truth itself. He replied to Jesus: "Truth? What is that?" He then released truth (in the person of Jesus) to be scourged and crucified. Pilate turned his back on truth. Men today do the same thing out of pride and human gain rather than accept truth for its own sake, which is, ultimately, to embrace God.

It is sometimes said that we cannot know the truth for certain. That is not correct. The very nature of the intellect is to seek the truth. God, who is the ultimate truth, made man in His own image and likeness. Man has a created intellect, patterned after the uncreated infinite intellect of Almighty God. God, who shared His gifts with us, including the gift of intellect, being a good God, surely would not create us with the inability to know the truth. God has given us an intellect whereby, even unaided by supernatural revelation, man can naturally come to the conclusion that God exists and he can learn many things about God from the created world. God desires that we know Him and love Him. To know Him is to know the truth. Too often, however, emotions get in the way of man's arriving at sound intellectual conclusions; the will is hindered by feelings, prejudices and inclinations based simply on what one has always thought, but not necessarily on what one has thought out, using sound logic.

Man has sought out truth since the foundation of the world. He also has accumulated knowledge over the centuries. Great philosophers, especially gifted in using their intellects to seek truth, have aided the world in developing the science of human reason, cultivating reasoning skills with order and precision, without error. When emotions and prejudices are set aside, one can be open to orderly mental processes whereby he can reach the truth about any specific issue under consideration.

True faith, true science and correct reason will never be in contradiction since all truth comes ultimately from God. True faith should never be contrary to reason, although, at times, faith may lead us beyond what we know by natural reason (e.g., the existence of three persons in one God). It is contrary to reason to believe that God could contradict himself. If

Christians would hold contradictory views on the same thing, yet claim that each position is God's, that would be a denial that truth is one. If some held that there is but one person in God while others held the position that there are three persons in God, these contradictions clearly could not both be true. Truth is the conformity of the mind with reality. The number of persons really existing in the Godhead is the one true answer. Contradictions cannot all be true when one is speaking about the same thing, at the same time and in the same respect.

There is only one true answer to the question of how many persons there are in God, namely three, God the Father, God the Son and God the Holy Spirit. The same is true about the other basic questions of our faith. How many sacraments did Jesus give His Holy Church? Is Holy Communion only a symbol of the Lord's body and blood or is it really the Lord Jesus under the appearance of bread and wine? Is there a hell? Contradictory answers to these questions cannot all be true. God's Word tells us that we should "have reason for the faith that is in us." Our faith must never be unreasonable.

If the faith be true, it stands on truth and it must be one. "There is one Lord, one faith, one baptism" (Ephesians 4:5).

While we can know many truths about God by reason, e.g., His existence, His eternity, His goodness, etc., yet, so that we may not miss these truths, and because some truths are beyond the reach of the mind unaided by divine revelation, God sent His Son as man into this world, saying, "I am the Truth" (John 14:6). "I was born for this, I came into the world for this: to bear witness to the truth; and all who are on the side of truth listen to my voice" (John 18:37).

DISCUSSION QUESTIONS

1. Can polls determine truth?

Polls do not determine truth but merely the opinions of people. They may not even be representative of the opinions of the majority of people if they are not conducted properly or if the questions asked are slanted in order to obtain a certain desired answer.

2. Why does sincerity in itself not guarantee possession of the truth?

One may be very sincere in thinking that something is true when, in fact, one may be mistaken in judgment. Objective truth requires that the mind conform with reality.

3. Explain: "Humility is truth."

"Humility is truth" means that one must seek the truth for its own sake. Sometimes one has to swallow pride in order to accept the truth because the truth, at times, may hurt.

4. Define objective truth.
Objective truth is the conformity of the mind with reality.

5. Explain: "Truth is one."
"Truth is one" means that in objective truth there is only one answer that is true at the same time and in the same respect.

6. What is subjectivism?
Subjectivism is any view of human nature and human activity which denies the objective order of reality.

7. Does what we experience necessarily guarantee truth to our minds? Explain your answer.
Experience does not guarantee truth because one can be mistaken in judging experiences. Emotion, failure of the senses, etc., can cause one to be mistaken, however sincere he may be.

8. What is a false conscience?
A false conscience is a judgment made by the mind when it wrongly decides that something is lawful when in fact is is unlawful, or vice versa. The error is due either to the use of false principles or because the mind was darkened or confused in its reasoning process.

9. Explain: "Absolute norms of faith and morality are from above, not from man."
Absolute norms of faith and morality are from God. Popular-opinion polls do not determine what is true faith and correct morality. The absolute norms, the supreme determining factor, is God himself. Man must seek to know the will of God as made manifest in divine revelation and as taught by the Church which Jesus founded and to which Jesus said: "Anyone who listens to you listens to me" (Luke 10:16).

10. Why can true faith and right reason never be in conflict?
True faith and right reason can never be in conflict because all truth comes ultimately from God. God is truth itself and whatever is of truth is of God and God is immutable (unchanging) truth.

11. Why is unity of faith among Christians needed if all are to have true faith?
Truth is one. Contradictions on the same subject at the same time and in the same respect cannot all be true. If all Christians were to have the true faith as given us by Jesus Christ and they interpreted it in a true manner, they would not have hundreds of interpretations. They would have one faith.

12. What did Jesus promise His Church to keep it in the truth?
Jesus promised His Church the Holy Spirit, the Spirit of Truth, to keep it in the truth (John 15:26-27).

13. Why are doctrines important?
Doctrines are important because they concern truths about God and His Incarnate Son, Jesus Christ, and the Church Jesus founded as necessary for the

salvation of souls. Sound doctrine is important to keep the members of the Church in one faith.

14. Why is unity of faith among Christians necessary to convert the world to Jesus, "The Way, the Truth and the Life"?

Disunity among Christians keeps much of the world from true faith in Jesus Christ. Instinctively, men of right reason know that truth is one. When the world sees hundreds of differing Christian denominations it is hindered in recognizing Jesus Christ as the Son of God made man and His Church as His mystical body.

15. Explain: "Truth does not change."

Since all truth comes from God and God in His very nature is immutable, truth in itself cannot change.

16. Explain: "Scientists do not create the truths of science."

Scientists do not create the truths of science, they merely discover the laws established by God in the very nature of things when He created the world.

CHAPTER 6

Angels

Angels are completely spiritual persons. The angels are pure spirits possessing sheer intelligence and will, but without physical bodies. Angels are pure spirits because they have no body and do not depend for their existence or activity on matter. The intelligence of angels is next to God's. Jesus said that not even the angels of heaven know the final day of judgment (Matthew 24:36). He was praising their great knowledge. St. Thomas Aquinas said that the angel is "the most excellent of creatures because he bears the strongest resemblance to God."

Angels, since they have no corporeal bodies, cannot be seen or felt by the senses of man. They are invisible to man. We do not know whether God first created angels or the material world. We do know from Sacred Scripture and the Fourth Lateran Council of the Catholic Church that God created angels before He made man. The existence of angels has been defined by the Church twice: at the Fourth Lateran Council (*Denzinger* 800) and the First Vatican Council (*Denzinger* 3002).

Some modernists have claimed that the angels are mere messages of God or figures of speech. It is a doctrine of the Catholic faith, however, that angels exist and that they are intellectual persons. This was solemnly defined in 1215 by the Fourth Lateran Council. It decreed: "God by His infinite power created from the beginning of time, both the spiritual and the corporeal creature, namely the angelic and the mundane, and afterward the human, a kind of intermediate creature composed of body and spirit." The First Vatican Council reaffirmed the same doctrine in 1869. Pope Paul VI, in issuing the *Credo of the People of God,* mentioned "the pure spirits which are also called angels," as being a required part of Catholic faith.

In 1950, Pope Pius XII, in the encyclical *Humani Generis* for the universal Church, reprimanded those who did not regard the angels as personal beings. The *General Catechetical Directory*, 1971, required that the teachings of Catholic faith include the angels as objects of Catholic faith. Sacred Scripture, the constant Tradition of the Holy Catholic Church, the Fathers of the Church and the great theologians of the centuries, all testify that angels are real persons; spiritual beings under God.

The angels are too little appreciated and too much ignored. Modernists, in explaining away the existence of angels as real persons, speak of them as "personifications of divine attributes" or "as traces of an original polytheism," or "as relics of Babylonian and Persian legends," or "as mere stand-ins for God's presence and activity in the world." Our theological knowledge of the angels, however, rests solidly on Divine Revelation. Natural reason alone cannot prove their existence. Their creation is a free act of God.

Karl Rahner (*Encyclopedia of Theology*, "angels") wrote: "The existence of the angels is not mythology," "cannot be disputed," "they are more creatures," "like man they were created for a supernatural goal, the vision of God," and "they freely decided in favor of this goal." "Their grace came from Christ . . . who is their Head," and "around this Word they form a true society of persons."

Although the angels are without physical bodies they have a real, permanent and essential relationship to the material world. They are not just "furnishings of heaven." They have a cosmic function in relationship to the material world. They act as "powers or principles" of this world.

John Cardinal Wright, when he was head of the Vatican's Congregation for the Clergy, wrote: "The angels confirm us in the faith and increase our hope and love for God. This is not the least of the ways in which they accomplish their principal purpose to praise with adoration their infinite, transcendent God and to express their love and loyalty. This is their primary function, their joy supreme. To meditate in diverse manners His presence, His guidance, His power to all other creatures, especially to man. This is also their role in history."

The late Cardinal Wright, in his above-mentioned reflections on the angels, discussed St. Joan of Arc and her "unshaken insistence that the Archangel Michael had commanded her and that she simply followed his instructions along with those of St. Margaret and St. Catherine, her 'voices.' The influence of her apparitions on history is beyond measure, as Winston Churchill is the most recent and eloquent to have testified in his *History of the English-Speaking People*. Certainly the most important of her voices was the archangel's. Without his guidance of Joan, the future of Europe and America could not possibly have been the same."

The angels are definitely a part of the Christian message. The Bible mentions the angels 148 times in the Old Testament and 74 times in the New Testament. While the term "angel" is generally applied only to those who remained faithful to God, the devils, fallen angels, are also angels by nature. The Old and New Testaments of the Bible mention the devils 115 times and Satan 33 times.

Satan is the chief of the fallen angels. Satan is the enemy of God and humanity and all that is good. Other names used for Satan are the devil, Beelzebul, Belial and Lucifer. Satan is identified with the serpent which tempted Eve (Genesis 3).

Satan, being the adversary of God, tempts human beings to defy God's laws (Wisdom 2:24; 1 Chronicles 21:1; Job 1:6-12). Satan obviously was not certain that Jesus was God made man, for even Jesus was subjected to temptation by Satan in the wilderness (Matthew 4:1-11). The Pharisees accused Jesus Christ of "casting out devils through Beelzebul, the prince of devils" (Matthew 12:24).

The New and Old Testaments warn against Satan. The apostle St. Paul warned the Corinthians against the temptations of Satan (1 Corinthians 7:6). There are many references to Satan in Sacred Scripture teaching that a personal, malign force is at work in the world attempting to pervert the designs of God.

It is most important that Christians be aware of the good angels and be open to their influence in our lives. If we ignore the good angels, we place ourselves in the serious danger of being open to the influence of the fallen angels.

Sacred Scripture and Tradition primarily show the good angels with God in heaven as His "court," and of enjoying the Beatific Vision (seeing God face to face even as He is). Before attaining the Beatific Vision, however, they were tested. It was a single and total test, not an extended one, as was man's test. Their free decision did not involve any predetermination affecting man's salvation or perdition (*Denzinger* 428, 907), though its results for or against God remain a factor affecting man, either helping or impeding him as he freely works out or fails to work out his own salvation.

Some angels failed the test: "The devil and the other demons were created good by God but made themselves evil," declared Lateran Council IV (1215) (*Denzinger* 427, 428); they fell into grievous sin and were cast into hell, as in 2 Peter 2:4 — "God did not spare them: he sent them down to the underworld and consigned them to the dark underground caves to be held there till the day of Judgment."

"As a consequence of Adam's sin, man is subject to the power of the devil," according to the Council of Trent (*Denzinger* 788, 793). Christ Jesus designated the devil as "the prince of the world" (John 14:30), whose dominion, in principle, Jesus conquered by His redemption. "I shall not talk with you any longer, because the prince of this world is on his way. He has no power over me, but the world must be brought to know that I love the Father and I am doing exactly what the Father told me" (John 14:30-31).

The devils, with God's permission, can inflict moral and physical in-

79

jury on mankind, as was the case in Paradise (temptations and seductions). "Be calm but vigilant, because your enemy the devil is prowling round like a roaring lion, looking for someone to eat. Stand up to him, strong in faith and in the knowledge that your brothers all over the world are suffering the same things" (1 Peter 5:8-9). The devil, however, cannot force man's free will to sin. "You can trust God not to let you be tried beyond your strength and with any trial he will give you a way out of it and the strength to bear it" (1 Corinthians 10:13). The devils also can cause man physical evil (Tobit 3:8; Job 1:12). Scripture relates the devil taking forceable possession of a human body, commanding man's bodily organs and the lower powers. The devil cannot force the higher powers of the soul, the intellect and will. Temptations come from the world, the flesh or the devil. Temptations from the world are found in bad example and the psychological pressure to conform. Temptations of the flesh are the urges of concupiscence, carnal and spiritual, as man's fallen nature has built-in tendencies to the seven capital sins. Temptations coming direct from the devil are the result of demonic instigations which encourage every form of avarice or selfishness so as to lead one to pride, and through pride to all other sins. The devil is an intelligent (fallen) angel and plays on every human weakness of man. The devil works not only to separate man from God but to separate men from one another. Disunity among Christians does not have the good angels as its source and inspiration.

Scripture speaks of the devil as the spirit of division and the "father of lies." Jesus said of the devil: "He was a murderer from the start; he was never grounded in the truth; there is no truth in him at all; when he lies he is drawing on his own store, because he is a liar, and the father of lies" (John 8:44).

Jesus Christ himself drove out evil spirits from people and gave this power to His disciples and to the Church, which is exercised in the rite of exorcism. Diabolic intervention, however, is extraordinary and one must guard against attributing to devils what comes from natural causes. At the same time, one must avoid rationalistic unbelief in attempting to explain away entirely diabolical influences. The devils will obviously work to keep men from true faith, to become confused in the faith or not to live it.

In Rome, in the Church of St. Peter in Chains, one can see the chains which tradition says held Peter in prison, guarded by sentries. The first pope of the Church awoke to find his cell bright with light. "Then suddenly the angel of the Lord stood there, and the cell was filled with light. He tapped Peter on the side and woke him. 'Get up!' he said, 'Hurry!' — and the chains fell from his hands. The angel then said, 'Put on your belt and sandals.' After he had done this the angel next said, 'Wrap your cloak round you and follow me.' Peter followed him, but had no idea that what the angel did was all happening in reality; he thought he was seeing a vision. They passed through two guard posts one after the other, and reached the iron gate leading to the city. This opened of its own accord; they went through it and had walked the whole length of one street when suddenly the angel left him. It was only then that Peter came to himself. 'Now I know it is all true,' he said. 'The Lord really did send his angel and has saved me from Herod and from all that the Jewish people were so certain would happen to me' " (Acts 12:6-11).

The early authors of the Church are almost unanimous in confirming that all believers have Guardian Angels. Some few among them held that only believers had Guardian Angels, but they were the exception. Agreement was virtually unanimous, too, that even unbelievers have Guardian Angels. One can hold as certain that baptized persons have a special, individual Guardian Angel. It is possible that unbaptized persons may share an angel with many persons. St. Gregory and St. Jerome attested that every human being has one throughout his entire life. Our Lord said: ". . . their angels in heaven are continually in the presence of my Father in heaven" (Matthew 18:10).

The Bible speaks of the very great number of angels: "millions" (Hebrews 12:22), "thousands upon thousands" (Revelation 5:11), "legions" (Matthew 26:53). Karl Rahner wrote: "It is an arbitrary decision to put the angels in definite 'choirs' and 'hierarchies'. . . . Like everything created they are correctly thought of as different in nature from one another. . . . Each has its own individual history; each is always active, and not only at particular moments."

Angels can have an effect on one another, passing on knowledge, etc. In the practical realm, Guardian Angels can bring people together to do the work of the Lord. It is important to speak to one's Guardian Angel as to a person. The good angel prays with us, adores with us. The angel is especially pleased when one goes in adoration to adore the Real Presence of Jesus Christ in the Most Blessed Sacrament (Chapter 16).

The work of the good angels is to lead men to faith in the existence of God; to faith and love of Jesus Christ and His Holy Church. Finally, the good angels lead men to venerate the Mother of Jesus, who is their queen as well as queen of saints in heaven and men upon earth.

The doctrine of the existence of the angels is not intended simply as another line on our checklist of Catholic doctrines. Our faith in the angels means they intervene in history. They have done so, and continue to do so in our individual lives. Padre Pio, the stigmatic priest who died in 1968 and who had special devotion to the angels, once amazed a person by saying that he would get the desired information through his Guardian

Angel. The individual asked: "Can you actually hear the angel?" Abruptly, the stigmatic priest asked: "Do you think I am deaf?" Our experiences with the angels may not be as graphic as that of the mystics; they are, nonetheless, real in our lives. The more we open our souls in faith to their existence, the more effective they will be.

The angels praise God in heaven and they reflect His glory on earth. The angels are created even more in the image of God than are men. We are a little less than the angels. "What is man that you should spare a thought for him, the son of man that you should care for him? For a short while you made him lower than the angels; you crowned him with glory and splendor" (Hebrews 2:6-8).

The angels are a part of that spiritual communion of God's intellectual persons and they act and interact in their relationships, not only with God, but with each other and with us. We are destined for that same place, which will be home forever with all the holy angels and saints. Our Guardian Angel is our constant companion, not only on this earth but if we achieve the glory of heaven, our Guardian Angel will be our companion for all eternity.

While man is a little less than the angels and even Jesus Christ "was for a short while made lower than the angels" (Hebrews 4:9), the human intellect of Christ was brought to a more perfect fulfillment in the Beatific Vision than the angel's spiritual intellect. According to St. Thomas Aquinas and Pope Pius XII, the soul of Jesus had the Beatific Vision from the moment of its creation.

The angel's will is incomparably superior to the human will. When he wills, he wills with all his power, and there will be no change, no drawing back. Before acting, he has all the necessary information about what he wills; the angel sees all the consequences of his act of will. When he acts, in what he does, there is no struggle or conflict. He destroys all opposition with irresistible might. His power is enormous; he could slay millions as he did the thousands of Sennacherib's army or the Egyptians of Pharaoh.

The angels move from place to place faster than light, in a fraction of a second. They are independent of matter, space or time. Finally, no two angels are alike; each is different. In fact, some claim that each angel is a new species (we humans are all of the same species).

St. Thomas Aquinas said of the angels: "They guide the stars, sun, moon, planets — each has an angel" (imagine the number of angels there must be if scientists are correct when they believe that there are billions of galaxies)! Cardinal John Henry Newman said that "as we move ourselves, God cooperating and willing it, so nature, seasons, rivers, etc., are moved by angels, God so directing."

The angels, by their nature, are superior to all other creatures, including men, and possess a higher perfection of intellect, will and power. ". . . The angels in their greater strength and power make no complaint or accusation against them in front of the Lord" (2 Peter 2:12). Angels understand differently than men do. We must make acts of the mind by proceeding from one truth to the knowledge of another truth. Humans with discursive reasoning are limited by physical senses when they think, judge, study and act. Humans gradually and with effort arrive at an understanding or at new knowledge. Angels immediately grasp the entire truth, the whole subject in a single glance. They see the principle and the conclusion at the same time. All consequences and all aspects are immediately understood by the angels. The angels are not limited by senses or material things.

We speak of our vocation in life. The single or religious life, the married life, are spoken of as vocations from God. How often do we consider the vocation of our Guardian Angel? Our Guardian Angel has a vocation which concerns us. The Guardian Angel is to lead his assigned person on earth to adore God, to be loyal to God's Word in the Church of Christ, and to venerate God's mother, the queen of all the holy angels. The angel of each person on earth discovers the vocation of his charge much more easily and sooner than does the human person himself.

As the holy angels were the precursors of the first coming of the Lord, so they will be for His second coming and so they are for His constant coming to men through the years. The coming of the Lord, new comings, are preceded by the coming of the angels. So, as each one grows closer to the Lord, the work of his angel is effective. From all eternity, God chose each person's angel just for him. God did this in His infinite love. The Guardian Angel has perfect awareness of his mission and responsibility toward you. His vocation is to stay by your side, protect and inspire you and to lead you in the true way of life, to the Way which is Jesus.

For those who actively and consciously accept their angel, there is the experience of a celestial companion. "I myself will send an angel before you" (Exodus 23:20-24). To remove the angels from our consciousness and not to work together with them is to remove the harmony of the advance of God to men, and men to God, according to the plan of the Almighty. Those who advance in union with their angels eventually learn to do all things in union with their angels.

To mention but some of the accounts of angels in the history of salvation: Angels were introduced in the history of Israel, and then into the life of Christ and the Church; it was an angel who told Joseph not to put Mary aside quietly because the child she was carrying was of God; the Angel Gabriel had first come to Mary with the message that she was the chosen mother of the Holy One.

While the world slept and ignored the birth of the Savior, not so the angels. They first announced the good news to the lowly shepherds. Christ Jesus, in the Garden of Olives, sorrowful unto death, with His sweat becoming as blood, is comforted by an angel while the apostles slept.

The angel kept guard at the empty tomb upon the resurrection of Jesus Christ. As our divine Lord ascended into heaven, it was two angels who directed the apostles to the mission for which they were left behind. An angel appeared to Peter in his dream, directing him to the baptism of the pagan centurion, Cornelius. As noted in the Book of Revelation, the angels will have a role in the final judgment at the end of the world.

When in the Garden of Olives, Christ freely surrendered himself to those who captured Him, He reminded Peter: "Do you think that I cannot appeal to my Father who would promptly send more than twelve legions of angels to my defense?" (Matthew 26:53)

Just before that, after singing some psalms and leaving for the Mount of Olives, Jesus had said to the apostles: "You will all lose faith in me this night, for the Scripture says 'I shall strike the shepherd and the sheep of the flock will be scattered.' But after my resurrection, I shall go before you to Galilee." It was Peter who protested the loudest: "Though all lose faith in you, I will never lose faith" (Matthew 26:30-34). Note that our Lord here directed that after His resurrection, He would go before them to Galilee. We notice later that it is angels who have to remind Peter and the other disciples not to look in the empty tomb for the risen Jesus, but to look in Galilee.

Sacred Scripture is the message of God to humanity. In Scripture we are able to confirm the mission which God entrusts to the angels. If one were to cut out all the passages in the Bible in which angels are mentioned, we would end up not only with a considerably reduced version of the Bible but one which lacked a great deal of meaning.

The angels guard the way to the tree of life (Genesis 3:24); they prevent the hand of Abraham from striking his son, Isaac (Genesis 22:11-12). The Mosaic Law is given by means of God's angels' ministries (Acts 7:52; Galatians 3:19; Hebrews 2:2). Angels assist Elijah (1 Kings 19:5); they assist Isaiah (Isaiah 6:6); they assist Ezekiel (Ezekiel 40:2). An angel punishes Heliodorus (2 Maccabees 3); an angel guides the young Tobias (Tobias). Another angel dissuades the prophet Balaam from cursing God's people (Numbers 22); an angel kills every firstborn of men and animals during the Passover night as he moves among the Egyptians, whose pharaoh would not let the Israelites, God's people, go. The angel goes before the Israelites in the desert (Exodus 23:20). There are many other references in the Old Testament. We already have hinted at the multiple involvements of angels in salvation history.

The Church, as has been the constant Christian Tradition, looks upon the angels as protectors, advisors and guides of men on their way to heaven. The divine liturgy of the Church entrusts the members of the Church to the custody of angels, this custody being an essential factor for salvation, because God sends forth His graces to men through the action of angels. Remember, Jesus Christ is head and king of angels as well as of men and all grace flows from Jesus Christ. Several Masses are dedicated to the angels, e.g., to the Guardian Angels, to the Archangels, etc.

Modern technology does not exclude, in the Church's mind, the importance of angels. The need of Guardian Angels for protection from accidents still exists. The Church invokes the aid of angels in blessing trains, ships, airplanes, etc. Angels are asked to go before the travelers to keep them from danger.

Recent popes have confirmed the Church's faith in the angels. Pius XI frequently recommended to visitors devotion to the angels. He would bid farewell to prelates in charge of any mission by saying: "May the Lord guide your way and His angel go before you." Pope John XXIII revealed that when he visited Pius XI, when he was appointed apostolic delegate to Turkey and to Greece, in order to undertake a delicate mission, the pope entrusted to him this most beautiful secret: "When I have to have a difficult conversation with someone, then I beg my Guardian Angel to speak to the Guardian Angel of the person with whom I have to deal."

Pope Pius XII, October 3, 1958, spoke to pilgrims from the United States urging them to foster familiarity with their Guardian Angels: "They were in the cities that you visited, they were your companions. . . . Didn't Christ say that the children's angels contemplate the face of the Father in heaven (Matthew 18:10)? When the children become adults, will they be abandoned by their Guardian Angels?" He then affirmed that the angels "are constantly concerned for your salvation and sanctification. You will spend an eternity of joy with the angels; learn now to know them."

According to Cardinal Danielou: "The greatest among the saints and men of God have always lived on familiar terms with the angels, from St. Augustine to John Henry Newman." St. Ignatius of Loyola and St. John of the Cross proposed to fervent souls that they imitate the serenity of angels. Angels love silence and peace and when one practices the virtue of silence one experiences the serenity, the peace of the angels. Silence means more than "not to talk." It consists chiefly in a silence of the heart, the love for recollection. Its first fruit is reverence. It elevates one into the world of the truths of faith where the Lord is met in a more personal knowledge and love.

One who practices this silence in union with the angels is led on the road to purgation from sin, to uprightness of Christian life, and is fortified against dissipation, distraction and superficiality in the world. After one learns in time to practice this silence in meditation, he arrives at "being able to listen." This involves a readiness for receiving. One learns to see things in a new way. Sacred Scripture takes on a deeper meaning as the Word of God, and many biblical passages become enlightened. The angels carry the light of God to men. There will follow from *silence* and *listening*, the virtue of *obedience*.

So important are the angels that in 1968 Pope Paul VI mandated the Holy Cross Fathers in Europe of the "Opus Sanctorum Angelorum" (Work of the Holy Angels) to preach the angels biblically and forcefully so that they will be our helpers at this time in history. This religious community has a special apostolate to carry out this mission given them by the Church. Those who get deeply into the *Work of the Holy Angels* make a *promise* to their Guardian Angels, and some, with special permission and guidance, make an act of *consecration* to their angels.

The angels help one to make Jesus Christ the center of one's life. United to the holy angels one is helped to live in union with Jesus Christ, in obedience to the Church and in veneration of God's mother. Pope Pius XII said: "We must be linked up with the Holy Angels; we must form with them one strong family because of the times that are to come."

Some spiritual writers have thought that the trial of the angels consisted in knowledge revealed to them by God that one day the Son of God would become man. This caused envy in some of the angels who revolted against this intention of God. It was a blow to their pride. Man is of a lower nature than the angels, yet God would not become an angel but rather take on the nature of lowly man who, in part (his body), is composed of the elements of earth's matter.

"God has never said to any angel: *You are my Son, today I have become your father;* or: *I will be a father to him and he a son to me.* Again, when he brings the First-born into the world, he says: *Let all the angels of God worship him.* About the angels, he says: *He makes his angels winds and his servants flames of fire,* but to his Son he says: *God, your throne shall last for ever and ever;* and: *his royal sceptre is the sceptre of virtue; virtue you love as much as you hate wickedness. This is why God, your God, has anointed you with the oil of gladness, above all your rivals.* And again: *It is you, Lord, who laid earth's foundations in the beginning, the heavens are the work of your hands; all will vanish, though you remain, all wear out like a garment; you will roll them up like a cloak, and like a garment they will be changed. But yourself, you never change and your years are unending.* God has never said to any angel: *Sit at

86

my right hand and I will make your enemies a footstool for you.
The truth is they are all spirits whose work is service sent to help those who will be the heirs of salvation" (Hebrews 1:5-14).

In the revelation to the angels that the Word would be made flesh, also involved was the fact that the incarnation would be taking place through a woman. Not only would the Christ be king of the angels, but a woman would be their queen. Angels of a higher nature would be required to adore the God-Man and venerate above all God's creature, the Virgin-Mother.

Whatever, precisely, the trial of the angels was, what is known is that the good angels accepted in humility, reverence and union of wills, the will of Almighty God. Satan and his followers would have none of it. Thus, Satan and his followers were cast into hell. The good angels passed into glory where they behold God face to face even as He is.

The good Guardian Angel of each man was involved in the trial of the angels and obviously remained on the side of God. The Guardian Angel of each man beholds the face of God now in the beatific vision.

While each one should have a special devotion to his or her Guardian Angel, it is to be remembered, in practical devotion, that all the good angels are on the side of man and are concerned about his salvation and the glory of God.

DISCUSSION QUESTIONS

1. Describe the nature of angels.
Angels are persons without corporeal bodies but with keen intellects and wills.

2. Is belief in the existence of angels optional to Catholic faith? Explain your answer.
The existence of angels is defined and required for faith in sincere Catholics.

3. On what does our knowledge of the angels rest? (Our source?)
Our knowledge of the angels rests solidly on Divine Revelation and defined doctrines of the Catholic Church.

4. What is the relationship of angels to the material world?
The angels are as powers or principles of the material world. They guide different aspects of the created universe.

5. How frequently are the good angels and the fallen angels mentioned in Sacred Scripture?
Good angels are mentioned 148 times in the Old Testament and 74 times in the New Testament. In both Old and New Testaments the devils are mentioned 115 times and Satan 33 times.

6. What does Sacred Scripture say of Satan?

Sacred Scripture speaks of Satan as a personal, malign force at work in the world attempting to pervert the designs of God. Satan is the chief of fallen angels and he is spoken of as the devil, Beelzebul, Belial and Lucifer.

7. What can happen to men who are not open to the works of the good angels?

Those who are not open to the works of the good angels endanger themselves to being open to the influence of the fallen angels.

8. How does the devil tempt human beings?

The devil tempts human beings by suggestions encouraging every form of avarice or selfishness in order to lead one to pride, and through pride to all other sins. Temptations arise from the world, the flesh or the devil. The devil can play on the weaknesses of fallen human nature, such as concupiscence, to lead one from God.

9. What limitations are placed on the devil in taking possession of human beings?

The devil cannot force the higher faculties of the soul to his bidding, viz. intellect and free will.

10. How does the Guardian Angel react to one's prayer life?

The Guardian Angel prays with us, adores with us.

11. What is the work of the good angels?

The work of the good angels is to lead men to faith in God, in Jesus Christ and His Holy Church, and, finally, to veneration of God's mother. The angels lead men to adore Jesus in the Blessed Sacrament. The angels lead us to unity in faith in obedience to Church authority.

12. Compare the angels to men.

Both angels and men have free intellects and wills. An angel is pure spirit without a body, whereas man, in addition to his spiritual soul, has a body. The angels are higher in nature than men because they do not have the limitations man has because of his body. Men and angels, however, have a spiritual union with each other. Angels have the same grace in them as humans have, and men are destined to spend eternity with the angels.

13. Was the intellect of Jesus as man lower than that of the angels?

The intellect of Jesus had infused knowledge, like Adam when he was first created, only on a superior level for Jesus was God in His Person. The human soul of Jesus always had the beatific vision, seeing God face to face.

14. Can an angel change his mind and will? Explain your answer.

The angel can never change his mind or will. The angel has a higher perfection of intellect and will and sees the consequences of his actions, so he can never repent.

15. How did St. Thomas Aquinas regard the angels and the universe?

According to St. Thomas Aquinas, the angels guide the stars, sun, moon and planets.

16. How do the angels understand as compared with human beings?

Angels immediately grasp knowledge whole and entire without reasoning processes, whereas man must do discursive reasoning to come to conclusions.

17. Explain: The angels precede the coming of the Lord.

Scripture itself indicates the angels at work as the coming of the Lord unfolds over the centuries leading to the salvation of mankind.

18. Explain: One devoted to the angels learns to love silence.

The angels lead us in silent contemplation to greater enlightenment of the truths and reality of God. Silence is needed for listening to the Lord so as to grow in His love.

19. Describe, basically, the trial of the angels.

The trial of the angels, whatever it may have been, was, basically, acceptance of the will of God. Some, in their pride, refused to accept God's will.

CHAPTER 7

Sanctifying Grace

Before considering *sanctifying grace*, which is a permanent quality of that soul which is free of serious sin, attention should be given to *actual grace*. Actual grace is fleeting. It comes and goes. It is not a constant quality of the soul.

Actual grace is a help from God which enlightens the mind or strengthens the will to perform supernatural actions which glorify God and lead to heaven. It is sometimes a help from God to overcome temptations and to avoid evil. Actual grace then is a temporary supernatural intervention by God for these purposes. Actual grace is a passing divine assistance given when man needs God's help to retain, regain or grow in the supernatural grace called "sanctifying," which we are going to deal with in this chapter. One cannot grow in sanctifying grace without first responding to actual grace.

A help from God to overcome temptation; the inspiration to pray and to grow in closer union with God; the strong desire growing in the heart to approach Jesus in the sacraments, or to stop in at the nearby Catholic church for a visit to our Divine Lord in the Most Blessed Sacrament — all these are actions of God drawing our soul. We may accept these actual graces of God moving us or we may reject them. We are free. God never forces. Jesus said: "No one can come to me unless he is drawn by the Father who sent me" (John 6:44). That action of God drawing us to Him is called "actual grace." If we respond to His drawing, whether it be to more fervent prayer, more generous works of charity, the sacraments, or whatever it may be, the result will be that through the merits of Christ, His grace, which sanctifies, will flood our soul yet more.

The promise of God's help in trials and temptations is recorded in 1 Corinthians 10:13. "The man who thinks he is safe must be careful that he does not fall. The trials which you have had to bear are no more than people normally have. You can trust God not to let you be tried beyond your strength, and with any trial he will give you a way out of it and the strength to bear it."

Jesus Christ by His death on the cross earned for us all grace, sanctifying as well as actual grace. We read in Hebrews how Jesus Christ became one with mankind, defeated the forces of evil and promised help (actual grace) to those men who are tempted.

"As it was his purpose to bring a great many of his sons into glory it was appropriate that God, for whom everything exists and through whom everything exists, should make perfect, through suffering, the leader who would take them to their salvation. For the one who sanctifies, and the ones who are sanctified, are of the same stock; that is why he openly calls them *brothers* in the text: *I shall announce your name to my brothers, praise you in full assembly;* or the text: *In him I help;* or the text: *Here I am with the children whom God has given me.*

"Since all the *children* share the same blood and flesh, he too shared equally in it, so that by his death he could take away all the power of the devil, who had power over death, and set free all those who have been held in slavery all their lives by the fear of death. For it was not the angels that he took to himself; he took to himself *descent from Abraham.* It was essential that he should in this way become completely like his brothers so that he could be a compassionate and trustworthy high priest of God's religion, able to atone for human sins. That is, because he has himself been through temptation he is able to help others who are tempted" (Hebrews 2:10-18).

It is most important to grasp the meaning of sanctifying grace as given us by Jesus Christ in divine revelation and as discussed in the remainder of this important chapter. Without understanding sanctifying grace we will not comprehend much of the meaning of the rest of our Christian faith. It is essential to understand what is meant by this grace before we can understand the nature of the Church as the *Mystical Body of Christ,* the subject of our next chapter. Then, too, without this understanding, one would not comprehend the Church's teachings on redemption, sin, heaven, hell, purgatory, the need for the sacraments, etc. It would be well to review this chapter often.

There are many negative ideas about what sanctifying grace is. Some see grace simply as being without mortal sin. While no soul in mortal sin can have sanctifying grace, the reality of the quality of this grace is something positive and not simply the lack of serious sin.

Nor is sanctifying grace simply a ticket to heaven whereby God looks the other way to have your sins covered over. Admittedly, no one can enter heaven without the power of this grace in the human soul. It is a supernatural quality of the soul and nothing visible to human eyes can compare with it. St. Paul speaks of grace in all his epistles of the Bible, including the short one to Philemon.

The underlying meaning of grace is that it is freely given. Man does not deserve grace nor does he, strictly speaking, merit it. The word "grace," from the Latin word "gratia," simply means favor or gift freely given.

In biblical language grace refers to the unmerited gift given by God proceeding from His benevolent disposition. Man has no claim to grace. It is not owed us by God according to our human nature. It is a totally gratuitous gift from God given us from God's love and mercy.

Sanctifying grace is a gift which is entirely supernatural, above the nature of man. It is more than the gifts of nature. Grace is not a natural gift like the blessings of good health or natural wealth needed to live well in this world. To simply call grace a "gift from God" is not sufficient. It is a "supernatural gift from God." The effects of this supernatural gift preserved until death will mean eternal life with God in heaven. One can attain the Beatific Vision only if he has grace in his soul at the moment of the death of the body.

No one has the right to the Beatific Vision, whereby the man saved will see God face to face in heaven, even as He is. That is supernatural to man, above human nature, to actually enter into the happiness of God. The essence of grace then, is, properly, its gratuity. If God had created man only for natural happiness, without any promise of eternal life in heaven with the Beatific Vision, man would have received from God all that was proper to him as man. Grace is not proper to man as man. It is above his nature as man.

If God had made it possible for souls to enter limbo[1] only, man would have no right to complain that he was deprived of that which was due him. Limbo is the abode of souls excluded from the vision and glory of the Beatific Vision in heaven. Such souls do not suffer any other punishment. Souls in limbo enjoy the happiness that would have been human destiny if man had not been elevated to the supernatural order. If the ultimate destiny of each one of us was only natural happiness in limbo, that would be worth striving for because it would fulfill all our natural capacities.

Jesus Christ never used the expressions "sanctifying" or "actual

---

[1]The Catholic Church has never defined the existence of limbo, although it has repeatedly supported the fact by its authority. There are two kinds of limbo. The limbo of the Fathers was the place where saints of Old Testament times remained until Christ had redeemed the world. The limbo of infants is the permanent state of infants who die in original sin, without baptism, but are innocent of any personal sin. The great majority of approved theologians teach that infants who die in original sin suffer no "pain of sense." They are, rather, simply excluded from the Beatific Vision. St. Thomas Aquinas said: "They rejoice because they share in God's goodness and in many natural perfections" (*De Maio*, V, 3). One can say souls in limbo are perfectly happy, but this means natural happiness, not supernatural happiness. The early Church Fathers wrote of limbo.

grace." The Savior surely did speak about them. One time Jesus used the word "gift" in speaking about that grace which is like living waters. It is recorded in John's Gospel (4:6-29) when the Samaritan woman met Jesus at Joseph's well. Jesus said to her, "Give me a drink." The woman thought of natural water only and Jesus elevated her thoughts. The woman is offered actual grace on this occasion because if she would respond to God's drawing, then sanctifying grace would come to her soul permanently if she repents of her sins, confesses them, and embraces the God of love in Jesus.

Jesus said to the Samaritan woman: "If thou didst know the *gift* of God, and who it is who sayeth to thee, *Give me to drink,* thou perhaps wouldst have asked of him, and he would have given thee living water" (Douay-Rheims version 4:10). The Jerusalem Bible (4:14) translates it this way: "If you only knew what God is offering. . . . The same could be said to many Christians today. "If thou didst know the *gift* of God," or "*If you only knew what* God is offering." Jesus gives a very strong hint at the answer to our inquiry, "What is the gift of sanctifying grace?" when He says to the Samaritan woman: "The water that I shall give will turn into a spring inside him, welling up to *eternal life.*"

This brings us to a basic definition of sanctifying grace. *Sanctifying grace is a sharing in the life of God.* Shortly, we shall see the scriptural basis for defining this grace as a share in God's own life.

By grace a supernatural state of being is infused into the soul by God and permanently inheres in it. This sanctifying grace is also called *habitual* or justifying grace. It is habitual in the sense that, unlike actual grace which is temporary or fleeting, sanctifying grace is a constant supernatural quality of the soul which sanctifies a person inherently and makes him or her just, holy and pleasing to God. No soul can enter heaven unless it has sanctifying grace.

Just as the soul is the vital principle of a human being's *natural* life, so sanctifying grace is the vital principle of the *supernatural* life. This grace is not a substance but a real *quality* that becomes part of the soul. It is not the same as the supernatural virtue of charity, by which a person loves God above all things for His own sake and loves others for God's sake. Supernatural charity is always infused with the state of sanctifying grace. One cannot have[2] charity without, at the same time, possessing

---

[2]The virtue of charity is based on divine faith, belief in God's revealed truths. It is infused and not acquired by merely human efforts. One who has lost charity and grace by serious sin may still possess the virtues of faith and hope. Possessing faith and hope he can still respond to actual grace drawing him to repentance and to restoration to the state of grace and the virtue of charity.

grace. Charity belongs to the will while sanctifying grace belongs to the entire soul, mind, will and affections.

While we commonly use the word "grace," our divine Lord is quoted directly in Sacred Scripture as speaking of His "life" in us. It is *zōē* (life) which Jesus Christ said He has in common with the Father and which He would share with men. Obviously, Jesus was not speaking of natural life, which men already had.

How much more beautiful and communicative would be the reality of the supernatural gift of grace if we had grown accustomed to calling grace "a sharing in the life of God" rather than simply speaking of our being in "the state of grace." Many, unfortunately, interpret the words "state of grace" to mean a stationary condition, that is, something fixed, unmoving or making no progress. Grace, however, is not stationary. In the spiritual life one either grows or moves ahead in grace or one falls behind.

In Scripture, Jesus Christ, the Son of God made man, referred many times to grace as our sharing in His divine life:

"As the Father raises the dead and gives them life, so the Son gives life to anyone he chooses. . ." (John 5:21).

"I tell you most solemnly, whoever listens to my words, and believes in the one who sent me, has eternal life; without being brought to judgment he has passed from death to life" (John 5:24).

"For the Father, who is the source of life, has made the Son the source of life; and, because he is the Son of Man, has appointed him supreme judge" (John 5:26).

"You study the scriptures, believing that in them you have eternal life; now these same scriptures testify to me, and yet you refuse to come to me for life!" (John 5:39).

"It is my Father who gives you the bread from heaven, the true bread; for the bread of God is that which comes down from heaven and gives life to the world. . ." (John 6:32-33).

"I am the bread of life. He who comes to me will never be hungry; he who believes in me will never thirst. . ." (John 6:35).

"I am the living bread which has come down from heaven. Anyone who eats this bread will live for ever; and the bread that I shall give is my flesh, for the life of the world" (John 6:51).

"I tell you most solemnly, if you do not eat the flesh of the Son of Man and drink his blood, you will not have life in you. Anyone who does eat my flesh and drink my blood has eternal life, and I shall raise him up on the last day. For my flesh is real food and my blood is real drink. He who eats my flesh and drinks my blood lives in me and I live in him. As I, who am sent by the living Father, myself draw life from the Father, so whoever eats me will draw life from me. This is the bread come down from heaven; not like the bread our ancestors ate: they are dead, but anyone who eats this bread will live for ever'' (John 6:35-58).

"I have come so that they may have life and have it to the full" (John 10:10). "I am the resurrection. If anyone believes in me, even though he dies, he will live, and whoever lives and believes in me will never die" (John 11:25-27).

"I am the Way, the Truth and the Life. No one can come to the Father except through me" (John 14:6).

"These are recorded so that you may believe that Jesus is the Christ, the Son of God, and that believing this you may have life through his name" (John 20:31).

The Apostle John, as noted above, quoted extensively from the words of Jesus Christ concerning grace as a participation in the life of God within us. Observe carefully the repeated references to "life."

By sanctifying grace we possess not only *human* nature but *divine* nature. St. Peter made this clear in his second letter, where he wrote of the special gifts God has given us so that "you will be able to share the divine nature" (2 Peter 1:4). Sharing in the nature of God we are elevated above all God's natural creation, even above our own human nature so that we share in the very nature of God, giving us power to know and to love as God knows and loves himself.

Grace then is a *power*. It gives us the power of God to participate in His divine life. Upon earth we live under the veil of faith. In heaven the veil of faith will be lifted, we shall see God directly and know and love with His very own life. "Now we are seeing a dim reflection in a mirror; but then we shall be seeing face to face. The knowledge that I have now is imperfect; but then I shall know as fully as I am known" (1 Corinthians 13:12).

Countless quotations could be drawn from Sacred Scripture to demonstrate that sanctifying grace elevates us from mere human nature to participation in the divine nature whereby we share in the very life of God. Only a few more should suffice, however:

"If it is certain that death reigned over everyone as the consequences of one man's fall, it is even more certain that one man, Jesus Christ, will cause everyone to reign in life who receives the free gift that he does not deserve, of being made righteous. Again, as one man's fall brought condemnation on everyone, so the good act of one man brings everyone life and makes them justified" (Romans 5:17-18).

"Intellectually they are in the dark, and they are estranged from the life of God, without knowledge because they have shut their hearts to it" (Ephesians 4:18).

"But when Christ is revealed — and he is your life — you too will be revealed in all your glory with him" (Colossians 3:4).

"From Paul, appointed by God to be an apostle of Christ Jesus in his design to promise life in Christ Jesus" (2 Timothy 1:1).

What each one needs to do is to meditate on the beautiful divine reality of grace as a "sharing in the life of God." To be able to recite those words may be very accurate, but the inner appreciation, the drinking of that living water, is something else — profound, real, divine. We need to probe the depths, to enter into deeper water, to accept the fullness of the divine reality in what is meant by sanctifying grace elevating us above the mere human level to participate in the divine nature. In discovering, by spiritual experience in faith, the gift, "what God is offering," we will be renewed in the light that is Jesus.

Sanctifying grace is given to the soul for the first time at baptism. It is the beginning of eternal life in the soul. The death of the body is a lifting back of the curtain, the dark glass, as it were, through which we now see and behold God only vaguely. The natural death of the body and its eventual entrance into heavenly glory, is the opening up, the blossoming into a full realization of the eternal life which has already been ours upon earth.

St. Paul, the apostle, who wrote much of the New Testament under divine inspiration, became so conscious of his union with Christ through grace that, in spiritual joy, he exclaimed: "I live now not with my own life but with the life of Christ who lives in me" (Galatians 2:20). Another time, the same apostle wrote: "Life to me, of course, is Christ, but then death would bring me something more" (Philippians 1:21).

Created grace is a freely given gift of God, distinct from God himself, which leads us to share in His life. It has "degrees" in the sense that it may be actual or habitual, external or internal, medicinal or elevating. Uncreated grace, on the other hand, is the indwelling of the Most Blessed Trinity in the soul. Uncreated grace does not have "degrees" because God the Father, God the Son and God the Holy Spirit come to live in the soul as in a temple. "Your body, you know, is the temple of the Holy Spirit, who is in you since you received him from God. You are not your own property. You have been bought and paid for. That is why you should use your body for the glory of God" (1 Corinthians 6:19-20). "The temple of God has no common ground with idols, and that is what we are — the temple of the living God. We have God's word for it: *I will make my home among them and live with them; I will be their God and they shall be my people.* Then *come away from them and keep aloof, says the Lord. Touch nothing that is unclean, and I will welcome you and be your father, and you shall be my sons and daughters, says the Almighty Lord"* (2 Corinthians 6:16-18).

St. John the Apostle, who waxed eloquent in contemplating our union with Jesus Christ and our sharing in His divine life, once cried out, in effect, that it would be wonderful even to have so great a God call us His children; even that would have been a great condescension on God's part, but the fact is that we are not only called but are, in truth, the children of God. That is the marvel of it.

"Think of the love that the Father has lavished on us, by letting us be called God's children; and that is what we are. Because the world refused to acknowledge him, therefore it does not acknowledge us. My dear people, we are already the children of God but what we are to be in the future has not yet been revealed; all we know is, that when it is revealed we shall be like him because we shall see him as he really is. Surely everyone who entertains this hope must purify himself, must try to be as pure as Christ" (1 John 3:1-3).

The Apostle Paul in his letter to the Church in Galatia also was taken up with the profundity of our adoption in Christ as the children of God.

"Let me put this another way: an heir, even if he has actually inherited everything, is no different from a slave for as long as he remains a child. He is under the control of guardians and administrators until he reaches the age fixed by his father. Now before we came of age we were as good as slaves to the elemental principles of this world, but when the appointed time came, God sent his Son, born of a woman, born a subject of the Law, to redeem the subjects of the Law and to enable us to be adopted as sons. The proof that you are sons is that God has sent the Spirit of his Son into our hearts: the Spirit that cries, 'Abba, Father,' and it is this that makes you a son, you are not a slave any more; and if God has made you son, then he has made you heir" (Galatians 4:1-7).

Our adoption as children of God is much more profound and real than earthly adoptions in which parents legally adopt a child, no matter how precious the relationship which develops. The legal father who has adopted a son does not give his very life to that child. In the case of sanctifying grace, however, God actually infuses a participation of His own divine life into the soul. He seals the soul with His very own Son, Jesus Christ.

At the same time that we become one in Jesus Christ by the infusion of sanctifying grace into the soul, we do not lose our identity. We are specially created persons, made in God's own image and likeness. Now, God's special creatures, made to His own image and likeness, are elevated above the mere natural level of mankind. We become the children of God. Natural human parents share their human life with their children. God likewise shares His very divine life with us.

Having become one in Jesus Christ, He lives in us and we live in Him.

That is what makes us the people of God of the New Covenant. We become as branches attached to the vine which is Jesus Christ. We, then, are members of the Mystical Body of Christ, the Church, which is the subject of our next chapter.

DISCUSSION QUESTIONS

1. Define actual grace.

Actual grace is a temporary help from God which enlightens the mind or strengthens the will to perform supernatural actions which glorify God and lead to heaven. It also is a help from God to overcome temptations.

2. What is the spiritual result in a soul responding to actual grace?

While actual grace is a help from God, drawing a soul to himself, those who respond to actual graces glorify God by growing in sanctifying grace.

3. Give some practical examples of actual graces presented to a human person.

Any person, place, thing or thought which inspires us to come back or closer to God is an actual grace. A sermon, the good example of a friend, an inspiring book, God's beauty in nature, the desire to repent, all are examples of actual graces.

4. From what source does the Church obtain its concepts of sanctifying grace?

Divine revelation reveals to us the real meaning of sanctifying grace.

5. Why is it so important to grasp the meaning of sanctifying grace?

It is important to grasp the meaning of sanctifying grace or we will never appreciate or understand other basics of our faith, such as: the nature of the Church, redemption, sin, heaven, hell, purgatory, the need for the sacraments, etc.

6. What is the underlying meaning of the word "grace"?

The underlying meaning of grace is that it is a free gift of God.

7. Does God owe it to man's nature to give him sanctifying grace?

God does not owe it to human nature to give man grace because grace is above human nature. Human nature would be complete according to its own nature even without grace.

8. Why is sanctifying grace a gift which is supernatural rather than merely natural?

Sanctifying grace is not a natural gift such as the natural blessings of health or prosperity. It is entirely supernatural, elevating man above human nature.

9. Why would limbo have been a sufficient reward to make man perfectly happy?

Limbo would have been a sufficient reward to man for it would respect every natural human quality of man, fulfilling perfectly man's *natural* capacity for happiness.

10. Did Jesus use the word "grace"?

Jesus is not recorded as using the word "grace" but at least once He called it "gift" when speaking to the Samaritan woman: "If you but knew the gift of God. . . ."

11. What is the basic definition of sanctifying grace?
The basic definition of sanctifying grace, drawing from divine revelation, is that it empowers human beings to participate in the divine nature. By grace we share in God's life.

12. What are the effects of sanctifying grace?
The effects of sanctifying grace are that we are elevated above human nature by participation in the divine life, empowered to live the life of God in heaven in eternal happiness.

13. Are charity and sanctifying grace the same?
Charity and sanctifying grace are not the same although they always go together. Charity is a supernatural virtue by which human beings love God above all things for His own sake, and others for the love of God.

14. Why is sanctifying grace also called "habitual" grace?
Sanctifying grace also is called "habitual" grace because unlike actual grace, which is temporary or fleeting, sanctifying grace habitually remains in a soul so long as that soul is free from mortal sin.

15. How, as recorded in Sacred Scripture, did Jesus Christ frequently speak of grace?
Jesus Christ, as recorded in Scripture, frequently spoke of grace as His life given to men. "I have come that they may have life. . . ." This means divine life.

16. Is sanctifying or habitual grace stationary?
Sanctifying grace is not stationary. One grows in grace and should grow in it daily.

17. How did the Apostle Paul view grace?
St. Paul, the apostle, understood grace as the life of Christ in us making for our becoming one in Christ: "I live now not with my own life but with the life of Christ who lives in me" (Galatians 2:20). "For me to live is Christ, to die is gain" (Philippians 1:21).

18. What is meant by the body of the Christian being a temple of God?
The Christian in sanctifying grace becomes a temple of God because the Spirit of God dwells in him. The entire Blessed Trinity, called uncreated grace, dwells in the human being who is in the state of grace.

19. Do Christians lose their own identity in their oneness with grace through prayer?
Christians do not lose their personal identity when they become one in Christ and possess the life of God by participation in the divine nature.

CHAPTER 8

The Nature of the Church

A major cause of tension among Christians, and sometimes even within the ancient Church of Jesus Christ founded almost 2,000 years ago, is the lack of a common understanding of the divine nature of the Church. Some look upon the Church as if it were merely a natural organization. Some have such a shallow understanding of the Church that they think it is an obstacle to union with Jesus Christ.

The Church and Jesus Christ are one. The Apostle Paul, converted from the faith of the Jews, a leader among the fanatical Pharisees, became the most dynamic of Christ's apostles, although he was not one of the original 12. It was this great convert to the Christian faith who wrote the largest portion of the New Testament of the Bible, and whom we have to thank as God's instrument of divine revelation for giving us a deeper understanding of the nature of the Church as the "Body of Christ."

Sometimes a person is heard to say: "I believe in God. I'm all for Jesus Christ. I believe in Jesus Christ. It's the Church I have trouble with. I can take my Bible, study it, pray and have union with God without the need of a church." What these statements reveal is a lack of understanding and faith in the divine nature of the Church. There are more than 80 million unchurched people in the United States, many of whom consider themselves some kind of "Christian." Those with an understanding of the divine nature of the Church as the *Body of Christ*, and who know some history, realize that the world would not have a Bible if Jesus Christ had not given us the Church.

St. Paul originally had the name Saul. He was born in Tarsus of Cilicia (Acts 22:3). As "Saul" he was a feared enemy of the early Christians. Just before he was converted "Saul was still breathing threats to slaughter the Lord's disciples. He had gone to the high priest and asked for letters addressed to the synagogues in Damascus that would authorize him to arrest and take to Jerusalem any followers of the Way, men or women, that he could find" (Acts 9:1-2).

The conversion of "Saul," the fanatical Pharisee, to the devout Christian believer "Paul," was sudden and dramatic. It was to affect his entire future theology of the faith, especially concerning the nature of the Church.

"Suddenly, while he was traveling to Damascus and just before he reached the city, there came a light from heaven all around him. He fell to the ground, and then he heard a voice saying, 'Saul, Saul, why are you persecuting me?' 'Who are you, Lord?' he asked, and the voice answered, 'I am Jesus, and you are persecuting me. Get up now and go into the city and you will be told what you have to do.' The men traveling with Saul stood there speechless, for though they heard the voice they could see no one. Saul got up from the ground, but even with his eyes wide open he could see nothing at all, and they had to lead him into Damascus by the hand. For three days he was blind, and took neither food nor drink.

"A disciple called Ananias, who lived in Damascus, had a vision in which he heard the Lord say to him, 'Ananias.' When he replied, 'Here I am, Lord,' the Lord said, 'You must go to Straight Street and ask at the house of Judas for someone called Saul, who comes from Tarsus. At this moment he is praying, having had a vision of a man called Ananias coming in and laying hands on him to give him back his sight.'

"When he heard that, Ananias said, 'Lord, several people have told me about this man and all the harm he has been doing to your saints in Jerusalem. He has only come here because he holds a warrant from the chief priests to arrest everybody who invokes your name.' The Lord replied, 'You must go all the same, because this man is my chosen instrument to bring my name before pagans and pagan kings and before the people of Israel; I myself will show him how much he himself must suffer for my name.' Then Ananias went. He entered the house, and at once laid his hands on Saul and said, 'Brother Saul, I have been sent by the Lord Jesus who appeared to you on your way here so that you may recover your sight and be filled with the Holy Spirit.'' Immediately it was as though scales fell away from Saul's eyes and he could see again. So he was baptized there and then, and after taking some food he regained his strength.

"After he had spent only a few days with the disciples in Damascus, he began preaching in the synagogues, 'Jesus is the Son of God.' All his hearers were amazed'' (Acts 9:3-21).

Those words, "I am Jesus, and you are persecuting me," never left the mind of Paul. Jesus of Nazareth, who had died, who had risen from the dead and who ascended into heaven, had now appeared to this leader among the Jews and identified himself with His followers. Jesus had not said, "Saul, why do you persecute those who believe in me, and follow me?" Jesus identified himself with His followers, His Church: "Why do you persecute ME?" Saul, now Paul, converted to faith in Jesus Christ as the Son of God, grew in faith and wisdom. Paul made three famous missionary journeys serving as a "chosen instrument" of Jesus in the conversion of many to the Christian faith.

Paul never forgot his former days when he persecuted Jesus. He had stood and watched the stoning of Stephen, the first Christian martyr. "Saul entirely approved of the killing" (Acts 7:60). After his baptism, the new convert Paul went into the desert of Arabia for three years. That time in the desert enabled him to meditate on the revelation he had received, and to prepare his soul for new light. Paul developed a profound understanding of the Church being one with Jesus Christ, so much so that repeatedly in his writings St. Paul refers to the Church as "the Body of Christ."

"The fact is, brothers, and I want you to realize this, the Good News I preached is not a human message that I was given by men, it is something I learned only through a revelation of Jesus Christ. You must have heard of my career as a practicing Jew, how merciless I was in persecuting the Church of God, how much damage I did to it, how I stood out among other Jews of my generation, and how enthusiastic I was for the traditions of my ancestors.

"Then God, who had specially *chosen* me while I was *still in my mother's womb*, called me through his grace and chose to reveal his Son in me, so that I might preach the Good News about him to the pagans. I did not stop to discuss this with any human being, nor did I go up to Jerusalem to see those who were already apostles before me, but I went off to Arabia at once and later went straight back from there to Damascus. Even when after three years I went up to Jerusalem to visit Cephas and stayed with him for fifteen days, I did not see any of the other apostles; I only saw James, the brother of the Lord, and I swear before God that what I have just written is the literal truth. After that I went to Syria and Cilicia, and was still not known by sight to the churches of Christ in Judaea, who had heard nothing except that their onetime persecutor was now preaching the faith he had previously tried to destroy; and they gave glory to God for me" (Galatians 1:11-24).

"In his body lives the fullness of divinity, and in him you too find your own fulfillment, in the one who is the head of every Sovereignty and Power" (Colossians 2:9).

"Now the Church is his body, he is its head" (Colossians 1:18).

"Christ is head of the Church and saves the whole body" (Ephesians 1:23).

"And to some, his gift was that they should be apostles; to some prophets; to some, evangelists; to some, pastors and teachers; so that the saints together make a unity in the work of service, building up the body of Christ. In this way we are all to come to unity in our faith and in our knowledge of the Son of God, until we become the perfect Man, fully mature with the fullness of Christ himself.

"Then we shall not be children any longer, or tossed one way and another and carried along by every wind of doctrine, at the mercy of all the tricks men play and their cleverness in practicing deceit. If we live by the truth and in love, we shall grow in all ways into Christ, who is the head by whom the whole body is fitted and joined together, every joint adding its own strength, for each separate part to work according to its function. So the body grows until it has built itself up, in love." (Ephesians 4:11-16).

Someone has taken the trouble to count the number of times the Apostle Paul referred to the Church as "the Body of Christ" and came up with the number 64. St. Paul in his epistles presents the Church as the extension of Jesus Christ in time and space. The apostle considers Christ in two ways: the natural physical now-risen Christ and the Mystical Body of Christ the Church. He identifies our Lord with the sum total of believers (Galatians 2:16). He says that in baptism we are immersed, buried in Jesus Christ (Romans 6:3). The apostle tells us that Christ has many members and that we are members of His body. (1 Corinthians 12:12; Galatians 3:27 ff). He uses the human body as an analogy to show how many organs, many parts, each sharing their life with the whole, form one body. He concludes: "Now you together are Christ's body; but each of you is a different part of it" (1 Corinthians 12:27).

St. John the Apostle quotes Jesus Christ using the allegory of the vine and the branches. The sap in the vine we can see as representing sanctifying grace (dealt with in Chapter 7) which is a participation in the divine nature, a sharing in the life of God.

"I am the true vine, and my Father is the vinedresser. Every branch in me that bears no fruit he cuts away, and every branch that does bear fruit he prunes to make it bear even more. You are pruned already, by means of the word that I have spoken to you. . . . As a branch cannot bear fruit all by itself, but must remain part of the vine, neither can you unless you remain in me. I am the vine, you are the branches. Whoever remains in me, with me in him, bears fruit in plenty; for cut off from me you can do nothing. Anyone who does not remain in me is like a branch that has been thrown away — he withers; these branches are collected and thrown on the fire, and they are burnt. If you remain in me and my words remain in you, you may ask what you will and you shall get it" (John 15:1.7).

The doctrine of the Church as the Mystical Body of Christ is not the fruit of a gradual doctrinal development over the years. It has no history. It is simply revealed by Jesus Christ himself, as seen in the allegory of the vine and the branches. It is wholly contained in the words of the Savior to Paul on the road to Damascus: "I am Jesus, and you are persecuting me."

St. Paul presents the Church not simply as a natural organization but as a *living organism*, a *divine organism*, "the body of Christ." Spiritual writers since at least the middle of the ninth century have added the word "Mystical" when speaking of the Church as the "Body of Christ." This distinguishes the Church as Christ's body from the sacramental body of Christ (studied in Chapter 16) and from the natural, physical body of Christ that was born of Mary, died on the Cross and ascended into heaven where He reigns in His risen physical body now glorified. He is king at the right hand of God the Father.

Every living body requires a head and a soul. The soul of the Mystical Body of Christ is the Holy Spirit. The head is the adorable person of Jesus Christ, God become man. Baptized believers are the members. The Holy Spirit dwells in the Church and in every Christian in the state of sanctifying grace as in His temple (Romans 8:9-11; 1 Corinthians 3:16, 6:19). Jesus is in the Church and its members as a principle of unity, movement and life (1 Corinthians 12:4-11). "Bear with one another charitably, in complete selflessness, gentleness and patience. Do all you can to preserve the unity of the Spirit by the peace that binds you together. There is one Body, one Spirit, just as you were all called into one and the same hope when you were called. There is one Lord, one faith, one baptism, and one God who is Father of all, over all, through all and within all. Each one of us, however, has been given his own share of grace, given as Christ allotted it" (Ephesians 4:2-7).

The descent of the Holy Spirit, the Spirit of Truth, whom Jesus promised to send after His ascension by interceding with God the Father, took place on Pentecost (Acts 2:1-13). It is sometimes called "the birthday of the Church" because with the pouring of the Spirit of the Lord upon the early Church, the Church comes to completion in the sense that it is now firmly established and prepared to grow and spread to all the nations. With the descent of the Holy Spirit, the Church is fully indwelt by its soul, empowering the Church to keep the truth of Jesus Christ and to sanctify souls.

As a branch could not live unless it were part of the vine or trunk of the tree, so, we cannot live in Christ without staying united to the "whole Christ," as St. Augustine called the Church. We need others for our life in Christ. In future chapters we shall see that Christians do not administer the sacraments to themselves. Jesus Christ acts in His sacraments to glorify the Father and to bring grace to man. Jesus does this through His Mystical Body, the Church.

While for St. Paul the most descriptive figure of the Church was "the Body of Christ," yet Jesus used many other images, as did the various biblical writers.

"In the Old Testament the revelation of the kingdom is often made under the form of symbols. In similar fashion the inner nature of the Church is now made known to us in various images. Taken either from the life of the shepherd or from cultivation of the land, from the art of building or from family life and marriage, these images have their preparation in the books of the prophets.

"The Church is, accordingly, a sheepfold, the sole and necessary gateway to which is Christ (Jn. 10:1-10). It is also a flock, of which God foretold that he would himself be the shepherd (see Is. 40:11; Ex. 34:11 ff.), and whose sheep, although watched over by human shepherds, are nevertheless at all times led and brought to pasture by Christ himself, the Good Shepherd and prince of shepherds (see Jn. 10:11; 1 Pet. 5:4), who gave his life for his sheep (see Jn. 10:11-16).

"The Church is a cultivated field, the tillage of God (1 Cor. 3:9). On that land the ancient olive tree grows whose holy roots were the prophets and in which the reconciliation of Jews and Gentiles has been brought about and will be brought about again (Rom. 11:13-26). That land, like a choice vineyard, has been planted by the heavenly cultivator (Mt. 21:33-43; see Is. 5:1 ff.). Yet the true vine is Christ who gives life and fruitfulness to the branches, that is, to us, who through the Church remain in Christ without whom we can do nothing (Jn. 15:1-5).

"Often, too, the Church is called the building of God (1 Cor. 3:9). The Lord compared himself to the stone which the builders rejected, but which was made into the cornerstone (Mt. 21:42; see Acts 4:11; 1 Pet. 2:7; Ps. 117:22). On this foundation the Church is built by the apostles (see 1 Cor. 3:11) and from it the Church receives solidity and unity. This edifice has many names to describe it: the house of God in which his family dwells; the household of God in the Spirit (Eph. 2:19,22); the dwelling place of God among men (Apoc. 21:3); and, especially, the holy temple. This temple, symbolized in places of worship built out of stone, is praised by the Fathers and, not without reason, is compared in the liturgy to the Holy City, the New Jerusalem. As living stones we here on earth are built into it (1 Pet. 2:5). It is this holy city that is seen by John as it comes down out of heaven from God when the world is made anew, prepared like a bride adorned for her husband (Apoc. 21:1 ff.).

"The Church, further, which is called 'that Jerusalem which is above' and 'our mother' (Gal. 4:26; cf. Apoc. 12:17), is described as the spotless spouse of the spotless lamb (Apoc. 19:7; 21:2 and 9; 22:17). It is she whom Christ 'loved and for whom he delivered himself up that he might sanctify her. . ." (*Dogmatic Constitution on the Church, Lumen Gentium,* 6).

Jesus used the word "Church" only twice and which the evangelists identified with *Ekklesia*, meaning, congregation or assembly of the faithful. Jesus spoke of two kinds of kingdoms, the earthly kingdom and the heavenly kingdom. We will reach the heavenly kingdom if, on earth, we live up to the standards of His kingdom.

In a sense, the Church began with the birth of human society. However, the foreshadowing of the Church takes place with the call of Abraham and the formation of the chosen people which eventually grows into the Church.

The Catholic Church teaches that the Church is necessary for salvation. Jesus Christ founded the Catholic Church in order to continue His work of redemption for all men even to the end of time. Understanding the Church as the Mystical Body of Christ, we can see how the Church is an extension of the redemption and incarnation to the present day.

While Jesus Christ is the invisible head of the Church, this Church founded by our Lord, Jesus Christ, is a *visible community*. Our divine and loving Savior founded His Church upon the apostles and built it upon the rock of the papacy. The original 12 chosen by Jesus were called "disciples" during the period in which Jesus was instructing them. Following the ascension of our Lord into heaven, they are called "apostles." They gathered in the upper room in Jerusalem where the Last Supper had been celebrated (Mark 14:14; Luke 22:12) and where the Holy Spirit visibly manifested himself in the form of tongues of fire on Pentecost Sunday (Acts 2:1-13). Since Judas, who betrayed our divine Lord, had committed suicide in his despair, after the ascension Peter stood up to speak to his spiritual brothers on the importance of electing someone to take his place. "As the lot fell to Matthias, he was listed as one of the twelve apostles" (Acts 1:26).

Our divine Lord instructed that His Church should have visible qualities of leadership and with one man as the chief visible head.

"Then Simon Peter spoke up, 'You are the Christ,' he said, 'the Son of the living God.' Jesus replied, 'Simon, son of Jonah, you are a happy man! Because it was not flesh and blood that revealed this to you but my Father in heaven. So I now say to you: You are Peter and on this rock I will build my Church. And the gates of the underworld can never hold out against it. I will give you the keys of the kingdom of heaven: whatever you bind on earth shall be considered bound in heaven; whatever you loose on earth shall be considered loosed in heaven' " (Matthew 16:16-20).

Other visible qualities of the Church will be discussed in the chapters on the sacraments where we shall see that Jesus acts today, using visible signs of water, bread, wine, oil, etc.

The Church is the People of God who have been baptized into Jesus Christ and who share the one same true faith that is from God. The Church is a community, God's family, who together share the life of

106

Christ, the invisible head. With the pope, the successor of St. Peter, as the world's chief bishop and visible head, and with the other Catholic bishops in union with the pope, God's People are kept in the one true faith through the power of the Holy Spirit, who lives in the Church as its soul. In this Church, which is also called the Mystical Body of Christ, we have the Mass and the sacraments which give glory to God and grace to souls. In this Catholic Church "there is one Body, one Spirit, just as you were all called into one and the same hope when you were called. There is one Lord, one faith, one baptism, and one God who is Father of all, over all, through all and within all" (Ephesians 4:4-6). $_{STOP}$

As the *community* of believers in Jesus Christ, the Church is the assembly (*ekklesia*) of all with a unified faith. The Church is also the *fellowship (koinonia)* of all who are united in their common love for the Savior. As the *kingdom (basileia)*, the Church is the fulfillment of the ancient prophecies which told of the reign of the Messiah. As the *Mystical Body of Christ*, the Church is the *communion* of all those made holy by the grace of Jesus Christ.

Pope Pius XII wrote a magnificent encyclical letter to the world *On the Mystical Body of Christ, (Mystici Corporis Christi*, 1943) which had a profound effect in leading members of the Church to contemplate "the grand and inestimable privilege of our intimate union with a Head so exalted."

"That the Church is a body is frequently asserted in Sacred Scripture. 'Christ,' says the Apostle,' is the Head of the Body of the Church.' (Col. 1:18). If the Church is a body, it must be an unbroken unity according to those words of Paul: 'Though many we are one body in Christ.' (Rom. 12:5). But it is not enough that the Body of the Church be an unbroken unity; it must also be something definite and perceptible to the senses, as Our predecessor of happy memory, Leo XIII, in his encyclical, *Satis cognitum*, asserts: 'the Church is visible because she is a Body.' Hence they err in a matter of divine truth, who imagine the Church to be invisible, intangible, something merely 'pneumatological,' as they say, by which many Christian communities, though they differ from each other in their profession of faith, are united by an invisible bond. . . .

"Only those are really to be included as members of the Church who have been baptized and profess the true faith and who have not unhappily withdrawn from Body-unity or for grave faults been excluded by legitimate authority. 'For in one Spirit,' says the Apostle, 'were we all baptized into one Body, whether Jews or Gentiles, whether bond or free.' (1 Cor. 12:13). As therefore in the true Christian community there is only one Body, one Spirit, one Lord, and one Baptism, so there can be only one faith. (Eph. 4:5). And so if a man refuse to hear the Church, let him be considered — so the Lord commands — as a heathen and a publican. It follows that those who are divided in faith or government cannot be living in one body such as this, and cannot be living the life of its one divine Spirit (Matt. 18:17).

"Because Christ the Head holds such an eminent position one must not think that He does not require the Body's help. What Paul said of the human organism is to be applied likewise to this Mystical Body: 'The head cannot say to the feet: I have no need of you' (1 Cor. 12:29). It is manifestly clear that the faithful need the help of the Divine Redeemer, for He has said: 'Without Me you can do nothing' (John 15.5), and in the teaching of the Apostle, every advance of this Body towards its perfection derives from Christ the Head. Yet this, too, must be held, marvelous though it appears: Christ requires His members. First, the person of Jesus Christ is borne by the Supreme Pontiff, who in turn must call on others to share much of his solicitude, lest he be overwhelmed by the burden of his pastoral office, and must be helped daily by the Church praying. Moreover, our Savior does not rule the Church directly in a visible manner and so in carrying out the work of Redemption He wishes to be helped by the members of His body. This is not because He is indigent and weak, but rather because He has so willed it for the greater glory of His unspotted Spouse. Dying on the Cross He left to His Church the immense treasury of the Redemption; towards this she contributed nothing. But when those graces come to be distributed, not only does He share this task of sanctification with His Church, but He wants it in a way to be due to her action. Deep mystery this, subject of inexhaustible meditation; that the salvation of many depends on the prayers and voluntary penances which the members of the Mystical Body of Jesus Christ offer for this intention and on the assistance of pastors of souls and of the faithful, especially of fathers and mothers of families, which they must offer to our divine Savior as though they were His associates. . . .

"That such a love, solidly grounded and undivided, may abide and increase in our souls, we must accustom ourselves to see Christ in the Church. It is Christ who lives in the Church, who teaches, governs and sanctifies through her. . . ." (Pius XII, *Mystici Corporis Christi*).

The Catholic Church has defined itself since the Council of Trent (1545-1563) as a union of human beings who are united by the profession of the same Christian faith, and by participation of and in the same sacraments under the direction of their lawful pastors, especially of the one representative of Christ on earth, the Bishop of Rome. Each part of this definition is intended to exclude all others from actual and vital membership in the Catholic Church, e.g. apostates and heretics who do not profess the same Christian faith, non-Christians who do not receive the same

108

sacraments, and schismatics who are not submissive to the lawful pastors of the Church under the pope.

The Second Vatican Council (1962-65) recognized the above as the objective reality which identifies the fullness of the Roman Catholic Church. It was qualified subjectively so as to include all who are baptized and profess their faith in Jesus Christ. They are related to the people of God, upon whom He bestows the special graces of His Divine Providence.

Those who do not have the *fullness* of true faith in union with the Roman Catholic Church, with the pope as visible head, are in some manner joined with the Mystical Body of Christ provided they are baptized and profess faith in Jesus Christ as Lord, God and Savior. It is difficult to describe the exact position of Christians not in full union with Rome with ecumenical sensitivity. Some have explained it as "imperfect membership" in the Mystical Body. Whatever the case, those not in full union of faith and practice with the Roman Catholic Church in some way lack the *fullness* of faith Jesus Christ intended for His Church upon earth. Acting with a sincere conscience, if through no fault of their own they do not recognize the fullness of true faith to be found in the Catholic Church, they can surely be saved.

The Second Vatican Council spoke as follows on the matters discussed above:

"This holy Council first of all turns its attention to the Catholic faithful. Basing itself on scripture and tradition, it teaches that the Church, a pilgrim now on earth, is necessary for salvation: the one Christ is mediator and the way of salvation; he is present to us in his body which is the Church. He himself explicitly asserted the necessity of faith and baptism (see Mk. 16:16; Jn. 3:5), and thereby affirmed at the same time the necessity of the Church which men enter through baptism as through a door. Hence they could not be saved who, knowing that the Catholic Church was founded as necessary by God through Christ, would refuse either to enter it, or to remain in it.

"Fully incorporated into the Church are those who, possessing the Spirit of Christ, accept all the means of salvation given to the Church together with her entire organization, and who — by the bonds constituted by the profession of faith, the sacraments, ecclesiastical government and communion — are joined in the visible structure of the Church of Christ, who rules her through the Supreme Pontiff and the bishops. Even though incorporated into the Church, one who does not however persevere in charity is not saved. He remains indeed in the bosom of the Church, but 'in body' not 'in heart.' All children of the Church should nevertheless remember that their exalted condition results, not from their own merits, but from the grace of Christ. If they fail to respond in thought, word and deed to that grace, not only shall they not be saved but they shall be the more severely judged.

"Catechumens who, moved by the Holy Spirit, desire with an explicit intention to be incorporated into the Church are by that very intention joined to her. With love and solicitude mother Church already embraces them as her own.

"The Church knows that she is joined in many ways to the baptized who are honored by the name of Christian, but who do not however profess the Catholic faith in its entirety or have not preserved unity or communion under the successor of Peter. For there are many who hold sacred scripture in honor as a rule of faith and of life, who have a sincere religious zeal, who lovingly believe in God the Father Almighty and in Christ, the Son of God and the Savior, who are sealed by baptism which unites them to Christ, and who indeed recognize and receive other sacraments in their own Churches or ecclesiastical communities. Many of them possess the episcopate, celebrate the holy Eucharist and cultivate devotion of the Virgin Mother of God.[1] There is furthermore a sharing in prayer and spiritual benefits; these Christians are indeed in some real way joined to us in the Holy Spirit for, by his gifts and graces, his sanctifying power is also active in them and he has strengthened some of them even to the shedding of their blood. And so the Spirit stirs up desires and actions in all of Christ's disciples in order that all may be peaceably united, as Christ ordained, in one flock under one shepherd. Mother Church never ceases to pray, hope and work that this may be achieved, and she exhorts her children to purification and renewal so that the sign of Christ may shine more brightly over the face of the Church.

"Finally, those who have not yet received the Gospel are related to the People of God in various ways. There is, first, that people in which the covenants and promises were made, and from which Christ was born according to the flesh (see Rom. 9:4-5): in view of the divine choice, they are a people most dear for the sake of the fathers, for the gifts of God are without repentance (see Rom. 11:29). But the plan of salvation also includes those who acknowledge the Creator, in the first place amongst whom are the Moslems: these profess to hold the faith of Abraham, and together with us they adore the one, merciful God, mankind's judge on the last day. Nor is God remote from those who in shadows and images seek

---

[1]The Vatican Council II fathers were referring here to Eastern churches which have a valid priesthood and valid bishops as the footnote of the official document refers to Pius XI, Litt. Encycl. *Rerum Orientalium*, Sept. 8, 1928; AAS 20 (1928) p. 287. Pius XII, Litt. Encycl. *Orientalis Ecclesiae*, April 9, 1944: AAS 36 (1944) p. 137.

the unknown God, since he gives to all men life and breath and all things (see Acts 17:25-28), and since the Savior wills all men to be saved (see 1 Tim 2:4). Those who, through no fault of their own, do not know the Gospel of Christ or his Church but who nevertheless seek God with a sincere heart, and, moved by grace, try in their actions to do his will as they know it through the dictates of their conscience — those too may achieve eternal salvation. Nor shall divine providence deny the assistance necessary for salvation to those who, without any fault of theirs, have not yet arrived at an explicit knowledge of God, and who, not without grace, strive to lead a good life. Whatever good or truth is found amongst them is considered by the Church to be a preparation for the Gospel and given by him who enlightens all men that they may at length have life. But very often deceived by the Evil One, men have become vain in their reasonings, have exchanged the truth of God for a lie and served the world rather than the Creator (see Rom. 1:21 and 25). Or else, living and dying in this world without God, they are exposed to ultimate despair. Hence to procure the glory of God and the salvation of all these, the Church, mindful of the Lord's command, 'preach the Gospel to every creature' (Mk 16:16) takes zealous care to foster the missions." (*Dogmatic Constitution on the Church, Lumen Gentium* 14,15,16).

With the descent of the Holy Spirit, the Church is fully indwelt by its soul empowering the Church to keep in the truth and sanctify souls.

DISCUSSION QUESTIONS

1. Who was St. Paul before his sudden conversion?

Before his conversion, St. Paul was known as "Saul." He was born in Tarsus of Cilicia. He was a Jew, a fanatical Pharisee. After his sudden conversion he became the most dynamic apostle, although he was not one of the original 12.

2. What did Jesus Christ say to St. Paul at his conversion that especially influenced his theology on the nature of the Church?

The words of Jesus to St. Paul, "I am Jesus, and you are persecuting me," contained the seed for his discernment of the identity of the members of the Church with Jesus Christ, making Jesus one with those who believe in Him.

3. What term does St. Paul repeatedly use in his epistles to describe the Church?

St. Paul frequently speaks of the Church as "the Body of Christ."

4. What allegory did Jesus Christ himself use, as quoted by the Apostle John, to explain our oneness in a divine organism, Christ?

Jesus, as quoted in St. John's Gospel, used the allegory of the vine and the branches.

5. What allegory did St. Paul use for the Church as the Body of Christ?

St. Paul used the allegory of the human body to explain how the many members of the human body share a common life. So it is with the many members of the Church. With Christ living in all by faith and grace, they form one Mystical Body of Christ.

6. Where did the doctrine of the Mystical Body of Christ come from? Was it a gradual doctrinal development within the Church?

The doctrine of the Church as the Mystical Body of Christ was not a gradual doctrinal development of the Church. It was revealed directly by Jesus Christ as seen in the allegory of the vine and the branches and in His words to St. Paul on the road to Damascus when Jesus identified himself with His followers.

7. Why is the Catholic Church more than an organization?

The Catholic Church is not simply a natural organization but a divine living organism because it shares in the divine life and possesses the powers of Jesus Christ and there is an inner spiritual communion through grace of all the members or at least a union in faith, if some are not in the state of grace.

8. Who are the head, soul and members of the Mystical Body of Christ?

The head of the Mystical Body is Jesus Christ, the soul is the Holy Spirit and the members are all those baptized and possessing faith in Jesus Christ as Lord, God and Savior.

9. How would you respond to this statement: "I can save my soul without the Church. I simply believe and serve Jesus Christ"?

A person can no more save his soul without the Church than a branch can live apart from the vine. The Church is "the Body of Christ" and is necessary for those with faith in order to receive the sacraments, the teachings of Jesus Christ who speaks through His Church with the guidance of the Holy Spirit and who governs His Church for the glory of God and the salvation of souls. The Apostle Paul repeatedly spoke of the necessity of union of all believers in Christ. In St. Paul's analogy of the body (1 Corinthians 12:12-30) each part of the human body needs the other parts to live.

10. Name at least five descriptive figures for the Church from Sacred Scripture besides "the Body of Christ."

Other descriptive figures for the Church besides "the Body of Christ" are: a sheep-fold; a building made up of many bricks fit together, with Christ the cornerstone; the vineyard; the union of husband and wife in marriage; spotless spouse of the spotless lamb, etc.

11. Where did the Church have its beginnings?

The beginnings of the Church are really found in the placing of man upon earth, with his fall and the promise of a Redeemer. A foreshadowing takes place at the call of Abraham. With the coming of Christ, His life, death and resurrection and, finally, the descent of the Holy Spirit on Pentecost, the Church is established.

12. Why did Jesus Christ found the Church?

Jesus Christ founded the Church to continue His work of redemption, to bring to men His teachings so they could have faith and receive through the Church His redemptive grace of salvation.

13. What is meant by: "the Church as established by Jesus Christ is a visible community"?

When we speak of the Church as a "visible" community we mean that the Church is not simply a spiritual quality of faith whereby men individually and independently put their faith in Jesus, rather, just as Jesus is both God and Man so the Church is both human and divine and has visible qualities. Jesus established His Church with basic organization, namely Peter (as pope) and the apostles as bishops who were given authority. The sacraments have visible signs to them, etc.

14. Give a brief description of the nature of the Church.

The nature of the Church is to be a communion of believers baptized into Jesus Christ, who share one faith and are under the authority of the pope and bishops in communion with him. This Church has the Holy Spirit for its soul, which is also the Spirit of Truth. Together Jesus, the Holy Spirit and baptized members with faith form one living divine organism for the salvation of man and the glory of God the Father.

15. What is meant by the "visible" and "invisible" head of the Church?

The invisible head of the Church is its founder, our Lord Jesus Christ. The visible head of the Church is the pope who is the vicar of Christ Jesus on earth.

16. How has the Catholic Church defined itself since the Council of Trent (1545-1563)?

From the time of the Council of Trent (1545-1563) the Church has strictly defined itself as a union of human beings, united by the profession of one faith in Jesus Christ, participating in the same sacraments under the direction of lawful pastors, especially of the one chief representative of Christ on earth, the bishop of Rome. This, in brief, is the objective reality of the Roman Catholic Church.

17. How did the Second Vatican Council relate others outside full union with the Roman Catholic Church to the membership of the Mystical Body?

Subjectively, the Mystical Body of Christ recognizes all baptized persons who profess faith in Jesus Christ, although this is not the perfect union in faith intended by our Lord, who built His Church upon the rock of the papacy.

18. Can Christians not in full and perfect union with the Roman Catholic Church be saved?

Baptized Christians who are sincere in their faith, even though not in full union with the Roman Catholic Church, can be saved if they follow the dictates of their conscience, namely the truths of Jesus Christ's revelation insofar as they understand them.

19. Can people who are not Christian be saved?

People who are not Christian can be saved but their salvation must come in some way through Jesus Christ who is the one universal Savior of all mankind. If through no fault of their own they do not know Jesus Christ and His Gospel, they nevertheless try in their lives to do the will of God as they come to know God in the world, they can be saved through the grace of Jesus Christ as it comes to them in another way. The ordinary way intended by God is through the Church founded by Jesus Christ.

20. What did the Second Vatican Council say about those who know the Catholic Church is the true Church but do not join it, or being a member, leave it?

Jesus Christ affirmed the necessity of the Church which men enter through baptism, and they cannot be saved who, knowing that the Catholic Church was founded as necessary by God through Christ, would refuse either to enter it, or to remain in it.

21. Describe those who are fully incorporated into the Roman Catholic Church.

Those are fully incorporated into the Roman Catholic Church who possess the Spirit of Christ, accept all the means of salvation given to the Church together with its entire organization, and who, by profession of faith, the sacraments, ecclesiastical government and communion, are joined in the visible structure of the Church of Christ, who rules the Church through the pope and bishops in union with the pope.

22. Does membership in the Catholic Church automatically guarantee salvation?

Membership in the Catholic Church does not automatically guarantee salvation. One must persevere in charity. One must die in the state of sanctifying grace.

23. Name the three categories of people who are not Christian but for whom the Church nonetheless holds out hope for salvation. Explain how they can be saved.

The Church holds out the hope of salvation for the descendents of God's chosen people, the Jews to whom the covenants and promises were first made and from whom Christ was born according to the flesh. There are also people who believe in one true God, especially the Moslems, who profess the faith of Abraham. Then there are those who are sincere, but without explicit knowledge of God, who seek Him with a sincere heart. These people can be saved through the grace of Jesus Christ as whatever good or truth is found among them is a preparation for the Gospel and in some way comes from God. Living according to a good conscience, worshiping God accordingly, they can in some way receive grace from Jesus Christ for their salvation since it is through no fault of their own that they do not possess the fullness of true faith.

CHAPTER 9

The Blessed Virgin Mary

As Abraham was the man of faith in the Old Testament, Mary, the Mother of Jesus, is presented in the New Testament as the woman of faith. The Sacred Scriptures themselves provide the most promising area for a deeper understanding both for Catholics and other Christians. Protestant scholars have been discovering more about Mary in the New Testament of the Bible.

Mary and the papacy have long been considered obstacles to unity between Catholics and their separated brethren. Some years ago, however, a 12-member task force of Catholic and Protestant scholars issued a 336-page volume, "Mary in the New Testament," and said: "We found more to discuss about Mary than we did about Peter."

Studies by Protestants and Catholics have found in the Bible a theological portrait of the Mother of Jesus emphasizing her faith-commitment to God's will and her Son's saving work. There is some difference between Catholic and Protestant interpretations regarding Mary joined to the saving work of Jesus. The Catholic Church sees in Mary "a faultless image, that which she herself desires and hopes wholly to be" (*Constitution on the Sacred Liturgy*, 103).

Abraham's son Isaac was born of the aged Sarah. The Gospel offers a comparison between the faith of Abraham and Mary's faith in God's power to bring forth the Messiah from her virginal womb. God brought forth the Messiah to save mankind independently of the will of the flesh and the will of man (John 1:13). However, God required a free, loving response from Mary. God bestows His favor as He chooses, when He chooses, whether in the barren Sarah or in the Blessed Virgin Mary "because nothing is impossible to God" (Luke 1:37; see Genesis 18:14). Thus Jews and Christians both honor Abraham as "our father in faith." In the Gospel, Mary is the "Mother in faith, the mother of believers."

Catholic understanding of Mary has become even more profound since the Second Vatican Council (1962-65). In its *Dogmatic Constitution on the Church* (Lumen Gentium) the council devoted its entire eighth and last chapter to *Our Lady*. Key statements on Mary also are found in the *Constitution on the Sacred Liturgy*.

The council, in considering the divine liturgy of the Church and the way it unfolds the entire mystery of Christ's life in the course of the year so that the mysteries or events of Christ's redemption are "in some way made present at all times," spoke as follows:

"In celebrating this annual cycle of the mysteries of Christ, Holy Church honors the Blessed Mary, Mother of God, with a special love. She is inseparably linked to her Son's saving work. In her the Church admires and exalts the most excellent fruit of redemption, and joyfully contemplates, as in a faultless image, that which she herself desires and hopes wholly to be." (*Constitution on the Sacred Liturgy* No. 103).

The Catholic Church considered the union of Mary with the Church to be so important that the council fathers did not want to develop a separate document on Mary, but incorporated a chapter on Mary into the constitution which discussed the very nature of the Church. Members of the Church were told: "Joined to Christ the head and in communion with all his saints, the faithful must in the first place reverence the memory 'of the glorious ever Virgin Mary, Mother of God and of our Lord Jesus Christ.' (52, also from the Canon of the Roman Mass).

"The Virgin Mary, who at the message of the angel received the Word of God in her heart and in her body and gave Life to the world, is acknowledged and honored as being truly the Mother of God and of the Redeemer. Redeemed, in a more exalted fashion, by reason of the merits of her Son and united to him by a close and indissoluble tie, she is endowed with the high office and dignity of the Mother of the Son of God, and therefore she is also the beloved daughter of the Father and the temple of the Holy Spirit. Because of this gift of sublime grace she far surpasses all creatures, both in heaven and on earth. But, being of the race of Adam, she is at the same time also united to all those who are to be saved; indeed, 'she is clearly the mother of the members of Christ . . . since she has by her charity joined in bringing about the birth of believers in the Church, who are members of its head.' (St. Augustine, *De S. Virginitate*, 6:PL 40, 399). Wherefore she is hailed as pre-eminent and as a wholly unique member of the Church, and as its type and outstanding model in faith and charity. The Catholic Church, taught by the Holy Spirit, honors charity. The Catholic Church, taught by the Holy Spirit, honors her with filial affection and devotion as a most beloved mother." (*Dogmatic Constitution on the Church*, 53).

The Gospels of Matthew, Luke and John illustrate stories of the birth and childhood of Jesus so as to relate the meaning of Mary to Christ and to the Church. In her "pilgrimage of faith," the earthly association of Mary with Jesus, even to "union with her Son unto the cross" (*Dogmatic Constitution on the Church, 58*), depicts her as a perfect "type of the Church

— in the order of faith, charity and perfect union with Christ" (*Dogmatic Constitution on the Church*, 63). The council referred to Mary as "the exalted Daughter of Sion" in whom "the times are fulfilled," after the long waiting for the promise, "and the new plan of salvation is established when the Son of God has taken human nature from her that he might in the mysteries of His flesh free men from sin" (*Dogmatic Constitution on the Church*, 55). Daughter of Sion in the Old Testament referred to the people of Israel who had been promised the Messiah. Mary of Nazareth, who is the daughter of her people, fulfills all the longings of Israel for its Messiah. In her the promise is realized. "She stands out among the poor and humble of the Lord who confidently hope for and receive salvation from Him" (*Dogmatic Constitution on the Church*, 55).

Mary is foreshadowed at the very dawn of creation, when, after the fall of Adam and Eve, God says to the serpent: "I will make you enemies of each other: you and the woman, your offspring and her offspring. It will crush your head and you will strike its heel" (Genesis 3:15). This scriptural quotation from the first pages of the Bible is often called the *Protoevangelium* (first Gospel) because it contains the promise of a Redeemer. Traditionally the woman is understood as Mary and her offspring as Jesus Christ, her Son. Here already, in the promise of the Redeemer, the woman Mary is joined to Jesus Christ, her Son, even though centuries were needed to fully understand the great promise God had made.

As time marches on, Isaiah the prophet records in his seventh chapter, verses 13-14, the words ascribed to the fulfillment of God's promise:

"Listen now, House of David: are you not satisfied with trying the patience of men without trying the patience of my God, too? The Lord himself, therefore, will give you a sign. It is this: the maiden is with child and will soon give birth to a son whom she will call Immanuel."

Mankind learns in time, with the coming of the Messiah, the Christ, and the foundation of the Church, that the woman of Genesis, the virgin of Isaiah, is she who becomes the Mother of Jesus Christ, but remains ever a virgin. It is the Blessed Virgin Mary. The prophet Isaiah, more than any other Old Testament prophet, according to biblical students, foreshadows numerous incidents in Jesus' life (Isaiah 2:1-5; 7:10-17; 9:1-6; 11:1-5).

St. Paul recognized the instrumentality of Mary whom God used in giving mankind its Redeemer. ". . . when the appointed time came, God sent his son, born of a woman, born a subject of the law, to redeem the subjects of the law and to enable us to be adopted sons" (Galatians 4:4).

Christian writers as early as the mid-second century compared Mary, whom they called the "new Eve," with the first Eve. The first Eve was disobedient and the second or "new Eve" was obedient. This is the oldest title after the Gospel records, for Mary. The first Eve listened to the evil

117

angel and the "new Eve" listened to the good Angel. St. Jerome said: "Death through Eve, life through Mary."

Already in the fourth century Christians held that Mary remained a virgin all her life. It is a dogma of Catholic faith that the Mother of Jesus conceived without carnal intercourse, gave birth to Christ without injury to her virginity, and remained a virgin all her life. Mary is "ever-virgin." The Old Testament in the famous Immanuel prophecy of Isaiah already foretold Mary's virginal conception. Mary's virginity includes: virginity of *mind*, virginity of the *senses* and virginity of the *body*. Virginity of the mind has reference to the constant virginal disposition of her soul; virginity of the senses means that Mary had freedom from any inordinate movement toward sexual desire; virginity of the body means that Mary always possessed her physical integrity. While the doctrine of the Church refers primarily to Mary's bodily integrity, her perfect virginity in every respect is also held as part of Church teaching.

The early Fathers of the Church held to the perpetual virginity of Mary. Early writers saw many references to Mary in the Old Testament. The Cloud above the Tabernacle of the Old Law, the Presence of God in the Holy of Holies, the Presence which only the High Priest could approach on one day in the year, the Day of Atonement, all are seen as types of the Holy Spirit overshadowing the Blessed Virgin. Her womb became a tabernacle and the New Temple of God, the most sacred Holy of all Holies.

We can conclude that no man could enter that sanctuary of God, except Jesus Christ himself, as the prophecy of Ezekiel pointed out: the gate of Jerusalem is closed; only God may enter through it, and it still remains closed, even after the entry of the Lord (44:1-2).

It is important that the perpetual virginity of Mary be preserved in the minds of people because it is a defined dogma of Catholic faith. This dogma of faith affects other key dogmas. This perfect virginity of Mary is connected to the dogma of Christ's divinity. Her virginity reflects on her relationship to the Church as its perfect model. The Church is the spotless bride of Christ of which Mary is the perfect exemplar.

The bodily origin of Jesus Christ was so arranged in the plan of God that the God-Man was brought into union with our race, becoming one with it, without binding Him under the sin of the first head of humanity, Adam. Jesus Christ was the New Adam, the New Head of the human race. The redemption of man would be a second creation, a recreation in the Spirit. The origins of Christ had, of necessity, to be untouched by the sin which man had brought upon himself. Consequently, a virgin birth was necessary.

The union of God and man in Jesus Christ, by the Second Person of the

Most Blessed Trinity, the Word being made flesh is prefigured immediately in Sacred Scripture by the perfect union of maternity and virginity in Mary. If God will become man, and such is the divine intention, then Mary, by the power of Almighty God, i.e., the overshadowing of the Holy Spirit, can be simultaneously perfect mother and absolute virgin. This unique role of Mary, and the holiness that accompanied it, enables Mary to be not only the perfect model of the Church but of every vocation within it; motherhood, marriage, consecrated virginity, the purity expected in the single state. Mary has always been a model for those in religious life. She is a model to priests and to disciples, bringing forth Christ.

Pope St. Leo I, among others of the early Church, in 449 defined the perpetual virginity of Mary. He wrote to Emperor Flavian:

"Jesus Christ was born of the Holy Spirit and the Virgin Mary. . . . She brought Him forth without the loss of virginity, even as she conceived Him without its loss. . . .

"The Son of God, therefore, came down from His heavenly throne without relinquishing the glory of His Father, and entered this lower world by way of a new order and a new mode of birth. . . . By way of a new mode of birth, insofar as virginity inviolate which knew not the desire of the flesh supplied the material of flesh. From His Mother the Lord took nature, not sin. Jesus Christ was born from a virgin's womb, by a miraculous birth. And yet His nature is not on that account unlike to ours, for He that is true God is also true Man."

The Council of the Lateran, under Pope St. Martin I, defined that anyone who denied that Mary was the Mother of God, or that the Word of God was brought forth from her "while her virginity remained intact also after the birth," should be anathema.[1]

At the wedding feast of Cana, Mary is present as the "Daughter of Zion" who welcomes the Messianic Bridegroom. She is there as the model

---

[1]Arguments proposed by those who would deny the perpetual virginity of Mary on the grounds that she had other children, because St. Luke uses the expression "first-born" (2:7) and the Gospels mention several men as "brethren" of Jesus, do not stand up when these expressions are considered in the entire context of Scripture. Also used against Mary's virginity is the Confraternity edition translation of St. Matthew 1:25: "and he did not know her till she brought forth her first son." The Jerusalem Bible, however, translates this "though he had not had intercourse with her, she gave birth to a son." In Oriental idiom, nothing is said about the future.

St. Luke (2:7) does not mean Mary had other children when he uses the expression "first-born." This was a technical expression. The firstborn son had to be consecrated to Yahweh, and bore special rights and duties.

There were, obviously, no other children when Jesus was 12 years old and was found in the temple after Mary and Joseph lost Him. Jesus is only named "Son of of the Church, the new People of God, the spotless Bride of Christ. The power of Mary's intercession is seen on this occasion when Christ says, "Woman, why turn to me? My hour has not come yet" (John 2:4). Still, His mother said to the servants, "Do whatever he tells you" (John 2:6). Our Lord changes the gallons of water in six stone water jars into the most precious wine. That miracle also signifies the Holy Eucharist, the changing of wine into the Precious Blood of Jesus Christ. Christ also sanctifies marriage by His presence. Mary has a unique role in all of this.

On Calvary Jesus again calls His mother "woman." Mary stands "by the cross of Jesus." The Apostle John, the only apostle at the foot of the Cross, recorded the words of the dying Savior in the very supreme act of redeeming the world. "Woman, behold your son. . . . Behold your mother" (John 19:26-27). Our Lord was not acting here simply as an individual son providing for His mother's natural care. Everything Jesus did and said from the Cross had a universal redemptive significance. John represents the entire Church in being given Mary as his mother.

The significance of "woman" used from the Cross is seen in its use at the Last Supper when the Savior gave His farewell discourse. Jesus strengthens His followers by recalling an example from the Bible: "A woman in childbirth suffers, because her time has come; but when she has given birth to the child she forgets the suffering in her joy that a man has been born into the world" (John 16:21). Israel's longing for the Messianic age had been compared to labor pain and the Daughter of Zion had been promised a progeny that would include all races, all nations. Mary on Calvary symbolizes the "woman" who becomes the Mother of the Church, but in herself is the model of mother Church, the new Israel, the new People of God, universal Mother, Jew and Gentile alike, having brought forth the head of the Mystical Body without pain at Bethlehem, Mary becomes the mother of the members of the Mystical Body on Calvary with great pain.

Mary" in St. Mark 6:3. Also Jesus would have entrusted Mary to a son of her own if there had been other sons (St. John 19:26-27) or at least it would not have been necessary for Mary to be taken into the home of John thereafter. Even the sons of women who died giving birth to their first son were called "firstborn." St. Jerome said that "firstborn" meant simply that no children preceded.

The several men mentioned in the Gospels as the "brethren" of Jesus are distinct from the apostles and are shown to be hostile to the preaching of Jesus. Since the Hebrew language had no explicit word to distinguish immediate blood brothers from cousins, the term does not mean brothers in the restricted sense used today. St. Matthew and St. Mark call St. James the Less and Joseph brethren of Jesus (Matthew 13:55; Mark 6:3), yet they also report them to be the sons of Mary, the wife of Cleophas (Matthew 27:56; Mark 15:40).

After the ascension of Jesus into heaven Mary is mentioned again in the Acts of the Apostles. She is at the center of the apostles gathered in the upper room, praying, awaiting the fulfillment of the promise of Christ that the Holy Spirit would be sent. After the Holy Spirit has overshadowed her at the Annunciation (Luke 1:35), Mary awaited the birth of Jesus, the head of the Mystical Body, the Church. Now in the upper room, the Cenacle, Mary awaits the coming of the Holy Spirit and the birth of Jesus in His Church (*Dogmatic Constitution on the Church*, 59; *Decree on the Missionary Activity of the Church*, 4).

The early Christians needed to defend the mystery of Jesus Christ, that He was true God, true Man, the Second Person of the Holy Trinity, the Word made flesh, who redeemed us by His death on the Cross, rose from the dead and ascended into heaven. Much of the knowledge contained in defined dogma arose from the Church's clarifications in defending the mystery of Jesus Christ and of Christian life. At the Council of Ephesus 431, the third ecumenical council defined the title of Mary as Theotokos, (Mother of God; Bearer of God). Mary as the Mother of God thus became a dogma of faith. The truth was upheld that the Son of Mary is actually the Son of God and Jesus is the God-Man. Jesus is Son of God, Son of Mary. When the council's decision was announced the people of Ephesus began to dance in the streets with joy.

To the present day the title "Mother of God" protects the central truth of the Incarnation even if some Western Christians, separated from descendants of ancient Christians, find the title difficult, almost pagan, as if the infinite Creator could have a mother. However, for Roman Catholics as well as for the Eastern Orthodox, this doctrine plays a key role in protecting the doctrine of the divinity of Christ.

In Jesus Christ there are two natures: a human nature and a divine nature. There is only one Person in Jesus Christ. One cannot speak of a *human person* in Jesus, only of a *human nature*. The Person born of Mary was the eternal Son of God, therefore divine. Mary represented the human race in freely accepting its Savior. Once she fully understood the will of God, that she would preserve her virginity and still be a mother, Mary answered the Angel Gabriel, "Let what you have said be done to me" (Luke 1:38). Speaking for all of humanity at the Annunciation in accepting the world's Redeemer, Mary was again present at the climax of our redemption on Calvary where Jesus as universal Redeemer spoke in giving mankind its spiritual Mother and in giving Mary all of mankind as her spiritual children.

To deny that Mary is truly the Mother of God is to deny that Mary gave birth to any kind of person. There is only one person in Jesus Christ, the Eternal Son of God the Father, who is equal to God the Father and

God the Holy Spirit. If Jesus is true man as well as true God, and that He is by faith divinely revealed, Jesus is then a person, not two persons. In conceiving by the power of the Holy Spirit the Second Person of the Holy Trinity, Mary became the mother of the Word made flesh, the Mother of God. All our Catholic theology flows from the dogma of faith that Mary is the Mother of God.

St. Ignatius of Antioch (died circa 107) wrote to the Ephesians: "Our God Jesus Christ was carried in Mary's womb, according to God's plan of salvation." The title *Theotokos* (Mother of God) was used by Origin (c. 185-254). St. Gregory Nazianzen, writing about 382, said: "If anyone does not recognize the holy Mary as Mother of God he is separated from the divinity."

Ancient spiritual writers concluded that the vocation of Mary to become the Mother of God required a special richness of divine friendship in grace. They emphasized the relationship between Mary's divine maternity and her fullness of grace declared in the angelic salutation, "Hail, highly favored one" (kecharitoméne).

Note that the angel did not salute the Blessed Virgin with her name "Mary." Rather heaven gave her the name "Full of Grace," a title which, it is recognized in time, means that Mary was conceived free of original sin. This privilege is rightfully titled the Immaculate Conception.

The special place of Mary in salvation history is recognized in Gospel times and has continued through the centuries. The downplaying of devotion to Mary, which took place among many separated Christians after the Protestant revolt in the early 16th century, did not typify early reformers among them. As a deeper and common biblical understanding of Mary develops between Christian denominations separated from Rome, it is to be hoped that it will serve as one more link toward Christian unity.

The words quoted by Mary in her *Magnificat* (Luke 1:48), "All generations will call me blessed," have been fulfilled in every century, with the praise and prayers of many Christian artists vying with one another to portray the beauty of the most beautiful woman God ever made. The beauty of God's mother is to be seen not simply in a beautiful body, but in her spirit. Byzantine art seems to have attempted to depict the whole Mary, body and spirit.

There is an incident from the public life of Jesus when a woman from the crowd who had been listening to Jesus suddenly praised His Mother. "Happy the womb that bore you and the breasts you sucked!" Jesus replied, "Still happier those who hear the word of God and keep it!" (Luke 11:27-28). It was not a put-down of Mary. It was praising Mary for the right reason, not simply because she conceived and gave birth to Christ and nursed Him physically. More important, her total person, her soul, her great faith as seen in Elizabeth's praise of Mary's faith: "Of all women you are the most blessed, and blessed is the fruit of your womb. Why should I be honored with a visit from the mother of my Lord? . . . Yes, blessed is she who believed that the promise made her by the Lord would be fulfilled" (Luke 1:42-45). For these same reasons the early Church Fathers said, "Mary conceived Jesus in her heart before she did in her womb."

While it is true, and scripturally based, that Mary is the "Woman of Faith," we must go further in considering her the Mother of Grace and that she has a continuing involvement in God's plan of salvation even today. If we look at Mary only as the "Woman of Faith" we are looking only at the historical, biblical Mary and not at her present role in heaven where she is described as the "Mediatrix of Grace." Her power of intercession is greater than all the angels and saints because of her closeness to God, because she is the "Mother of God."

Vatican II said, "the Blessed Virgin is invoked in the Church under the titles of Advocate, Helper, Benefactress and Mediatrix. This, however, is so understood that it neither takes away anything from nor adds anything to the dignity and efficacy of Christ the one Mediator" (*Dogmatic Constitution on the Church*, 62).

Christians turned more and more to Mary as a model of faith and holy response to Jesus Christ. Mary in authentic Catholic faith and devotions has always been seen as inseparable from her Son, Jesus Christ. The sense of a communion between Mary in heaven and the members of her Son upon earth has grown stronger with the centuries. The intercession of Mary is powerful but still her prayers ascend to the Father in, with and through Jesus Christ. An example of this is seen at the wedding feast of Cana, already described. Being greater than all angels and saints, the power of Mary's intercession is greater than all these.

When Pope Paul VI promulgated the *Dogmatic Constitution on the Church*, November 21, 1964, with special mention of its eighth chapter dedicated to Mary, he called upon Christians to invoke our Lady frequently by the title "Mother of the Church." This concept was not new. As early as St. Augustine (d. 430), Mary was recognized as the "Mother of the members of Christ." She was already regarded in the early centuries as Mother of the members of the Mystical Body of Christ.

"This motherhood of Mary in the order of grace continues uninterruptedly from the consent which she loyally gave at the Annunciation and which she sustained without wavering beneath the cross, until the eternal fulfillment of all the elect. Taken up to heaven she did not lay aside this saving office, but by her manifold intercession continues to bring us the gifts of eternal salvation. By her maternal charity, she cares for the brethren of her Son, who still journey on earth surrounded by dangers and difficulties, until they are led into their blessed home" (*Dogmatic Constitution on the Church*, 62).

The solemn definition of the Immaculate Conception of Mary, declaring her sinless from the first moment of her existence, was not made until 1854. This teaching, however, is *implicit* in the writings of the Greek and Latin Fathers. St. Ephrem (c. 306-73) spoke to Christ and Mary with these words: "You and Your mother are the only ones who are totally beautiful in every way. For in You, O Lord, there is no stain, and in Your mother no stain."

What was necessary in defining the Immaculate Conception was to preserve the role of Jesus Christ as the universal Savior. Jesus Christ is the Savior of all, even Mary. How could this be if she was never with sin, not even Original Sin? Chief credit for a clear explanation goes to the Franciscan John Duns Scotus (c. 1266-1308), who developed the idea of pre-redemption in order to reconcile Mary's being conceived without Original Sin even though her conception came before the coming of Christ and His redeeming death.

By a special prevenient grace Mary was created free of Original Sin. That grace, which came in advance to the saving redemptive acts of Jesus Christ, was, nonetheless, merited by Jesus Christ for His own mother. God is not tied down to time or space. As Mary stood beneath the Cross, suffering with her Son by compassion, as Co-Redemptrix, freely consenting in His labors, sufferings and death for the salvation of the human race, Jesus was suffering too for the special privilege of His mother, her unique privilege of the Immaculate Conception.

As Co-Redemptrix, Mary is not equal to Jesus Christ in His redemptive acts because she herself required redemption by her Son. Jesus, the one essential Savior and Mediator, merited mankind's salvation. Mary, however, has a subjective role as she does in the application of Christ's merits for those whom the Savior has objectively redeemed.

At the moment of the creation of the soul of Mary, God stepped in and prevented from happening what should have happened. As a descendant of Adam and Eve, Mary too should have been conceived in the state of Original Sin. But God redeemed Mary so perfectly that the moment of her creation was also the moment of her redemption. They coincided and Mary was created free of all sin. In defining the doctrine Pope Pius IX said:

"The most holy virgin Mary was, in the first moment of her conception, by a unique gift of grace and privilege of almighty God, in view of the merits of Jesus Christ the Redeemer of mankind, preserved free from all stain of original sin."

The doctrine of Mary's assumption into heaven, body and soul, was defined by Pope Pius XII in 1950. This dogma states that "Mary, the immaculate perpetually Virgin Mother of God, after the completion of her earthly life, was assumed body and soul into the glory of heaven."

We have historical records showing that Mary's Feast of the Assumption was celebrated as early as A.D. 400 (Epiphanius), when it was called "Mary's dormition, or transition" (Mary's going to sleep, her passing).

The doctrine of Mary's Assumption is part of oral tradition handed down from the first century. The Church does not rely on Scripture for this belief, although implicitly the Church reasons from Mary's fullness of grace (Luke 1:28) that she remained preserved from the consequence of sin, the corruption of the body after death and the postponement of bodily happiness in heaven until the end of the world. If Mary's bodily integrity is assured in the doctrine of her perpetual virginity, it would be fitting that it not be subject to destruction after death. Also, since Mary and Christ are presented in the Scriptures and doctrines of the Church as inseparable, with Mary sharing so closely in Christ's redemptive mission on earth, it is fitting to conclude that Mary would join Christ in bodily glorification.

The assumption of Mary into heaven is, obviously, a part of the universal faith of the Catholic Church, for when Pope Pius XII questioned the bishops of the world prior to defining the Assumption as a dogma of faith, the Catholic bishops all but unanimously stated their belief that this is part of Divine Revelation.

When the Church defined the dogmas of Mary's Immaculate Conception and Assumption, it was not declaring new doctrines for the Church. The Church was, rather, reaffirming and solemnly defining what was already the faith of the Church.

Developing in the modern world in recent years is what is known as devotion to the Immaculate Heart of Mary. Devotion to the Immaculate Heart of Mary[2] has gained international prominence since the Fatima apparitions of 1917 where the Blessed Mother announced, "God wishes to establish in the world devotion to my Immaculate Heart."

There is more to devotion to the Immaculate Heart of Mary than honoring the physical heart of the Blessed Virgin, although her physical heart exposed is a sign and symbol of her compassion and love for the faithful as the Mother of the Church. As the perfect Christian, as Mother and Model

---

[2]The development of the Fatima messages and devotion to the Immaculate Heart of Mary are to be found more extensively in the books, *Rediscovering Fatima* (Our Sunday Visitor Book Department) and *Fatima Today*, Christendom Publications, Box 87, Front Royal, VA 22630.

of the Church, the perfect exemplar of all that the Church is and hopes to become — all this is understood in the expression "Immaculate Heart of Mary."

Devotion to the Immaculate Heart of Mary is a call to faith and love such as Mary manifested upon earth and the love and grace, through her most powerful intercession after Christ, which she continues to lavish upon the world today.

The approved apparitions of Mary, which the Church permits the faithful to accept on human faith, rather than divine faith (in the sense of public revelation which is required of Catholic faith), may be believed by the faithful as helpful to their spiritual welfare. The Church, after careful investigation, has approved certain reported apparitions and messages in this manner since they are in harmony with the Scriptures and doctrines of the Church. Pope Pius XII spoke of Fatima as "the reaffirmation of the Gospels."

Other examples of approved appearances of Our Lady are Banneux (Belgium, 1933); Beauraing (Belgium 1932-33); Guadalupe (Mexico, 1531); Knock (Ireland, 1879); La Salette (France, 1846); Lourdes (France, 1858), and Our Lady of the Miraculous Medal (France, 1830). These apparitions tell us of the motherly love and concern Mary has for us yet today.

The messages of Our Lady of Fatima with her request for devotion to her Immaculate Heart as the will of God, is considered the most significant of Marian apparitions for modern times. The messages, when studied in depth, reveal that Mary reaffirms major doctrines of Catholicism and calls mankind back to her Son in the Holy Eucharist and to loyalty to the magisterial teachings of the Church, especially of the Holy Father. Also contained in the messages was a reminder of the punishment mankind can bring upon itself when it falls into the error of materialism and the spirit of atheism.

The Rosary is the most popular devotional prayer in honor of God's Mother and is, in reality, directed to meditation on the mysteries of Jesus Christ. The Rosary then is, when prayed properly, Christ-centered.

Pope Paul VI, February 2, 1974, issued an apostolic exhortation (*Marialis Cultus*) to the world for the right ordering and development of devotion to the Blessed Virgin Mary. In it, among many other things, he spoke of the Rosary:

"It has also been more easily seen how the orderly and gradual unfolding of the Rosary reflects the very way in which the Word of God, mercifully entering into human affairs, brought about the Redemption. The Rosary considers in harmonious succession the principal salvific events accomplished in Christ, from His virginal conception and the mysteries of His childhood to the culminating moments of the Passover — the blessed Passion and the glorious Resurrection — and to the effects of this on the infant Church on the day of Pentecost, and on the Virgin Mary when at the end of her earthly life she was assumed body and soul into her heavenly home. It also has been observed that the division of the mysteries of the Rosary into three parts not only adheres strictly to the chronological order of the facts but, above all, reflects the plan of the original proclamation of the faith and sets forth once more the mystery of Christ in the very way in which it is seen by St. Paul in the celebrated "hymn" of the Letter to the Philippians — kenosis, death and exaltation (2:6-11).

"As a Gospel prayer, centered on the mystery of the redemptive Incarnation, the "Rosary is therefore a prayer with a clearly Christological orientation. . . ."

The Second Vatican Council in its statements on Mary said that practice and exercises of devotion to Mary were to "be treasured as recommended by the teaching authority of the Church in the course of centuries. . . ." On February 2, 1965, two months and two days after the council's declaration on Mary (eighth chapter of the *Dogmatic Constitution on the Church*) was promulgated, Pope Paul VI said: ". . . Ever hold in great esteem the practices and exercises of the devotion to the most blessed Virgin which have been recommended for centuries by the Magisterium of the Church. And among them we judge well to recall especially the Marian Rosary and the religious use of the Scapular of Mount Carmel."

The origin of the Brown Scapular of Mount Carmel has a long history, and those of the Carmelite Order trace their beginnings back to the spiritual sons of Elijah the prophet who lived on Mt. Carmel in Palestine. They pondered the Word of God in their hearts. When Jesus founded the Church there was a group of hermits who believed themselves to be the spiritual sons of Elijah. As descendants of this great Old Testament prophet, they developed a deep devotion to the Mother of God. They became known as "The Brothers of Our Lady of Mt. Carmel." From the Carmelites the Church received the devotion of the Brown Scapular, according to an authenticated apparition of our Blessed Mother to St. Simon Stock, who became the superior general of the Carmelite Order in 1246 at Aylesford, England, since the Carmelites had moved to the West with the Saracen invasion. Today, however, on Mt. Carmel in the Holy Land, one can still visit the cave which tradition holds to have been the cave of Elijah. There one discovers a magnificent shrine, built over the cave on the mountain, in honor or Our Lady of Mt. Carmel.

For centuries popes have approved of the wearing of the brown cloth scapular and have even, at times, fostered this devotion. Pope Pius XII spoke of the wearing of the Brown Scapular as a sign of our consecration to the Immaculate Virgin. The Church does not teach that any spiritual power comes from the scapular itself, but rather comes from the prayers of the Church and the power of Mary's intercession, when Catholics wear the scapular with love for the Immaculate Heart of Mary.

The approved devotions to Mary, if understood and practiced correctly, have their roots in scriptural revelations and the doctrines of the Church. A widely used prayer of consecration to the Immaculate Heart of Mary reads as follows:

"Virgin of Fatima, Mother of mercy, Queen of heaven and earth, Refuge of sinners, we consecrate ourselves to your Immaculate Heart. To you we consecrate our hearts, our souls, our families, and all we have.

"And in order that this consecration may be truly effective and lasting, we renew today the promises of our Baptism and Confirmation; and we undertake to live as good Christians — faithful to God, the Church and the Holy Father. We desire to pray the Rosary, partake in the Holy Eucharist, attach special importance to the first Saturday of the month and work for the conversion of sinners.

"Furthermore we promise, O most holy Virgin, that we will zealously spread devotion to you, so that through our consecration to your Immaculate Heart, and through your own intercession, the coming of the Kingdom of Christ in the world may be hastened. Amen."

DISCUSSION QUESTIONS

1. What do Protestant and Catholic scholars see in common in the Bible concerning Mary?

Protestant and Catholic scholars recognize in common that Mary is a model of faith-commitment to doing the will of God.

2. What major difference remains between Protestant and Catholic views on Mary in Scripture?

Protestant and Catholic scholars do not have a common understanding regarding the union of Mary with the saving work of her Son, Jesus. Catholics see Mary as actively cooperating in the saving Redemption, but always as dependent on Christ.

3. What has contributed in recent history to a more profound understanding of Mary among Catholics?

Catholics have made a more thorough study of Sacred Scripture and rooted their teachings on Mary even more firmly in Sacred Scripture, as noted in the eighth chapter of the *Dogmatic Constitution on the Church* which was dedicated to Our Lady.

4. How did Vatican Council II compare the Daughter of Zion with Mary?

Vatican Council II saw the Daughter of Zion in the Old Testament, which referred to the people of Israel awaiting the fulfillment of the promised Messiah, as being fulfilled in Mary, the Mother of the Messiah. In Mary all the longings of Israel for its Messiah are fulfilled.

5. When is Mary first spoken of in the Bible?

Mary is first referred to in the Bible in its first book, Genesis, immediately after the fall of Adam and Eve, when God promises that a Redeemer will be born of a woman who will be an enemy of the devil.

6. What is meant by the Protoevangelium?

The Protoevangelium, or "first Gospel," has reference to Genesis 3:15 when God promises our first parents in the Garden that all hope is not lost, that a Savior will come to crush the forces of evil which has just conquered them.

7. What is the Sign of Redemption promised in Isaiah?

The sign of Isaiah (seventh chapter) is the promise that a virgin would have a child who would be called Immanuel, which means "God with us." Biblical students have commonly seen in Isaiah, as no other Old Testament prophet, foreshadowings of the coming Messiah, who would be a descendant of David. (Isaiah 2:1-5, 7:10-17, 9:1-6.

8. How did the early Christian writers compare Eve with Mary?

The first Eve was disobedient and brought death. Mary, the New Eve, was obedient to God's will and brought life.

9. Explain what is meant by the perfect virginity of Mary.

The perfect virginity of Mary means she remained perpetually a virgin, not only in her body but in her mind and in her senses. There was no disposition to inordinate sexual desires.

10. Name some Old Testament accounts which are seen as prefigurements of Mary's perpetual virginity.

Old Testament foreshadowings of Mary's perpetual virginity include: the cloud above the tabernacle; the presence of God in the Holy of Holies; the gate of Jerusalem remaining closed even after the Lord had entered.

11. Why is the dogma of Mary's virginity so important?

The doctrine of Mary's perpetual virginity is important because it protects our faith in the divinity of Jesus Christ.

12. What does Mary's virginal motherhood prefigure?

Mary becoming a mother while remaining a virgin immediately prefigures God becoming man while remaining God. Jesus is true God and true man.

13. How is Mary a model to various vocations in life?

Mary, by her special privileges, is a model to all major vocations: marriage; motherhood; consecrated virginity; purity in the single state; apostles bringing forth Christ.

14. Indicate the various riches of doctrine contained in the marriage feast at Cana.

129

The miracle of Cana and the presence of Christ there sanctifies married love, symbolizes the Holy Eucharist where wine is changed into the Blood of Jesus. Wrought at Mary's request, it demonstrates the power of her intercession.

15. Why were all of Christ's words from the Cross of universal significance?

Jesus Christ was the one essential mediator and high priest on the Cross and everything done and said had that significance. Nothing was of private concern but universal in scope, namely, the salvation of the world.

16. Who did the Apostle John represent at the foot of the Cross?

The Apostle John represented all of mankind, the entire Church, in receiving Mary as his spiritual mother and being declared the son of Mary by Christ the High Priest.

17. How did the need in the early Church to clearly define Jesus Christ as the true Son of God lead to the definition of Mary as the Mother of God?

It was necessary for the early Christians to have it clearly defined that Jesus was the Second Person of the Most Blessed Trinity, true God. This definition meant, as seen at the Council of Ephesus, 431, that Mary is truly the Mother of God.

18. Who did Mary represent in her response at the Annunciation?

When Mary answered her "fiat" at the Annunciation she represented all of humanity in accepting its Savior.

19. What contradiction results if it is denied that Mary is the Mother of God?

To deny that Mary is truly the Mother of God is to deny that Mary's child was a person. It would say Mary gave birth to a human nature that had no person.

20. From what dogma of faith does all Catholic theology on Mary flow?

All Catholic teaching on Mary flows from the truth that Mary is the Mother of God.

21. What is meant by the Immaculate Conception?

The Immaculate Conception was a special privilege granted to Mary whereby she was conceived free of Original Sin.

She was always in grace from the first instant of her conception in the womb of St. Anne.

22. Was Christ criticizing the woman who praised the Mother who bore and nursed him?

Christ did not criticize the woman who praised his mother (Luke 11:27-28). Rather Jesus praised Mary's faith and her response to that faith as had St. Elizabeth (Luke 1:42-45).

23. Why is it important that we consider Mary beyond her role as Woman of Faith?

Although Mary's role in Scripture as Woman of Faith shows her as a perfect model of faith doing God's will, now, she is the Mother of Grace and today intercedes for us in heaven.

24. What is meant by the statement: "Mary and Christ are inseparable"?

"Mary and Jesus are inseparable" means that Mary as cooperator is always involved with Jesus in God's saving plan for mankind. Yet, today, her intercession is to the Father through Jesus in the unity of the Holy Spirit, whose spouse she is.

25. Explain how Mary as Mediatrix of Grace does not detract from Christ as mediator.

The doctrine of Mary as Mediatrix does not detract from the power of Christ as the one essential mediator because her graces and privileges are entirely dependent on the redeeming acts of her Son, Jesus Christ.

26. Did the dogmas of the Immaculate Conception (1854) and the Assumption (1950) represent new doctrines of faith for Catholics?

The dogmas of Mary's Immaculate Conception and Assumption were merely solemn definitions of the constant faith of the Church, now clarified for all to know and believe firmly. What was implicit was now, with clarity, made explicit. What was already believed was now defined.

27. What special difficulty needed to be reconciled before the Church defined the dogma of the Immaculate Conception?

In solemnly defining the dogma of the Immaculate Conception of Mary, the Church was careful to protect the role of Jesus Christ as the universal Savior. The privilege of Mary being always without sin was due to prevenient grace from Christ.

28. How did the doctrine of the Assumption develop?

The doctrine of the Assumption was held by the early Christians, although not solemnly defined until 1950. It is part of oral tradition and is also consequential to Mary's fullness of grace (Luke 1:28) and of her having been conceived immaculate.

29. Do the authenticated apparitions such as Lourdes and Fatima represent new Catholic doctrines for Catholics?

Authenticated apparitions such as Lourdes and Fatima do not represent new Catholic doctrines, but they are reaffirmations of the Gospels and of the faith of the Church.

30. What is meant by devotion to the Immaculate Heart of Mary?

Devotion to the Immaculate Heart of Mary refers to our responding to God's Word in faith and love as Mary did upon earth and also of recognizing her role of Mediatrix of Grace in her love and concern for us yet today as Mother of the Church.

31. Summarize the Fatima message.

The Fatima message is essentially a call to devotion to the Immaculate Heart of Mary, a return to her Son Jesus Christ, especially in the form of eucharistic reparation and in total fidelity to the Church and loyalty to the papacy and its teaching authority.

32. Explain how the Rosary properly prayed is "Christ-centered" and a "Gospel prayer."

The Rosary properly prayed means meditating on the 15 Mysteries of Christ which is the soul of the Rosary. The chief Gospel events of the saving mysteries of Jesus Christ become the center of meditation when praying the Rosary.

33. How is it possible that devotion to Our Lady of Mount Carmel and the Brown Scapular has roots in the Old Testament?

The Brown Scapular was given to the Carmelite Order by Our Lady of Mount Carmel. The Carmelite Order traces its beginnings back to the spiritual sons of Elijah, the prophet on Mount Carmel.

CHAPTER 10

Church History

The history of the Catholic Church began almost 2,000 years ago when the Church was founded by Jesus Christ, our Lord, God and Savior. However, the Church was already prepared for in the history of the people of Israel in the "old alliance" or "old covenant." One could go back even further and say that the Church was present "in figure" at the very beginning of the world.

When God created man and he fell, the immediate plan of God (Genesis 3:15) was to send a Redeemer which mankind learns in time is the Son of God, the Word made flesh. Jesus Christ founded the Church so that the fruits of His redemption would be available for all men of all nations until the end of the world. Jesus founded His Church upon Peter, the prince of the apostles. Jesus promised that His Church would endure until the end of the world. (Matthew 28:20).

The greatest event in the entire history of salvation took place when the Son of God, the Second Person of the Most Holy Trinity, as the Word of God, was made flesh in the womb of the Blessed Virgin Mary through the "overshadowing" of the Holy Spirit. Jesus then climaxed His Incarnation by dying on the Cross for the redemption of the world, rose from the dead, ascended into heaven and sent the Holy Spirit upon the Church on Pentecost.

The promise of a Redeemer was kept alive in the hearts of men by the patriarchs and prophets whom God sent to His Chosen People, as recorded in the Old Testament. The Gentiles, or heathen nations, namely those who became separated from Divine Revelation, held on to the hope of a Redeemer but only in a vague and corrupt manner. These other nations fell into idolatry.

Evidence of the promise of a Redeemer, however distorted, is to be found in recorded reports of rumors that circulated in the pagan world. Seutonius and Tacitus, pagan Roman historians, wrote that the world was full of rumors about a mysterious power which was to come out of Palestine and rule the whole world. These authors recorded that the reports had been handed down from ancient traditions and that, at the time of Christ, the world was full of such rumors. Among the Greeks there was a legend that the son of their highest god would become man and be born of a virgin mother in order to redeem our fallen race. In A.D. 64 the emperor of China sent ambassadors to the West in search of the divine teacher who was foretold in the ancient books of China. Arriving in India, they discovered the religion of Buddha and embraced that religion, thinking it to be true. There were many other confused ancient beliefs of pagan gods who appeared in human form.

The people of Israel were among the smallest of nations and often were "stiff-necked" and not faithful to God. Yet, the one true God chose these people as His very own to keep alive the hope of the coming of the Redeemer of the world. These "chosen people of God" foreshadowed in their history the future kingdom of God on earth — the coming of the Savior who would establish the Church. As shown in the preceding chapter, all their longings were fulfilled in the Blessed Virgin Mary, "the exalted Daughter of Sion" in whom "the times are fulfilled" after the long wait for the promise, "and the new plan of salvation is established when the Son of God has taken human nature from her in the mysteries of his flesh that he might free men from sin" (*Dogmatic Constitution on the Church*, 55).

The Chosen People of God were set, by divine power, in Palestine, in the midst of great and ancient nations, though Israel itself was small and comparatively insignificant. The kingdoms of Babylonia, Assyria and Persia were to the east and north. Egypt was to the south. The Macedonian and Roman empires were to the west. The Prophet Ezekiel called Jerusalem the "gate of the nations." Palestine was the gateway to Africa and to Asia and it had a waterway to India through the Red Sea. The Chosen People of God, who kept hope in the promised Messiah, spread into all the great lands, preparing the way for the apostles of Jesus Christ to go forth from Jerusalem after Pentecost and take the Good News of the Savior to "all the nations" (Matthew 28:19).

The world was in the darkness of sin when Jesus came. The Gentile nations had fallen into idolatry, making gods out of things of creation. Crimes were sometimes committed in the name of worship. There was widespread immorality. God's Chosen People, the Jews, in spite of themselves and their sinfulness, were protected by God and continued to worship the one true God, Yahweh.

The highly developed nations of Rome and Greece, with all their culture, still worshiped false gods. Venus was worshiped by impurity. Bacchus was worshiped by drunkenness and Mars by bloody revenge. There was little unity in family life. Slavery abounded. "Cultured" people questioned whether slaves were human beings. There were public games in the circus where gladiators and captives were compelled to kill one another for the amusement of the crowds. This was the way of the world when Christ came at the "appointed time" (Galatians 4:4).

For the most part, the Jews, God's Chosen People, did not accept Jesus Christ as the long-promised Messiah. Jerusalem did not recognize God's moment (Luke 19:42). Some of the Jews accepted Jesus Christ as the Messiah, the Redeemer promised in Genesis 3:15 and mentioned again and again by the prophets through the centuries. Among them were Mary and the apostles. The Jews who did not accept Christ continued as a people to believe in one true God but they did not believe that God the Father sent His Son who became man in Jesus Christ. They accepted the faith of the Old Covenant, but did not believe it had been fulfilled. The Jews remain our ancestors in faith, under the one Fatherhood of God.

"Even though the Jewish authorities and those who followed their lead pressed for the death of Christ (See John 19:6), neither all Jews indiscriminately at that time, nor Jews today, can be charged with the crimes committed during His Passion. It is true that the Church is the new People of God, yet the Jews should not be spoken of as rejected or accursed as if this followed from Holy Scripture. Consequently, all must take care, lest in catechizing or in preaching the Word of God, they teach anything which is not in accord with the truth of the Gospel message or the spirit of Christ" (*Declaration on the Relation of the Church to Non-Christian Religions*, 4, Vatican II).

Jesus Christ had commanded the apostles to preach the Good News "to all nations," Jews and Gentiles alike. They were given the gift of tongues at Pentecost, when the Holy Spirit descended with a mighty wind and as tongues of fire (Acts 2:1-13) and people from various nations understood them and were converted to Jesus Christ. The apostles then went to the various nations to preach the Gospel. Just as Jesus Christ was persecuted and put to death, so it was to happen to His first apostles. Only St. John, although attempts on his life were unsuccessful, died naturally in old age.

The preaching of the original apostles was verified by the miracles which accompanied their preaching of the Good News. The shedding of the blood of the apostles and of the early Christians became the seed for more conversions. The apostles first preached to the Jews, but most of them did not accept faith in Christ. Our Lord foretold the destruction of Jerusalem because His own people would not accept Him and this prophecy was fulfilled in the year 70 when the Roman army, under Titus, destroyed Jerusalem. Even the temple in Jerusalem was destroyed. It had been the very center of worship and its destruction signified the end of both the old law and the unity of the Chosen People who did not accept Jesus Christ.

Basically, the Church began to operate in the first century much as it does today. There was the divine liturgy (the Mass) and the sacraments. Evidence of the sacraments can be found in Sacred Scripture itself. (See Acts 2:42; Acts 8:17; Acts 19:6; Acts 13:3; Ephesians 5:32; James 5:14 and John 20:21-23.) There was a hierarchy in the early Church, too, one which is, basically, present in the Catholic Church today. The Bible repeatedly signifies the special authority of St. Peter, the first pope. It was Peter who presided over the special functions of the apostles. In addition to the special authority of St. Peter, the early Church had deacons, priests and bishops.

"Let all be obedient to the bishop as Jesus to the Father, to the priests as to the apostles, and to the deacons as God's law. . . . Partake of the one Eucharist; for one is the body of the Lord Jesus Christ and one is the chalice of his blood, one altar and one bishop with the priests and the deacons" (St. Ignatius of Antioch, writing to Philadelphians, A.D. 107).

St. Peter left Jerusalem and began his apostolic journeys, which finally took him to Rome. Persecution of the early Christians by the Roman emperors had already begun when St. Peter, the first pope, was still living. The first persecution was under Nero, beginning about A.D. 64. According to tradition, St. Peter was martyred under Nero and was buried at the foot of the Vatican Hill. The first Christian emperor, Constantine, built a basilica over the site. It was replaced by the present St. Peter's Basilica at Vatican City, Rome. St. Paul also died during the persecution under Nero. Sts. Peter and Paul are traditionally honored together in the Catholic Church. Christians were killed by the thousands in the streets. Nero set Rome afire, but he blamed the Christians for it. Archeologists, encouraged by Pope Pius XII who ordered excavations under the high altar of St. Peter's Basilica, uncovered evidence that St. Peter did, in fact, go to Rome and was buried on Vatican Hill.

In the first centuries everything, it seemed, including the civil powers, were opposed to the spread of Christianity. Yet, the faith spread to the nations of the world. In A.D. 150 St. Justin wrote: "There is no people, neither among the barbarians, nor the Greeks, nor any known tribe, where prayers and thanksgivings are not offered to God in the name of Christ crucified." By the end of the first century the Church Jesus Christ had founded was being called "catholic" because it had spread to all the known nations, fulfilling the command of Jesus Christ to preach the Gospel "to all nations." The word "catholic" means universal.

While there was almost uninterrupted persecution of the early Church for some 300 years by the powerful Roman Empire, yet, faith in Jesus Christ spread everywhere. Lies were spread against the Christians by the pagans, which caused Christians to be under constant suspicion. There were 10 great persecutions. During the persecutions the popes remained strong and firm in guiding the faithful in the faith. The Christians would gather in the catacombs (undergound tunnels bored through soft rock) outside Rome to celebrate secretly the Holy Eucharist, the Mass as it is commonly called today. Occasionally wider spaces were made in the catacombs to form rooms where the Eucharist was offered. One can still visit the catacombs today to discover pictures and inscriptions on the tombs and walls of the ancient catacombs of the first centuries. These pictures, medals and inscriptions identify the faith of the early Christians with the Catholic faith of today.

St. Irenaeus, bishop of Lyons, who wrote around the year 200, left a list of the popes of the first and second centuries. "With the Church of Rome all churches must agree on account of her higher rank" (Adversus Haereses 3,3).

In 313 the Emperor Constantine, together with Licinius, who fought for the freedom of religion for Christians in the East, issued the Edict of Milan. This edict of toleration, granted religious tolerance to pagans and to Christians alike. It made Sunday a day of rest. It forbade public business and servile work on the Lord's Day. Eventually the Christian religion became the chief religion of the Roman Empire, since Constantine not only gave the Church full liberty, but honored popes and bishops. The mother of Constantine, St. Helena, brought the Holy Cross and many sacred relics to Rome from Jerusalem.

The forces of evil are never inactive. Christ had foretold false prophets. Many were led into heresy through internal conflicts within the Church. God, however, can draw good out of all things, even out of things evil. The disturbances to the faith had the good effect of requiring the Church to define clearly its teachings, crystalizing important doctrines as dogmas of faith if people were to consider themselves in union with the Church Jesus Christ himself had founded, and not with some merely human version of it.

Some of the chief heresies the Church had to struggle against were Arianism (318), which denied the divinity of the Son of God who became one with Jesus Christ; Macedonianism (381), which denied the divinity of the Holy Spirit; Pelagianism (about 400), which denied original sin and the necessity of grace. The heresy of Pelagianism had the consequence of attacking many of the divine truths of Christianity. There were the Nestorians (428), who taught that there were two persons in Christ, one human and one divine. The Monothelites (680) taught that there was one will in Christ, the divine will, but no human will. This was contrary to Jesus becoming true God and true man. The Sacred Scriptures say that Jesus became a man in all things except sin. The Iconoclasts (787) attacked the veneration of holy images.

Holy and learned men, known today as the *Fathers of the Church*, from both the East and the West, wrote against the heresies threatening the early Church. This protected the purity of the faith and, at the same time, aided in spreading the clear doctrines about Jesus Christ and His Holy Church. The Catholic Church with its chief teachers, the pope and the bishops, beginning with the Council at Jerusalem in the year 51 and the 21 ecumenical councils which have followed, found it necessary to oppose false teachings and to define true doctrines.

The great Fathers of the Church in the East were St. Athanasius (c. 296-373), St. Basil (c. 329-379), St. Gregory Nazianzen (c. 330-390), and St. John Chrysostom (c. 347-407). They are sometimes called the Greek Fathers. The chief Western, or Latin, Fathers were: St. Ambrose (c. 340-397), St. Augustine (354-430), St. Jerome (343-420), and St. Gregory the Great (c. 540-604). The period of the Western Fathers was about one century later than that of the Eastern Fathers. The greatest of the Western Fathers is considered to be St. Augustine of Hippo. His ideals influenced Western Christian civilization. Most of his writings are still in existence. These include 232 books, more than 350 sermons and 260 lengthy letters. He wrote 93 major works, which include *On the Trinity, On Teaching Christian Doctrine*, and *On the Faith and the Creed*. For 800 years the Christian theology of St. Augustine dominated the West until the time of St. Thomas Aquinas. Never in the history of the world had a religion caused so many people to surrender to its idealism as did that of Jesus Christ.

It is generally held that the last of the Western Fathers (Latin) was St. Isidore of Seville (c. 560-636). Last of the Eastern Fathers (Greek) was St. John Damascene (675-749).

Monasticism originated in the third century. It had for its inspiration the three evangelical counsels encouraged by Jesus: poverty, chastity and obedience. St. Benedict (c. 480-547) founded the Benedictine Order and wrote the famous rule blending prayer, study, work, silence and mortification.

The Church of the early centuries faced the Barbarian invasions. Nations were scattered and these scattered nations in turn conquered other nations so that within 500 years the face of Europe was changed.

The Western world was now composed of new nations, although these "nations" were more like tribes than nations. These tribes which formed the new nations had high ideals of self-respect and personal liberty. Being loyal to their tribe, to their relatives and having a great respect for womanhood — this nobility of spirit lent itself to conversion to Christianity. The pope and bishops sent priests and missionaries to work among the new people, to make treaties, etc. The Church was most conscious of its mission from Christ to the nations. The Church became the spiritual teacher and mother to these people, sharing with them the knowledge and love of Jesus Christ. Schools and churches were established among these peoples.

If it had not been for the Catholic Church, all of Europe would have fallen and the ancient Greek and Roman cultures would have been entirely lost. The Church converted the nations, rather than fight them. Monasticism proved an invaluable help to the Church during these years.

Looking at the Church at the time of the Barbarian invasions, from a natural point of view, it would have seemed that the Church would end. In every century,though, there have been predictions that the Church would end. This is true even in our own day. Still, the Church survives and lives a more vibrant life when each crisis has passed. The result of the migration of nations was that the Church made many more converts and laid the foundation for a new Europe.

One of the next crises the Church faced was the spread of Mohammedanism. The followers of Mohammed organized a "holy war" against all outsiders and within 100 years they had built an empire which stretched from Spain to India. The Mohammedans were relatively easy on Christians when they first conquered a country and many Christians gave up their faith to win the favor of their conquerors. Later, books defending Christianity were sent into these countries. Then the Mohammedans manifested their religious intolerance and forced Christians to become Mohammedans or die.

Mohammed, a native of Arabia, began preaching in Mecca in A.D. 610. He denied the Blessed Trinity and taught that there is only one God and Mohammed is his prophet. External observances were emphasized at the expense of self-discipline. Mohammed's heaven was a place of beautiful trees, filled with fruits, in which there were all the sensual delights. The great tenet of Mohammed's faith was "God alone is God, and Mohammed is his prophet." Mohammed developed a religion which was a mixture of Judaism, Christianity and paganism.

Christians responded with their own sacred wars known as the "Crusades." Basically, the Crusades were waged by Christian nations to deliver the Holy Land and the Sepulcher (the burial place) of Jesus Christ, from the oppression of the Mohammedans (Moslems). The word "Crusader" is from the word "cross," as the Crusaders wore the cross on their breasts as a sign of their undertaking. Sometimes God permits tragedies to unite Christians in love and common purpose. The preaching of the Crusades motivated the people toward a holier life. There were eight principal Crusades in the 11th through the 13th centuries, the first (1096-99) and the eighth was in 1270.

The Turkish power was finally broken when the pope motivated the Christian nations, calling the faithful to recite the Rosary and the Angelus in all Christian lands and to rise to physical resistance. Through the efforts of Pope Pius V, Don Juan of Austria formed a mighty fleet and defeated the Turkish navy in the great victory of Lepanto in 1571. On the sea, the Turkish power was broken. The combined Christian fleets completely destroyed the invading armada, liberating Christians and, thereby, Europe from being overrun by Moslems. The Christians were inspired in their battle by the image of God's Mother, the miraculous image of Our Lady of Guadalupe in the ship of Prince Andrea Doria. The pope ascribed the victory to the Queen of the Rosary, since he had sponsored the Rosary for victory.

The popes as temporal rulers seem strange to modern times. The Church, however, was born into a world which was largely pagan. It had to Christianize the nations and to use the circumstances of the time to serve the cause of Christ. It is never fair to judge history in terms of our own times. The Middle Ages refer to that period of European history which began with the coronation of Charlemagne in 800 and ended with the invasion of Italy by the French in 1494. Charlemagne is the name given to Charles the Great, the ruler of the Frankist Empire. It made up the larger portion of western and middle Europe. Among the Franks the Church had been reorganized by St. Boniface and more closely united with the Holy See at Rome. This great English monk was successful in his work and it resulted in the crowning of Charlemagne as head of the Holy Roman Empire. Charlemagne sought the spiritual and temporal welfare of the people in union with the pope as visible head of the Church. Mistakenly the period is sometimes called the Dark Ages, and it is said to have continued into the 13th century with the false implication that "enlightenment" did not come until the Protestant Reformation in the 16th century. In reality, the period was an Age of Faith. Charlemagne gathered holy and learned men around himself. The period saw the founding of monasticism and the spread of the great Benedictine monasteries. It was a period of realignment and Christian advances in conversion and education. It was the monks who, during the invasions, preserved the works of the great Latin and Greek writers. Unfortunately Charlemagne was not succeeded by great men, and his empire was divided into three parts among his grandsons.

After the seventh century, when the emperors moved to Constantinople, thereby abandoning their rights, the people turned to the pope for protection because Rome and Italy were exposed to the invasions of Barbarian nations. Due to the will of the people, therefore, the popes had to act as rulers. Pope Stephen II appealed to Pepin, king of the Franks, when the Lombards attempted the conquest of Rome and the emperor in the East did not answer the call for help. In this way the Lombards were defeated and Rome saved. Pepin gave back to the pope the Patrimony of St. Peter, laying the keys of the cities taken from the Lombards on the tomb of St. Peter to express possession of the papal lands by the Holy See. The son of King Pepin was Charlemagne, who reaffirmed this decision of his father, thus marking the beginning of temporal power for the popes. The pope thus became temporal ruler of Rome and the surrounding area. This proved advantageous for the Church for some time. Finally, however, disputes arose.

In 1054 the Eastern Schism arose in the Church while the ordinary Christians were not aware of the mutual excommunications hurled between the pope in the West and the patriarch in the East. The Crusaders and the sacking of Constantinople caused bitterness which brought the schism to the popular level, where it has endured for more than 900 years. It was not essentially theological differences which caused the separation of Christians in the East from those in the West. Prejudice, stemming from abuses, scarred the memories of Eastern Christians. After 900 years of separation, the Catholic Church and the Orthodox communities remain close in faith and communications are gradually being restored. The separation is often called the "Greek Schism." When the Christians of the East separated from Rome, they kept their bishops, which meant they did not lose the powers of the priesthood which Jesus gave His apostles. The schism of the West, called the Great Schism, was not a schism in the strict sense of the word because it did not involve doctrine, but was due to political influence as a result of which the popes lived for a time in Avignon, France.

The High Middle Ages cover the years from approximately 1050 to 1450. Some historians use the term "Middle" to express the period between ancient and modern times. The strength of leadership shown by Pope Hildebrand (Pope Gregory VII) demonstrates not only how the Church, but society as well, was saved and prospered. The High Middle Ages witnessed the development of science and art. Great cities developed and magnificent cathedrals were built which still stand as monuments of faith. Convents, universities and libraries developed. Medical science was an important branch of university studies. Serfs were freed and new inventions enabled the cultivation of more land, producing a greater supply of food. Parishes developed their own schools.

In the High Middle Ages, St. Albert the Great and Roger Bacon initiated modern science. Bacon was an English monk and wrote *The Secrets of Art and Nature*. During this period there was the birth of philosophy and theology known as Scholasticism. St. Thomas Aquinas (1225-74), one of the greatest theologians the Church has ever known, was largely responsible for Scholasticism (Thomism). He was a student of St. Albert the Great. Vatican Council II (1962-65) still looked to the philosophy and theology of St. Thomas Aquinas as having a special place in the training of future priests. Scholasticism uses many of the philosophical principles and insights of Aristotle and Neoplatonism for a synthesis of human and divine wisdom.

Even though heresies such as the Albigensian heresy which, among other things, denied the sacraments, arose during the High Middle Ages, the Church continued to advance the cause of Christ. The Fourth Lateran Council (1215) used the term "transubstantiation" to express the faith of the Church in the Real Presence of Jesus Christ in the Holy Eucharist.

During this time mendicant orders developed, such as those founded by St. Francis of Assisi and by St. Dominic Guzman. St. Francis of Assisi inspires people to the present day with his manner of life. The Franciscans (Order of Friar's Minor) were approved by Pope Innocent III in 1209. St. Dominic's followers became the Order of Preachers, approved by Pope Honorius III in 1216. St. Thomas Aquinas was one of the most celebrated members of the Dominican Order.

The Church had great and holy men and women even during the decline of the Middle Ages. The Church suffered when the papacy fell too much under the control of the king of France during the Avignon papacy. The removal of the papal court from Rome is often called the Babylonian Captivity of the popes. The Schism of the West was a division caused by more than one man *claiming* to be pope. It lowered the trust of Christians in the papacy and encouraged civil rulers to infringe on the affairs of the Church. It also led to the false opinion that general councils of the Church have greater authority than the pope. It must be remembered that in reality there has never been more than one pope at a time in the history of the Church. There is always only one successor to St. Peter.

The schism, with two, then three men claiming to be pope, was ended by the Council of Constance (1414-1418), after 40 years of confusion. In the strict sense there was no Schism of the West, for there was always only one lawfully elected pope. It was the great spirituality and influence of St. Catherine of Siena which brought the pope back from "exile" to live again in Rome.

The "Protestant Reformation," as it is often called, was really a religious revolt which began in Germany. There were many causes which gradually led to the breakup among Christians at the beginning of the 16th century. The world was in change. Cities grew; trade and commerce developed. Emphasis was placed on the money a man owned, rather than on land devoted to agriculture to provide stable family life. The control of capital by a few determined what the majority could and would do. The Church resisted this but acquired wealth itself which was not well used. A division developed among the "higher" and "lower" clergy. Bishops were often chosen from the nobility and from wealthy families. Such churchmen were more interested in the things of the world than in the souls of men and the glory of God. Priests tending to the spiritual needs of souls were often financially poor and had to find other work to make a living, in addition to their priestly administrations. At the beginning of the 16th century, the peasants in Germany (as well as Austria), began to rise against such abuses.

In brief then, failure, neglect and the laxity of some Church leaders paved the way for a divided Christendom into hundreds of bickering churches. The Church as such was still a holy organism. There were even great saints at that time, but a general purification in many quarters was needed.

John Wycliff and John Hus sowed ideas before Martin Luther which set the stage for what happened. These men taught that every Christian can interpret the Bible for himself without the guidance of the Church. They taught that the Church is an *invisible* society, existing only in the hearts of the "predestined." Wycliff and Hus rejected the fact that Jesus Christ instituted the hierarchy of pope and bishops and the priesthood itself. They said that the wrongs done by spiritual and temporal rulers deprives them of the right to govern or own property. They supported the right of subjects to judge and rebel against such men.

Martin Luther was born in Eisleben, Saxony, November 10, 1483. Scholars hold that Martin Luther developed a neurosis known as scrupulosity, which affected his theology. It appeared to him that nothing could be good enough for God. Man could not be good, only evil. Luther claimed to discover God's mercy in 1519, stating that man is saved by faith and confidence in God the Father, not by good works. He literally absorbed the Bible, calling it the "story of hope." "Faith alone" became the emphasis of his theology. Luther's 95 theses developed into a jealous dispute between the Dominicans and Luther, who was an Augustinian. Disputes developed over the subject of indulgences which, obviously, in some cases, were an abuse of official Church teaching. Luther said: "For I myself did not know what the indulgences were, and the song threatened to become too high for my voice." Luther himself was more the occasion than the cause of the Protestant Revolt. Many unfortunate circumstances led to the disunity which resulted, including political meddling in Church affairs.

Martin Luther frequently doubted the rightness and wisdom of his own position. Replacing papal authority with private interpretation of the

Bible, Luther's middle-class church became ripe for revolt. With the theories of Wycliff and Hus preceding Luther, men found the opportunity now to strike out against all authority, political as well as spiritual. The Peasant's Revolt in Germany ended with the loss of much blood. Luther wrote in the pamphlet, *Against the Murderous and Thieving Hordes of Peasants*: "Let everyone who can, slay, smite and stab."

There were abuses in the Church at the time of the Protestant Revolt and reforms were needed, but not the kind that took place and divided Christendom. Men must be changed by religion, not religion by men. The revolt resulted in hundreds of Protestant denominations. Without a central visible head, the pope, the rock on which Christ founded His Church, with bishops also under the authority of the pope, there was little to hold the divided Christians together except their vague faith in Jesus Christ. The many contradictory interpretations of the Bible permitted among Protestants had the effect of replacing the Church with a book and no official sanction to teach or interpret with authority.

In the Catholic Church a "counter-reformation" took place after the Protestant Revolt. Rather than trying to change the nature of the Church itself, the official Catholic Church worked to correct the abuses of certain churchmen and to strengthen the faith and morals of all the Church's members. Pope Paul III called the Council of Trent (1545-1563), which established rules for the promotion of faith and morals. The council worked to lay down standard doctrines which a Catholic must believe to be a sincere Catholic.

The Catholic Church did not remain entirely on the defensive. A period immediately followed the Protestant Revolt in which a positive approach was taken to reform weaknesses. The reforms of the Council of Trent began to take effect with the election of Pope Pius V in 1566. Pope Pius V lived in poverty, contrary to the spirit of the Renaissance, which began in the 14th century. It reached its height in the early 16th century and represented a turning to pagan Greek culture and scholarship in the midst of profound social changes and discoveries. Pope Pius V, being devoted to the Passion of Jesus Christ, declined to wear rich robes. He had great devotion to Mary and her Rosary. Respect for the authority of the papacy began to return to the hearts of people. The sacraments were frequented and Catholics became better educated in Catholic doctrines.

Then too, with the discovery of the New World, missionaries were sent abroad, especially from Spain. Millions of conversions took place. These converts replaced in even greater numbers those lost to the ancient Church of Christ because of the revolt in Europe. The appearance of Our Lady of Guadalupe near Mexico City in December 1531 to Juan Diego, an early convert in the New World, had a profound effect in the conversion of
144

millions. Our Lady left her image imprinted on his garment which was made of simple cactus fiber. The miraculous picture can be seen there to the present day.

A spirit of liberalism with little respect for authority, which holds that man has no responsibility except to satisfy every human desire, continues to prevail in the world today. The Church continues to battle against these false theories which arose from the Renaissance and the Protestant Revolt. Liberalism holds that man's mind is greater than any other power. God himself is ignored. This thinking was developed in the 17th century and matured with a "reign of terror" in the 18th. Rationalists known as "Freethinkers" arose. They refused to accept any authority in intellectual or religious matters, saying that there was no such thing as absolutes in the possession of certain knowledge. In France, Francois Marie Arouet, whose pen name was Voltaire (1694-1778), was their great prophet. He led a life of blasphemy and immorality and had as his goal the destruction of the Church. Jean-Jacques Rousseau, born in Geneva, Switzerland, in 1712 (d. 1778), became a hero to the Enlightenment cause. He taught that the world could be saved by education, if education were founded on the desires of human nature and not controlled by authority or any ideas from the past. Freemasonry, founded in London July 24, 1717, adopted "free thought" and spread swiftly through the world. The French Revolution, the religious and political upheaval which began in France in 1789, influenced the whole world. The oath of allegiance to civil authority affected the Catholic Church because it implied a denial of the faith. There were many martyrs as a result, a massive dissolution of religious orders, and the secularization of Church property.

The French Revolution demonstrated the total confusion, chaos and disbelief which can result when men seek unbridled freedom. At that time it was strongly argued that the clergy should be free to marry. Such revolutions, if they succeed, end up destroying all freedom. Representative of such revolutions were the Enlightenment, Rationalism, private interpretation, Josephinism and Gallicanism. Liberalism was condemned by Pope Pius IX in 1864 in the *Syllabus of Errors* (Denzinger, 2977-80).

A study of the Catholic Church in the 19th century shows that the Church Jesus founded is able to endure every human problem and attack. In both the 19th and 20th centuries the Church has been blessed with exceptionally holy popes. There was a treaty of peace, signed at Vienna in 1815, which ended the War of Nations in Europe with Napoleon. In the first part of the 19th century the Church worked hard to defend its rights against the new governments in Europe. A strong revival of Catholicism took place in the various countries of Europe. The 19th century produced some great saints concerned with Catholic education and the formation of youths, such as St. John Bosco, the founder of the Salesians. The appearance of Jesus' Mother at Lourdes, France, in 1858 also contributed to a revival of interest in things Catholic. Pope Pius IX reigned from 1846 until 1878, the longest reign of any pope since St. Peter. This pope was very influential in bringing new strength and influence to the Catholic Church in the world. Pope Leo XIII (1878-1903) became the champion of the working man at a time when there were many problems with industry, social revolutions, etc. The world was blessed with an extraordinary saint in Pope St. Pius X (1903-1914). His principal aim was "to restore all things in Christ, in order that Christ may be all and in all." He sought to teach and defend Christian truth and law. Pius X is called the "Pope of the Catechism" and the "Pope of the Holy Eucharist." He called for the thorough religious education of youths under the Confraternity of Christian Doctrine (CCD). He also recommended early and frequent Holy Communion. This sainted pope was followed by two other outstanding leaders in the papacy, Pius XI and the scholarly Pius XII.

During the 19th century the evils of atheistic communism were born, even though its philosophy was conceived years earlier. The plan of communism began to take shape in Russia with the revolution of 1917. Nikolai Lenin was the leading personality in that revolution. Lenin succeeded in putting into effect the political-economic system of Karl Marx, who wrote *Das Kapital* and the *Communist Manifesto* in cooperation with Frederick Engels. The philosophy of communism is dialectical materialism, which claims that matter and not spirit, and certainly not an infinite God, is the primary reality in the universe. It claims that material force in conflict (dialectic) explains all progress in the world. It claims that economics is the sole basis of human civilization.

Communism is a shifting expediency that defies analysis because it does not operate on truth, but only on what will promote its own cause even if falsehood will help it obtain its end, which is world revolution, the overthrow of existing society, so as to put communism in power everywhere. The Communist powers have taken over country after country, even murdering millions to achieve the goal of world domination. During the very months (March 1917 to November 1917) when Lenin was leading the overthrow of the provisional government in Russia, Jesus' Mother, now known as "Our Lady of Fatima," was appearing (May 13, 1917-October 13, 1917) each month, warning that the errors of Russia would spread throughout the world if mankind did not turn back to her Son, Jesus Christ.

Pope John XXIII was elected pope October 28, 1958. He was already an old man and many thought he would be merely an "interim" pope, after the great pontifical reign of Pius XII when authority in the Catholic

Church was greatly respected. Pope John XXIII reigned for about five and a half years and his reign and decisions affected the history of the Catholic Church for future generations. It was this pope who convoked the Second Vatican Council (1962-65). This 21st worldwide council was for the purpose of renewing the life of the Church, to reform structures and institutions which needed updating and to discover ways and means of promoting unity among all Christians. ("Separated brethren, as non-Catholic Christians have come to be known, represent at least 500 different denominations, and if every little denomination be considered, the number goes into the thousands.)

Pope John lived for only four of the council's sessions. The council's first work was on the *Constitution on the Sacred Liturgy*, which brought about great changes in the structure and language of the Mass, without in any way changing its divine nature as sacrifice and sacrament, as given to us by the Lord Jesus Christ. The Church, however, did not do away entirely with Latin. A total of 2,860 bishops of the world participated in this 21st Ecumenical Council of the Catholic Church. For reasons of health and denial of exit visas from communist-dominated countries, 274 bishops were not able to participate.

Vatican Council II did not change any doctrines of the Church as some mistakenly thought. Greater participation of the laity in the divine liturgy was made possible as a result of Vatican II. The reforms of the liturgy brought the Mass and the sacraments of the Church closer to the people. Vatican II made the members of the Church more aware that all baptized members, not simply the clergy and Religious, are the Church and share various functions and responsibilities in spreading the faith of Christ to the ends of the world. The nature of the Church as missionary and the fact that all are to participate in that mission became more clear to many Catholics.

Vatican II, while it called for shared responsibility, in no way abdicated authority. All the teachings of the preceding 20 ecumenical councils were upheld. The council opened the Scriptures more fully for the faithful in their liturgical participation.

After the council, certain abuses set in, misrepresenting the Second Vatican Council. Some of the Liberalism and Modernism of former centuries began to surface. Some who did not read the times correctly interpreted the abuses as the reforms of Vatican II. As a result, in some quarters of the Church, a reaction set in resisting some of the authentic changes which the council intended without in any way changing the 2,000-year-old faith and morals of the Catholic Church. Even some priests and nuns became confused, or at least, resisted proper Church authority. It has been the history of the Church that after an ecumenical council a period of confusion follows, and Vatican II was no exception. When the 16 documents of Vatican II are properly implemented in the lives of Catholic people, however, the authentic Church renewal will ensue.

Pope Paul VI, who succeeded Pope John XXIII and completed the Second Vatican Council, had to meet the challenge of the troublesome 13 years following the council. July 25, 1968, this pope issued an encyclical, *Humanae Vitae* (Of Human Life), which restated the teaching of the Church which prohibits artificial birth control. It became the occasion for some theologians to defy the authority of the pope. Some even used the public media to make known their disagreements. Dissent against papal authority became widespread, resulting in scandal. A "contraceptive mentality" became widespread and contributed to the "abortion mentality." All this had a weakening effect on many marriages. Divorce statistics greatly increased to the point that many feared that the family as the basic unit of society was in grave jeopardy.

The disobedience of many to papal authority after Vatican II demonstrated the chaos which results when proper respect does not exist for the authority that Jesus Christ established in His Church. As time continued, the divine wisdom behind *Humanae Vitae* began to be realized, however late. Natural family planning, which works in harmony with nature, as opposed to artificial means which are contrary to nature, gradually came to the awareness of Christian peoples. The Church began to work hard to instruct its members on the meaning of holiness in marriage and on the importance of not practicing sinful artificial birth control. Some of the greatest champions for education in natural family planning were lay people themselves, who organized "Couple to Couple leagues."

The world was shocked when the friendly and smiling Pope John Paul I, who succeeded Paul VI August 26, 1978, reigned only 33 days. In three months, August through October 1978, the world saw three different popes. October 16, 1978, the Catholic Church was given its first non-Italian pope in 455 years. Cardinal Karol Wojtyla of Krakow, Poland, took the name Pope John Paul II and was well received.

Pope John Paul II went directly to the bishops, priests, Religious and people of the world. Shortly after his election, he announced a pilgrimage to Mexico, where he prayed before the miraculous image of Our Lady of Guadalupe. June 2-20, 1979, he made a triumphal return to his homeland in Poland. In October of that same year, the pontiff visited the United States and spoke to the United Nations. In the succeeding years the pope visited many nations of the world carrying the message of Jesus Christ and His Church to the masses.

May 13, 1981, a 24-year-old Turk, Mehmet Ali Agca, was arrested (and later convicted) for the shooting of Pope John Paul II in St. Peter's

Square. The pope came within minutes of death and spent months recuperating. Investigations continued the following year and by 1983 evidence had surfaced indicating Bulgarian and Soviet complicity in the assassination attempt. Investigators in Italy, Turkey and West Germany were convinced that Agca did not act alone, but was only one cog in a complex international plot to kill the pope. Other arrests were subsequently made. Italian Minister of Defense Lelio Lagorio on December 21, 1982, said, "The assassination of the charismatic figure of the pontiff presents itself as a precautionary and alternative solution instead of a project of a Russian military invasion of Poland. The Bulgarian trial in this crime, therefore, raises and justifies the most acute worries of international politics."

May 13, 1982, Pope John Paul II went to Fatima, Portugal, to thank the Mother of God for having spared his life one year before. During his homily in the Cova da Iria at Fatima the pope said:

". . . On this very day last year, in St. Peter's Square in Rome, the attempt on the pope's life was made, in mysterious coincidence with the anniversary of the first apparition at Fatima, which occurred May 13, 1917. I seemed to recognize in the coincidence of the dates a special call to come to this place. So, today I am here. I have come in order to thank the Divine Providence in this place which the Mother of God seems to have chosen in a particular way."

While in Fatima Pope John Paul II consecrated the world to the Immaculate Heart of Mary with special mention of Russia. The pope had invited the bishops of the world to join in repeating the acts of Pius XII who had consecrated the world and then Russia.

". . . I am here, united with all the pastors of the Church in that particular bond whereby we constitute a body and a college, just as Christ desired the apostles to be in union with Peter.

"In the bond of this union, I utter the words of the present act, in which I wish to include, once more, the hopes and anxieties of the Church in the modern world. Forty years ago and again 10 years later, your servant Pope Pius XII, having before his eyes the painful experience of the human family, entrusted and consecrated to your Immaculate Heart the whole world, especially the peoples for which you had particular love and solicitude. This world of individuals and nations I, too, have before my eyes today, as I renew the entrusting and consecration carried out by my predecessor in the See of Peter: the world of the second millennium that is drawing to a close, the modern world, our world of today!"

January 25, 1983, Pope John Paul II signed a revised Code of Canon Law for the Church representing 24 years of preparations. The revised code of 1,752 canons went into effect Nov. 27, 1983, the first day of Advent.

The revised code, which was personally reviewed by John Paul II, bringing Church law into harmony with Vatican Council II, was designed to put a positive emphasis on the living of the Christian life.

The changing style of the papacy became evident soon after the death of Pope Paul VI, who was referred to as "the suffering pope." Pope John Paul I, who succeeded him, gave an image of a relaxed and "smiling" pope. When his 33-day reign ended with his abrupt death, he was succeeded by Pope John Paul II who would be a pastoral pope of the people, anxious to use modern technology to evangelize the world to Jesus Christ. At the same time, the world's first Polish pope made it obvious that his role was universal and that he would uphold all the doctrinal traditions of the Church.

DISCUSSION QUESTIONS

1. When did the Church begin?

Strictly speaking, the Catholic Church began almost 2,000 years ago when Jesus built his Church on Peter and sent the Holy Spirit on Pentecost. God had the Church in mind, however, from the time He created the world and placed man upon the earth.

2. What was the greatest event in salvation history?

The greatest event in salvation history was the Incarnation, God becoming man.

3. Is there any evidence that people outside of Israel believed in a promised Redeemer?

There is evidence of distorted beliefs in the Redeemer in the many rumors which circulated in the world at the time Christ came. These beliefs could have come down from the time of the promise made to mankind in Genesis 3:15 and from the Israelites who traveled to other nations.

4. Why was Israel considered to be a strategic location in the world?

Israel had a strategic location because it was at the crossroads of civilization and great nations had to cross through Israel to journey to various parts of the world.

5. Describe the condition of the world at the time Jesus came.

The world was in the darkness of sin when Jesus came. Almost every kind of immorality existed, even among the cultures of Greece and Rome.

6. What did the Second Vatican Council say about the Jews and the death of Jesus Christ?

All Jews of Jesus' time, as well as Jews of today, cannot be blamed for the crimes committed against Jesus which led to His death.

7. To whom did the apostles first preach?

The apostles first preached to the Jews, God's chosen people.

8. Did the structure of the Church of the first centuries differ radically from the Church today?
Basically, the Church of the first century was the same in structure as today, with pope, deacons, priests and bishops.

9. When did the pagan Roman emperors begin to persecute the early Christians?
The Roman Emperor Nero began the persecution of Christians while St. Peter was still living. Both St. Peter and St. Paul suffered martyrdom under Nero.

10. When was the early Church first called "Catholic"?
By the end of the first century the Church had spread to the nations of the known world and was called "Catholic," which means "universal" or "all nations."

11. What are the catacombs of Rome and what value do they have to the faith today?
The catacombs are underground burial places outside Rome which the early Christians used for the celebration of the Eucharist. Inscriptions in these catacombs remain which reaffirm the constant Catholic faith through the centuries.

12. What important contribution did the writings of St. Irenaeus make?
St. Irenaeus, about the year A.D. 200, wrote a list of the popes of the first two centuries.

13. Why was the Edict of Milan significant to the development of the early Church?
The Edict of Milan in 313 granted religious freedom to pagans and Christians alike, but eventually worked in favor of Christian expansion.

14. Were there heresies against which the Church had to struggle in the early centuries?
The Church had to struggle against misrepresentations of the true faith from the very first centuries. There was Arianism, which became very widespread, denying that Jesus Christ was truly divine. There were other heresies denying original sin, and the nature of Christ as true God and true Man at the same time.

15. What is meant by the "Fathers of the Church"?
The Fathers of the Church were saintly writers of the early centuries whom the Church recognizes as special witnesses of the true faith. Antiquity, orthodoxy, sanctity and approval by the Church are their chief characteristics.

16. What is monastic life and when did it originate?
Monastic life originated in the third century. It involves living together in community with the three evangelical counsels taken as vows: poverty, chastity and obedience.

17. What was one of the greatest crises faced by the early Church?

The barbarian invasions, also known as the "Migration of Nations," which caused the face of Europe to be changed within 500 years.

18. What is meant by Mohammedanism?

Mohammedanism is named after Mohammed, who combined paganism, Christianity and Judaism as a new form of religion.

19. How did Christians respond to the Mohammedans?

The Christians organized crusades to deliver the Holy Land and to rescue the sepulcher of Jesus Christ from a non-Christian people.

20. What is meant by the "Middle Ages"?

The "Middle Ages" refer to that period of European history which began with the coronation of Charlemagne in 800 and ended with the invasion of Italy by the French in 1494.

21. Is "Dark Ages" a correct expression for the Middle Ages?

The "Dark Ages" should rather be called an "Age of Faith."

22. How did the popes become temporal rulers?

The popes became "temporal rulers" not because they desired power but because the people sought leadership and protection from the barbarian nations.

23. Explain the "Eastern" or "Greek Schism."

The "Greek Schism" refers to the separation of Christians in the East from the pope and Christians of the West. Many natural factors, rather than theological differences were involved, especially politics. The split has existed since 1054.

24. What is meant by the "High Middle Ages"?

The "High Middle Ages" cover the period from approximately 1050 to 1450. There was much progress in the world at this time in science and art and the development of great cities. Some of the great theologians of the Church developed during these years.

25. Who was St. Thomas Aquinas and what influence did he have on the Church?

St. Thomas Aquinas was a student of St. Albert the Great and is largely responsible for developing Scholasticism (Thomism), using many of the philosophical principles and insights of Aristotle and Neoplatonism, coordinated into the synthesis of human and divine wisdom. Thomism has dominated Catholic philosophy and theology ever since.

26. What were some of the effects of the Avignon papacy?

The "Avignon papacy" weakened the influence of the popes on the life of the Church as the kings of France interfered in Church matters, wanting the popes in France for selfish motives.

27. What were some of the circumstances which led to the Protestant Revolt of the 16th century?

There were many causes which led to the Protestant Revolt of the early 16th century. There were economic, political and moral causes. Bishops sometimes were more interested in things regarding the state than those regarding souls.

28. What were the ideas which lead to the Protestant Revolt and who were the two men most responsible for expounding them?

The ideas of John Wycliff and John Hus paved the way for the Protestant Revolt. These included disregard for authority, private interpretation of the Bible, the rejection of a divinely established hierarchical Church, etc.

29. Was Martin Luther the cause of the Protestant Revolt?

Martin Luther was not the cause of the religious revolt of the early 16th century, but he was the catalyst for it. There were many causes for the sad situation which weakened or destroyed the influence of Christianity in the lives of many people.

30. Was a reform needed in the Catholic Church at the time of the Protestant Revolt?

A reform was needed, but not of the Catholic Church as such. Its official doctrines of faith and morals were intact. A reform was needed in the lives of Christians, including some clergy and Religious. Christian life at the time of the Protestant Revolt was at a low ebb.

31. Explain the "counter-reformation."

The "counter-reformation" was a period of Catholic revival from 1522 to about 1648. It was an effort by the Church to stem the tide of Protestantism by genuine reform within the Catholic Church. The main factors in the Counter-reformation were the papacy and the Council of Trent (1545-63).

32. Explain the Renaissance.

The Renaissance began in the 14th century and represented a return to the ancient pagan Greek and Roman cultures and scholarship.

33. What happened in the New World to offset the losses of the Protestant Reformation?

With the discovery of the New World the Catholic Church sent out many missionaries who by God's grace converted many millions, especially in Mexico where our Lady appeared in 1531 to Juan Diego. She is known as Our Lady of Guadalupe from her miraculous painting.

34. Explain "Liberalism."

Liberalism has little, if any, respect for authority and holds that a man's mind is greater than any other power. This spirit contributed to the Protestant Revolt and also to a movement of "Freethinkers" and Rationalists and, finally, to the French Revolution.

35. What special strength did the Church experience in the 19th and 20th centuries?

In the 19th and 20th centuries the Catholic Church was blessed by exceptionally learned and holy popes.

36. What special evil developed in the 19th century which bore much fruit in the 20th?

The ideals of communism were born in the 19th century. It was a political-economic system developed by Karl Marx and Frederick Engels but it was implemented in Russia when Nikolai Lenin overthrew the provisional government during the revolution.

37. Why did Pope John XXIII convoke the Second Vatican Council?

Pope John XXIII convoked the 21st Ecumenical Council to renew the life of the Church, to reform structures and institutions which needed updating and to promote Christian unity.

38. What reactions set in after the Second Vatican Council which brought much confusion to Catholics?

After Vatican Council II a spirit of dissension broke out in some quarters resulting in a disrespect for the authority of the Church. This dissension was especially intense among unfaithful theologians who publicly protested the encyclical of Pope Paul VI, *Humanae Vitae,* which upheld the traditional teaching that artificial birth control is immoral. Within little more than a decade it became obvious that the dissenters had done the cause of Catholicism a great disservice and confused many souls.

39. Explain the change of style in the papacy which took place after the death of Pope Paul VI.

Pope Paul VI was known as a "suffering pope." Pope John Paul I, who succeeded him, lived only 33 days and was known as the "smiling pope." Then, for the first time in 455 years, a non-Italian pope was elected. Pope John Paul II was from the Communist-dominated country of Poland and as a charismatic world figure went directly to the people, winning their love and respect.

CHAPTER 11

The Attributes of the Church
(Authority — Infallibility — Indefectibility)

Jesus Christ, the Son of God, Savior of mankind, founded a Church to continue His work. Jesus Christ is the Wisdom of God the Father who took on human flesh and soul.

Can you imagine the Word of God made flesh founding a Church with these qualities? 1. No authority. It would teach only opinions. 2. Fallible. It would be a Church to which, as Scripture records, Jesus Christ would promise the Holy Spirit as the "Spirit of Truth" but, at the same time, would say: "Remember, it's only human; it will speak in My name, but make mistakes." 3. Capable of changing to such a degree that it would no longer be essentially the way Jesus established it. It could be destroyed and something else could take its place.

The above supposed qualities of the Church, which Scripture tells us is the "Body of Christ," are certainly contrary to the very nature of God, contrary to Jesus Christ himself and the work He commissioned the apostles to accomplish, promising to be with the Church all days until the end of the world. Such weak human qualities are not divine and would not require a divine person become man to establish. They would promise us nothing. Yet, such is the kind of Church or churches some would have or at least describe when they speak of the mere human qualities they think a church or churches possess.

Jesus, the Word of God, spoke with authority and He came forth as light shining in the darkness (John 1:5). "And His teaching made a deep impression on them because, unlike the scribes, He taught them with authority" (Mark 1:22). "The Word was the true light that enlightens all men; and he was coming into the world . . . that had its being through him, and the world did not know him. . . . The Word was made flesh, he lived among us, and we saw his glory, the glory that is his as the only Son of the Father, full of grace and truth" (John 1:9-14).

"When Jesus spoke to the people again, he said: 'I am the light of the world; anyone who follows me will not be walking in the dark; he will have the light of life' " (John 8:12).

What happens then if we would conceive of a church which had no divine authority to speak for Jesus Christ in the world? We would be living in darkness. We would be unable to believe in anything with certain faith. We would be among those in the world who did not know Him. "He came to his own domain and his own people did not accept him. But to all who did accept him he gave power to become children of God, to all who believe in the name. . . ." (John 1:11-12)

If we deny the three traditional attributes or qualities which describe the Church Jesus Christ founded, we become guilty, in effect, of rejecting Jesus Christ as the Word of God made flesh. "And The Word was made flesh, he lived among us" (John 1:14). As seen in Chapter 8, the Church is a divine organism. It is the "Body of Christ," His Mystical Body. "Anyone who listens to you listens to me; anyone who rejects you rejects me, and those who reject me reject the one who sent me" (Luke 10:16).

Once we accept Jesus Christ in divine faith as the Son of God, Savior, the name through which God the Father is to be involved and by which the apostles worked miracles (Acts 3:6), and that from Jesus as Son and from the Father as from a single principle the Holy Spirit proceeds, which Spirit of truth descended on Pentecost to become the Soul of the Church — then we must accept the Church Jesus established as having the qualities of authority, infallability and indefectibility.

Believing Jesus Christ to be what we profess in the ancient creeds requires that we ascribe to Him a Church with like qualities, even though the human part of the Church, which is also divine, becomes marred in its members at times. Even the divine head in His sacred humanity permitted His people to desecrate His physical body; "from the sole of the foot to the head there is not a sound spot: wounds, bruises, open sores not dressed, not bandaged, not soothed with oil" (Isaiah 1:6).

If we accept faith in Jesus telling us that He is the eternal Son of God, the second person of the Most Blessed Trinity, come to earth to die on the Cross for the salvation of the world, to found a Church built on a rock, and then rise and ascend into heaven, leaving the Church, indwelt by the Holy Spirit, as His own Mystical Body, but to survive and teach only on human ingenuity, would this not be equivalent to saying, "God is dead"? It would at least have the God-Man say, in effect, "I gave you my teachings but now you are on your own until the end of the world. The Church is only a human institution, not a divine organism." Such would be contrary to divine revelation so clearly recorded in the Sacred Scriptures; contrary to common sense if one claims faith in Jesus Christ as true God and true man.

It would be an insult to Jesus Christ to say that His Church is defectible, that it could be destroyed. If the Church is, in its very nature, defectible, it would be only human, not divine. But the Church has qualities which are both human and divine, just as Jesus Christ is both human and

156

divine, having both a human nature and a divine nature possessed by His one divine person. The glorious attributes of the Church are not due to its being merely human, they are due to the divine qualities. Jesus himself said that "the Father is greater than I" (John 14:28). Jesus was not saying that the person of the Father is greater than the person of the Son, because all three persons in the Blessed Trinity are equal. He did indicate that the divine nature of God, which is infinite, is greater than His human nature, which is created.

The context in which Jesus revealed that the Father was greater was when He explained to the apostles that He would, together with the Father, give His Church the Holy Spirit.

"If you love me you will keep my commandments. I shall ask the Father, and he will give you another Advocate to be with you for ever, that Spirit of truth whom the world can never receive since it neither sees nor knows him; but you know him, because he is with you, he is in you.

"I will not leave you orphans; I will come back to you. In a short time the world will no longer see me; but you will see me, because I live and you will live. On that day you will understand that I am in my Father and you in me and I in you. Anybody who receives my commandments and keeps them will be one who loves me; and anybody who loves me will be loved by my Father, and I shall love him and show myself to him. . . .

"I have said these things to you while still with you; but the Advocate, the Holy Spirit, whom the Father will send in my name, will teach you everything and remind you of all I have said to you.

"Peace I bequeath to you, my own peace I give you, a peace the world cannot give, this is my gift to you. Do not let your hearts be troubled or afraid. You heard me say: I am going away, and shall return. If you loved me you would have been glad to know that I am going to the Father, for the Father is greater than I. I have told you this now before it happens, so that when it does happen you may believe. . . ." (John 14:15-21, 25-29)

Any divine qualities attributed to the Church then, such as authority, infallibility, indefectibility, are of God, the Holy Spirit, the Soul of the Church. This keeps the Church in the truth and enables the Church to teach and be preserved with the divine power of God himself. The Church being human as well as divine, manifests itself externally in a human way, just as the "Word was made flesh and lived among us" (John 1:14), and God manifested himself in Jesus through the human nature to which the Son was hypostatically united.

Attempts to make the Church Jesus established seem merely human and, therefore, not infallible and indefectible, are to distort history by claiming the Church does change its doctrines, such as on usury and its stance today compared with its former position when it condemned

157

Galileo for making the sun the center or pivot of our planetary system, rather than the earth. It is said, "Modern science holds that the sun is the center of our system of the Milky Way, and relative to its planets, the sun stands still while the earth is not the center, but moves around the sun. How then can the Church teach with the authority and infallibility of Jesus when it clearly condemned as false something that we now know with scientific certainty is true?"

As regards usury, the change has not been in the teachings of the Church but in the economic system of modern times. Usury, which was forbidden among the Jews and had reference to taking interest for a loan, was permitted by Jews in dealing with the Gentiles. Jesus, in the precept of charity, made no distinction between Hebrew and Gentile. *Charity must extend to all.* The Catholic Church still teaches that where something is loaned and later returned in kind only, no profit may be made by reason of the contract itself and *excessive* interest is forbidden.

What has changed today is the economic system. It has changed so that the function of money can fructify. The Church still condemns what was meant by usury in biblical terms. The Church's basic teaching on the subject has not changed. Injustice surrounding moneylending was and remains condemned. As the economic system changed, the circumstances under which an injustice is committed also have changed.

As for the Galileo case, which some use in an attempt to prove Church defectibility, or at least the inconsistency of the Church, the case is often misrepresented. The Catholic Church never condemned the position that the earth moves around the sun. What was condemned was Galileo's sneering at the Bible and his charge that the Bible was untrue for stating that the sun stood still. Galileo publicly and brazenly repeated the charge so that it became a public scandal. When he referred to the Bible as being ignorant and containing untruths, the Church took a stand to protect the inerrancy of Sacred Scripture.

In some ways Galileo was a genius, as Pope John Paul II pointed out Nov. 11, 1979. At the same time, Galileo, an upstart among scientists of his day, made mistakes scientifically as well as theologically. Galileo used the daily movement of the tides to prove the earth's rotation on its axis while he ridiculed Kepler's proposition that the moon exerts an influence on the tides.

The Congregation of the Index, in its 1616 censure, allowed Galileo to hold to his theory on the condition that he would use it as a working hypothesis, forbidding him to boast of it as an established fact, which it was not at that time. Scientists of the day were not in agreement with Galileo. Also, Galileo was not the originator of the concept of the centrality of the sun. Pythagoras had the idea first. It was not Galileo who reintroduced the Pythagorian centralization of the sun to astronomy. It was a Catholic priest, Father Nicholas Copernicus. In doing so, Father Copernicus did not ridicule the Bible. To his dying day Father Copernicus never drew any protest to his theory from the Holy See.

Galileo's arguments were inconclusive. He had reached the right conclusion but for the wrong reasons. He would have had no trouble with the Church if he had left the Bible out of it. Martin Luther in his *Table Talk* wrote of Copernicus in a bad light, saying: "This madman would subvert the whole science of astronomy, but Scripture tells us that Joshua bade the sun and not the earth to stand still." Another reformer, Melanchthon, widened his denunciation to include both Copernicus and Galileo.

The March 5, 1616, decree of the Congregation of the Index was a bad decision, but it did not involve an infallible teaching. Unfortunately, the congregation did not take into account that sacred texts are not always to be interpreted literally or scientifically. Even scientists today have no trouble saying, "the sun rises," or "the sun sets." Both are common expressions but they are based on appearance only. As stated in the chapter on revelation, the Bible is not a book of science but a book of religion. The Bible tells not how the heavens go, but how to go to heaven.

In no way did the decree reflect against papal infallibility. The pope at the time was Pope Paul V, and he would not sign the decree. The pope wrote to Cardinal di Zoller as follows: "The Holy Church has not condemned the opinion of Copernicus, nor was it condemned as heretical but only as rash. . . ." The pope then added: "If anyone could demonstrate it to be necessarily true, it would no longer be rash." Recent scholarship also has shown that the document which led to Galileo's trial in Rome (1633) was a forgery. It had been planted in the Roman Curia by an unscrupulous official. It falsely accused Galileo of having been enjoined 17 years before not to teach the Copernican theory.

The above two examples are used to indicate how some yet today attempt through historical distortions to explain away the divine attributes of the true Church of Jesus Christ and the qualities which He promised would always endure. Jesus promised that His Church would never be destroyed but would always remain essentially as He established it.

History clearly demonstrates that the ancient Church placed on this earth by our Lord, God and Savior, is the Catholic Church. This Church was established with Peter as the first visible head on earth. It was given authority by our divine and loving Savior in matters of faith and morals. The authority given the Church was the very authority which God the Father had given to Jesus Christ and which He in turn gave to His Church.

"As the Father sent me, so I am sending you" (John 20:21).

"All authority in heaven and on earth has been given to me. Go, therefore, make disciples of all the nations; baptize them in the name of the Father and of the Son and of the Holy Spirit, and teach them to observe all the commands I gave you. And know that I am with you always; yes, to the end of time" (Matthew 28:19-20).

The words of Jesus Christ quoted above, according to St. Matthew, were the very last words Jesus Christ spoke to the remaining 11 apostles, the first bishops of the Church, after His resurrection and before His ascension into heaven. According to St. Luke, after promising to send the Holy Spirit upon the Church not many days hence, Jesus, just before ascending into heaven, spoke as follows:

". . . You will receive power when the Holy Spirit comes on you, and then you will be my witnesses not only in Jerusalem but throughout Judea and Samaria, and indeed to the ends of the earth" (Acts 1:8).

The chief powers which Jesus Christ gave to His Church in order to bring the fruits of the redemption to mankind were threefold: 1. To teach, 2. To govern, and 3. To sanctify.

The authority given the Church to teach in the name of Jesus is clearly seen in Matthew 28 (above). "Teach them to observe all. . . ."

The authority Jesus gave His Church to govern is recorded in the Gospels of St. John and St. Matthew:

"After the meal Jesus said to Simon Peter, 'Simon son of John, do you love me more than these others do?' He answered, 'Yes, Lord, you know I love you.' Jesus said to him, 'Feed my lambs.' A second time he said to him, 'Simon son of John, do you love me?' He replied, 'Yes, Lord, you know I love you.' Jesus said to him, 'Look after my sheep.'' Then he said to him a third time, 'Simon son of John do you love me?' Peter was upset that he asked him the third time, 'Do you love me?' and said, 'Lord, you know everything; you know I love you,' Jesus said to him, 'Feed my sheep' ''(John 21:15-17).

Jesus instructed the first pope, St. Peter, to feed the entire flock, lambs and sheep. Peter was given the primacy of authority in the Church. It is a primacy of jurisdiction, the possession of full and supreme teaching, legislative and sacerdotal powers in the Catholic Church.

Peter had been promised the primacy when Jesus Christ told him that he was to be the rock on which the Savior would build His Church.

"Simon son of Jonah, you are a happy man! Because it was not flesh and blood that revealed this to you, but my Father in heaven. So I now say to you: You are Peter and on this rock I will build my Church. And the gates of the underworld can never hold out against it. I will give you the keys of the kingdom of heaven: whatever you bind on earth shall be considered bound in heaven; whatever you loose on earth shall be considered loosed in heaven" (Matthew 16:17-19).

According to the ordinance of Jesus Christ, Peter was to have successors in his primacy over the universal Church and for all time. The First Vatican Council (1869-70) defined that it is heretical to deny that "in virtue of the decree of Our Lord Jesus Christ himself, blessed Peter has perpetual successors in his primacy over the universal Church" (*Denzinger*, 3058). The First Vatican Council followed the precedent of the Second Council of Lyons (1274) and the Council of Florence (1450) in further defining that the bishops of Rome are the successors of Peter in the primacy (*Denzinger*, 3058).

One has but to study history to discover the 264 popes, one succeeding another, since the time of St. Peter.

The authority of the Church to sanctify, to dispense the grace Jesus merited for us, is done primarily through the Sacrifice of the Mass and the sacraments. In Matthew 28:19-20 is seen the power of the Church to baptize. In Luke 22:19 we read where Jesus gave the first priests and bishops of the Church the power to change bread and wine into His body and blood so that members of the Church might receive the divine life of Jesus Christ, grace, unto eternal life. In John 20:23 Jesus Christ gives His priests the Holy Spirit so as to forgive sins in His name.

Unity among His followers was important to Jesus Christ, as is evidenced in John 17:17 where Jesus prayed that we might be consecrated in the truth. Jesus promised to be with His Church until the end of the world. Jesus gave His Church authority, with primacy vested in Peter and his successors, so that all might remain one. "May they all be one. Father, may they be one in us, as you are in me and I am in you, so that the world may believe it was you who sent me" (John 17.21). Recall our chapter on truth, "Truth: What Is It?" and it is easy to understand why Jesus prayed for unity "so that the world may believe it was you who sent me." Contradictions in the name of faith on the same things and at the same time cannot be true. Whenever men have not remained loyal to and united in faith to Peter and his successors, disunity has resulted. Disunity is contrary to the will of Jesus Christ.

When it is stated that the Church is infallible, with the primacy of teaching authority vested in the pope, it has reference to freedom from error in teaching the universal Church in matters of faith or morals. This doctrine was solemnly defined by the First Vatican Council.

"The Roman Pontiff, when he speaks *ex cathedra* — that is, when in discharge of the office of pastor and teacher of all Christians, by virtue of his supreme apostolic authority, he defines a doctrine regarding faith or morals to be held by the universal Church, by the divine assistance promised to him in Blessed Peter, is possessed of that infallibility with which the divine Redeemer willed that his Church should be endowed in defining doctrine regarding faith or morals; and therefore such definitions are irreformable of themselves, and not in virtue of consent of the Church" (*Denzinger* 3074).

For the pope to speak infallibly, the *first* condition is that he speaks *ex cathedra*. *Ex cathedra* is the term used to describe the pope teaching from the chair of authority as visible head of all Christians. The pope in this case is speaking (teaching) as shepherd of all the faithful with the full weight of his apostolic authority, not merely as another bishop or private theologian. A *second* condition is that he has the intention of declaring something unchangeably true. The *third* condition, already mentioned, is that it must concern faith or morals.

The source of the infallibility is the Holy Spirit, who assists or guides and protects the supreme teacher of the Church from error and from misleading the faithful of the Church. Jesus promised the Church that together with the Father he would send the Holy Spirit, the "Spirit of Truth."

"I am the Way, the Truth and the Life. No one can come to the Father except through me" (John 14:6).

"I shall ask the Father, and he will give you another Advocate to be with you for ever, that Spirit of truth whom the world can never receive since it neither sees nor knows him; but you know him because he is with you, he is in you" (John 14:15-17).

"When the Advocate comes, whom I shall send to you from the Father, the Spirit of truth who issues from the Father, he will be my witness. And you too will be witnesses, because you have been with me from the outset" (John 15:26).

"Still, I must tell you the truth: it is for your own good that I am going because unless I go, the Advocate will not come to you; but if I do go, I will send him to you. And when he comes, he will show the world how wrong it was, about sin, and about who was in the right. . . ." (John 16:7-8).

"But when the Spirit of truth comes he will lead you to the complete truth, since he will not be speaking as from himself, but will only say what he has learned. . . . (John 16:13).

"I came into the world for this: to bear witness to the truth; and all who are on the side of truth listen to my voice" (John 18:37).

"Anyone who listens to you listens to me; anyone who rejects you rejects me; and those who reject me reject the one who sent me" (Luke 10:16).

The infallibility of the Church, as vested primarily in Peter and his successors, follows from the words of Christ and the nature of the Church as the Mystical Body of Christ. Christ said, "I am the light of the world" (John 8:12; 9:5). He promised the "Spirit of truth" to His Church which would speak in His name, saying He would be with His Church always until the end of time (Matthew 28:20). Jesus promised that the gates of hell would never prevail against His Church (Matthew 16:18).

If the Church ever officially taught falsehood, the gates of hell, the father of lies, would have prevailed against His Church. From this we can reason to the third attribute of the Church, indefectibility. This attitude refers to the imperishable duration of the Church and its immutability until the end of the world. Vatican Council I declared that the Church possesses "an unconquered stability." It said of the Church: "built on a rock, she will continue to stand until the end of time" (Denzinger 3013, 3056). The Church now is and will always remain the institution and divine organism of salvation founded by Jesus Christ.

Indefectibility means that the Church is essentially unchangeable in its doctrines, its constitution, and in its liturgy. Modifications which do not affect the nature or substance of the Church can be made. The essence of what Jesus Christ established will always remain. We have His word for that. "I am with you always; yes, to the end of time" (Matthew 28:20). Indefectibility refers to the universal Church while individual local churches, whole dioceses, even the church in an entire country could be lost to the true faith.

The fact that local churches can and do decay is the reason why any dissent from the true faith and the authority of the Church which speaks for Jesus Christ is so serious. Sometimes some claiming to be "Catholic" have dissented from official positions of the Church. They contribute nothing to the life of the Church but, rather, serve to destroy themselves, if left unchecked, by eating away at the very source of their life. Universally, however, we have the divine promise that the Church will never be destroyed.

While infallibility is specifically assigned to the pope, as described above, there also is episcopal infallibility. This means that when the bishops of the Catholic Church are gathered in a general council, or, scattered over the earth, they propose as one a teaching of faith or morals to be held by all the faithful, they are preserved from error. This assurance of freedom from error is provided, however, only if they speak in union with the bishop of Rome, the pope, and their teaching is subject to his authority.

The *magisterium* of the Church refers to its teaching authority, vested in the bishops, as successors of the apostles, under the Roman pontiff who is the successor of St. Peter. The supreme teaching authority is vested even in the pope alone as Vicar of Jesus Christ on earth and visible head of the Catholic Church. The magisterium is classifed as *extraordinary* and *ordinary*. Extraordinary is the exercise of the Church's teaching authority in a solemn way, as in formal declarations of the pope or of

163

an ecumenical council of the world's bishops when the council is approved by the pope. When the extraordinary magisterium forms solemn definitions, that is dogmas, which are doctrines taught by the Church to be believed by all the faithful as part of divine revelation, then such conciliar decisions or papal definitions bind the consciences of all the faithful in matters of faith and morals and are infallible. Ordinary magisterium refers to the normal, day-to-day teaching of the Church and also must be adhered to.

Some have wrongly supposed and even taught that Catholics are required to believe or obey the pope only when he speaks *ex cathedra* in solemnly defining a doctrine of faith or morals. They claim that unless the Church makes an infallible pronouncement in a formal way one is free to dissent. Such is contrary to the official teachings of the Church as clearly explained at the Second Vatican Council (1962-65).

"Bishops who teach in communion with the Roman Pontiff are to be revered by all as witnesses of divine and Catholic truth; the faithful, for their part, are obliged to submit to their bishops' decision, made in the name of Christ, in matters of faith and morals, and to adhere to it with a ready and respectful allegiance of mind. This loyal submission of the will and intellect must be given, in a special way, to the authentic teaching authority of the Roman Pontiff, even when he does not speak *ex cathedra* in such wise, indeed, that his supreme teaching authority be acknowledged with respect, and sincere assent be given to decisions made by him, conformable with his manifest mind and intention, which is made known principally either by the character of the documents in question, or by the frequency with which a certain doctrine is proposed, or by the manner in which the doctrine is formulated.

"Although the bishops, taken individually, do not enjoy the privilege of infallibility, they do, however, proclaim infallibly the doctrine of Christ on the following conditions: namely, when, even though dispersed throughout the world but preserving for all that amongst themselves and with Peter's successor the bond of communion, in their authoritative teaching concerning matters of faith and morals, they are in agreement that a particular teaching is to be held definitively and absolutely. This is still more clearly the case when, assembled in an ecumenical council, they are, for the universal Church, teachers of and judges in matters of faith and morals, whose decisions must be adhered to with the loyal and obedient assent of faith.

"This infallibility, however, with which the divine redeemer wished to endow his Church in defining doctrine pertaining to faith and morals, is co-extensive with the deposit of revelation, which must be religiously guarded and loyally and courageously expounded. The Roman Pontiff, head of the college of bishops, enjoys this infallibility in virtue of his office, when, as supreme pastor and teacher of all the faithful — who confirms his brethren in the faith (see Luke 22:32) — he proclaims in an absolute decision a doctrine pertaining to faith or morals. For that reason his definitions are rightly said to be irreformable by their very nature and not by reason of the assent of the Church in as much as they were made with the assistance of the Holy Spirit promised to him in the person of blessed Peter himself; and as a consequence they are in no way in need of the approval of others, and do not admit of appeal to any other tribunal. For in such a case the Roman Pontiff does not utter a pronouncement as a private person, but rather does he expound and defend the teaching of the Catholic faith as the supreme teacher of the universal Church, in whom the Church's charism of infallibility is present in a singular way. The infallibility promised to the Church is also present in the body of bishops when, together with Peter's successor, they exercise the supreme teaching office" (*Dogmatic Constitution on the Church*, 25).

While doctrines of faith and morals solemnly defined are irreformable, a careful distinction must be made between doctrine and Church discipline. There are divine laws and Church-made laws. Revealed divine laws would be a part of doctrine in the sense that laws which come directly from God can never change. The God-Man Jesus Christ gave His Church the power to make laws and dispense with laws which it has made. "Whatever you bind on earth shall be considered bound in heaven; whatever you loose on earth shall be considered loosed in heaven" (Matthew 16:19).

Divine laws flow from the eternal law of God and the very nature of God in himself. God is the ruler of the universe and His eternal laws embrace both the physical and moral laws. In nature, the norms of physical laws are necessarily fulfilled, such as in gravity or the expansion of matter by heat. In moral laws, since God respects the free will of man, the norm may or may not be fulfilled. Still, truth remains and man sins when he does not fulfill the divine moral law.

The eternal moral law of God is known by man in two ways: naturally and supernaturally. Natural law, coming from God, is known by human beings discovering the truth by the unaided light of human reason. St. Thomas Aquinas called it "nothing else than the rational creature's participation in the eternal law" (*Summa Theologica*, 1a, 2ae, quest. 91, art. 2). Supernaturally, human beings know the eternal law from divine revelation to which they are able to respond with the help of God's grace. This revealed divine law spans the whole circuit of the special communications from God of His will "through the prophets" in times past and in our time "through his Son" (Hebrews 1:1).

The Catholic Church uses its God-given authority to govern when it makes laws and changes laws according to times and circumstances. However, the Church can never change divine laws but must rather protect through the power of the Holy Spirit the interpretation of divine laws according to the eternal will of God and exhort the faithful to fulfill the divine will.

DISCUSSION QUESTIONS

1. What kind of Church would have resulted if Jesus had promised it no divine attributes?

If Jesus had founded the Church without authority, infallibility or indefectibility we would still be living in darkness, we could have no certainty in faith, and the Church He founded would no longer exist. He would have promised us nothing in that case.

2. Why is it tantamount to denying Christ if one denies the three attributes of authority, infallibility and indefectibility in the Church?

The Church is the Mystical Body of Christ, one with Christ. If one claims His Church has no authority, that it can make mistakes in teaching faith or morals and be destroyed, he is denying the very nature of Christ who identified himself with His Church and said that all authority had been given Him, that His Church would speak for Him and that He would be with us all days, even unto the end of the world.

3. To what are the glorious attributes of the Church attributed?

The glorious attributes of the Church are not due to the human beings who now govern the Church in Jesus' name, but due to the divine power of the Holy Spirit working through and in them.

4. How could Jesus say, "The Father is greater than I"?

When Jesus said, "The Father is greater than I," He had reference to the divine nature being superior to the human nature with which the Son of God had become hypostatically united.

5. Who was the Advocate Jesus promised to send upon the Church in conjunction with His Father?

Jesus promised that when He had ascended into heaven together with the Father He would send the Holy Spirit upon the Church as its Advocate to assist it in its work.

6. Why did Jesus indicate it was expedient that He depart physically from this earth?

Jesus said that the Advocate, the Holy Spirit of truth, would not come to the Church unless He (Jesus) departed to heaven. This would enable the Church to spread to all the nations of the world, guided by the Holy Spirit, and not be limited simply to one part of the world.

7. Has the Church changed its teachings on usury from earlier centuries?

The Church has not changed its teachings on usury. What has changed is the economic system under which injustices may occur.

8. Why did the Church protest against Galileo in 1616?

In 1616 the decree of the Congregation of the Index placed Galileo under a disciplinary prohibition to protect the faithful from the disturbing effect of a then-unproved hypothesis. Galileo had been imprudent in ridiculing certain passages of the Bible.

9. Did the decision of 1616 concern papal infallibility?

The Galileo affair did not involve papal infallibility, as it involved the utterance of no doctrine and nothing was defined. Also, the pope did not sign any decree.

10. What authority did Jesus give His Church?

Jesus gave His Church the authority to teach, to govern and to sanctify.

11. What special authority did Jesus give the papacy in the person of St. Peter?

St. Peter was given the primacy of authority in the Church; it is a primacy of jurisdiction, the full and supreme teaching authority, legislative and sacerdotal powers.

12. What is a major purpose of the papacy as instituted by Jesus Christ?

A major purpose of the papacy is to keep the Church united in faith.

13. Answer this statement: Defined doctrines are irreformable until the pope redefines or changes a defined doctrine.

Defined doctrines of the Church, called dogmas of faith, can never be changed. No pope can change a defined doctrine. They are irreformable.

14. What three conditions are necessary for the pope to teach infallibly?

For the pope to teach infallibly there must coexist three conditions: 1. He must be teaching on faith or morals. 2. He must be teaching as the universal pastor, *ex cathedra*, to the whole world. 3. He must have the intention of declaring a doctrine unchangeably true.

15. What is the source of the Church's infallibility?

The source of the Church's infallibility is the Holy Spirit which Jesus promised.

16. Does the New Testament indicate that Jesus would keep His Church in the truth?

The New Testament repeatedly speaks of the promise of Jesus to keep His Church in the true faith. Jesus promised that the gates of hell would never prevail against it (Matthew 16:19). In Chapters 14, 15 and 16 of St. John's Gospel there are many recorded words of Jesus promising the "Spirit of truth." St. Luke 10:16 says that the disciples of Jesus would speak in His name. Jesus promised to be with His Church until the end of the world. (Matthew 28:20).

17. Show from Sacred Scripture that Jesus promised the Church indefectibility.

Indefectibility is also implied in the promise of Jesus to keep His Church in the true faith through the "Spirit of truth." Also, the direct words of Jesus to the first pope, St. Peter, "On this rock I will build my church. And the gates of the underworld can never hold out against it. . . ." (Matthew 16:18).

18. Explain: The Universal Church could never be destroyed, but local churches could be destroyed.

Local churches refer to the diocese and the church in a certain part of the world. Whereas the Church could never be destroyed entirely from the face of the earth, yet, the true faith could disappear from a diocese or even an entire nation.

19. When is it possible for bishops to teach infallibly?

Bishops can teach infallibly only when, even while dispersed throughout the world, they teach amongst themselves in union with Peter's successors in matters of faith or morals, and are in agreement that a particular teaching is to be held definitively and absolutely. Also, in an ecumenical council, when together with the pope, they teach in like manner.

20. Why is the assent of the faithful not required for infallible Church teachings?

For a teaching of the Church to be infallible the assent of the faithful is not required, for the authority of true faith comes not from the people but from above. The infallibility comes from the Holy Spirit.

21. What can change in the Church and what can never change?

Laws which the Church itself has made can change, but the eternal laws of God and defined doctrines can never change.

CHAPTER 12

The Four Marks of the Church

Once a person has put his faith in Jesus Christ as true God, true man, Son of God incarnate, and in the fact that Jesus Christ did found a Church, there are certain marks which that Church must necessarily possess. The marks of the Church are clear signs or characteristics which point to the Church which Jesus Christ established. The four essential marks, *one, holy, universal* and *apostolic*, were first fully enumerated in the Nicene-Constantinople Creed. Since the Eastern Schism and the Protestant Reformation, which resulted in many hundreds of Christian denominations, the four marks have become the means of identifying the true Church.

There are repeated incidents of individuals traveling all the way from atheism to agnosticism and, finally, to belief that Jesus Christ is true God and true man who was sent to earth by the first person of the Blessed Trinity to redeem mankind from its sins. Such a person then finds himself facing the dilemma of many churches which claim to be the Church Jesus established.

The person who accepts the Word of God as divinely inspired discovers the clear pronouncement of Jesus Christ that He would establish a Church, not churches (Matthew 16:18-19). It is a contradiction of right reason to suppose that Jesus Christ could found more than one true Church. Truth is one. The Apostle Paul speaks clearly about the need to remain in one faith, in one Lord after one baptism.

"Do all you can to preserve the unity of the Spirit by the peace that binds you together. There is one Body, one Spirit, just as you were all called into one and the same hope when you were called. There is one Lord, one faith, one baptism, and one God who is Father of all, over all, through all and within all" (Ephesians 4:3-6).

The words of Jesus Christ that He would build one Church upon Peter and that it would never be destroyed requires that the Church He founded be in the world yet today. If the true Church established by Jesus faded away, if it were destroyed, then Jesus Christ did not keep His promise to preserve and abide with His Church always, even to the end of time. If Jesus did not keep His promise, then He was not God. The need for the

169

true Church founded by Jesus Christ to remain always and be present in the world yet today is that important. To put one's faith in Jesus Christ is to place one's faith in the existence of His one Church until the end of the world.

There is no room for claiming that we can have faith simply in Jesus Christ while different members may belong to many different Christian denominations. Such is not the "one flock and one shepherd" Jesus speaks of in St. John's Gospel (John 10:16). Jesus surely did not intend many branches of a church when these hundreds of branches represent disagreeing faiths. He prayed for unity, not division.

The Apostle Paul speaks again of the need for unity in the true Church of Christ in writing to the Romans. "Just as each of our bodies has several parts and each part has a separate function, so all of us, in union with Christ, form one body, and as parts of it we belong to each other" (Romans 12:4-5).

When Jesus raised Lazarus from death to life He prayed to His heavenly Father aloud "for the sake of all those who stand around me." He concluded with, "so that they may believe it was you who sent me" (John 11:42). Another time Jesus prayed "so that the world may believe it was you who sent me" (John 17:21). Reason tells us that true faith requires oneness. Just before giving the requirement for the world to believe it was God the Father who sent Him, Jesus prayed for unity in His followers:

"As you sent me into the world, I have sent them into the world, and for their sake I consecrate myself so that they too may be consecrated in truth. I pray not only for these, but for those also who through their words will believe in me. May they all be one. Father, may they be one in us, as you are in me and I am in you, so that the world may believe it was you who sent me" (John 17:18-21).

Jesus Christ explicitly asserted the necessity of faith and baptism. He thereby affirmed at the same time the necessity of the Church which men must enter through baptism.

The Second Vatican Council clearly stated the necessity of the Church for salvation rather than merely some vague or general faith in Jesus Christ without a church.

"This holy Council first of all turns its attention to the Catholic faithful. Basing itself on scripture and tradition, it teaches that the Church, a pilgrim now on earth, is necessary for salvation: the one Christ is mediator and the way of salvation; he is present to us in his body which is the Church. He himself explicitly asserted the necessity of faith and baptism (see Mark 16:16; John 3:5), and thereby affirmed at the same time the necessity of the Church which men enter through baptism as through a door. Hence they could not be saved who, knowing that the Catholic Church was

170

founded as necessary by God through Christ, would refuse either to enter it or to remain in it.

"Fully incorporated into the Church are those who, possessing the Spirit of Christ, accept all the means of salvation given to the Church together with her entire organization, and who — by the bonds constituted by the profession of faith, the sacraments, ecclesiastical government, and communion — are joined in the visible structure of the Church of Christ, who rules her through the Supreme Pontiff and the bishops. Even though incorporated into the Church, one who does not however persevere in charity is not saved. He remains indeed in the bosom of the Church, but 'in body' not 'in heart.' All children of the Church should nevertheless remember that their exalted condition results, not from their own merits, but from the grace of Christ. If they fail to respond in thought, word and deed to that grace, not only shall they not be saved, but they shall be the more severely judged.

"Catechumens who, moved by the Holy Spirit, desire with an explicit intention to be incorporated into the Church, are by that very intention joined to her. With love and solicitude mother Church already embraces them as her own" (*Dogmatic Constitution on the Church*, 14).

All men must belong to the true Church of Jesus Christ, which history itself attests to be the Catholic Church, since truth does not change and only the Catholic Church with the pope as visible head and Jesus Christ as invisible Head has been in the world since the days of Jesus Christ and His apostles. This does not mean that everyone not formally and fully in membership will be damned. They may be saved through membership *by desire*. One who is sincere and desires all that God wants of him or her, even if that person through no fault of his own does not come to the realization that the Catholic Church is the one true Church of Jesus Christ, is already a member of the Church *by desire*. Those, however, who come to the full realization of the truth of the Catholic Church must act on it.

One cannot be satisfied with possessing part of the true faith when the *fullness* of true faith is known to be available and willed by Jesus Christ. Jesus told His apostles to go forth and teach everything, "all things" he had commanded, not just part. When we recognize truth we must also accept and live by all of it.

Scripture tells us to have a "reason for the hope that you all have." While faith may often go beyond reason the two are never contrary. Here one needs to recall the chapter on truth (Chapter 5) to determine the reasonableness of oneness in faith and why our divine and loving Savior insisted on oneness in His followers. St. Peter, the first pope, spoke similarly:

"No one can hurt you if you are determined to do only what is right; if you do have to suffer for being good, you will count it a blessing. *There is no need to be afraid or to worry about them.* Simply *reverence the Lord* Christ in your hearts, and always have your answer ready for people who ask you the reason for the hope that you all have. But give it with courtesy and respect and with a clear conscience, so that those who slander you when you are living a good life in Christ may be proved wrong in the accusations that they bring. And if it is the will of God that you should suffer, it is better to suffer for doing right than for doing wrong" (1 Peter 3:13-17).

The second mark of the true Church is holiness. The Catholic Church possesses holiness in its founder, who is clearly Jesus Christ. It is holy in its teachings and provides all the means necessary to lead a holy life. A study of the sacraments will indicate how Jesus Christ lives and acts in the world today through His Church, forgiving sin and bringing people to the divine life of grace ever more abundantly. An honest study of history reveals in every age holiness in many of the Church's members and always extraordinary holiness in some. The lives of the saints through the centuries testify to that.

Jesus prayed for holiness in His Church, as seen in His prayer for His apostles. Miracles have been present in the Catholic Church throughout every age, starting with Jesus Christ himself.

While some Catholics live bad moral lives, such do not discredit the essential holiness of the Church because these individuals are not using the means of holiness available to them and will have to render an accounting of their souls. Jesus said that "the kingdom of heaven is like a dragnet cast into the sea that brings in a haul of all kinds. When it is full, the fishermen haul it ashore; then, sitting down, they collect the good ones in a basket and throw away those that are no use. This is how it will be at the end of time: the angels will appear and separate the wicked from the just to throw them into the blazing furnace where there will be weeping and grinding of teeth" (Matthew 13:47-50).

The man who has faith in Jesus Christ as Son of God, Savior, in looking for the one true Church in its fullness, will have to conclude that this Church must be universal. It must be a Church offering true faith for all nations. There is a unity to the human race. We are all descendants of Adam and Eve. As there is one Lord and Jesus Christ is universal Savior, there must be one faith for the one human race. The true faith cannot be different for different countries and different cultures. There is "one Lord, one faith, one baptism" (Ephesians 4:5).

"For of all the names in the world given to men, this is the only one by which we can be saved" (Acts 4:12). "But God raised him high and gave him the name which is above all other names so that *all beings* in the heavens, on earth and in the underworld, *should bend the knee* at the name of Jesus and that every tongue should acclaim Jesus Christ as Lord, to the glory of God the Father" (Philippians 2:9-11). Jesus instructed His apostles, "Go, therefore, make disciples of all the nations; baptize them in the name of the Father and of the Son and of the Holy Spirit" (Matthew 28:19). The word "Catholic" means "all nations" or universal. The one true faith in the one true God and in His Son made man who died on the Cross for our salvation and rose again from the dead and ascended into heaven, such faith was for every nation. This is the one true religion. No longer can there be different nations and cultures with different gods, different religions. There is one God and one true religion. The Church of Jesus must, of necessity, be universal or Catholic because of who Jesus is.

The word "Catholic" was first used, according to recorded history, by St. Ignatius of Antioch (c. A.D. 35-c. 107) in a letter to the Smyrneans (8:2). Jesus had founded the true Church with true faith in the one true God for all nations, and by the end of the first century it was spreading to the known nations of the world and was then rightly called Catholic as it still is today.

The person who has come to faith in Jesus Christ as Lord, God, Savior, and concluded that His Church must be one, holy and universal, likewise will find the necessity for the true Church to be apostolic. Apostolicity is that quality of the Catholic Church which is derived from and descended from the original apostles upon whom Jesus Christ built His Church, with Peter as the chief apostle. In the Catholic Church there is an apostolicity of origin. The Church was first organized by the original apostles chosen, formed and ordained by Jesus Christ. There is an apostolicity of teaching because what the Church teaches now is essentially the same as what was taught by the apostles. As will be seen in the chapter on Holy Orders, there is an apostolic succession in office, because there has been an unbroken historical transmission of episcopal powers from Jesus Christ to the apostles to all bishops today who are in union with the bishop of Rome.

The mark of apostolicity is also connected to the fact that truth is immutable. Truth does not change. The Catholic Church, being the one true Church of Jesus Christ, possessing true faith in its fullness, must have a history which extends back to the original apostles, making the Church truly apostolic.

No other church has any historical basis to claim it has all the marks of the Roman Catholic Church: One, Holy, Catholic and Apostolic.

The Roman Catholic Church during its almost 2,000 years of existence has had to struggle, not only with movements from without but against movements from within which have at times posed as Catholicism. A

173

great heresy the Church has had to contend with is known as *Modernism*. It is a theory about the origin and nature of Christianity. According to Modernism, there is no such thing as absolute truth. Religion is essentially a matter of experience. There is no objective revelation from God to the human race on which our faith is based. Modernism claims there are no reasonable grounds for credibility in the Christian faith based on miracles or the testimony of history. For the *Modernist*, faith would be uniquely from within, part of human nature, "a kind of motion of the heart," hidden and unconscious. It attempts to remove the supernatural from religion.

To use Modernist terms, faith is a "feeling for the divine" that cannot be expressed in words or doctrinal propositions, a natural instinct belonging to the emotions.

Modernism was condemned by Pope St. Pius X in two documents in 1907, *Lamentabili* and *Pascendi*. The effects of the great heresy of Modernism were thereby quieted for some years, but its proponents used the aftermath of the Second Vatican Council (1962-65) as the occasion to surface its false ideas. Many of the faithful, even clergy and Religious in some cases, became confused as Modernism often presented itself as being in the "spirit of Vatican II."

Modernism wages a continued assault on the papacy. It attacks Catholic dogma and fosters abuses in the divine liturgy, since it has no respect for authority. Modernism is in conflict with Catholicism, although some of its adherents sow great confusion by calling themselves "Catholic" while attempting to teach in the name of the Church the very things which the Catholic Church condemns.

Modernism promotes relativism, which justifies almost everything and treats everything as of equal value. It tends to eliminate everything which requires effort or inconvenience in obeying God's commandments. Its attacks against Catholic dogma result in confusion and false ecumenism. Pope Paul VI warned about this in his encyclical *Ecclesiam Suam*: "The desire to come together as brothers must not lead to a watering down or whittling away of truth. Our dialogue must not weaken our attachment to our faith. Our apostolate must not make vague compromises concerning the principles which regulate and govern the profession of the Christian faith both in theory and practice."

Modernism not only has affected theology, philosophy and catechetics, even as taught to children, but it contains social, economic and political principles favoring socialism and Marxism. It tends to weaken opposition to atheistic materialism and communism. Secular Humanism's *Manifesto* condones suicide and advocates abortion, artificial birth control (contraception), euthanasia, sexual perversions and divorce. It is

174

destructive in that it spreads immoral sex-education programs free of parental control.

The most violent but often subtle attacks of Modernism are aimed at the pope, the hierarchy and the priesthood as well as at Religious. They are aimed at the pope because he is the chief Vicar of Jesus Christ on earth. They are aimed at bishops and priests because they act as the bridge between God and man. They are aimed against Religious because as consecrated persons they are engaged in important apostolic endeavors in the work of the Church. Modernism has been effective in recent times in affecting even some of the clergy and Religious.

A book of this nature on *The Catholic Faith* would not be complete without at least a brief warning that whereas the Church founded by Jesus Christ does, indeed, have divine attributes of authority, infallibility and indefectibility and the marks of oneness, holiness, universality and apostolicity, yet, it must still struggle against the forces of evil which have always attempted to destroy it by every means. The divine promise for the universal Church remains, however, "the gates of the underworld can never hold out against it" (Matthew 16:18).

DISCUSSION QUESTIONS

1. Would it have been possible for Jesus Christ to have founded more than one true Church?
Truth is one. It is a contradiction to suppose that Jesus Christ could have founded more than one true Church. If they were the same, they would not be two or more but one. Jesus, being Truth itself, could not found contradicting churches but only one true Church.

2. Why does denial of the continued existence of the true Church amount to denial that Jesus Christ is God?
Jesus promised that His Church would never be destroyed. Being God, He had to keep His word. To claim Jesus did not keep His word is to say He is not God.

3. Why could it not be the will of Jesus Christ to have had many different branches of His Church with a plurality of doctrines?
Jesus is truth and stands for unity of faith. He prayed intensely for unity in His followers. Where there are contradictions on the same subjects, there is not truth. Jesus, being truth itself, could not will falsehoods.

4. Why did Jesus pray that His followers remain one so that the world may believe that God the Father had sent Him?
Right reason tells us that truth is one. When Christians contradict one another on the same subject it is obvious they cannot all be speaking the truth. This is why Jesus prayed that His followers might remain one "so that the world may believe that you [Father] have sent me" (John 17:21). The scandal of divisions among

Christians has hindered the conversion of the world to faith in Jesus Christ.

5. Does membership in the one true Church guarantee salvation?

Mere membership in the true Catholic Church does not guarantee salvation. One must live the faith in charity and die in the state of grace in order to be saved.

6. How can persons be saved who never came to realize that the Catholic Church is the true Church?

Persons who, through no fault of their own, do not realize that the Catholic Church is the true Church of Jesus Christ can be saved if they sincerely strive to do the will of God as they understand it. In this way they are members by desire.

7. What happens to a person who dies knowing that the Catholic Church is the true Church but refused to join it and live according to its teachings?

If a person knew the Catholic Church is the true Church but died outside of it, refusing to live by its teachings, he could not be saved because he refused to do the will of God as he knew it.

8. How can the Catholic Church be holy when there are bad Catholics?

Holiness of the Catholic Church does not mean that each and every member is necessarily holy. Jesus compared the Kingdom of God to a net that takes in all kinds of fish, good and bad. Only the good are found fit for heaven. Those who have been given the gift of true faith but who refuse to live according to it, that is, making use of its special graces, will be held more seriously accountable.

9. Why does the true faith have to be universal?

The true faith has to be universal or for all nations because there is one God and there is a unity of the human race. Jesus died for all men, establishing a Church for all nations. Truth itself is universal, for all.

10. What is meant by the apostolicity of the true Church?

The apostolicity of the Church means the Church has a history going back to the original apostles upon whom Jesus built His Church with Peter as the chief apostle in authority. The teaching of the Church today is apostolic for it is essentially the same as given the apostles by Jesus Christ and passed on through the centuries.

11. What is Modernism?

Modernism is a heresy, already condemned by Pope Pius X. It denies any certainty or unchangeableness in faith. There are no concepts of absolutes but everything is relative, gained by personal experience on the natural level. It amounts to the denial of the supernatural and divine unchanging faith. After Vatican II, the spirit of Modernism surfaced in many quarters in the Church affecting even some of the clergy and Religious.

CHAPTER 13

Divine Liturgy
and the Sacraments
of the Church

The divine liturgy of the Church refers to the official public worship of the Catholic Church as distinguished from private devotion. Liturgy refers to the Holy Eucharist, often called "the Mass," and the administration of the seven sacraments. Before studying the meaning of the Holy Eucharist, or the Mass as sacrifice and sacrament, as well as each of the other six sacraments of the Church, we shall discuss in this chapter the general meaning of the liturgy.

"The Church is a worshiping community. In worship it praises God for his goodness and glory. It also acknowledges its total dependence on God, the Father, and accepts the gift of divine life which he wishes to share with us in the Son, through the outpouring of the Spirit. Worship creates, expresses and fulfills the Church. It is the action in and by which men and women are drawn into the mystery of the glorified Christ.

"Faith and worship are intimately related. Faith brings the community together to worship; and in worship faith is renewed. The Church celebrates Christ's life, death, resurrection in its liturgy; it proclaims its faith in his presence in the Church, in his word, in the sacramental celebrations; it gives praise and thanks, asks for the things it needs, and strengthens itself to carry out its commission to give witness and service" (*Sharing the Light of Faith*, National Catechetical Directory, 112).

"For it is the liturgy through which, especially in the divine sacrifice of the Eucharist, 'the work of redemption is accomplished,' and it is through the liturgy, especially, that the faithful are enabled to express in their lives and manifest to others the mystery of Christ and the real nature of the true Church. The Church is essentially both human and divine, visible but endowed with invisible realities, zealous in action and dedicated to contemplation, present in the world, but as a pilgrim, so con-

177

stituted that in her the human is directed toward and subordinated to the divine, the visible to the invisible, action to contemplation, and this present world to that city yet to come, the object of our quest (see Hebrews 13:14). The liturgy daily builds up those who are in the Church, making of them a holy temple of the Lord, a dwelling-place for God in the Spirit (see Ephesians 2:21-22), to the mature measure of the fullness of Christ (See Ephesians 4:13)" (*Constitution on the Sacred Liturgy*, Vatican II, 2).

One begins to understand the reality of what the divine liturgy is when he realizes that whenever there is authentic liturgy the very person of Jesus Christ is at work, worshiping God the Father in the unity of the Holy Spirit. To understand the liturgy we must understand something about the holy priesthood.

What is a priest? According to Sacred Scripture Jesus Christ is the eternal High Priest. Chapters 7, 8 and 9 of Hebrews explain the superiority of the priesthood of Jesus Christ and of His worship and mediation, especially in His sacrifice on the Cross, which we shall see is perpetuated every time the Sacrifice of the Mass is offered.

To answer the question, "what is a priest?" — he is an authorized mediator who offers a true sacrifice in acknowledgment of God's supreme dominion over human beings and in expiation for their sins. A priest is the reverse of a prophet. A prophet communicates God to the people. A prophet speaks for God. A priest mediates from the people to God. Jesus Christ was, in fact, both prophet and priest (as well as king) and carries out these roles yet today in His holy Church, His Mystical Body.

Jesus Christ, true God and true man, is the first, last and the greatest priest of the New Covenant. He is the eternal High Priest who offered himself physically on the Cross once and for all, a victim of infinite value for the redemption of all men for all time. Now He continuously renews or perpetuates that selfsame Sacrifice of the Cross on the altar through the Church. Certain men have been especially ordained to act in the name of Jesus Christ and perpetuate through the divine liturgy, the Mass and the Sacraments that which Jesus Christ accomplished physically in history almost 2,000 years ago.

A priest, then, is essentially one who offers sacrifice. Jesus Christ was anointed High Priest in His mother's womb at the moment of the Incarnation, at the moment when the Word of God assumed human flesh as Mary said, "Let what you have said be done to me" (Luke 1:38).

The human nature of Jesus was created in both His body and soul. The hypostatic union took place at the moment of the Incarnation, when "the Word was made flesh, and and he lived among us" (John 1:14). The eternal Son of God was joined substantially to this created body and soul of Jesus so that His body, soul, divinity are one, and Jesus Christ is now

178

the anointed eternal High Priest destined to offer himself in sacrifice for the redemption of the world.

The very nature of Jesus Christ is to be priest, to offer sacrifice. He came to earth to die in sacrifice. In our chapter on the holy priesthood, we shall see that Catholic priests are not priests of their very nature, but by *participation* in the one priesthood of Jesus Christ. Thus Catholic priests offer sacrifice in the name of Jesus Christ. They act "in persona Christi" (in the person of Christ).

The 10th chapter of Hebrews makes clear that Jesus not only is essentially the High Priest, as the chapters immediately before outline, but that His very first movement of soul, in His human intellect and will, was a priestly act of offering himself in sacrifice, which would be carried out physically as an adult man.

"Bulls' blood and goats' blood are useless for taking away sins, and this is what he said, on coming into the world: *You who wanted no sacrifice or oblations, prepared a body for me. You took no pleasure in holocausts or sacrifices for sin; then I said, just as I was commanded in the scroll of the book, 'God, here I am! I am coming to obey your will'* " (Hebrews 10:4-7).

Already in the Old Testament (the Old Covenant), God's people had a liturgy or rituals of worship carried out according to the prescriptions of God. They were but types of the perfect adoration to come in Christ Jesus. Jesus at the beginning of His ministry respects the temple and goes there to teach (Matthew 21:23; Luke 19:47). It was this same temple of the Old Covenant where bulls' blood and goats' blood were once offered but were not effective for the forgiveness of sins. So Jesus came to offer His own body and His own blood in Sacrifice on the Cross for the redemption of the world.

On the night before he died, just as there were strict prescriptions for the ritual under the Old Covenant, so Jesus would lay down basic regulations for the perfect adoration in the New Covenant which He was about to establish.

"Now as they were eating, Jesus took some bread, and when he had said the blessing he broke it and gave it to the disciples. 'Take it and eat'; he said 'this is my body.' Then he took a cup, and when he had returned thanks he gave it to them. 'Drink all of you from this,' he said, 'for this is my blood, the blood of the covenant, which is to be poured out for many for the forgiveness of sins.' " (Matthew 26:26-29).

What makes official divine liturgy in the Roman Catholic Church is not simply whether the prayers be public but whether Jesus Christ the High Priest is present and is acting as priest in His holy Church in the public divine work of worship. The very word "liturgy" comes from two

Greek words, *laos* (people) and *ergon* (work), and means a *public work*, or public duty or service. Applied to Catholic worship it means a public duty, service, work which God's creatures owe the Creator and render God in, with and through Jesus Christ the High Priest. Whenever an official liturgy of the Church is conducted, Jesus Christ the priest is present and acting for the glory of God the Father, in the unity of the Holy Spirit and for the salvation of man. This is why this chapter began by saying that to understand liturgy, one must have an appreciation of the holy priesthood.

The divine liturgy then is the exercise on earth of the priestly office of Jesus Christ, as distinct from His role as teacher and ruler of His people. Christ performs this priestly role as head of His Mystical Body, the Church, so that head and members together offer the sacred liturgy or worship. The function is twofold. First, to give glory and praise to God. That is worship. Second, to obtain grace for the people of God. That is sanctification.

The Second Vatican Council reminded us that in the liturgy the Body of Christ, through the power of the Holy Spirit, gives first of all glory to God and then grace to men.

"To accomplish so great a work, Christ is always present in his Church, especially in her liturgical celebrations. He is present in the Sacrifice of the Mass not only in the person of his minister, 'the same now offering, through the ministry of priests, who formerly offered himself on the cross,' but especially in the eucharistic species. By his power he is present in the sacraments so that when anybody baptizes it is really Christ himself who baptizes. He is present in his word since it is he himself who speaks when the holy scriptures are read in the Church. Lastly, he is present when the Church prays and sings, for he has promised 'where two or three are gathered together in my name there am I in the midst of them' (Matthew 18:20).

"Christ, indeed, always associates the Church with himself in this great work in which God is perfectly glorified and men are sanctified. The Church is his beloved Bride who calls to her Lord, and through him offers worship to the eternal Father.

"The liturgy, then, is rightly seen as an exercise of the priestly office of Jesus Christ. . ." (*Constitution on the Sacred Liturgy*, 7).

All seven sacraments of the Church were instituted by our Lord and Savior, Jesus Christ. Whenever any one of the seven sacraments is administered the very person of Jesus Christ, the High Priest, is present and acts, giving adoration and glory to God the Father and bestowing grace upon mankind. The priest at the altar, in the confessional, at the baptismal font, is essentially Christ the High Priest acting, or rather, Christ the High Priest is acting in the visible priest we see and he shares in the priestly powers of Christ, who was once upon the earth and now is in heaven. In the case of each sacrament administered, the ordained man is acting "in persona Christi" (in the person of Christ). Christ Jesus accomplishes all these things through the instrumental cause of the ordained priest.

Because the ordained priest acts "in persona Christi," he has no right "to do his own thing" in offering Mass or administering the sacraments. He is not acting in his own name but in the name and person of Jesus Christ. The only authority he has is to act in harmony with the authority which Jesus Christ gave to His universal Church, His Mystical Body, which, in turn, has bestowed authority upon the priest through Holy Orders.

The sacraments are the acts of Jesus Christ extended in time and space. Through the sacraments, Jesus Christ does today in His Mystical Body what he once did physically upon earth. This is why the divine liturgy is referred to as "celebrating the sacred mysteries of Christ." What Jesus did in His physical body upon earth almost 2,000 years ago, He accomplishes today in His Mystical Body unto the glory of God the Father so as to sanctify men.

Through the divine liturgy, through the sacraments of the Church, what Jesus did in history when He was physically upon earth, He does today in His Mystical Body, the Church. The term "Mystery of Faith" is often used when speaking of the Holy Eucharist. The liturgy of the Mass perpetuates the Sacrifice of the Last Supper which Jesus offered Holy Thursday evening and which He offered physically on the Cross Good Friday afternoon. All this Jesus accomplishes sacramentally at every Holy Mass in what is called the divine liturgy of the Mass.

The definition of the sacraments *in general* should then become more meaningful to us: "The Sacraments are the acts of Christ Jesus extended in time and space." We see this, by faith, especially in the Mass which perpetuates the sacrifice of the Cross. In the other sacraments, too, Jesus accomplishes today in souls and for the glory of the Father what He accomplished when He was on earth.

The definition of a sacrament *in particular*, long familiar to Catholics, is still valid. "A sacrament is an outward sign instituted by Jesus Christ to give grace." It would be more complete to add, "and to give glory to God." Our definition then could well read: "A sacrament is an outward sign instituted by Jesus Christ to give glory to God and grace to man." God is always the beginning and the end, the chief purpose of all things divine. Every sacrament validly administered is to the praise of God, and the sacraments always give grace if they are participated in and

181

received with a right supernatural disposition. The amount of grace received from any particular sacrament will depend upon the dispositions of one's soul.

A sacrament is a sensible sign which indicates an action by Jesus Christ to give an invisible grace. Inward sanctification is given to the soul properly disposed. We are familiar with signs in daily life. There are road signs, the clock, a map, etc. These signs signify something as do the outward signs of the sacraments: water, oil, bread, wine, words, actions.

Natural signs, such as the road sign, do not contain power within themselves to cause what they signify. The sign which says, "Lone Tree five miles ahead" does not cause the little village to exist five miles ahead. In the case of the seven sacraments instituted by our loving Savior, Jesus Christ, however, the sacraments do have the power within themselves to cause what they signify. Jesus Christ in His very person does act in and through the sacraments. This is why the Church officially declares "that when anybody baptizes it is really Christ himself who baptizes. . . . The liturgy, then, is rightly seen as an exercise of the priestly office of Jesus Christ." It is Jesus Christ who forgives sin when Catholics go to confession and receive the absolution of the priest. It is Jesus Christ who confirms, changes bread and wine into the Body, Blood, Soul and Divinity of Jesus Christ, etc.

This is the manner in which we must view the sacraments. They contain the real person of Jesus Christ, acting here and now, applying the graces of His redemption which He earned by His life, death and resurrection. While every example limps, the pictures sometimes seen of the cross on Mt. Calvary, with seven fountains of life-giving water flowing down to us today, do convey a divine truth. Jesus merited all grace for us by the sacrifice of His death on the cross. The seven sacraments do serve as channels to dispense the infinite merits of His saving graces. We must, however, see by faith the very person of our loving Savior present and acting in each one of the seven sacraments.

Each of the seven sacraments, which we shall study one at a time, has a definite purpose and assistance to the spiritual life as instituted by Jesus Christ. The sacraments accompany us from the birth to burial. We can see that in the supernatural realm the sacraments correspond to seven major aspects of human life.

NATURAL	SUPERNATURAL
BIRTH	BAPTISM
GROWTH-STRENGTH	CONFIRMATION
FOOD & DRINK	HOLY COMMUNION
DISEASE — BURDENED WITH GUILT	CONFESSION

GOVERNMENT   HOLY ORDERS
PROPAGATION OF RACE   MATRIMONY
DANGER OF DEATH   ANOINTING OF SICK

Each of these seven sacraments has a purpose and gives a special grace which no other sacrament can give. While each of the sacraments gives a particular grace according to the need of our state and/or occasion in life, yet each one gives an increase of sanctifying grace when worthily received. Each sacrament, while giving glory to God, brings an increase of the sharing in the life of God to the soul which will provide for a higher and happier place in heaven for all eternity.

Unfortunately, outside the Catholic Church among the many hundreds of different Protestant denominations where the apostolic chain has been broken, people have been deprived of most of the sacraments of Jesus Christ. With the exception of baptism and matrimony, which can be valid for Protestant Christians under the proper conditions, they have been deprived of the validity of the sacraments, and most do not believe that Jesus Christ gave His Church seven sacraments. Most of these non-Catholics do not consider matrimony a sacrament, but only a contract. It is one of the sad results of division among Christians. Many have lost the powers of the ordained priesthood of Jesus Christ which are required to effect five of the seven sacraments.

The sacraments are essential to the authentic and full Christian life, being an extension of the redeeming acts of Jesus Christ. The sacraments bring us into contact with Jesus Christ the High Priest.

DISCUSSION QUESTIONS

1. Who essentially is it who acts in the divine liturgy of the Catholic Church?
     Jesus Christ the High Priest acts in the liturgy, the Mass and the sacraments.

2. Why is it said that the liturgy involves the exercise of the priesthood of Jesus Christ?
     The liturgy is an exercise of the priesthood of Jesus Christ because His very powers and person are present whenever there is an official liturgy and Jesus is essentially the High Priest who acts.

3. What is the difference between prophet and priest, and which role did Christ exercise on earth?
     A prophet is one who speaks for God and communicates from God to the people. A priest mediates from the people to God. Jesus is priest, prophet and king.

4. What essentially is a priest?
     A priest is essentially one who offers sacrifice to God.

5. When was Jesus Christ anointed High Priest?

Jesus Christ was anointed High Priest at the moment God created His body and soul in the womb of Mary when Mary answered, "Let what you have said be done to me" (Luke 1:38).

6. What is the essential nature of Jesus Christ?

The essential nature of Jesus Christ is that He is High Priest who offered himself in sacrifice for the sins of the world.

7. What was the first act of the soul of Jesus Christ when He was created as man?

The first act of the soul of Jesus when He was created, according to Hebrews 10, was to acknowledge, upon coming into the world, that sacrifices of the Old Covenant were not pleasing to God and that He would take on a body to offer himself in sacrifice.

8. Why is it said that Jesus was born to die?

Jesus was born to die in the sense that the high point of His ministry was to offer himself in sacrificial death upon the Cross for the redemption of the world.

9. Why did the Sacrifice of Jesus Christ replace the sacrifices of the Old Covenant?

The sacrifices of the Old Covenant were merely symbolic, only types of the perfect sacrifice of Jesus to come. They had no power to take away sin.

10. What determines when worship is official liturgy?

Worship is official liturgy when the very person of Jesus Christ is present and acts, as in the Mass and the seven sacraments. It is public worship in the sense that it is an official action of the Mystical Body of Christ, the Church, in Christ's power and name.

11. What is the twofold function of liturgy?

The twofold function of the liturgy is to glorify and praise God and give grace to men.

12. When the priest conducts liturgy, what is meant when it is said that he acts "in persona Christi"?

The Catholic priest shares in the powers of Christ the High Priest, and whenever he conducts an official priestly act the very person of Jesus acts in and through him.

13. Why is it contrary to authentic liturgy and the law of the Church for a priest to improvise his own liturgy?

Since the Catholic priest does not act in his own name but in the name and person of Jesus Christ, he may not "do his own thing," that is, improvise his own liturgy, for it is not his but that of Christ in His Mystical Body. It is public divine worship, not private.

14. Why is the liturgy called "celebrating the mysteries of Jesus Christ"?

The liturgy is sometimes called "celebrating the mysteries of Jesus Christ" because the liturgy contains the power to make present sacramentally what Christ did and merited for us almost 2,000 years ago.

15. Distinguish the sacraments in *general* from a sacrament in *particular*.

In *general* the sacraments are the acts of Jesus Christ extended in time and space. In *particular* each sacrament has a particular outward, sensible sign signifying what it causes in giving grace to man.

16. Explain why Jesus Christ instituted *seven* sacraments and not just one when all seven give the same sanctifying grace?

Jesus instituted **seven** sacraments (while each one gives an increase of sanctifying grace if received with proper dispositions of soul) because each sacrament has a special purpose depending on our state or need in life at a particular time. In addition to an increase of sanctifying grace, each sacrament gives a special sacramental grace.

17. Explain: "The sacraments contain the powers of Jesus Christ which they signify."

The sacraments not only signify, they actually cause to happen what they signify. The sacraments have the very power of Jesus Christ who acts within them.

18. Do Christians separated from the Catholic Church have the seven sacraments?

Because Christians separated from Catholicism have lost the powers of Christ's ordained priesthood, they also have lost five of the sacraments which need ordained priests to administer them. Only baptism and matrimony are valid for Protestants.

CHAPTER 14

Baptism and Confirmation

There are three acts of Jesus Christ which incorporate a person more and more intimately into our divine and loving Savior, Jesus Christ. There are three sacraments which seal a person in Jesus Christ forever, so that never again is that person the same. It is God's will that every one of us be sealed for all eternity with at least two of these indelible marks of Jesus Christ.

The three sacraments which place an indelible seal of Jesus Christ upon the soul for all eternity are Baptism, Confirmation and Holy Orders. In another chapter the indelible seal of Holy Orders will be discussed, whereby one is given a special charism with the powers of Jesus Christ the High Priest.

Baptism is a sacrament in which by the water and the word of God a person is not only cleansed of all sin but is reborn in Jesus Christ. Through Baptism one is given sanctifying grace for the first time, thereby sharing in the life of God for the first time. The matter for the correct administration of Baptism is natural water, which is poured or sprinkled on a person, or in which a person is immersed.

Jesus made it very clear that Baptism is essential for salvation. "I tell you most solemnly, unless a man is born through water and the Spirit, he cannot enter the kingdom of God" (John 3:5).

Jesus commanded His apostles to teach all nations and to baptize. "He who believes and is baptized will be saved" (Mark 16:16). "Go, therefore, make disciples of all the nations; baptize them in the name of the Father and of the Son and of the Holy Spirit" (Matthew 28:19).

Scripture, God's own word, again and again points out the power and importance of Baptism:

"But when the kindness and love of God our savior for mankind were revealed, it was not because he was concerned with any righteous actions we might have done ourselves; it was for no reason except his own compassion that he saved us, by means of the cleansing water of rebirth and by renewing us with the Holy Spirit which he has so generously poured over us through Jesus Christ our savior. He did this so that we should be justified by his grace, to become heirs looking forward to inheriting eternal life. This is doctrine that you can rely on" (Titus 3:4-7).

While the indelible seal of Holy Orders gives a special charism, the powers of Jesus Christ the High Priest, there is a sense, even if different in essence from the Sacrament of Holy Orders, where everyone who is baptized shares in the priesthood of Jesus Christ. It is called the priesthood of the faithful or the priesthood of the baptized.

"The Church is also a priestly people (see Revelation 1:6). All of its members share in Christ's priestly ministry. By regeneration and the anointing of the Holy Spirit, the baptized are consecrated as a priestly people. Though the ministerial or hierarchial priesthood differs, not only in degree but in essence from the priesthood of the faithful, nevertheless, they are interrelated" (*National Catechetical Directory*, 93).

While not to be confused with the priesthood received in Holy Orders, everyone baptized shares in the priesthood of Jesus Christ through the indelible seal. The indelible mark or seal of Christ in Baptism is not a decoration simply to beautify the soul but adds a quality, indeed a power of Christ, to the soul. We all become a priestly people by Baptism into Jesus Christ. It is strengthened in Confirmation and constantly nourished and exercised by the Holy Eucharist.

Baptism gives a person the right to heaven. It also gives one the right to receive the other sacraments of the Church when that person is properly disposed. The baptismal seal empowers one to participate in the liturgy of the Church as a priest of the faithful, since all the baptized are a priestly people. This is to say all the baptized are identified with Christ the High Priest but their priestly sharing is not of the same essence as the ministerial priesthood. Through the seal of Baptism one is empowered to offer in union with the Mystical Body of Christ the Sacrifice of the Mass to God the Father. For the faithful to do this, however, there is needed a priest of Holy Orders to produce the Victim, that is, to consecrate the bread and wine into the Body, Blood, Soul and Divinity of our Lord and Savior, the Mediator, Jesus Christ.

If one were not baptized but went to Holy Mass, he could kneel, stand, sit, make the responses, sing like an angel. While all his external participation might appear more excellent than anyone else present, still, if that person were not sealed with Christ in Baptism he would not have the power to offer the Victim Jesus Christ to God the Father so as to participate in the adoration which is of infinite value. The seal of Baptism gives one a power, the power of the priesthood of the faithful to glorify the Father, in, with and through Jesus Christ in the unity of the Holy Spirit.

"Mother Church earnestly desires that all the faithful should be led to that full, conscious, and active participation in liturgical celebrations which is demanded by the very nature of the liturgy, and to which the

Christian people, 'a chosen race, a royal priesthood, a holy nation, a redeemed people' (1 Peter 2:9, 4-5) have a right and obligation by reason of their baptism" (*Constitution on the Sacred Liturgy*, 14).

When the Church uses the expression "indelible character" referring to seal of Christ imprinted upon the soul through the sacraments of Baptism, Confirmation and Holy Orders, its meaning is derived from the ancient Greek term "charassein," which is used in the Bible to describe an image or inscription engraved in a permanent way on a medal, coin or piece of stone. "In these three sacraments a character is imprinted on the soul, that is, an indelible spiritual sign which makes their repetition impossible" (Council of Trent).

The indelible mark of Christ, imprinted on the soul for all eternity through Baptism, Confirmation and Holy Orders, is for the honor and glory of God and the soul that is saved, and the shame and punishment of the soul that is lost. "For anyone who wants to save his life will lose it; but anyone who loses his life for my sake, and for the sake of the gospel, will save it. What gain, then, is it for a man to win the whole world and ruin his life? And indeed what can a man offer in exchange for his life? For if anyone in this adulterous and sinful generation is ashamed of me and of my words, the Son of Man will also be ashamed of him when he comes in the glory of his Father with the holy angels" (Mark 8:35-38; see Luke 9:24-26).

There are various accounts in God's word of the seal of Christ on the soul that is incorporated into Christ's Mystical Body.

"Remember it is God himself who assures us all, and you, of our standing in Christ, and has anointed us, marking us with his seal and giving us the pledge, the Spirit, that we carry in our hearts" (2 Corinthians 1:21-22).

"Now you too, in him, have heard the message of the truth and the good news of your salvation, and have believed it; and you too have been stamped with the seal of the Holy Spirit of the Promise" (Ephesians 1:13).

"Guard against foul talk; let your words be for the improvement of others, as occasion offers, and do good to your listeners, otherwise you will only be grieving the Holy Spirit of God who has marked you with his seal" (Ephesians 4:29-30).

If we consider in faith the indelible seal of Jesus Christ which is stamped upon the soul for all eternity, it is breathtaking. The seal which bestows upon the human soul the copy of Jesus Christ mysteriously and radically changes the person who receives it by an immutable participation in Christ's holy priesthood. In virtue of the sacramental character which Christians are given, they are anointed with something similar to

188

what occurred in Jesus Christ's humanity when the eternal Son of God united himself with our lowly human nature. Eternity became time. The God who is everywhere became somewhere. By Baptism we are incorporated into the Body of Christ which is the Church, identified with Jesus Christ.

The hypostatic union (God-man) is the root from which grace sprang, giving to our humanity an infinite dignity in Jesus Christ. We do not become infinite. Only Jesus Christ in His divinity is infinite. The seal-character of Jesus Christ which we receive is the source of grace. We become like Jesus Christ, the heavenly vine of which we are the branches.

Because there is a radical change when a person is baptized, one should never say, "I *was* baptized," as if it is something once accomplished and ends there. It is more proper to say "I *am* baptized," for the effects are eternal and our lives, henceforth, are to be lived in Jesus Christ, because in Christ we adore the Father and grow ever more and more into the likeness of Jesus Christ as we grow in sanctifying grace, our sharing in the life of God. We are sealed in the likeness of Jesus Christ permanently, in "the radiant light of God's glory and the perfect copy of his nature" (Hebrews 1:3).

The Sacrament of Baptism makes one a member of the Church. It is necessary for salvation. "He who believes and is baptized will be saved" (Mark 16:16). Baptism gives one a share in the life of God for the first time, and marks the beginning of "everlasting life" of which Jesus spoke. By Baptism "we are able to share the divine nature" (2 Peter 1:4). Through the grace given in Baptism "we are children of God" (Romans 8:17). Coming into the world in the state of original sin inherited from Adam and Eve and without grace, one must be baptized in order to be saved. While one need not receive all the sacraments to be saved, Baptism is necessary, and none of the other six sacraments can be received validly unless one is first baptized.

While the priest is the ordinary minister of Baptism (just as the bishop is the ordinary minister of Confirmation), anyone can baptize in case of necessity. If a non-baptized person is in danger of death, anyone, with the right intention of doing what the Church intends when it baptizes, may baptize. God used the most plentiful element on the earth, water, as the necessary matter for this sacrament. There must be a union of the pouring action of the water (or profuse sprinkling so as to make the water flow) and pronouncing the words: "I baptize you in the name of the Father and of the Son and of the Holy Spirit." Normally the water is poured over the head.

Every sacrament is an outward (sensible) sign. Water is a sign of cleansing and life. Baptism washes all sin from the soul and bestows a sharing in the life of God (grace) for the first time. The theological virtues of faith, hope and charity are infused into the soul at the time of Baptism.

For those who have never been given the opportunity to come to the knowledge of Jesus Christ and His Church and the need for Baptism, such as those in pagan lands, it is possible for them to be saved through Baptism *by blood*, or Baptism *by desire*. Some through the centuries have died for the faith by martyrdom before they had the opportunity to receive Baptism by water. Having laid down their lives for Jesus Christ they could be saved by Baptism of Blood. "A man can have no greater love than to lay down his life for his friends" (John 15:13).

Baptism *by desire* is based on perfect love of God. One may come to faith in the existence of God, and even though the Christian message has not been preached to him (or, having heard the message of Christ, he formed the intention to be baptized, yet entered eternity before receiving Baptism of Water). In such cases, if he developed a perfect love for God and desired to perform his will in all things, Christ Jesus then acted outside the sacraments to forgive sin and bestow grace. Only Baptism of Water, however, imprints the seal of Jesus Christ on the soul.

When an adult, who has been baptized in one of the hundreds of non-Catholic but Christian denominations, comes to the fullness of faith found in Catholicism and desires full and formal membership in the Catholic Church, there is no need for rebaptism as Baptism can never be administered more than once. Sacred Scripture speaks of "one baptism" and there is a common bond between Catholics and Protestants by their baptism in Christ. When there is doubt about the validity of a former Baptism, then the one making a profession of faith into full communion with the Catholic Church is baptized privately and conditionally. When Baptism is administered "conditionally" the priest, just before pouring the water and saying the proper words, says, *"If you are not baptized*, I baptize you. . . ."* In this circumstance, it is not a matter of being baptized a second time. If the first attempted Baptism was not valid, this is a true and first Baptism for the person. If the first Baptism was valid, then the "conditional" Baptism is no Baptism at all.

It is not proper simply to accept a certificate that one has been baptized into one of the many non-Catholic Christian denominations. The present norms of the Church concerning conditional Baptism of doubtfully baptized persons reads "if after serious investigation it seems necessary because of reasonable doubt," the person making the profession of Catholic faith is to be baptized privately. A study of the many different Christian denominations reveals that some do not fulfill all the conditions for Baptism, i.e., the flowing of water, the union of words and flowing of wa-

190

ter, the invocation of the entire Blessed Trinity, Father, Son and Holy Spirit.

Children who die without Baptism and who have not reached the age of reason, according to St. Thomas Aquinas, will have perfect *natural* happiness in limbo. St. Thomas Aquinas, along with the great majority of theologians, approved by the Church, held that infants who die in original sin suffer no "pain of sense." They do not grieve because they are deprived of heaven because pain of punishment is proportioned to personal guilt of which the infants have none. The Church, however, has never solemnly defined the existence of limbo. And though it teaches that Baptism in some form is necessary for salvation, it is possible that God does provide in some way for the salvation of unbaptized infants. In any case, God does not owe heaven to any of us, it is above our nature. Even if limbo, a place of perfect natural happiness, was all that was opened to any of us, it would be well worth striving to obtain. Eternal perfect *natural* happiness, even though excluded from the full blessedness of the Beatific Vision, while not suffering any punishment, would involve a great gift from God. Heaven, however, involves supernatural happiness.

Confirmation is the sacrament in which a person, already baptized, is strengthened by the Holy Spirit in order to profess the true faith and faithfully live up to one's profession. Confirmation gives one the grace to witness the true faith to others. The matter of the sacrament is the laying on of hands and the anointing with chrism. The celebrant of Confirmation, normally the bishop, dips his right thumb in the chrism and makes the Sign of the Cross on the forehead of the one to be confirmed, as he says: "Be sealed with the Gift of the Holy Spirit." A priest may administer Confirmation to children in danger of death when the bishop is not available.

When we are only baptized, we are, as it were, *infant* Christians. Confirmation makes us *adults* in our faith. Once a person is given the gift of faith which is infused at Baptism, along with the theological virtues of hope and charity, one has an obligation to grow and mature in it, to share it with others. That maturing so that we may witness the faith in the world is a grace given us in Confirmation when the Holy Spirit comes to us in a new and special way and another special indelible mark of Christ is sealed upon the soul.

The Confirmation character assimilates a person more closely to Christ, the Teacher of Truth, the King of Justice, and the High Priest. According to St. Thomas Aquinas, the confirmation character gives a person the power and the right to perform actions that are necessary in the spiritual battle against the enemies of the faith. He distinguished the fighters of Christ, *the confirmed*, from the simple members of the Church, *the baptized*. Confirmation then is a grace and power from God, not simply

191

to preserve the faith for oneself, but to empower one to make public profession of what he believes. When one is open to the special graces of Confirmation he is given a sense of mission to extend his faith to others. Such is the special sacramental grace of Confirmation.

The seven gifts of the Holy Spirit are wisdom, understanding, counsel, fortitude, knowledge, piety, and fear of the Lord. The 12 fruits of the Holy Spirit are charity, joy, peace, patience, benignity, goodness, long-suffering, mildness, faith, modesty, continence and charity. These supernatural works, according to St. Paul, manifest the presence of the Holy Spirit in one's life. Performing them, one recognizes God's presence by the happiness he experiences while others sense the divine presence in witnessing these good works (see Galatians 5:22-23).

Confirmation is our Pentecost. On that first Pentecost there was an outpouring of the Holy Spirit witnessed in signs by the mighty wind and the tongues of fire (Acts 2). The same Holy Spirit is available today to those whose hearts and souls are open to receive Him. The seal of Confirmation permanently marks one as a witness to Jesus Christ and gives a person the strength even to shed his blood for Christ, if necessary. Confirmation brings the soul then a strengthening by the Holy Spirit and thus completes Baptism. While Confirmation is not strictly necessary for salvation, as is Baptism, yet it is eminently important in contributing to Christian perfection and there is a grave obligation to receive it in due time. One who makes a profession of Catholic faith for reception into full communion with the Catholic Church may receive the Sacrament of Confirmation from the priest who receives him or her into the Church.

What the Prophet Ezekiel (36:27) foretold of God is realized in Confirmation. "I shall give you a new heart and place a new spirit within you; I shall remove the heart of stone from your bodies and give you a heart of flesh instead. I shall put my spirit in you, and make you keep my laws and sincerely respect my observances."

Let us ask the Lord Jesus to release in us the living waters of the Holy Spirit. May He open our hard hearts, soften our own difficult spirits which have often resisted the action of the divine life within us, and create a new spirit within us. Then may we reach out to all around us to share the spirit of the living Lord, Jesus Christ.

DISCUSSION QUESTIONS

1. What does one receive for the first time at Baptism?
One receives sanctifying grace for the first time at Baptism.

2. What permanent or indelible quality does one receive at Baptism?

Baptism imprints on the soul the indelible mark of Jesus Christ, called by Sacred Scripture "the seal of Christ."

3. What three sacraments give an indelible mark of Jesus Christ to the soul?

Baptism, Confirmation and Holy Orders imprint an indelible mark or character of Jesus Christ upon the soul.

4. What is meant by "Priesthood of the Faithful"?

The "Priesthood of the Faithful" refers to the indelible seal of Jesus Christ imprinted upon the soul at Baptism, which incorporates one into Jesus Christ the High Priest, giving the soul the power to receive other sacraments and to worship as a member of Jesus Christ at the Sacrifice of the Mass.

5. How does the priesthood of the faithful differ from the ordained priesthood of Holy Orders?

The priesthood of the faithful differs from the priesthood of Holy Orders not only by degree but in its very essence. The priesthood of the faithful is common to all baptized Christians, while the ministerial priesthood of Holy Orders is a different and special seal of Jesus Christ empowering the soul in a unique way.

6. What power does the indelible mark of Baptism give a person?

The indelible mark of Baptism empowers one to participate in the Liturgy of the Mass, to offer to God the Father the Victim which is Jesus Christ, once an ordained priest of Holy Orders has consecrated bread and wine. It empowers one to receive other sacraments of the Church which Jesus Christ instituted.

7. Why cannot the Sacraments of Baptism, Confirmation and Holy Orders be repeated for the same person?

Baptism, Confirmation and Holy Orders may not be repeated for the same person because they imprint upon the soul an indelible spiritual seal which is eternal.

8. Will one who loses his soul and is condemned to hell still retain the indelible marks of Christ on his soul which he received from Baptism, Confirmation or Holy Orders?

The indelible marks of Christ received from the sacraments will remain upon the soul for all eternity for the honor and glory of God and the soul of the person who is saved. It will be to the shame and punishment of the one who is lost.

9. What does Baptism do for the soul?

Baptism gives one a sharing in the life of God (grace) for the first time. It makes one a child of God. It imprints an indelible mark of Jesus Christ upon the soul for all eternity. It infuses into the soul the theological virtues of faith, hope and charity. Baptism makes one a member of the Church, Christ's Mystical Body.

10. Is it possible to receive any of the other sacraments validly before Baptism?

No sacrament may be received validly until one is first baptized, as Baptism is like the door through which we enter the Church.

11. For the valid administration of Baptism, what is necessary?

For the valid administration of Baptism one must have the intention of doing what the Church, Jesus Christ himself, intends by Baptism. One must use water, which must flow, while reciting the words: "I baptize you in the name of the Father and of the Son and of the Holy Spirit."

12. Explain Baptism of Blood? Of Desire? what do these fail to bestow upon the soul?

Baptism of Blood is received by a person who has not been able to be baptized by water but is martyred for his/her faith in Jesus Christ. Baptism of Desire comes when one has perfect love of God but has no opportunity to be baptized by water. Only Baptism of Water confers the eternal and indelible mark of Jesus Christ upon the soul.

13. According to the understanding of limbo, would infant souls that go there be punished?

Infants in limbo are not punished. They suffer no pain of sense but are perfectly happy in a natural way.

14. What does Confirmation do for a baptized person?

Confirmation completes Baptism, assimilating a person more closely to Jesus Christ. It gives one strength to live an adult Christian life amidst the trials and temptations of the world, to suffer from enemies and to be able to die for the faith if necessary. It brings a strengthening in the Holy Spirit, who comes in a new and special way.

15. How does Confirmation make one an adult Christian?

Confirmation makes one an adult Christian because by the power of the Holy Spirit it gives grace to witness Christ to others and have a sense of mission for the salvation of other souls, not simply one's own.

Chapter 15

Confession — Sacrament of Reconciliation

There is something intrinsic in human nature whereby we are burdened with guilt, even on the natural level, when we do something wrong, especially when it involves a serious matter. Psychologically we are relieved when we are able to share our wrongdoings with another human being whom we can trust. It is so much a part of human nature that a profession (trained pyschologist) has been developed to help handle that need.

Alcoholics Anonymous (AA) is an organization to be admired. It has a five-step program in which the fifth step states: "Admitted to God, to ourselves and to another human being the exact nature of all our wrongs." Once one has admitted to another and, therefore, to oneself, that one has been guilty, has done wrong, one is ready to begin making amends. I've admired the humility of AA members making that fifth step and I even have witnessed, on occasion, the non-Catholic entering step five and making a total confession of life as complete and beautiful as ever made by a lifelong Catholic in the confessional.

Confession is good for the soul. It purifies and relieves the human spirit when we share our human problems and failures, our sins, if done in a prudent and honest manner. Our divine and loving Savior, Jesus Christ, knew this human need because God had made the human heart. Jesus elevated the confession of sins to the dignity of a sacrament in which His representatives, the priests, who act in His name and power and person, are able not only to listen to the confession of sins, but are empowered as well to grant the forgiveness of God when the penitents are properly disposed.

The Catholic Sacrament of Confession is more properly called the Sacrament of Repentance or Reconciliation. It also is commonly called the Sacrament of Penance. The word "confession" itself would apply to the act of voluntary self-accusation of one's sins to a qualified priest in order to obtain absolution. The Sacrament of Penance is for the forgiveness of sins, committed after Baptism, for which one is truly sorry.

In considering the confession of sins for forgiveness through the absolution of a priest, one should be aware of the seal of the confessional. The priest who is authorized to hear confessions has a grave duty to keep absolutely secret all sins revealed in sacramental confession and anything else said by the penitent which is related to the confession. There is the natural law, the divine law of Jesus Christ and the positive law of the Church which bind the priest to the seal of the confessional. Not only is the priest himself bound to the seal, but any other person who may overhear of discover what was confessed, has a serious obligation to keep absolute secrecy. If a priest broke the seal of the confessional, the Church would not permit him to practice his ministry again.

The Sacrament of Penance was instituted by Jesus Christ on the evening of the first Easter Sunday. It was Christ's Easter gift to His Church. Jesus had died on the Cross to redeem us from our sins. It is significant then, that His first acts upon speaking to the apostles after rising from the dead was to bestow on them the power of the Holy Spirit with the authority to forgive sins in His name.

"In the evening of that same day, the first day of the week, the doors were closed in the room where the disciples were, for fear of the Jews. Jesus came and stood among them. He said to them, 'Peace be with you,' and showed them his hands and his side. The disciples were filled with joy when they saw the Lord, and he said to them again, 'Peace be with you. As the Father sent me, so am I sending you.'

"After saying this he breathed on them and said:

'RECEIVE THE HOLY SPIRIT.
FOR THOSE WHOSE SINS YOU FORGIVE,
THEY ARE FORGIVEN:
FOR THOSE WHOSE SINS YOU RETAIN,
THEY ARE RETAINED'."

(John 20:19-23)

The only other time Scripture mentions God breathing upon people is when He created our first parents. God breathed into the nostrils of Adam the breath of life and Adam became a living being. Here, Jesus, the God-Man is giving the apostles, his first bishops and priests, the power to give supernatural life to spiritually dead souls.

In a former lesson on the sacraments we learned that it is Jesus who baptizes, who confirms, who consecrates, and it is Jesus Christ who forgives sin. The priest of Holy Orders has stamped upon his soul the very special indelible mark of Jesus Christ the High Priest, empowering the priest with the ministerial powers of Jesus Christ. When the ordained

196

priest performs a special priestly act in the name of Jesus Christ, he acts "in persona Christi" (in the person of Christ). So it is in the Sacrament of Confession. It is Jesus Christ who forgives sins through the powers of His own priesthood which He has shared with the ordained. It is the priesthood of Jesus Christ, Christ the priest, the God-Man, who forgives the sins of the repentant who confess.

Jesus Christ acts in all the sacraments. Just as it is Jesus who consecrates bread and wine into His living body and blood, so it is Jesus who forgives sins. The early Christians called the Sacrament of Penance "a second baptism." It is a good answer to those who cannot comprehend "how a mere man can forgive sins." A mere man, of course, does not forgive sins. It is Jesus Christ who acts in and through His priests. Most Christians believe that Baptism forgives sin for the first time. It washes away Original Sin inherited from our first parents. If one was older when baptized, then Baptism would wash away not only Original Sin but all the sins on the soul. If God can use a man as His instrument for the forgiveness of sin in Baptism, surely He can (and does) for sins committed after Baptism.

Many express the desire to have a sign from God that they enjoy His favor, that their sins have been forgiven. Every sacrament is an outward sign. The absolution of the priest, "I absolve you from your sins in the name of the Father, and of the Son and of the Holy Spirit" is God's sign to us that our sins have been forgiven. Jesus said to the first priests, "Whose sins you shall forgive, they are forgiven; whose sins you shall retain, they are retained." The priest needs to make a judgment for each person who desires forgiveness, whether to forgive or to retain. For this confession of sin is necessary. He needs information to judge.

Confession is not like a washing machine which automatically cleans. Something more is required on the part of the one confessing than the telling of sins in a general way. The confession must be objectively complete in that the penitent confesses every known mortal sin, according to their number and kind, which he has committed since his last worthy reception of the Sacrament of Penance. To conceal a mortal sin deliberately is to cut off the effectiveness of the sacrament and to be guilty of sacrilege. Only in extraordinary circumstances would one be permitted to abstain from an integral or complete confession, such as when one is not able to speak because of health or physical surroundings. Nevertheless, that person is obliged to confess all his mortal sins in his next confession.

The absolution of the priest requires the confession of sin. If there are no mortal sins to confess, it is sufficient to confess any previous sins from one's past life or any present venial sins. Every mortal sin *must* be confessed as well as the circumstances which may change the nature of the

197

sin. Venial sins may be confessed. While it is not strictly required to confess every venial sin, it is well to confess especially those small failings which are more common and which are keeping one from growing spiritually. One grows in grace and in the spiritual strength to avoid sin by frequent confession when one has only venial sins to confess.

Sorrow for sin is necessary in order to make a good confession. One should be sorry for sin because it offends God. There is perfect sorrow and imperfect sorrow. Perfect contrition is based on pure love of God. The motive for perfect sorrow flows from love for God whom one has offended while the motive for imperfect sorrow flows more from fear of God's punishment. Motives for imperfect contrition would include fear of the pains of hell, of losing heaven, of being punished by God even in this life for one's sins, the sense of disobedience or ingratitude toward God and the realization of having lost merit which one could have acquired for heaven. Both perfect and imperfect sorrow are good, but one should strive for perfect sorrow.

Imperfect contrition is sufficient for the remission of sin in the Sacrament of Penance. If one's contrition is *perfect* one's sins are forgiven even before sacramental absolution. However, one must make a good confession after committing mortal sin before one may receive our divine Lord in Holy Communion. One can know with certainty whether one has imperfect sorrow. Only an actual grace from God to which one responds would enable one to make a *perfect* act of contrition. One cannot know for certain that his contrition has been perfect. Moral certitude that one is in the state of sanctifying grace is necessary before going to Holy Communion. Therefore, a good confession after mortal sin is required by the Church before Holy Communion.

Repentance is necessary to make a good confession. The will must aim at detesting past sinful thoughts, words, deeds or omissions. One must retract his past sins, wish he had not committed them. In repenting, one desires to regain the state of grace, that is, friendship with God. There must be formed a desire not to commit the sin again and to take the necessary means to overcome the sin, including the occasions of the sin. There must be a firm purpose of amendment.

A final condition for making a good confession is the willingness to do the penance which the priest may give. One will be punished for every sin he commits. If he does not do sufficient penance in this life, it is required in the next. The penance given by the priest helps remit at least part of the temporal punishment due to forgiven sin. God in His mercy may forgive the sin, but the justice of God requires penance. The penance the priest gives us should be performed with care, as it has special merit in making satisfaction to God for one's past sins. Through the priest in the

Sacrament of Penance one has been especially commissioned with a particular kind of penance. The penance may be in the form of special prayers, acts of charity, Bible readings, etc.

In summary, then, to make a good confession five conditions are necessary:

1. Examination of conscience.
2. Sorrow for sins.
3. Having a firm intention of avoiding the sins in the future.
4. Confession of sins.
5. Being willing to perform the penance the priest may give.

It is a dogma of Catholic faith that only an ordained priest or bishop (not a deacon or lay person) has the power of Jesus Christ to forgive sin. By the Church's absolution, sins are truly and immediately forgiven. One who has fallen into serious sin should strive immediately to make an act of perfect contrition with the intention to go to confession as soon as it is reasonably possible. The Church teaches as a dogma of faith, according to the Council of Trent, that the sacramental confession of sins is ordained by God and is necessary for salvation for those who after baptism have fallen into grievous sin. Also, by virtue of divine ordinance, all grievous sins according to kind and number, together with those circumstances which change their nature, are subject to the obligation of confession.

For the validity of the Sacrament of Penance there are required acts both on the part of the penitent and on the part of the confessor. This is to say, there is required both the confession of one's sins with proper dispositions of heart on the part of the penitent and absolution on the part of the priest. The principal effect of the Sacrament of Penance is the reconciliation of the sinner with God and with his fellow members of the Mystical Body of Christ.

It is true that all sin is social. It has a bad effect on the Mystical Body of Christ. A good confession, therefore, effects reconciliation with fellow members of the Mystical Body of Christ as well as with God. Some today, however, so overstress the horizontal (our relationship with one another) that it would almost seem that forgiveness comes from our brother rather than from God himself. One might answer: "If I get myself reconciled with God and you get yourself reconciled with God, we'll all be reconciled with one another."

This is not to downplay the social qualities of sin. Sin is not just a matter of "God and me." Since sin separates one from God, it also separates one from union in Jesus Christ with others. The Apostle Paul explained it in 1 Corinthians 12:26: "If one part is hurt, all parts are hurt with it. If one part is given special honor, all parts enjoy it." It is like one member of the human body being seriously diseased. It is bad for the entire body. Yet, an organ of the body which is exceptionally healthy is good for the whole body. So it is in the body of Christ, the Church.

The Church under ordinary conditions requires individual confession and individual absolution. General absolution of more than one person at a time is permitted *only for serious reasons*. When general absolution may be validly given, the provision for general confession is that "the penitents who wish to receive absolution" are invited "to indicate this by some kind of sign." The penitents make a general formula of confession, e.g. "I confess to almighty God." One of the necessary dispositions for receiving valid absolution, when only general confession and general absolution are possible, is that the penitent must "resolve to confess in due time each one of the grave sins which he cannot confess at present." A penitent who goes merely to communal services where general absolution is given without having the intention of making an individual confession of mortal sins later does not receive absolution validly. Communal services, where a congregation prepares for confession by prayers, scriptural readings, homily, etc., and then each penitent goes to individual confession and receives individual absolution, are encouraged by the Church. The National Catholic Directory for the United States, *Sharing the Light of Faith*, spoke as follows:

"Jesus began his work on earth by calling people to repentance and faith: 'Reform your lives and believe in the gospel' (Mark 1:15). Conversion means turning from sin toward him — present in his Church, in the Eucharist, in his work, in our neighbor — with love and a desire for reconciliation.

"Jesus began his risen life by giving his apostles power to forgive sins (see John 20:23). The Sacrament of Reconciliation continues his work of forgiving and reconciling. It celebrates the prodigal's return to the eternal merciful Father, renewing the sinner's union with God — and also with the community, inasmuch as our sins harm our brothers and sisters.

"The revised ritual offers various forms and options for celebrating this sacrament. Among these are communal celebrations, which more clearly show its ecclesial nature. Penitents have a choice of the customary anonymity or a setting face-to-face with the confessor. A choice is also offered among various prayers and readings.

"The sacrament's traditional and essential elements are contrition, confession, absolution, and satisfaction. Contrition is heartfelt sorrow and aversion from sin as an offense against God, with the firm intention of sinning no more. It expresses a conversion, 'a profound change of the whole person by which one begins to consider, judge and arrange' one's whole life to conform more with Christ's values. Following the revised rite, the penitent confesses sins, makes an appropriate expression of sorrow, and

200

receives forgiveness and reconciliation from the priest in Christ's name. Afterward the penitent performs the agreed upon act of satisfaction (penance).

"The Sacrament of Reconciliation, including individual and complete confession and absolution, remains the ordinary way of reconciling the faithful with God and with the Church. The Church holds and teaches that this method of receiving the sacrament is necessary and willed by Christ. Individual confession and absolution cannot be easily or ordinarily set aside. Particular, occasional circumstances may render it lawful and even necessary to give general absolution to a number of penitents without their previous individual confession, though the obligation to confess serious sin still remains. The existence of these serious circumstances is identified by the local bishop in consultation with other bishops according to articles 31 and 32 of the Rite of Penance.

"Secrecy is essential for safeguarding the sacrament; both penitent and sacrament are protected by the priest's obligation to maintain secrecy. The penitent ought to exercise prudent care in speaking about his or her own confession.

"Frequent participation in this sacrament, even though one has not committed a serious sin, is a highly desirable way of celebrating ongoing conversion and making progress in holiness"(124).

MANNER OF GOING TO CONFESSION

One who makes a profession of faith in coming into full communion with the Church also makes a general confession of sins committed during his entire life. After his first confession, he need go back no further than his last good confession in his examination of conscience.

Priest opens confessional door:
Priest and Penitent: IN THE NAME OF THE FATHER, AND OF THE SON, AND OF THE HOLY SPIRIT. AMEN. (While making the Sign of the Cross.+)
Priest: MAY GOD, WHO HAS ENLIGHTENED EVERY HEART, HELP YOU TO KNOW YOUR SINS AND TRUST IN HIS MERCY.
Penitent: AMEN.
Priest: (Optional: Father may read a scriptural quotation.) NOW YOU MAY MAKE YOUR CONFESSION.
Penitent:[1] FATHER, MY LAST CONFESSION WAS _____ AGO. I AM

---

[1]In some parishes at this point the penitent begins confession immediately with the Sign of the Cross as the priest opens the confessional slide and blesses the penitent.

A (state of life). . . . THESE ARE MY SINS: (Give number and circumstances which change the nature of the sins). I AM SORRY FOR THESE AND ALL THE SINS OF MY PAST LIFE AND THOSE WHICH I CANNOT NOW REMEMBER. I HUMBLY ASK PARDON OF GOD AND PENANCE AND ABSOLUTION OF YOU, FATHER.

Priest: (Talks to you and gives you a penance and asks you to recite a good ACT OF CONTRITION. Father waits while you recite ACT OF CONTRITION.)

Penitent: "O MY GOD, I AM HEARTILY SORRY FOR HAVING OFFENDED YOU, etc. . . . "

Priest: (Penitent listens while Father gives absolution:) GOD, THE FATHER OF MERCIES, THROUGH THE DEATH AND RESURRECTION OF HIS SON HAS RECONCILED THE WORLD TO HIMSELF AND SENT THE HOLY SPIRIT AMONG US FOR THE FORGIVENESS OF SINS: THROUGH THE MINISTRY OF THE CHURCH MAY GOD GIVE YOU PARDON AND PEACE, AND *I ABSOLVE YOU FROM YOUR SINS IN THE NAME OF THE FATHER, AND OF THE SON, AND OF THE HOLY SPIRIT.* +

Penitent: AMEN.

Priest: GIVE THANKS TO THE LORD, FOR HE IS GOOD.

Penitent: HIS MERCY ENDURES FOREVER.

Priest: THE LORD HAS FREED YOU FROM YOUR SINS. GO IN PEACE.

Penitent: THANK YOU, FATHER.

(Re-enter main body of the Church for penance and thanksgiving.)

DISCUSSION QUESTIONS

1. Even on the natural level confession is good for the soul. Explain.

Confession, even on the natural level, is good for the soul because it purifies and relieves the human spirit by sharing human problems and failures with another trusted human being.

2. For what purpose did Jesus Christ institute the Sacrament of Penance?

Jesus Christ instituted the Sacrament of Penance for the forgiveness of sins committed after baptism, sins for which one is truly repentant.

3. What is meant by the Seal of the Confessional?

The Seal of the Confessional seriously binds a priest by natural law, divine law and positive law of the Church never to reveal the sins of anyone who confesses. The privilege of hearing confessions would be removed from a priest known to break the seal.

4. Why is Confession (Sacrament of Reconciliation) called Christ's Easter gift to us?

The Sacrament of Reconciliation or Confession is considered Christ's Easter gift to the Church because Jesus gave the apostles the power to forgive sin in His name on the evening of the first Easter Sunday, the day He rose from the dead.

5. Who forgives sins when a properly disposed penitent confesses?

In the reception of the Sacrament of Penance, it is Jesus Christ himself who forgives sin through the instrumentality of the ordained priest who shares Christ's priesthood through the indelible character of Holy Orders. The priest forgives us, but he does so in the very person of Jesus Christ.

6. Why is the Sacrament of Reconciliation like a second baptism?

The Sacrament of Reconciliation is like a second baptism because it forgives sins which we have committed after Baptism and for which we are sorry.

7. "A mere man cannot forgive sins." Reply.

Jesus is no mere man. He is the God-Man, and He forgives us our sins through the ordained priest who shares the priestly powers of Jesus Christ.

8. What is meant by an objectively complete confession?

An objectively complete confession, which is required for a good confession, means that the penitent must confess every known mortal sin according to number and kinds.

9. What is the state of soul of one who goes to confession but deliberately conceals a mortal sin? What must such a person do to become reconciled with God?

One who deliberately conceals a known mortal sin makes a sacrilegious confession, and none of his sins are forgiven. He also adds the mortal sin of sacrilege to the mortal sins already on his soul. To become reconciled with God, he must make a complete confession of all mortal sins committed since his last good confession.

10. What purpose does the Sacrament of Confession serve if one has only venial sins?

If one has only venial sin to confess, it is still well to go to confession with frequency because every sacrament gives grace. Such a reception of penance helps the soul to grow in grace and gives spiritual strength to avoid sin and to grow spiritually through a more intense union with Jesus Christ.

11. What is the difference between perfect and imperfect contrition?

Perfect contrition is sorrow for sin when the motive is pure love of God. Imperfect sorrow has as its motive fear of God's punishment.

12. What kind of contrition is required to make a good confession?

To make a good confession one must have at least imperfect contrition.

13. Why is confession required before Holy Communion if one is conscious of having committed a mortal sin since one's last good confession?

The Church itself requires a good confession before Holy Communion if one is conscious of having committed a mortal sin since one's last good confession. This is because moral certitude of being in the state of grace is required for Holy Communion.

14. What is meant by "firm purpose of amendment"?

By "firm purpose of amendment" is meant the firm intention not to commit the same sin again and to avoid the occasions which lead one to the sin. One must be willing to take the means necessary to overcome the sin.

15. What are the five things necessary for a good confession?

The five things necessary for a good confession are: examination of conscience; sorrow for past sins; firm intention of avoiding the sins in the future; complete confession; willingness to perform the penance the priest may give.

16. If one should fall into mortal sin in a moment of weakness, what should he do as soon as he realizes the state of his soul?

One who has fallen into mortal sin should strive to make an act of perfect contrition with the intention of going to confession as soon as reasonably possible.

17. What is the principle effect of the Sacrament of Penance?

The principle effect of the Sacrament of Penance is the reconciliation of the sinner with God and with fellow members of the Mystical Body of Christ.

18. Sin is social. Explain.

Sin is social because we are members of the Mystical Body of Christ, which is the Church. Just as greater grace in a saintly person is of spiritual benefit to the entire Mystical Body, as pointed out by the Apostle Paul (1 Corinthians 12), so the sin of any one of us causes a weakness to the same Mystical Body. An analogy is seen in the physical body: when one member is weak or sick, the rest of the body suffers because of it.

19. Why is general absolution without serious reason an abuse?

The Church forbids general absolution except when there are serious reasons. The Church, headed by the pope, has responsibility over the sacraments given it by Jesus Christ. The Church has declared it an abuse for a priest to give general absolution without sufficient reason. Normally each penitent must not only confess privately but receive absolution individually.

20. A man regularly goes to communal penance where general absolution is given without the intention of privately confessing his mortal sins. Are his sins forgiven?

If one regularly goes to communal penance where general absolution is given and has no intention of confessing his mortal sins privately later, he does **not** receive absolution and still remains in sin.

CHAPTER 16

Holy Eucharist — Sacrament

There are at least three ways in which the presence of Jesus in the world is recognized by the Church. Jesus is present in His Church, the Mystical Body of Christ upon earth. Jesus is present to the People of God in His Word. Finally, Jesus is present in the sacraments, preeminently in the Most Blessed Sacrament, the Holy Eucharist.

"To accomplish so great a work Christ is always present in his Church, especially in her liturgical celebrations. He is present in the Sacrifice of the Mass not only in the person of his minister, 'the same now offering, through the ministry of priests, who formerly offered himself on the cross,' but especially in the eucharistic species. By his power he is present in the sacraments so that when anybody baptizes it is really Christ himself who baptizes. He is present in his word since it is he himself who speaks when the holy scriptures are read in the Church. Lastly, he is present when the Church prays and sings, for he has promised 'where two or three are gathered together in my name there am I in the midst of them' (Matthew 18:20)" (Vatican II, *Constitution on the Sacred Liturgy*, Chapter I, Number 7).

Once the properly ordained Catholic priest pronounces the words of consecration, "This is my body . . . the cup of my blood," there is present in the Blessed Sacrament, under the appearance of bread and wine, the living Body, Blood, Soul and Divinity of our Lord and Savior Jesus Christ, true God and true Man.

The Holy Eucharist is one of the seven sacraments instituted by Jesus Christ to be received by the faithful. The Holy Eucharist was instituted not only to be received, like the other sacraments, but to be adored. This is because there is a constant abiding presence of Jesus Christ as long as the species of bread and wine remain. Jesus is adored in the Blessed Sacrament, not simply at the moment of consecration but before, during and after reception as well. As long as the physical properties of the species of bread and wine remain essentially unchanged, there is the Real Presence of Jesus Christ and the Sacrament of the Eucharist continues.

The presence of Jesus Christ, our Lord and Savior, is not simply a spiritual, mystical or symbolic presence in the Eucharist. It is a Real

Presence, a real substantial presence of the God-Man in sacramental form with His true Body, Blood, Soul and Divinity. Jesus Christ is most profoundly, directly and intimately present.

Once the ordained priest has pronounced the words of consecration, "This is my body . . . the cup of my blood," there is no longer present the substance of bread or wine. After the consecration only the *appearances* of bread and wine remain. This is what is meant when we say that the "species" of bread and wine remain but the substance of bread and wine no longer exist.

The Church has long used the term "transubstantiation" to describe its faith in the complete change of bread and wine into the living substance of the Body and Blood of Jesus Christ by a validly ordained priest during the consecration at Mass. *Trans* means across. There is a change across from the *substance* of bread to the substance of the Body of Jesus Christ and from the substance of wine to the substance of the Precious Blood of Jesus Christ. After transubstantiation, the accidents (appearances, species) do not inhere in any substance whatever. They are sustained in existence by the divine power. It is the only case of accidents existing without a subject or substance.

The faith of the Church from the time of the apostles has been that Jesus Christ exists with His Body, Blood, Soul and Divinity under the appearances of the consecrated bread and wine. The term to describe this faith, "transubstantiation," was developed later. The Eastern Fathers of the Church, before the sixth century, favored the expression *meta-ousiosis*, "change of being." The Latin or western part of the Church coined the word *transubstantiatio*, "change of substance." Transubstantiation was incorporated in the creed of the Fourth Lateran Council in 1215. The Council of Trent used the term, too, in defining the "wonderful and singular conversion of the whole substance of the bread into the body, and the whole substance of the wine into the blood" of Christ, and added, "which conversion the Catholic Church calls transubstantiation" (*Denzinger* 1652).

The Catechism of the Council of Trent[1] spoke of the Holy Eucharist as follows: "As of all the sacred mysteries bequeathed to us by our Lord and Savior as most infallible instruments of divine grace, there is none comparable to the most holy Sacrament of the Eucharist; so, for no crime is there a heavier punishment to be feared from God than for the unholy or irreligious use by the faithful of that which is full of holiness, or rather which contains the very author and source of holiness. This the Apostle

---

[1]The Catechism of the Council of Trent is among the best known catechisms in the Catholic Church. It is known also as the Roman Catechism (1566). The Council of Trent, seeing the need for solid religious instructions, ordered such a work.

wisely saw, and has openly admonished us for it. For when he had declared the enormity of their guilt who discerned not the body of the Lord he immediately subjoined: 'In fact that is why many of you are weak and ill and some of you have died' (1 Corinthians 11:30).

". . . That its institution was as follows, is clearly inferred from the Evangelist. 'Our Lord, having loved his own, loved them to the end' (John 13:1). As a divine and admirable pledge of this love, knowing that the hour had now come that he should pass from the world to the Father, that he might not ever at any period be absent from his own, he accomplished with inexplicable wisdom that which surpasses all the order and condition of nature. For having kept the supper of the Paschal lamb with his disciples, that the figure might yield to the reality, the shadow to the substance, 'he took bread, and giving thanks unto God, he blessed, and broke, and gave to the disciples, and said: 'Take you and eat, this is me.' In like manner also, he took the chalice after he had supped, saying: 'This chalice is the new testament in my blood; this do, as often as you shall drink it, in commemoration of me.' (Matthew 26:26-28; Mark 14:22-24; Luke 22:19-20; 1 Corinthians 11:24-25).

". . . How much this Sacrament differs from all the others is easily inferred. For all the other Sacraments are completed by the use of the material, that is, while they are being administered to someone. Thus Baptism attains the nature of a sacrament when the individual is actually being washed in the water. For the perfecting of the Eucharist on the other hand, the consecration of the material itself suffices, since neither (species) ceases to be a sacrament, though kept in the pyx.

"Again in perfecting the other sacraments there is no change of the matter and element into another nature. The water of Baptism, or the oil of Confirmation, when those sacraments are being administered, do not lose their former nature of water and oil; but in the Eucharist, that which was bread and wine before consecration, after consecration is truly the substance of the body and blood of the Lord.

"But although there are two elements, as bread and wine, of which the entire Sacrament of the Eucharist is constituted, yet guided by the authority of the Church, we confess that this is not many sacraments, but only one.

"Otherwise, there cannot be the exact number of seven Sacraments, as has ever been handed down, and as we decreed by the Councils of Lateran, Florence and Trent.

". . . When our Lord says: 'This is my body, this is my blood,' no persons of sound mind can mistake his meaning, particularly since there is reference to Christ's human nature, the reality of which the Catholic faith permits no one to doubt.

". . . The Apostle, after having recorded the consecration of bread and wine by our Lord, and also the administration of Communion to the Apostles, adds: 'But let a man prove himself, and so eat of that bread and drink of the chalice; for he that eateth and drinketh unworthily, eateth and drinketh judgment to himself, not discerning the body of the Lord' (1 Corinthians 11:28-29). If, as heretics continually repeat, the sacrament presents nothing to our veneration but a memorial and sign of the Passion of Christ, why was there need to exhort the faithful, in language so energetic, to prove themselves? By the terrible word 'judgment,' the Apostles show how enormous is the guilt of those who receive unworthily and do not distinguish from common food the body of the Lord concealed in the Eucharist. In the same epistle St. Paul had already developed this doctrine more fully, when he said: 'The chalice of benediction which we bless, is it not the communion of the blood of Christ? And the bread which we break, is it not the participation of the body of the Lord? (1 Corinthians 10:16). Now these words signify the real substance of the body and blood of Christ the Lord."

The Church Fathers of the first as well as succeeding centuries were most explicit about the faith of the Church regarding the Holy Eucharist. St. Ambrose wrote in his book *On Those Who are Initiated Into the Mysteries* that the true body of Christ is received in this sacrament, just as the true body of Christ was derived from the Virgin. St. John Chrysostom wrote many passages professing his faith in the Real Presence of Jesus in the Holy Eucharist: "His words cannot deceive, our senses are easily deceived." St. Augustine wrote: "To carry himself in his own hands is impossible to man, and peculiar to Christ alone; he was carried in his own hands when, giving his body to be eaten, he said, 'This is my body'" (In Psalm xxiii, Serm. i.n.10).

Other Church Fathers who wrote profoundly in early centuries declaring that the true body and blood of Jesus Christ are found under the veils of bread and wine were Justin, Irenaeus, St. Cyril, St. Denis, St. Hilary, St. Jerome, St. Damascene and a host of others.

Some, not understanding the power of God, have asked that if one places places the consecrated bread and wine under a microscope could there be seen the properties of body and blood. One would, in fact, see the natural properties of bread and wine. Those who know philosophy in depth know that with the physical eyes one never sees a substance but only accidents, and the accidents of bread and wine remain after the consecration. Jesus Christ is not present in the host and chalice in a physical manner but in a sacramental manner. It is a sacramental presence. Jesus Christ is actually present, the substance of Jesus' physical Body and Blood is actually present. This is a mystery of faith. We cannot possibly understand it in a natural way. It is brought about by the special divine power of God.

The Council of Trent declared it a dogma of faith that Jesus Christ becomes present in the Sacrament of the Altar by the transformation of the whole substance of the bread into His body and of the whole substance of wine into His blood. Also, a dogma of faith, the accidents of bread and wine continue after the change of the substance. Also, the whole Christ is present under either of the two consecrated species.

After the consecration has been completed, the body and blood of Jesus Christ are *permanently* present in the Holy Eucharist. This permanent presence of Jesus in the Holy Eucharist also was declared a dogma of faith by the Council of Trent. This is important to remember, lest carelessness creep in with a breakdown of reverence justifying such false concepts as Jesus is only present in the "meal," and even present to us only by reason of our love for one another. There is a permanent presence of Jesus, and not simply for the duration of the Communion service or while someone is present before the Blessed Sacrament. Even if all withdrew from before the tabernacle, there is still the Real Presence of Jesus Christ with His Body, Blood, Soul and Divinity.

The sanctuary lamp or candle burns constantly in the Catholic church when there is present in the tabernacle the consecrated host. Catholics are requested to genuflect upon entering the Church and before entering their pews when the Blessed Sacrament is reserved in the tabernacle. They also are asked to be ever conscious of the presence of the Blessed Sacrament and to act accordingly. The Council of Trent defined as a dogma of faith that the adoration of *Latria* must be given to Jesus Christ present in the Holy Eucharist. *Latria* is essentially adoration given only to God.

Visiting the Blessed Sacrament is an ancient practice among devout Catholics. Praying before the tabernacle which contains the sacramental presence of Jesus Christ is highly recommended. The Blessed Sacrament is reserved for the purpose of adoration by the faithful and so that the Eucharist is available for the sick and those in danger of death. The Sacrament of the Eucharist may be taken to hospitals or homes of those who are shut in and not able to come to the church for Mass.

The Catechism of the Council of Trent in explaining the Catholic meaning of the Real Presence, that Jesus Christ is whole and entire in the Holy Eucharist, used very graphic expressions to relate the truth.

"In this Sacrament are contained not only the true body of Christ and all the constituents of a true body, such as bones and sinews, but also Christ whole and entire. . . . The word 'Christ' designates the God-man, that is to say, one Person in whom are united the divine and human natures; that the Holy Eucharist, therefore, contains both, and whatever is included in the idea of both, the Divinity and humanity whole and entire, consisting of the soul, all the parts of the body and the blood — all of which must be believed to be in this Sacrament. In heaven the whole humanity is united to the Divinity in one hypostasis, or Person; hence it would be impious, to suppose that the body of Christ, which is contained in the Sacrament, is separated from His Divinity.

". . . Some things are contained in the Sacrament because they are united to those which are expressed in the form. For instance, the words 'This is my body,' which comprise the form used to consecrate the bread, signify the body of the Lord, and hence the body itself of Christ the Lord is contained in the Eucharist by virtue of the Sacrament. Since, however, to Christ's body are united his blood, his soul, and his Divinity, all of these also must be found to coexist in the Sacrament; not, however, by virtue of the consecration, but by virtue of the union that subsists between them and his body. All these are said to be in the Eucharist *by virtue of concomitance*. Hence it is clear that Christ, whole and entire is contained in the Sacrament; for when two things are actually united, where one is, the other must also be.

"Hence it also follows that Christ is so contained, whole and entire, under either species, that, as under the species of bread are contained not only the body, but also the blood and Christ entire; so in like manner, under the species of wine are truly contained not only the blood, but also the body and Christ entire.

"But although these are matters on which the faithful cannot entertain a doubt, it was nevertheless wisely ordained that two distinct consecrations should take place. First, because they represent in a more lively manner the Passion of our Lord, in which his blood was separated from his body; and hence in the form of consecration we commemorate the shedding of his blood. Secondly, since the Sacrament is to be used by us as the food and nourishment of our souls, it was most appropriate that it would be instituted as food and drink, two things which obviously constitute the complete."

The Council of Trent also declared it a dogma of faith that when either consecrated species is divided the whole Christ is present in each part of the species. Whether one receives under both forms or only one, whether one receives a large host or a particle of host; whether one drinks a large portion or small, Christ Jesus is whole and entire.

All the sacraments give grace if they are received with worthy dispositions of heart. The Holy Eucharist, however, is primary for growth in the divine life. All grace and truth come by Jesus Christ (John 1:17) and they are, therefore, poured into the soul most abundantly when our Lord and Savior is received with purity and holiness, that is, in the state of sanctifying grace.

"I tell you most solemnly, if you do not eat the flesh of the Son of Man and drink his blood, you will not have life in you. Anyone who does eat my flesh and drink my blood has eternal life, and I shall raise him up on the last day. For my flesh is real food and my blood is real drink. He who eats my flesh and drinks my blood lives in me and I live in him. As I, who am sent by the living Father, myself draw life from the Father, so whoever eats me will draw life from me. This is the bread come down from heaven; not like the bread our ancestors ate: they are dead, but anyone who eats this bread will live for ever" (John 6:53-58).

The entire sixth chapter of St. John's Gospel is excellent to read meditatively. Jesus was the perfect teacher. He said, "I am the bread of life." (John 6:35). When our divine Lord tells us that He will give us His body to eat and His blood to drink, murmuring breaks out among the Jews who argue with one another, saying, "How can this man give us his flesh to eat?" (John 6:53). Finally, they begin to walk away when Jesus continues His discourse on the Holy Eucharist. Jesus becomes all the more emphatic, the more they murmur. He had begun by feeding five thousand with five loaves and had 12 baskets left over. Jesus next walked on water, indicating His power over the elements of the earth. At the marriage feast at Cana He had changed six stone water jars of water into the choicest wine (John 2:1-12). If Jesus can change wine into water "and his disciples believed in him" they should have faith in Him that He can change wine into His precious blood and bread into His sacred body.

Jesus, being the perfect teacher, had the ability to know what was in the heart of man, when he saw every last one of that crowd described in John 6 depart with many of His disciples saying, "This is intolerable language. How could anyone accept it?" (John 6:60). If they had misunderstood Jesus and He had meant only that He would give them bread and wine which would be merely symbolic of His body and blood, Jesus would have clarified himself, calling them back, "You have misunderstood me. . . ." On the contrary, Jesus meant exactly what He said and He said it with repetition. He let them depart.

Finally, Jesus stands there with the Twelve, the crowd having departed. "Do you also wish to go away?" Simon Peter, destined to be the first pope, answered, "Lord, who shall we go to? You have the message of eternal life, and we believe; we know that you are the Holy One of God" (John 6:67-69). Even then this sixth chapter of John concludes by telling us that even one of the Twelve, Judas Iscariot, was a devil.

Faith in the Real Presence of Jesus Christ in the Holy Eucharist was the moment of truth for the disciples of Jesus and for that vast crowd following Him until then. It is the moment of truth for us as well. At every Mass the priest proclaims the Eucharist a "Mystery of Faith" immediately after the twofold consecration. When Peter chose to stay with the Lord his profession of faith was not a proclamation that he understood the mystery, but that he believed it, that he had faith in the Christ as the Son of God. It was saying in effect: "I don't understand by human reason, but if you say it Lord, I believe it because you are the Christ, the Son of the living God.

The Holy Eucharist is the fountain of all graces. It contains the fountain itself of heavenly gifts and graces. It contains Jesus Christ, the author of all the sacraments. The Catechism of the Council of Trent, comparing the Holy Eucharist to a fountain, considered the other sacraments as rivulets because the Eucharist, which contains the author of grace, contains the source of whatever goodness and perfection the other sacraments possess.

The worthy reception of our divine Lord in Holy Communion increases the life of grace in the soul. Just as natural food can be of no value to a dead body, so Holy Communion can be of no avail to a soul which does not live by the Spirit. This sacrament, instituted under the form of bread and wine, signifies that the object of its institution is not to recall the soul to divine life, but to preserve and increase the soul's sharing in the life of God. The greater the degree of sanctifying grace in one's soul at the moment of death, the higher and happier place in heaven one will have for all eternity.

For those who receive our loving Lord in the state of grace with fitting disposition of heart, this reception invigorates and delights the soul and can be compared to the manna "containing every delight, satisfying every taste" (Wisdom 16:20). Holy Communion can remit venial sins. St. Ambrose said: "That daily bread is taken as a remedy for daily infirmity" (*De Sacramentis*, Book IV, Chapter 6). "But," says the Catechism of Trent, "these things are to be understood of those sins for which no actual affection is retained."

The Holy Eucharist strengthens one against temptation. There is power in the sacred mysteries, which contain Jesus Christ himself, so as to preserve us pure and unsullied from sin and strengthen us to overcome temptations. The fervent and frequent reception of our divine Lord in Holy Communion weakens the hold of concupiscence on a person. Inflaming the soul with the fire of divine charity, it consequently extinguishes the strength of concupiscence.

The reception of the Lord's Body, Blood, Soul and Divinity brings with it the promise of eternal glory. St. Thomas Aquinas taught that those who frequently receive our divine Lord in Holy Communion will wear a special

212

badge of eternal glory. This badge will be for both the body and soul. "Anyone who does eat my flesh and drink my blood has eternal life, and I shall raise him up on the last day" (John 6:54). Those who receive the grace of this sacrament enjoy great peace and tranquility of conscience on earth and are assured of a glorious resurrection which may be compared to Elijah, who, from the strength of the bread baked on the hearth, walked to Mount Horeb, the mount of God. So too, invigorated by the strengthening power of Holy Communion, men in every age can ascend to unfading glory and bliss in heaven.

It is possible to receive special spiritual fruits for the soul by desiring strongly with lively faith and charity to receive our Lord sacramentally, even when, because of circumstances, one is not able. If the entire fruits of a sacramental Holy Communion are not possible, one can receive at least great fruits from such a SPIRITUAL COMMUNION of desire.

The first preparation for Holy Communion must be to distinguish the eucharistic bread from ordinary bread and recognize in faith that this is truly the body and blood of the Lord, of Him whom the angels adore in heaven. Another necessary preparation is to examine whether we are at peace with and love our neighbor. "So then, if you are bringing your offering to the altar and there remember that your brother has something against you, leave your offering there before the altar, go and be reconciled with your brother first, and then come back and present your offering" (Matthew 5:23-24). As indicated earlier in this chapter, we must also carefully examine our conscience to see if it is free of mortal sin. If it is not, before Holy Communion it must be blotted out, forgiven by God through contrition and sacramental confession. The Council of Trent defined that no one conscious of mortal sin and having an opportunity of going to confession, however contrite he may deem himself, is to approach the Holy Eucharist until he has been purified by sacramental confession (Session 13, Chapter 7, Canon 2). The one receiving must have the right intention of close union with Jesus Christ and of growth in divine life.

The present regulation for fasting before Holy Communion requires one hour's abstinence from solid food and drink before the actual reception of the sacrament. Medicine, when necessary, may always be taken.

The Church desires frequent reception of Holy Communion, even daily when possible. The Second Vatican Council stated: "It is clear that the frequent or daily reception of the Blessed Eucharist increases union with Christ, nourishes the spiritual life more abundantly, strengthens the soul in virtue and gives the communicant a stronger pledge of eternal happiness. . . ."

"In accordance with the custom of the Church, communion may be received by the faithful either kneeling or standing. One or the other way is to be chosen, according to the decision of the episcopal conference, bearing in mind all the circumstances, above all the number of the faithful and the arrangement of the churches. The faithful should willingly adopt the method indicated by their pastors, so that communion may truly be a sign of the brotherly union of all those who share in the same table of the Lord.

"When the faithful communicate kneeling, no other sign of reverence towards the Blessed Sacrament is required, since kneeling is itself a sign of adoration.

"When they receive communion standing, it is strongly recommended that, coming up in procession, they should make a sign of reverence before receiving the Blessed Sacrament.[2] This should be done at the right time and place, so that the order of people going to and from Communion should not be disrupted" (*Eucharisticum Mysterium*, an Instruction issued by the Sacred Congregation of Rites, May 25, 1967).

The bread used for the Holy Eucharist must be made from wheat in accordance with the tradition of the entire Church. It must be unleavened in accord with the tradition of the Latin Church. Water is to be used with the wheaten flour in preparation of the bread. It is forbidden to add other ingredients, and if a large amount of any other ingredient is added, the result is invalidating matter for the consecration to take effect.

After one has received our Lord in Holy Communion the Real Presence remains from 15 to 30 minutes or until the body has digested the species. Pope Pius XII said that even after the Mass has ended we ought not interrupt the hymn of divine praise within us but prolong our thanksgiving. Of private prayer after Communion, the Sacred Congregation of Rites under Pope Paul VI in the 1967 instruction *Eucharisticum Mysterium* wrote as follows:

"On those who receive the Body and Blood of Christ, the gift of the Spirit is poured out abundantly like living water (see John 7:37-39), provided that this Body and Blood have been received sacramentally and spiritually, namely, by that faith which operates through charity.

"But union with Christ, to which the sacrament itself is directed, is not to be limited to the duration of the celebration of the Eucharist; it is to be prolonged into the entire Christian life, in such a way that the Christian faithful, contemplating unceasingly the gift they have received, may make their life a continual thanksgiving under the guidance of the Holy Spirit and may produce fruits of greater charity.

---

[2]In some parishes a genuflection is the custom. Each one genuflects when the person in front of him is receiving so as to cause no disruption. Eastern Rite Catholics have the custom of a profound bow and Sign of the Cross.

"In order to remain easily in this thanksgiving which is offered to God in an eminent way in the Mass, those who have been nourished by holy communion should be encouraged to remain for a while in prayer."

Not everyone who receives our divine Lord in Holy Communion receives the same measure of grace. The divine life of God is poured more abundantly into the soul with greater faith and charity. Jesus gives grace to the soul according to the dispositions of heart with which one receives. As long as Jesus is sacramentally present in the one who has communicated, Jesus is pouring His saving graces, the merits of His redemption into that soul. Therefore, one ought not become distracted after Holy Communion but should make a fervent thanksgiving.

DISCUSSION QUESTIONS

1. What are the three chief ways that Jesus Christ is present in the Church today?

The three chief ways that Jesus Christ is present in the Church today are: 1. The Most Blessed Sacrament. 2. The Word of God or the Scriptures when read in Church. 3. The Church or People of God, which makes up the Mystical Body of Christ.

2. Which is the preeminent manner of Christ's presence in the Church?

The preeminent presence of Jesus Christ is in the Sacrament of the Holy Eucharist, where He is really and substantially present with His Body, Blood, Soul and Divinity.

3. What is meant by Real Presence?

Real Presence means the real, living, substantial presence of the Body, Blood, Soul and Divinity of our Lord and Savior, Jesus Christ.

4. What is meant by the "species" of the Holy Eucharist?

"Species" is a word used to describe the accidents or appearances which the senses of the body can perceive after the consecration of the bread into the Body of Jesus and the wine into the Blood of Jesus. The color, shape, size, taste, roughness, smoothness, etc., all these accidents of bread and wine remain after the consecration.

5. Explain: The sacrament continues in the Holy Eucharist so long as the consecrated species continues. In the other sacraments the sacrament is completed after their administration.

The Sacrament of Holy Eucharist differs from all the other sacraments in that only this sacrament continues permanently, that is, as long as the accidents of bread and wine remain. All the other sacraments are completed once they have been administered to someone. Christ Jesus acts in all seven sacraments. Only in the Holy Eucharist does His real presence continue.

6. Name some of the Church Fathers of the early centuries who wrote on the Holy Eucharist. What essentially, in substance, did they write?

Early Church Fathers who wrote on the Holy Eucharist were St. Ambrose, St. John Chrysostom, St. Augustine, St. Justin, St. Irenaeus, St. Cyril, St. Denis, St. Hilary, St. Jerome, St. John Damascene and many others. In substance all spoke of the Real Presence of the Body, Blood, Soul and Divinity of Jesus Christ under the appearances of consecrated bread and wine.

7. Respond to this statement: "Jesus is present in the Holy Eucharist only during the ceremonies of the Mass and while someone is present before the Blessed Sacrament."

It is not true to say that the Real Presence of Jesus is reserved to the time of the eucharistic ceremonies or when one is present before the Blessed Sacrament. The presence of our divine Lord is continuous. For that reason the sanctuary lamp must continuously burn before the Most Blessed Sacrament.

8. Explain what is meant by the adoration of the Blessed Sacrament called "latria."

The special adoration called "latria" which is due God alone is given to the Most Blessed Sacrament because it contains the Real Presence of the God-Man, Jesus Christ.

9. Why is the Most Blessed Sacrament reserved in the tabernacle?

The Most Blessed Sacrament is reserved in the tabernacle for the purpose of adoration by the faithful and so that the Holy Eucharist is available to be taken to the sick and those in danger of death.

10. Explain. The whole Christ is present under either species by virtue of concomitance.

The Church speaks of the Real Presence of Jesus Christ, whole and entire, under either of the consecrated species **by virtue of concomitance**, not simply by virtue of the consecration. One must be careful in interpreting what is meant here. There is a twofold or separate consecration of the bread and wine. The priest consecrates the bread only into the Body of Jesus. However, where part of Jesus is, the whole Jesus is. The power of the consecration brings the Body of Jesus, but by necessity, or concomitance, since Jesus cannot be divided, there also comes His blood, His soul, His divinity, the whole and entire Jesus Christ. The same happens with the consecration of the wine. If the blood of Jesus substantially replaces the substance of wine, Christ Jesus, whole and entire is made present.

11. What happens to the sacrament when the species are divided?

Jesus Christ, whole and entire, is present in each part, however big or small, of the species of consecrated bread and wine.

12. Which of the seven sacraments is most important to our Catholic faith regarding the Real Presence?

The Holy Eucharist is the most important for growth in divine life, called sanctifying grace.

13. Why is the sixth chapter of St. John's Gospel important to our Catholic faith regarding the Real Presence?

The sixth chapter of St. John's Gospel deals with the promise of the Holy Eucharist. First it shows Christ's power over natural elements. He multiplies natural bread, just as His sacred Body will not diminish through the centuries with millions eating Him. He walks on water. So, too, Jesus has power over bread and wine to change them into His Body and Blood. Jesus is emphatic in John 6 that He will not give natural bread as God did for Moses in the desert but that He himself is the Bread of life, come down from heaven. When the crowd finds His promise to be too much and it breaks out in murmuring and walks away, Jesus, rather than weakening His promise, intensifies the meaning of His words. He will really give us himself to eat and drink. In fact, says Jesus, we cannot be saved unless we eat His Body and drink His Blood. Holy Communion is necessary for eternal life, as emphasized in John 6.

14. Why is the Holy Eucharist called "the fountain of all graces"?

The Holy Eucharist is called "the fountain of all graces" because it contains the very author of all grace, Jesus Christ himself. Jesus Christ is the source of whatever goodness and perfection the other sacraments possess. Compared to the Holy Eucharist, the other sacraments are, as it were, rivulets.

15. What effects does the reception of Holy Communion have on a person?

The effects of the reception of our divine Lord in Holy Communion:

1. Sanctifying Grace, the sharing in God's life, is increased, thus permitting a higher place in heaven.

2. It remits venial sins when one is not attached to them.

3. It weakens the hold of concupiscence on a person.

4. It contains the pledge of eternal glory for both body and soul.

5. It brings spiritual delight to the soul.

16. When can Holy Communion remit venial sin?

Holy Communion can take away venial sin only when one has no attachment or actual affection for the sin.

17. Explain what is meant by "Spiritual Communion."

"Spiritual Communion" refers to the **desire** to receive our Lord in the Sacrament of the Holy Eucharist when one is not able to receive sacramentally. Jesus Christ can grant special graces to a soul for desiring to receive Him.

18. What preparations are necessary for a good Communion?

Preparations necessary for a good Holy Communion are:

1. Making the distinction that the eucharistic bread is not ordinary bread but the true Body, Blood, Soul and Divinity of our Lord and Savior, Jesus Christ, true God and true Man.

2. Examining our conscience to see that we are at peace and love with all our neighbors.

3. Examining our conscience to make certain we are free of every mortal sin.

4. Having the right intention of union with Jesus Christ and growth in grace.

5. Fasting for one hour before receiving Communion.

19. What does the Church request of a person after receiving our Lord in Holy Communion?

After we have received our divine Lord in Holy Communion, the Church desires that we spend some time in private prayer, prolonging our thanksgiving in union with Jesus Christ, who is sacramentally present within us for at least 15 minutes and up to 30 minutes. Those who make a more fervant Communion please God more greatly and receive a greater abundance of grace from the sacrament.

CHAPTER 17

The Holy Eucharist As Sacrifice

As the Second Person of the Most Blessed Trinity, Jesus Christ always existed. His divine person is eternal. As man, the body and soul of Jesus was created in time, being hypostatically joined to His eternal person. What then was the first thought that passed through the human intellect and will of Jesus Christ, the God-Man, when the human nature of Jesus Christ was created? According to an encyclical of Pope Pius XII, the soul of Jesus Christ, as mentioned in an earlier chapter, beheld the beatific vision from the moment of His conception in the Virgin Mother Mary.

Having always the use of the higher faculties of the soul, the intellect and will, there was a first act of intellect and will in the created human soul of Jesus Christ. The 10th chapter of Hebrews gives us the answer after telling us how the Old Law with its sacrifices was powerless to do what Jesus Christ would accomplish in His perfect sacrifice.

"Bulls' blood and goats' blood are useless for taking away sins, and this is what he said, on coming into the world: *'You who wanted no sacrifice or oblation, prepared a body for me. You took no pleasure in holocausts or sacrifices for sin; then I said, just as I was commanded in the scroll of the book, 'God, here I am! I am coming to obey your will.'*

"Notice that he says first: *You did not want* what the Law lays down as the things to be offered, that is: *the sacrifices, the oblations, the holocausts and the sacrifices for sin*, and *you took no pleasure in them*; and then he says: *Here I am! I am coming to obey your will*. He is abolishing the first sort to replace it with the second. And this *will* was for us to be made holy by the *offering* of his body made once and for all by Jesus Christ" (Hebrews 10:4-10).

That act of intellect and will, formed at His coming into the world, Jesus Christ carried out physically on the Cross on the first Good Friday.

Jesus Christ offered the one perfect sacrifice of infinite value to make satisfaction to God the Father for the sins of the entire world for all time. All through His life, then, Jesus was always marching, as it were, toward Calvary. The shadow of the Cross looms up from the time of His infancy. His sacrifice is consummated on Calvary when He says, " 'It is accomplished'; and bowing his head he gave up his spirit" (John 19:30).

The Sacrifice of the Cross, offered physically once on the Cross, is perpetuated at every Holy Sacrifice of the Mass. The Council of Trent declared as a dogma of faith: In the Sacrifice of the Mass, Christ's Sacrifice on the Cross is made present, its memory is celebrated, and its saving power is applied. Also, in the Sacrifice of the Mass and in the Sacrifice of the Cross, the sacrificial victim and the primary sacrificing priest are the same; only the nature and the mode of offering are different.

Expressed in simple terms, to be present at the Sacrifice of the Mass is to be present at the Sacrifice of the Cross first offered by Jesus Christ the High Priest on Mount Calvary almost 2,000 years ago. The sacrifice offered in the Mass today is the same sacrifice as that offered on the Cross. On Mount Calvary Jesus Christ made the offering in a physical manner, actually shedding His precious blood in a bloody manner and dying a physical death with the separation of His soul from His body.

Sacred Scripture is clear that the physical death of Jesus Christ was offered once and for all and cannot be repeated. "Christ, as we know, having been raised from the dead will never die again. Death has no power over him any more. When he died, he died once for all to sin, so his life now is life with God; and in that way, you too must consider yourselves to be dead to sin but alive for God in Christ Jesus" (Romans 6:9-11).

God is not bound down by space or time. Jesus Christ, the God-Man, can offer the selfsame sacrifice to God the Father in a mystical manner. He does this through the Sacrament of the Holy Eucharist. As will be explained in this chapter, Jesus offers today through the Mass the selfsame Sacrifice of the Cross without repeating the *physical* death in a bloody historical manner. But the same sacrifice is offered. One who was present at the foot of the Cross on Mount Calvary on that first Good Friday afternoon was no more present to the Sacrifice of the Cross than a person is today who is present at the Sacrifice of the Mass. Only the manner of offering is different. It was once offered physically. Today it is offered sacramentally.

"At the Last Supper, on the night he was betrayed, our Savior instituted the eucharistic sacrifice of his Body and Blood. This he did in order to perpetuate the sacrifice of the Cross throughout the ages until he should come again, and so to entrust to his beloved Spouse, the Church, a memorial of his death and resurrection: a sacrament of love, a sign of unity, a bond of charity, a paschal banquet in which Christ is consumed, the mind is filled with grace, and a pledge of future glory is given to us.

"The Church, therefore, earnestly desires that Christ's faithful, when present at this mystery of faith, should not be there as strangers or silent spectators. On the contrary, through a good understanding of the rites and prayers they should take part in the sacred action, conscious of what they are doing, with devotion and full collaboration. They should be instructed by God's Word, and be nourished at the table of the Lord's Body. They should give thanks to God. Offering the Immaculate Victim, not only through the hands of the priest but also together with him, they should learn to offer themselves. Through Christ, the Mediator, they should be drawn day by day into ever more perfect union with God and each other, so that finally God may be all in all" (Vatican II, *Constitution on the Sacred Liturgy*, 47-48).

"This sacrifice is not merely a rite commemorating a past sacrifice. For in it Christ by the ministry of the priests perpetuates the Sacrifice of the Cross in an unbloody manner through the course of the centuries. In it too he nourishes the faithful with himself, the Bread of Life, in order that, filled with love of God and neighbor, they may become more and more a people acceptable to God" (*General Catechetical Directory*, 58).

Sacrifice is the highest form of adoration, in which a duly authorized priest, in the name of the people, offers a victim in acknowledgment of God's supreme dominion and of total human dependence on God. When there is sacrifice the victim is at least partially removed from human use, more or less destroyed in submission to the divine majesty. It is not merely an oblation which offers something to God. A sacrifice immolates or gives up what is offered to God. The gift or victim is something precious which is entirely surrendered.

In the Old Testament, before the coming of Jesus Christ, sacrifice involved offering God some of the creatures which were precious to man. This was done to acknowledge God's sovereignty and man's dependence.

Under the Old Law which described the kind of sacrifices to be offered, there were two kinds required of man: bloody and unbloody. There were four kinds of bloody sacrifices: 1. The whole-burnt offering or holocaust. The victim, often an animal, was entirely consumed by fire, and this was done twice daily as a perpetual sacrifice. 2. Sin offering, which was to expiate misdeeds committed through ignorance or inadvertence; the victim was determined by the dignity of the person offended. 3. Guilt offering was required for sins demanding restitution. 4. Peace offerings were offered in thanksgiving or to fulfill a vow or were simply voluntary; in this kind of sacrifice part of what was offered was returned to the offerer to be eaten in a sacrificial meal.

Unbloody sacrifices, which were really oblations, were offerings of articles of solid or liquid food and also incense. These food offerings were made at every holocaust and peace offering but never at sacrifices for sin or guilt, except at the cleansing of a leper.

The idea of sacrifice in worship, then, is part of divine revelation extending from the early days of recorded divine revelation until the coming of Jesus Christ. Already in the first book of the Bible, Genesis 14:18-20, we read of sacrifice as Abraham returned from battle after rescuing Lot. Melchizedek greeted him and gave him a blessing in honor of his victory. Abraham in return offered him tithes because of his priesthood. Melchizedek is a priest who appears and disappears in Scripture with no genealogy offered. In the New Testament, the Epistle to the Hebrews, therefore, associates Christ's eternal priesthood with that of Melchizedek, making this early Old Testament priest, who offered bread and wine in sacrifice on that occasion, a foreshadowing of the eternal priesthood of Jesus Christ, who perpetuates His Sacrifice in the Mass today. The early Church Fathers saw in the sacrifice of Melchizedek the archetype of the eucharistic sacrifice. St. Augustine says: "The sacrifice appeared for the first time there which is now offered to God by Christians throughout the whole world."

While Jesus Christ allowed the Mosaic sacrifice in His day, He predicted the end of the temple and its worship (Mark 13:2; John 4:20-23). The Old Testament sacrifices would pass away and be replaced with the infinitely perfect sacrifice of Christ on the Cross, to be perpetuated in the Sacrifice of the Mass where bread and wine would be used. At the Last Supper Jesus instituted the Holy Eucharist, saying: "This is my body which will be given up for you; do this as a memorial of me. . . . This cup is the new covenant in my blood which will be poured out for you" (Luke 22:19-20).

The Apostle Paul throughout his writings identifies Jesus Christ as the Sacrificial Victim (1 Corinthians 5:7; Ephesians 5:2). This sacrificial victimhood is confirmed by the Catholic Epistles (1 Peter 1:19; 1 John 2:2). There is assumed the eternal nature of Christ's sacrifice (Revelation 13:8). The entire letter to the Hebrews is dedicated to the high priesthood of Christ, who by His perfect obedience has "offered one single sacrifice for sins, and then taken His place forever *at the right hand of God*" (Hebrews 10:12-13). Jesus is the eternal high priest, interceding now with His heavenly Father for sinful humanity, His brothers and sisters.

The Prophet Malachi (Malachi 1:10-11) speaks for God to the Jewish priests: "I am not pleased with you, says Yahweh Sabaoth; from your hands I find no offerings acceptable. But from farthest east to farthest west my name is honored among the nations and everywhere a sacrifice of incense is offered to my name, and a pure offering too, since my name is honored among the nations, says Yahweh Sabaoth."

Today, in the Roman Catholic Church, there is never a moment but that prophecy is fulfilled. At every moment of the day and night, somewhere throughout the world, in each of every 24 hours of every day, someplace the Sacrifice of the Mass is being offered perpetuating the Sacrifice of the Cross of Christ. Through the Prophet Malachi[1] God proclaimed the abolition of the Jewish cult of sacrifice and foretold a new, perfect sacrifice. The Sacrifice of the Cross in a bloody manner, at a historical day and definite location, cannot be meant, as this was offered in one place and time only. The prophecy is fulfilled in the Holy Sacrifice of the Mass, offered universally, perpetuating the Sacrifice of the Cross.

The sacrificial nature of the Holy Eucharist is seen in the fact that Jesus Christ made His body and His blood present under separate forms. The twofold[2] consecration, that is, separate consecration of body and separate consecration of blood, represent the real separation of the Body and Blood of Christ physically in the Sacrifice of the Cross. Sacramentally the separation in the twofold consecration perpetuates the Sacrifice of the Cross. The priest may never consecrate only one, the bread or wine; he must always consecrate both. This is because the nature of the Holy Eucharist must be both Sacrifice and Sacrament.

The very words that Jesus Christ used in instituting the Holy Eucharist reveal its sacrificial character. "This is my body which shall be given up for you"; "This is my blood, which shall be shed for you." These are biblical sacrificial expressions, "to give up the body" and "to shed blood." Furthermore, Christ makes clear that His Blood is the Blood of the Covenant. The Old Covenant of God with Israel concluded by proferring of bloody sacrifice (Exodus 24:8): "This . . . is the blood of the covenant which Yahweh has made with you . . ." The blood of the covenant is synonymous with saying the blood of sacrifice.

The original Greek words used in Luke, Matthew, Mark, indicate the *present tense* of the offering of Christ's blood in sacrifice. Biblical scholars assert this is true especially in Luke 22:20, where the pouring out of the chalice is asserted. Reference is thereby made to the present-day eu-

---

[1]Oldest tradition has referred the Prophecy of Malachi to the Holy Eucharist: Didache, 143; St. Justin, Dialogues, 41; St. Irenaeus, Adversus haereses, IV, 17, 5; St. Augustine, Tractatus adversus Judaeos, 9, 13).

[2]See Chapter 16 where it is explained that in *virtue of concomitance* the whole Christ is present under either of the consecrated forms, although the force of the words of consecration brings only the Body or the Blood of Jesus Christ, thus effecting the sacrifice.

charistic celebration. There is also the mandate: "Do this as a memorial of me" (Luke 22:19; see 1 Corinthians 11:24). The context is that the eucharistic sacrifice is to be a permanent institution of the New Testament.

When asked, "Where does it say in the Bible that the Mass is the Sacrifice of the Cross perpetuated?" we must say that from the beginning to the end of Sacred Scripture the message is there, first foreshadowed, then fulfilled. In the Old Testament, that is, under the Old Covenant, as shown above, there were bloody and unbloody sacrifices. The Sacrifice of the Mass is the unbloody representation of Christ's sacrifice of the Cross, marking the New Covenant Sacrifice, in contrast to the bloody sacrifices of animals in the Old Covenant. But it is a true sacrifice, only in an unbloody manner. The actual Body and Blood of Jesus Christ, the Perfect Priest and Victim, are made present and are offered to God the Father.

The Council of Trent said that Christ left a visible Sacrifice to His Church "in which that bloody sacrifice which was once offered on the Cross should be made present, its memory preserved to the end of the world, and its salvation-bringing power applied to the forgiveness of the sins which are daily committed by us" (*Denzinger* 938).

The Sacrifice of the Mass is a representation, that is, a making-present, as well as a memorial and an application of the saving graces of the Cross. The sacrificial Body and the sacrificial Blood of Christ are made present under the separate species so as to perpetuate Calvary's sacrifice. It is not a mere commemorative celebration but a true and proper sacrifice. The fruits of the Sacrifice of the Cross are applied to mankind. The Sacrifice of the Mass then draws its entire power from the Sacrifice of the Cross.

The Council of Trent said that Christ left a visible sacrifice to his Mass is not merely a sacrifice of praise and thanksgiving, but also a sacrifice of expiation and impetration. Expiation means atonement for wrongdoing; the making of satisfaction or reparation to God who has been offended by mankind's sins. Impetration refers to entreating or petitioning our God. Thus the Mass has all the qualities of prayer perfectly fulfilled: thanksgiving (the word Eucharist itself means "Thanksgiving"); adoration, petition and reparation. The adoration value is infinite because the chief priest is Jesus Christ himself offering himself as victim in love and reparation to His heavenly Father.

The intrinsic value of the Sacrifice of the Mass is infinite, because of the infinite dignity of the sacrificial gift and the primary sacrificial priest. The praise and thanksgiving value of the Sacrifice of the Mass is infinite as to its external value, that is, in its actual operation, since the adoration and thanksgiving are directed by Jesus Christ immediately to God who is the Infinite Being. As a propitiatory (atoning) and impetratory sacrifice, the Sacrifice of the Mass has a finite external value, since the operations of propitiation and petition refer to human beings who can only act and receive in a finite manner. This is why the Church offers the Sacrifice of the Mass repeatedly for the same intention. This is why devout Catholics request Masses to be offered to their intentions, making some sacrifice themselves in doing so.

It must be remembered that the Mass as sacrifice is directed or offered to God alone, as it is of infinite value. When offered in commemoration or honor of the Blessed Virgin Mary, the angels and/or saints, the purpose is to thank God for the grace and glory conferred on them and to appeal for their intercession.

In the strict sense there are no "private Masses." The Sacrifice of the Mass is always the self-sacrifice of Jesus Christ, the primary sacrificing priest. The Mass is also the Sacrifice of the Church to which Jesus Christ transmitted the Holy Eucharist as sacrifice and as sacrament. While only the ordained priest has the power to consecrate the bread and wine, yet all the baptized faithful offer the Victim to the Father, using the power of the indelible character received in Baptism.

"Initiated into the Christian mystery by Baptism and Confirmation (Chrismation), Christians are fully joined to the Body of Christ in the Eucharist. The Eucharist is the center and heart of Christian life for both the universal and local Church and for each Christian. All that belongs to Christian life leads to the eucharistic celebration or flows from it.

"It is a traditional theme of both the Eastern and Western Churches that Eucharist forms Church. Eucharist and Church are the basic realities, bearing the same names: Communion and Body of Christ. The Eucharist increases charity within the visible community. The other mysteries (sacraments) dispose people to participate fruitfully in the central mystery of the Eucharist. The Eucharist is also seen as the chief source of divinization and maintains the pledge of immortality.

"The Eucharist is a memorial of the Lord's passion, death and resurrection. This holy sacrifice is both a commemoration of a past event and a celebration of it here and now. Through, with, and in the Church, Christ's sacrifice on the Cross and the victory of His resurrection become present in every celebration.

"The eucharistic celebration is a holy meal which recalls the Last Supper, reminds us of our unity with one another in Christ, and anticipates the banquet of God's kingdom. In the Eucharist, Christ the Lord nourishes Christians, not only with His word but especially with His body and blood, effecting a transformation which impels them toward greater love of God and neighbor.

" 'By means of the homily the mysteries of the faith and the guiding principles of the Christian life are expounded from the sacred text during the course of the liturgical year. The homily, therefore, is to be highly esteemed as part of the liturgy itself' (Vatican II, Liturgy, 52).

"The Eucharist is also a Sacrament of Reconciliation, completing and fulfilling the Sacraments of Initiation. In each Eucharist we reaffirm our conversion from sin, a conversion already real but not yet complete. The Eucharist proclaims and effects our reconciliation with the Father. 'Look with favor on your Church's offering, and see the Victim whose death has reconciled yourself' " (Eucharistic Prayer III) (*Sharing the Light of Faith*, 120, National Catechetical Directory).

The above quotation from the *National Catechetical Directory* summarizes the Catholic faith on the Holy Eucharist as both Sacrifice and Sacrament. As in the Old Covenant sacrificial meals worshippers sometimes ate of the victim offered, so too in the perfect fulfillment in the New Covenant. The eucharistic banquet is a sacrificial meal wherein the Victim, who is Jesus Christ, is offered by the Church in Christ's own name, and in the power of His priesthood to God the Father, is also received and eaten in return. A sacrificial gift is presented to God the Father, through, with and in Jesus Christ. God the Father says in effect, "Thank you. And now I want to give you a gift in return. I accept the gift of My Son, and as a return-gift I give you My Son in Holy Communion."

When, in the eternal counsels of the Most Blessed Trinity, God knew He would create man, God also knew that man would sin and what would be the solution for man's redemption. The Second Person of the Trinity would become man and redeem mankind by His sacrificial death on the Cross. Marvel of marvels, every Sacrifice of the Mass tunes in to Calvary on Good Friday afternoon of that first Holy Week. In man's time, the past is made present, the Sacrifice of the Cross is perpetuated.

The Apostle Paul, after relating the manner in which our Lord instituted the Holy Eucharist at the Last Supper, added: "Until the Lord comes, therefore, every time you eat this bread and drink this cup, you are proclaiming his death" (1 Corinthians 11:26).

We defined sacrifice as the highest form of adoration, in which a duly authorized priest in the name of the people offers a victim in acknowledgment of God's supreme dominion and of total human dependence on God. It is in the very nature of man, when he adores his Creator in the most perfect way he knows how, to do so by offering sacrifice. So much is this in the very heart and nature of man that primitive peoples, having lost direct divine revelation, have been known to offer even human sacrifices. At one time, before the conversion of Mexico, up to 20,000 human sacrifices were offered in that part of the world alone each year. With the conversion to Christianity the people discovered that the God-Man Jesus

Christ had sacrificed himself as a perfect sacrificial gift and this was perpetuated at every Holy Mass. No need, therefore, for any other sacrifice. The need of the human heart to offer sacrifice is fulfilled in the Eucharistic Sacrifice.

While God is infinitely adored in every Sacrifice of the Mass, since Jesus Christ is the primary sacrificing priest, and it is chiefly directed to the glory of God, there is also special fruit of the Mass which accrues to the benefit of those persons for whom the Mass is, in a special manner, offered, whether they be living or dead. In *general*, the fruits of the Mass always accrue to the benefit of the universal Church, the entire Mystical Body, independently of the intention of the celebrating priest. This includes the living faithful and the poor souls in Purgatory, since every Mass is a sacrifice for the Church. In *particular*, however, special fruit is directed to those for whom the Mass is applied by the intention of those offering. There is also *personal* Mass-fruit which accrues to the celebrating priest as the representative of the primary Sacrificing Priest, Jesus Christ, and also to the co-sacrificing faithful, those who directly participate at Mass with faith and love. Since the applied fruits of the Sacrifice of the Mass to individuals are not mechanical, as is the case with the other sacraments, the measure of spiritual fruits received will depend on the quality of the dispositions of each one's soul.

The individual who participates at Mass with greater faith, greater love, with dispositions of special holiness, will give greater external glory to God, and receive greater benefits for himself and those for whom he offers the Sacrifice of the Mass.

For a Catholic with faith and love, believing the Sacrifice of the Mass to be what it is in reality should be enough to motivate one to participate at least every Sunday but oftener if possible. For one attempting to walk in the footsteps of Jesus Christ, the first day of every week, commemorating the Resurrection, is a special day, the Lord's day. It is a special day set aside for worship of God. The Lord Jesus, in giving us the Eucharistic Sacrifice to strike anew, as it were, the New Covenant which He himself inaugurated and which contains the perpetual sacrifice of His eternal priesthood, commanded, "Do this as a memorial of me" (Luke 22:19; 1 Corinthians 11:24). This command of our Savior, together with the third commandment, "Remember to keep holy the sabbath day," and the positive precept of the Church, marks every Sunday as a day when Catholics are bound under pain of mortal sin to participate in Holy Mass. The obligation begins at the age of seven, and, besides all Sundays, the serious obligation of participation in Mass extends by Church law to special Holy Days of Obligation.

Non-Catholics taking Catholic instructions, with the exception of receiving Holy Communion, should participate in the Sacrifice of the Mass each Sunday and Holy Day so as to be gradually incorporated into Catholic practices which will soon be their serious obligation.

"Each Sunday should be kept as a day for special personal renewal, free from work and everyday business. It is both a privilege and a serious duty of the individual Catholic, as well as the Catholic faith community, to assemble on Sunday in order to recall the Lord Jesus and His acts, hear the Word of God, and offer the sacrifice of His body and blood in the eucharistic celebration. This is, in fact, a precept of the Church, following the commandment of God" (*Sharing the Light of Faith*, National Catechetical Directory, 105).

DISCUSSION QUESTIONS

1. What was the first act of the intellect and will of Christ's created soul?

The first act of the human soul of Jesus Christ on coming into the world was a recognition that God wanted no sacrifice or oblation, that God took no pleasure in holocausts or sacrifices for sin, that is to say these sacrifices and offerings of the Old Covenant were ineffective. At the same time the soul of Christ, His intellect and will, recognizing that God had prepared a human body for Him, willed to offer it in sacrifice for the redemption of mankind as the perfect sacrifice with power to redeem the world from its sins.

2. What aspect is the same, and which is different, regarding the Sacrifice of the Cross and the Sacrifice of the Mass today?

The Sacrifice of the Cross and the Sacrifice of the Mass are one and the same sacrifice. The difference is in the manner of offering. One is bloody, as it was offered physically on the Cross at a historical time. The other, the Mass, is unbloody, under the form of the sacrament. Under both manners, the priest is the same, namely Jesus Christ. The victim of the sacrifice is the same, namely, Jesus Christ.

3. If the Mass is the Sacrifice of the Cross perpetuated, does Jesus Christ die a physical death again in the Mass?

Jesus does not suffer physically in the Sacrifice of the Mass. He does not undergo a physical death. That was once for all time. But since Jesus is true God, true man, he is not bound to time and space and can perpetuate the same sacrifice.

4. How do the faithful at Mass offer themselves with Jesus Christ, the victim?

The baptized faithful are members of the Mystical Body of Christ, the Church. In, with and through Jesus Christ the High Priest, who acts in the Mass through the instrumentality of the ordained priest at the altar, to consecrate and produce the victim of the sacrifice, all the baptized faithful in offering Jesus Christ the Head of the Church, offer themselves, too, since they are members of the head. The sacrifice of themselves is pleasing only because they are identified with Jesus Christ their head.

228

5. What kind of sacrifices were offered under the Old Covenant before Jesus Christ came?

Under the Old Covenant, before the coming of Jesus Christ who established the New Covenant, there were two general kinds of sacrifices offered by man: bloody and unbloody. There were four kinds of bloody sacrifices. The unbloody sacrifices were offerings of articles of solid or liquid food and also incense. The bloody sacrifices for various purposes consisted in the offering of animals in sacrifice. These sacrifices prefigured the Sacrifice of Christ on the Cross to come, as the Old Covenant sacrifices were powerless to take away sin. They were merely symbolic. In the Sacrifice of the Mass today, what is symbolized, Christ's Sacrifice, is actually perpetuated, made present.

6. How was the Sacrifice of Melchizedek a foreshadowing of the Sacrifice of the Last Supper and the Mass today?

Melchizedek met Abraham returning home victorious from battle. Melchizedek is a type of Jesus Christ, the eternal High Priest, because he appears mysteriously without genealogy and disappears without being heard from again. There is the application made in the New Testament comparing him in type to Jesus Christ. Melchizedek offered bread and wine in sacrifice. These are the materials used at the Last Supper and in the Mass today to perpetuate the Sacrifice of the Cross.

7. When does God, as mentioned in the Bible, begin to prepare His people for the Sacrifice of the New Covenant as seen in Christ's death on the Cross and the Mass today?

God himself, in the creation of man, obviously placed in man's heart the need for sacrifice in the worship of God. We see this very early in the Bible with the sacrifices of Cain and Abel. We see it with Abraham, called to sacrifice Isaac, his only son. We see it in the plagues in Egypt when Moses begs the Pharaoh, in the name of God, to "let my people go." Finally, after the Passover when the Israelites are saved by the blood of the sacrificed lamb, we see the beginning of a special annual paschal feast (Exodus 12). Christ as the Messiah "has been sacrificed" (1 Corinthians 5:7) and, according to John 1:29, became for those who believe in Him "the lamb of God that takes away the sin of the world." We can see throughout all the pages of the Old Testament, beginning with the first pages, the concept of sacrifice in the worship of God.

8. To what subject is the Epistle to the Hebrews especially dedicated?

The entire Epistle to the Hebrews is dedicated to the high priesthood of Jesus Christ, who offered himself in sacrifice for the remission of sins and continues His intercession for us as High Priest forever at the right hand of God.

9. What did the Prophet Malachi prophesy about the New Covenant under which we live today?

The Prophet Malachi (Malachi 1:10ff.) prophesied that in time to come, when the New Covenant replaced the Old Covenant, there would be a perpetual sacrifice offered around the clock. This is true today. At every hour of every day and night, some place in the world, a Catholic priest is offering the Sacrifice of the Mass in the name of Jesus Christ and the Church.

10. The perpetual sacrifice foreseen by Malachi for the New Covenant cannot re-

fer simply to the sacrifice of Christ's death on the Cross. Explain.

The prophesy of Malachi cannot refer simply to the sacrificial death of Jesus Christ on the Cross, for that was once in a physical manner. What the prophet foresaw was the perpetuation of Jesus' Sacrifice of the Cross in the Sacrifice of the Mass.

11. Why may the Catholic priest never consecrate unless there be a twofold consecration?

The Catholic priest must always consecrate both the bread and the wine to effect the Sacrifice of the Cross perpetuated as the Holy Eucharist because it is both sacrifice and sacrament and the Sacrament of the Lord's Body and Blood is never to be separated from Christ's sacrifice. The Last Supper was already a sacrifice. If there were only one consecration, no true sacrifice of the New Covenant would be perpetuated.

12. How do the very words of Jesus Christ, spoken in His act of consecrating at the institution of the Holy Eucharist, reveal the sacrificial character of the Eucharist?

The very words which Jesus Christ used in instituting the Holy Eucharist reveal its sacrificial nature. "This is my body which shall be given up for you. . . . This is by blood, which shall be shed for you." "To give up body" and "to shed blood" are sacrificial expressions familiar to biblical language. The people of the Old Covenant were familiar with sacrifices in worship. Jesus is saying that His own body and blood would be sacrificed under the New Covenant and this was to be perpetuated as He commanded the apostles to "do this as a memorial of me" (Luke 22:19).

13. Why does the Church teach that the Sacrifice of the Mass is more than a mere memorial of the Sacrifice of the Cross?

The Sacrifice of the Mass is more than a mere memorial of the sacrifice of the death of Jesus Christ on the Cross because it contains the reality of the sacrifice. The sacrifice of Jesus is perpetuated, not simply remembered. There is a making-present of the sacrifice.

14. To whom does the Church offer the Sacrifice of the Mass?

The Sacrifice of the Mass is of infinite value and is directed only to God. It is offered to God the Father in, with and through Jesus Christ in the unity of the Holy Spirit.

15. Why, in the strict sense, is there no such thing as "private Masses"?

There is no such thing as "private Masses" because every Sacrifice of the Mass is the Sacrifice of the Church offered by the primary sacrificing Priest, Jesus Christ, through the action of His Church with whom Christ has shared His holy priesthood. The entire Mystical Body shares in some way in every Mass.

16. The Holy Eucharist is a sacrifice which both commemorates a past event and celebrates it here and now. Explain.

The Holy Eucharist (see answer to 13) is indeed a memorial which commemorates a past event, but the reality is celebrated here and now. To be present at the Sacrifice of the Mass is to be present at the same Sacrifice that was offered on the Cross of Calvary almost 2,000 years ago. The sacrifice is the same. Only the manner of offering differs.

17. How is the Sacrifice of the Mass a sacrificial meal?
The Sacrifice of the Mass is a sacrificial meal because Jesus Christ, having perpetuated His Sacrifice of the Cross in His Church, offers His body and blood to be eaten and drunk.

18. How is the Sacrifice of the Mass a gift exchange?
The Sacrifice of the Mass is a gift exchange because the victim or gift given God the Father at Holy Mass is Jesus Christ, and the gift which the Father returns to us is also Jesus Christ, our Mediator with heaven.

19. Explain how *in general* the fruits of the Mass accrue to the universal Church?
In general the fruits of the Mass accrue to the universal Church because Jesus Christ, the head of the Mystical Body, offers for the whole Church, including, as the Mass itself states in its ritual, the souls in purgatory. Since no Mass is "private," every Mass affects the universal Church.

20. Explain how *in particular* the fruits of the Mass accrue to certain persons?
In particular the fruits of the Mass accrue to those for whom the Mass was applied in a special way by the priest offering and/or by the one who requested the Mass for a particular intention. There are personal fruits for the priest-celebrant and for those who are actually present at a given Mass and who participate with faith and love.

21. How seriously are we obliged to participate in the Sacrifice of the Mass, and when are we so obliged?
Catholics, beginning at the age of seven are bound under pain of mortal sin to participate in the Sacrifice of the Mass every Sunday and Holy Day of Obligation.

CHAPTER 18

Holy Orders

The Sacrament of Holy Orders is administered by the imposition of the hands of a validly consecrated bishop who is a successor to the original apostles who were ordained by Jesus Christ. This sacrament confers on a man the spiritual power and grace to sanctify others. There are three forms of sacramental orders, the diaconate, priesthood and episcopate. They are not three sacraments, but one sacrament which is separately administered with three successively higher sacramental effects.

Studying the nature and essence of the other sacraments, it will be realized that they depend on the Sacrament of Holy Orders to such an extent that without it some of them would not be possible. The only two sacraments that do not require a properly ordained priest in the strict sense are Baptism and Matrimony. While normally Baptism is administered by a deacon, priest or bishop, and Matrimony, by Church law, normally requires one in Holy Orders as its chief witness, the other five sacraments absolutely require an ordained priest or bishop for validity in every case.

The Sacrament of Holy Orders confers upon the soul of the man ordained a special indelible mark or character of Jesus Christ which will remain for all eternity. Each of the three stages of this sacrament imprint indelibly according to the order being received.

A deacon is a man specially ordained to the service of the Church's ministry. The bishop imposes his hands on the candidate before the consecratory prayer. The words spoken by the bishop at the ordination of a deacon are: "Lord, we pray, send forth upon them the Holy Spirit so that by the grace of Your seven gifts they may be strengthened by Him to carry out faithfully the work of the ministry." The deacon has as his role to assist priests in preaching, the conferral of baptism, performance of marriage, administrative work in parishes and such duties of service. Vatican Council II restored the permanent diaconate whereby some, rather than advancing to the priesthood, remain permanent deacons, living in the world, at times as married men.

The priesthood is the Sacrament of the New Covenant which was instituted by Jesus Christ at the Last Supper when our divine and loving Savior offered the first Sacrifice of the Mass ever offered. The priesthood

232

confers on a man the power to consecrate and offer the Body and Blood of Jesus Christ and to remit or retain sins. Only those in the Church ordained to the holy priesthood of Jesus Christ have this power.

There are two grades or levels of the priesthood: the presbyterate and the episcopate (bishop). Only a bishop can ordain priests, who must first have been ordained deacons. The matter for the sacrament in the ordination of priests is the imposition of the bishop's hands upon the head of the man to be ordained. This is done in silence before the consecration prayer. Then follows the required words as established by the Church: "We ask You, all powerful Father, give these servants of Yours the dignity of the presbyterate. Renew the Spirit of holiness within them. By Your divine gift may they attain the second order of the hierarchy and exemplify right conduct in their lives."

A bishop is a successor of the original apostles appointed and ordained by Jesus Christ. A bishop has received the *fullness* of the priesthood of Jesus Christ. The most distinctive power of the bishop is that in having the *fullness* of the priesthood he is empowered to ordain priests and other bishops. A priest cannot consecrate a bishop. Only a bishop can perpetuate the priesthood of Jesus Christ by the administration of the Sacrament of Holy Orders. A bishop in collegiality with the world's bishops, but always and only if together with and under the pope, has special teaching authority as part of the magisterium.

The bishop imposes his hands on the head of the bishop-elect as do other consecrating bishops. At least the principal consecrator must impose hands. This is done in silence before the consecratory prayer. The form of the sacrament required by the Church for the validity of consecrating a bishop are the words: "Now pour out upon this chosen one that power which flows from You, the perfect Spirit whom He gave to the apostles, who established the Church in every place as the sanctuary where Your name would always be praised and glorified."

To appreciate the Catholic priesthood one must consider in faith the priesthood of Jesus Christ. The ordination of Jesus Christ as the eternal High Priest was at the moment of the Incarnation when the eternal Word of God assumed human flesh in the womb of Mary. The words of Mary, "Let what you have said be done to me" (Luke 1:38), marked the moment of the ordination of Christ when the world was given its eternal High Priest. The role of Jesus as priest is ordained to offer sacrifice and prayer for humanity to His heavenly Father.

While Jesus Christ was upon earth in His physical body, He exercised His priestly office by every act of His will and every deed of His body. At the Last Supper Jesus offered the sacrifice of himself under the sacramental form, instituting the Holy Eucharist and the Sacrifice of the Mass, which sacrifice He offered in a bloody or physical manner on Mt. Calvary the next afternoon. At the Last Supper and on the Cross Jesus Christ united all His acts into one supreme sacrifice.

Together with His supreme sacrifice, Jesus Christ prayed as the High Priest and one essential mediator between man and God. His priestly prayer is recorded in the Gospel of St. John (17:1-26). Jesus Christ continues His priesthood forever in heaven as related by the Letter to the Hebrews: "He is living for ever to intercede. . ." (Hebrews 7:25; see Romans 8:34). This priestly intercession is intimately related to Christ's Sacrifice of the Cross, which He forever presents to the Father in the unity of the Holy Spirit. Because Christ's priesthood continues, there is efficacy to the Sacrifice of the Mass perpetuating Calvary's sacrifice.

The Catholic priest shares in the priesthood of Jesus Christ. He is an authorized mediator who offers a true sacrifice in acknowledgment of God's supreme dominion over men and for the expiation of their sins. The Catholic priest offers the Sacrifice of Christ which was first offered at the Last Supper and on Mt. Calvary. The priest mediates from the people to God. Through the ministry of the Church in its priests, Christ Jesus continually renews and perpetuates the Sacrifice of the Cross on our altars today.

Christ Jesus ordained the apostles as the first priests Holy Thursday evening when they were told to consecrate bread and wine into His body and blood as He had just done. The second essential priestly power which Jesus gave the apostles, the power to forgive sins in His name, was conferred by our divine Lord Easter Sunday evening. "Receive the Holy Spirit. For those whose sins you forgive, they are forgiven; for those whose sins you retain, they are retained" (John 20:23).

Vatican II in its *Decree on the Ministry and Life of Priests* (*Presbyterorum Ordinis*, December 7, 1965), after reminding us that the Lord Jesus makes His whole Mystical Body a sharer in the anointing of the Spirit by which He has been anointed (Matthew 3:16; Luke 4:18; Acts 4:27, 10:38), stated:

"However, the Lord also appointed certain men as ministers, in order that they might be united in one body in which 'all the members have not the same function' (Rom. 12:4). These men were to hold in the community of the faithful the sacred power of Holy Orders, that of offering sacrifice and forgiving sins, and were to exercise the priestly office publicly on behalf of men in the name of Christ. Thus Christ sent the apostles as he himself had been sent by the Father, and then through the apostles made their successors, the bishops, sharers in his consecration and mission. The function of the bishops' ministry was handed over in a subordinate degree to priests so that they might be appointed in the order of the priest-

234

hood and be co-workers of the episcopal order for the proper fulfillment of the apostolic mission that had been entrusted to it by Christ.

"Because it is joined with the episcopal order the office of priests shares in the authority by which Christ himself builds up and sanctifies and rules his Body. Hence the priesthood of priests, while presupposing the sacraments of initiation, is nevertheless conferred by its own particular sacrament. Through that sacrament priests by the anointing of the Holy Spirit are signed with a special character and so are configured to Christ the priest in such a way that they are able to act in the person of Christ the head.

"Since they share in the function of the apostles in their own degree, priests are given the grace by God to be the ministers of Jesus Christ among the nations, fulfilling the sacred task of the Gospel, that the oblation of the gentiles may be made acceptable and sanctified in the Holy Spirit. For it is by the apostolic herald of the Gospel that the People of God are called together and gathered so that all who belong to this people, sanctified as they are by the Holy Spirit, may offer themselves 'a living sacrifice, holy and acceptable to God' (Rom. 12:1). Through the ministry of priests the spiritual sacrifice of the faithful is completed in union with the sacrifice of Christ the only mediator, which in the Eucharist is offered through the priests' hands in the name of the whole Church in an unbloody and sacramental manner until the Lord himself come. The ministry of priests is directed to this and finds its consummation in it. . ." (*Decree on the Ministry and Life of Priests*, 2).

Without the priesthood we would be powerless to offer God the Father the infinitely perfect Sacrifice of the Cross perpetuated in every Holy Sacrifice of the Mass. Without the priesthood we could never receive the Body, Blood, Soul and Divinity of our Lord and Savior in Holy Communion. We need the ordained Catholic priest to have our sins forgiven in the Sacrament of Penance. Only the priest can administer the Sacrament of the Anointing of the Sick. The priesthood is needed for the Sacrament of Confirmation.

A man once ordained is always a priest. The faith of the Catholic Church is that the priestly character is indelible and therefore eternal. "You are a priest of the order of Melchizedek, and for ever" (Psalms 110:4). That is applied by the Church to all ordained to the Catholic priesthood. In the *strict sense*, there is no such thing as reducing a priest to the lay state because the indelible character of Christ's priesthood will remain upon the soul for all eternity. Once ordained, the priest has all the graces necessary to perform successfully the duties of the priestly state and bear fruit abundantly for Jesus Christ in His Church, unto the glory of God and for the sanctification and salvation of others.

When the Catholic priest acts "in persona Christi" (in the person of Christ) at the Sacrifice of the Mass, he does not say, "May this become the Body of Christ," or "May Christ change this bread into the Body of Jesus," or "this wine into the Blood of Jesus." Rather, the priest says: "THIS IS *MY* BODY. . . ." and "THIS IS THE CHALICE OF *MY* BLOOD. . . ." In the confessional the priest does not say, "May God forgive you your sins. . . ." The very person of Jesus Christ, the God-Man, acts in the priest again when in administering the Sacrament of Penance he says: "*I* ABSOLVE YOU FROM YOUR SINS IN THE NAME OF THE FATHER AND OF THE SON AND OF THE HOLY SPIRIT."

There is only one priesthood — the priesthood of Jesus Christ, which He shares with men, mere vessels of clay. The priesthood is the greatest calling upon earth. This in no way degrades the dignity and holiness of other vocations. It is just that the priesthood identifies men most intimately with Christ the High Priest.

"In all ages, priests have been held in the highest honor; yet the priests of the New Testament far exceed all others. For their power of consecrating and offering the body and blood of our Lord and of forgiving sins, which has been conferred on them, not only has nothing equal or like to it on earth, but even surpasses human reason and understanding.

"And as our Savior was sent by his Father, and as the Apostles and disciples were sent into the whole world by Christ our Lord, so priests are daily sent with the same powers, for the perfecting of the saints, for the work of the ministry, and the edifying of the body of Christ (Eph. 4:12)" (*Catechism of the Council of Trent*).

For a man to be validly ordained and be an authentic Catholic priest sharing the priestly powers of Jesus Christ, he must have been ordained by a bishop who is a true bishop of *apostolic succession*. Unfortunately, outside the Catholic Church this succession, sometimes called the "Apostolic Chain," has been broken. This means that ministers of various Christian denominations who cannot trace their ministry and ordination in an unbroken line back to Jesus Christ and the first apostles lack the powers of the priesthood.

At the time of the Protestant Revolt of the 16th century the Apostolic Chain was broken for those who separated from Rome, from the Vicar of Jesus Christ, the pope. There was a denial of special priestly powers. There was a loss of a valid ordained priesthood for the many Protestant denominations which sprang from the Protestant Reformation of the early 16th century. They held only to the common priesthood of all the faithful.

Ministers outside of the Catholic Church who cannot trace their ordination, the receiving of a commission in a lineal sequence from the

236

apostles, do not have any special powers of Jesus Christ beyond the ordinary baptized layman. Therefore, in these Protestant communities there is not effected the Body, Blood, Soul and Divinity of Jesus Christ in their communion services. There is no perpetuation of the Sacrifice of the Cross in their eucharistic services. However sincere and good, there is lacking all the special priestly powers of Jesus Christ which comes with the administration of the Sacrament of Holy Orders. These ministers lack the power to forgive sins in Jesus' name. There is no true Sacrament of Confirmation or of Anointing of the Sick in these communities because the priesthood of Holy Orders is needed for these sacraments which extend the acts of Christ in time and space.

The Eastern Orthodox churches share in the apostolic succession in having valid episcopal orders, even though they are not in collegial union with the Roman Catholic hierarchy. When the Orthodox broke from union with Rome they did not deny or give up the Sacrament of Holy Orders which confers the priesthood of Jesus Christ. They kept their bishops.

Some other Christians claim apostolic succession. Pope Leo XIII in the document *Apostolicae Curae* (Sept. 13, 1896), after careful study, decided in the negative regarding the validity of Anglican ordination. They were declared "absolutely null and utterly void" because of defect of form in the rite and defect of intention in the minister. Anglican orders in practice had been considered invalid, since Anglican clergymen who came into full union with the Catholic Church and desired to be ordained Catholic priests were required to be ordained by a Roman Catholic bishop. Since then a limited number of Anglicans have been ordained by Orthodox prelates whose orders were held to be valid by Rome.

The conclusion, then, is that with the exception of the Orthodox, and some other rare exceptions, outside the Catholic Church there is no true priesthood of Jesus Christ which requires apostolic succession. The apostolic chain has been broken for our separated brethren. This is one of the sad consequences of division among Christians. When realized by those who convert to Catholicism or come into full communion with the ancient Catholic Church, the light of discovering the fullness of true faith and the powers of Christ the Priest present in the Catholic Church brings great joy to souls.

"Only to the Apostles, and thenceforth to those on whom their successors imposed hands, is granted the power of the priesthood, in virtue of which they represent the person of Jesus Christ before their people, acting at the same time as representatives of their people before God.

"This priesthood is not transmitted by heredity or human descent. It does not emanate from the Christian community. It is not a delegation from the people. Prior to acting as representative of the community before the throne of God, the priest is the ambassador of the divine Redeemer. He is God's vice-regent in the midst of the flock precisely because Jesus Christ is head of tht body of which Christians are members. The power entrusted to him, therefore, bears no resemblance to anything human" (Pius XII, encyclical *Mediator Dei*, 40).

DISCUSSION QUESTIONS

1. What are the three forms or levels of the Sacrament of Holy Orders?

There are three forms or levels to the Sacrament of Holy Orders, the diaconate, priesthood and episcopate (bishop). These are one sacrament with successively higher sacramental effects.

2. What happens in the soul of the man ordained to one of the three levels?

An indelible character is sealed on the soul of a man who receives any one of the levels of the Sacrament of Holy Orders.

3. What is a deacon and what is his role?

A deacon is a man specially ordained to the service of the Church's ministry. He is authorized, with the bishop's permission, to preach. He may baptize solemnly, perform marriage ceremonies, distribute Holy Communion, administer parishes in matters where the priestly order is not required and perform various duties of service in the Church.

4. What are the special powers of the Catholic priest?

The Catholic priest has the chief priestly powers of consecrating bread and wine into the Body, Blood, Soul and Divinity of Jesus Christ, thereby perpetuating the Sacrifice of the Cross; he also has the power to forgive sins in Jesus' name. The priest also may administer the Sacrament of the Anointing of the Sick; Confirmation, under certain conditions (as well as other sacraments such as baptism and marriage ceremonies which do not strictly require priestly powers). The priest is **not** empowered to administer the Sacrament of Holy Orders.

5. What are the special powers of the bishop?

A bishop as a successor of the apostles has the **fullness** of the priesthood of Jesus Christ. His distinctive power is that he can ordain a priest or another bishop. In a diocese which he administers he also has special teaching duties. When a bishop teaches collegially with the pope and the other world bishops under the proper conditions, he is part of the teaching Church (magisterium) guaranteed infallibility. The teaching authority of bishops must always be together with and under the authority of the pope.

6. When was Jesus Christ ordained High Priest?

Jesus Christ was ordained High Priest at the moment of the Incarnation when He was conceived in the womb of Mary. At the response of Mary to the Archangel Gabriel, "let what you have said be done to me" (Luke 1:38), the Word was made flesh and dwelt among us, and the world had its High Priest.

7. What is the role of Jesus Christ as Priest?

The role of Jesus Christ as Priest is ordained to offer sacrifice and prayer for humanity to His heavenly Father.

8. When did Jesus Christ exercise His priesthood on earth?

While upon earth Jesus exercised His priesthood at every moment by every act of His will, intellect and body. At the Last Supper and in His Sacrifice on the Cross, Jesus Christ united all His acts into one supreme sacrifice.

9. How does the Catholic priest today continue the sacrificial acts of Christ's priesthood?

The Catholic priest shares in the priesthood of Jesus Christ and is thereby empowered to act on behalf of the Church in perpetuating the Sacrifice of the Cross and the Last Supper in every Holy Mass. The priest also has the power to forgive sins in the person of Jesus Christ.

10. When were the original apostles ordained?

The apostles were ordained into the fullness of the priesthood of Jesus Christ, that is, they were ordained bishops, Holy Thursday evening at the Last Supper.

11. What is meant by the statement that the function of the bishop's ministry is handed over in a subordinate degree to priests?

The function of the bishop's ministry is handed over in a subordinate degree to priests so that they might be appointed in the order of the priesthood and be co-workers of the episcopal order. The priest extends the authority and priestly power of the bishop into the local parishes, to wherever he performs priestly tasks. Jesus Christ ordained the apostles bishops with the fullness of the priesthood. The apostles obviously understood they could pass on their priestly power by degree, in a subordinate manner.

12. What would be lacking in a Christian's life if he had no validly ordained priest?

Christian communities without a valid priesthood would lack the Sacrifice of the Cross perpetuated in the eucharistic celebration which Catholics call the Sacrifice of the Mass. They would lack the sacramental Body, Blood, Soul and Divinity of Jesus Christ in Holy Communion. They would lack the Sacrament of Penance or Confession for the forgiveness of sin. They would not have the Sacrament of the Anointing of the Sick, nor would they have valid sacramental Confirmation.

13. Is it possible for an ordained Catholic priest to have the priestly character removed from his soul so that he can be strictly reduced to the lay state of life?

Once he is ordained a Catholic priest by an ordaining bishop who is a successor to the apostles, the indelible priestly character will remain on the priest's soul for all eternity. Even should a priest return to living a life of the laity, he is still a true priest of Jesus Christ forever. The priesthood is forever, and once he is ordained, the Church expects that one will live a priestly life henceforth.

14. Give some examples to explain how the Catholic priest acts in the person of Jesus Christ.

The Catholic priest acts "in persona Christi" (in the person of Jesus Christ) when he offers the Sacrifice of the Mass or confers any of the sacraments. As Vatican Council II indicated, it is Jesus who baptizes, consecrates, forgives sin, etc.

In consecrating bread and wine at Mass the priest says: "This is my body. . . .

239

This is my blood. . . ." In administering forgiveness with the Sacrament of Penance, he says: "I absolve you. . . ."

15. What is meant by apostolic succession?

Apostolic succession refers to the method by which the fullness of the priestly powers of Jesus Christ has been passed down from the apostles to bishops today. It has been by a succession of consecration through the laying on of hands, performing the functions of the apostles, receiving their commission in a lineal sequence from the apostles.

16. What was lost for the various Protestant communities when the apostolic chain was broken for them in their separation from the hierarchy of the Catholic Church?

See answer to question 12 above. In brief, the powers of the episcopacy which Jesus gave to the apostles were lost for various Protestant communities which separated from the Catholic Church, giving up their bishops.

17. Why does the Catholic Church recognize the priesthood of the Orthodox Churches?

The Roman Catholic Church recognizes that Orthodox Christians still have a valid priesthood because at the time of their separation from Rome they retained their bishops who were successors of the apostles in handing down the priestly powers of Jesus Christ. They are in schism, however, because they do not recognize the pope as the supreme pastor or bishop of the world.

CHAPTER 19

Matrimony

There are two sacraments instituted by Jesus Christ which are special sacraments of love. Now it was out of mercy and love that Jesus Christ instituted all of the sacraments, but two of them are special sacraments of love: the Holy Eucharist and Matrimony.

In the Sacrament of the Holy Eucharist Jesus Christ, the Son of God made flesh, becomes one with those who receive Him. In the Holy Eucharist God gives himself to us in love. In the Sacrament of Matrimony, where "two become one body" (Matthew 19:5), husband and wife give themselves to each other in love. Their love, by virtue of the sacrament, is supernaturalized. It is placed in Christ, and the sharing of their total lives in love becomes a means of glorifying God while growing in grace themselves.

In marriage there are roles designed by nature and nature's God for men as husbands and fathers and for women as wives and mothers. Today, unfortunately, many people isolate sex from marriage. In reality, marriage as intended by God is the lasting union of man and woman who agree to give and receive rights over each other for the performance of the act of generation and for the fostering of their love for each other.

Marriage by its very nature is a contract. As such, from the beginning, when God created Adam and Eve as the first man and woman, it was intended as a binding contract until death. When Jesus Christ came and established the New Law He raised marriage to the dignity of a sacrament. Thus the Christian husband and wife signify and enter into the mystery of that unity and fruitful love which exists between Jesus Christ and His Church. They help each other attain holiness, get to heaven, rear and educate their children in Jesus Christ.

The Second Vatican Council drew attention to the family as the domestic church, as a miniature Mystical Body, as it were, in referring us to Ephesians, which discusses the love of husband and wife in the Sacrament of Matrimony.

"Give way to one another in obedience to Christ. Wives should regard their husbands as they regard the Lord, since as Christ is head of the

Church and saves the whole body, so is a husband the head of his wife; and as the Church submits to Christ, so should wives to their husbands, in everything. Husbands should love their wives just as Christ loved the Church and sacrificed himself for her to make her holy. He made her clean by washing her in water with a form of words, so that when he took her to himself she would be glorious, with no speck or wrinkle or anything like that, but holy and faultless. In the same way, husbands must love their wives as they love their own bodies; for a man to love his wife is for him to love himself. A man never hates his own body, but he feeds it and looks after it; and that is the way Christ treats the Church, because it is his body — and we are its living parts. *For this reason, a man must leave his father and mother and be joined to his wife, and the two will become one body.* This mystery has many implications; but I am saying it applies to Christ and the Church. To sum up; you too, each one of you, must love his wife as he loves himself; and let every wife respect her husband" (Ephesians 5:21-33).

The contract of matrimony which was raised by Jesus Christ to the dignity of a sacrament is truly and properly one of the seven sacraments of the law of the Gospel. Matrimony as a sacrament was not introduced by men into the Church. St. Pius X in his decree *Sacra Tridentina Synodus* stated that "because of the grace given through Christ, it is superior to the marriage unions of earlier times. . . . Our holy Fathers, the councils, and the tradition of the universal Church have always rightly taught, matrimony should be included among the sacraments of the New Law."

The Creator established marriage as an intimate partnership of life and love and endowed it with its own proper laws. Rooted in the marriage contract as established by God is the irrevocable personal consent of both husband and wife. Marriage is an institution confirmed by divine law. It receives its stability from the human act by which partners mutually surrender themselves to each other. God himself is the author of marriage, and for the good of the partners, children and society, the indissoluble and sacred bond is not of human decision alone, but binding by and in the Son of God made Man, Jesus Christ.

The indissolubility of marriage until death is important to the entire human race, to the personal development of each partner and to the eternal destiny of each member of the family. When marriages are weakly bound because the contract is not held to firmly as intended by Almighty God, then the salvation of family members is made more difficult because the graces of Holy Matrimony are not being accepted and lived. Marriage by its very nature is ordered to the procreation and education of children, and in them it finds its crowning glory.

The intimacy of marriage demands total fidelity for the good of chil-

242

dren and for the mutual love of husband and wife. It demands an unbreakable unity between them.

✶ "Christ our Lord has abundantly blessed this love, which is rich in its various features, coming as it does from the spring of divine love and modeled on Christ's own union with the Church. Just as of old, God encountered his people with a covenant of love and fidelity, so our Savior, the spouse of the Church, now encounters Christian spouses through the sacrament of marriage. He abides with them in order that, by their mutual self-giving, spouses will love each other with enduring fidelity, as he loved the Church and delivered himself for it. Authentic married love is caught up into divine love and is directed and enriched by the redemptive power of Christ and the salvific action of the Church, with the result that the spouses are effectively led to God and are helped and strengthened in their lofty role as fathers and mothers. Spouses, therefore, are fortified and, as it were, consecrated for the duties and dignity of their state by a special sacrament; fulfilling their conjugal and family role by virtue of this sacrament, spouses are penetrated with the spirit of Christ and their whole life is suffused by faith, hope and charity; thus they increasingly further their own perfection and their mutual sanctification, and together they render glory to God" (Vatican II, *Church in the Modern World*, 48)‒end‒

There are four conditions to marriage: 1. There must be a union of opposite sexes. Marriage as intended by nature and God who created the nature of things, excludes all forms of unnatural, homosexual activities. 2. Marriage can be authentic only when it is entered into as a permanent union until the death of either spouse. Optional marriages, those intended only for a time, those entered into conditionally, are no true marriage before God. 3. Marriage is an exclusive union, which means that all other men and women, except this particular husband and this particular wife, are excluded from conjugal affections. Extramarital acts are a violation of justice and love and contrary to the marriage contract and sacrament. 4. The permanence and exclusiveness are guaranteed by a sacred contract. Those who live together without mutually binding themselves to such permanence and exclusiveness are living in the serious sin of concubinage. There is no such thing as "trial marriages." They are seriously sinful states.

What is seriously needed in today's society is to get back to respect for the fundamentals of human life, to respect the family as the basic cell of society. Children, the supreme gift of marriage, greatly contribute to the good of the parents. "It is not good that the man should be alone" (Genesis 2:18). The Creator "from the beginning *made them male and female*" (Matthew 19:4), desiring to associate husband and wife in a special way with His own creative work. The Creator blessed man and woman with the words, "Be fruitful, multiply. . ."(Genesis 1:28). True married love thus cooperates with the love of the Creator and Savior.

In an age when there is much talk about "equal rights," there is a need not to confuse roles. The father of the family has great need to manifest love and affection to his wife as such and as the mother of his children. The father is important in the minds of the children in assisting them to form a correct concept of God the Father. The strength (not simply physical) of the father, his understanding and forgiveness, together with justice and the various virtues, all bonded by love as he offers protection and means of livelihood to his children, is an image of God the Father. The mother, with her special womanly qualities of mercy, compassion, intercessory powers and tender love as the heart of the home, reflects the goodness, mercy and love of God in a special way as she complements her husband while he complements her.

So much do the parents represent God in authority and love to their children that God's own word commands us to "honor your father and your mother." To disobey, to dishonor one's parents, is to sin against God. "Let married people themselves, who are created in the image of the living God and constituted in an authentic personal dignity, be united together in equal affection, agreement of mind and mutual holiness. Thus, in the footsteps of Christ, the principle of life, they will bear witness by their faithful love in the joys and sacrifices of their calling, to that mystery of love which the Lord revealed to the world by his death and resurrection" (Vatican II, *Church in the Modern World*, 52).

The Catholic Church interprets the divine law as seriously forbidding the practice of artificial birth control. Contraception is seriously sinful. The Catholic Church does not require a married couple to have the maximum number of children physically possible for them, as some falsely claim. The Church teaches *responsible parenthood*. Couples are to bring into the world what children they can reasonably support and educate. The call of God is for generosity, not selfishness, in sharing God's creative power as co-operators. In condemning artificial birth control the Church forbids the separation of love-giving from life-giving and from acting in marriage contrary to nature.

The official position of the Catholic Church regarding the transmission of human life is sometimes misunderstood and more often misrepresented. Because of its importance, we quote in detail from the Second Vatican Council:

"The Council realizes that married people are often hindered by certain situations in modern life from working out their married love harmoniously and that they can sometimes find themselves in a position where

244

the number of children cannot be increased, at least for the time being: in cases like these it is quite difficult to preserve the practice of faithful love and the complete intimacy of their lives. But where the intimacy of married life is broken, it often happens that faithfulness is imperiled and the good of the children suffers; then the education of the children as well as the courage to accept more children are both endangered.

"Some of the proposed solutions to these problems are shameful and some people have not hesitated to suggest the taking of life: the Church wishes to emphasize that there can be no conflict between the divine laws governing the transmission of life and the fostering of authentic married love.

"God, the Lord of life, has entrusted to men the noble mission of safeguarding life, and men must carry it out in a manner worthy of themselves. Life must be protected with the utmost care from the moment of conception: abortion and infanticide are abominable crimes. Man's sexuality and the faculty of reproduction wondrously surpass the endowments of lower forms of life; therefore the acts proper to married life are to be ordered according to authentic human dignity and must be honored with the greatest reverence. When it is a question of harmonizing married love with the responsible transmission of life, it is not enough to take only the good intention and the evaluation of motives into account; the objective criteria must be used, criteria drawn from the nature of the human person and human action, criteria which respect the total meaning of mutual self-giving and human procreation in the context of true love; all this is possible only if the virtue of married chastity is seriously practiced. In questions of birth regulation the sons of the Church, faithful to these principles, are forbidden to use methods disapproved by the teaching authority of the Church in its interpretation of the divine law" (*Church in the Modern World*, 51).

On July 25, 1968, Pope Paul VI issued the encyclical letter *Humanae Vitae*, subtitled "The Right Order to Be Followed in the Propagation of Human Offspring." This was a fulfillment of the promise during Vatican II that the Holy Father after study by a commission would later pass judgment on matters of population, the family and births. In the encyclical the pope spoke authoritatively. He stated: "Equally to be excluded, as the teaching authority of the Church has frequently declared, is direct sterilization, whether perpetual or temporary, whether of the man or of the woman. Similarly excluded is every action which, either in anticipation of the conjugal act, or in its accomplishment, or in the development of its natural consequences, proposes whether as an end or as a means, to render procreation impossible."

Catholics are bound in conscience to accept this teaching authority of the Church as voiced by the Vicar of Jesus Christ, Pope Paul VI, and reaffirmed by his successors. Since 1968 few if any subjects of morality have been more repeatedly dealt with by the pope than that forbidding artificial birth control. It cannot be argued that it was not a defined moral teaching *ex cathedra*. One should study the words of Vatican II on the obligation to follow the teachings of the pope.

"Bishops who teach in communion with the Roman Pontiff are to be revered by all as witnesses of divine and Catholic truth; the faithful, for their part, are obliged to submit to their bishops' decision, made in the name of Christ, in matters of faith and morals, and to adhere to it with a ready and respectful allegiance of mind. This loyal submission of the will and intellect must be given, in a special way, to the authentic teaching authority of the Roman Pontiff, even when he does not speak *ex cathedra* in such wise, indeed, that his supreme teaching authority be acknowledged with respect, and sincere assent be given to decisions made by him, conformably with his manifest mind and intention, which is made known principally either by the character of the documents in question, or by the frequency with which a certain doctrine is proposed, or by the manner in which the doctrine is formulated" (Dogmatic Constitution on the Church, 25).

Pope Paul VI in his encyclical *Humanae Vitae*, reaffirming the constant principles of Church teachings which condemned unnatural and artificial means of birth control, proved providential in his assurance that the Church's magisterium could resolve the problem. The Church held firmly to the principle that unnatural methods were sinful. Great advancements have been made in the subsequent years to understanding the ovulation method, the times of fertility, etc. Couple-to-Couple Leagues have been formed in many dioceses explaining to others *Natural Family Planning*, which is safe and reliable. Understanding the ovulation method and natural family planning methods in harmony with the teaching of the Church has strengthened marriages both psychologically and spiritually as these couples continue to live in God's grace.

Dr. John Billings, who helped develop a natural family planning method that does not go contrary to nature, has said:

"Some people may immediately comment that the ideal family planning method should require no abstinence, and here, in my view, they reveal a profound ignorance of human psychology. Human beings are not to be regarded as super-beasts, as a materialistic view of evolution might propose. They are distinct within the animal kingdom by their ability to govern instinct by reason, and by their ability through the exercise of free will to act responsibly.

"The development of maturity of the human personality depends upon the ability to exercise self-control, and this maturity necessarily implies control of the most urgent and pressing impulse for physical gratification which lies within the realm of sexuality. No marriage is secure until the fidelity of the husband and wife have been demonstrated by their ability to accept abstinence, the need for which inevitably occurs in marriage at one time or another. Additionally the happiness of marriage finds its true basis in love, and the essence of love is generosity, the willingness to accept sacrifice for the welfare of the beloved. More than that, for the Christian, marriage has become a Sacrament, and the graces of the Sacrament which the husband and wife administer to each other take on a truly redemptive character when the husband and wife share in the selfless paschal mystery of the death and resurrection of Christ."

It is to be noted that the sharp percentage rise in the failure of Catholics to succeed in their marriages coincided with the rise of dissension against the authoritative teachings of the Church which condemned artificial birth control. Selfishness in marriage, a lack of generosity, plus not keeping one's marriage "in Christ," contribute largely to the breakdown in marriages. Thousands of Catholics who abide by the teachings of the Church, on the other hand, bear testimony by their good lives as to what strengthens marriage in Christ.

God's Word is clear that marriage lasts until death: "A wife is tied as long as her husband is alive. But if her husband dies, she is free to marry anybody she likes, only it must be in the Lord" (1 Corinthians 7:39). "A married woman, for instance, has legal obligations to her husband while he is alive, but all these obligations come to an end if the husband dies. So if she gives herself to another man while her husband is still alive, she is legally an adultress; but after her husband is dead her legal obligations come to an end, and she can marry someone else without becoming an adultress" (Romans 7:2-3). "For the married I have something to say, and this is not from me but from the Lord: a wife must not leave her husband — or if she does leave him, she must either remain unmarried or else make it up with her husband — nor must a husband send his wife away" (1 Corinthians 7:10-11). The direct words of Jesus on the indissolubility of marriage are clear: ". . . So then, what God has united, man must not divide" (Mark 10:9).

The frequency of divorce today, as granted by civil courts, in no way diminishes the seriousness of the marriage vows and the indissolubility of the sacramental marriage bond. Marriage lasts until death. When two baptized Christians have been validly joined in sacramental marriage and their marriage is consummated, there is no power on earth which can dissolve it except the death of one of the parties. When the Church has, in some cases, declared a marriage null and void, it was declared to have

247

been no true sacramental marriage from the beginning because of some defect. There is no such thing as divorce.

The validly married couple give each other the right to each other's bodies, and to refuse the marriage right and duty for selfish reasons is seriously sinful (see Corinthians 7:3-5). It is seriously sinful for wife or husband to separate indefinitely without a serious reason and without permission of the bishop.

The Catholic Church teaches that abortion, willfully causing the death of an unborn baby in any way, is murder. The unborn baby is a human being with the right to life. A Catholic who would willingly have an abortion or be the cause of another's having an abortion is automatically excommunicated from the Church.

The law of the Church requires that Catholics be married in the presence of a Catholic priest and two witnesses. When a dispensation is granted by the bishop for a Catholic to marry a person who is not Catholic, the Catholic party must promise to do all in his/her power to see that all the children resulting from the marriage are both baptized in the Catholic Church and educated in the Catholic faith. That the non-Catholic is not required to sign any written promises does *not* mean that those entering a mixed marriage of Catholic-Protestant (or Catholic/Jewish/Mohammedan) may bring their children up outside the Catholic faith. Rather, the responsibility falls upon the Catholic partner in the marriage to have an understanding and agreement with the intended spouse prior to the marriage that all the children will be baptized and educated as Catholics. The Catholic party must attest before the marriage that the non-Catholic party has been informed of the declaration and promise which the Catholic makes to continue living his/her faith in Jesus Christ and intends to continue living that faith in the Catholic Church, promising to share the Catholic faith with the children.

In rare cases the bishop may dispense from canonical form, since Matrimony is one sacrament that an ordained priest is not required to administer. The man administers Matrimony to the woman and the woman administers Matrimony to the man at the time of the exchange of their marriage vows. Normally, they can do this by Church law, which heaven respects according to the words of Jesus Christ, only in the presence of a Catholic priest and at least two other witnesses. To attempt marriage without the priest and without a dispensation from the bishop is to enter into an invalid marriage which is not marriage at all but a sinful union.

The normal place for a Catholic to marry, even in the case when he has a dispensation for a mixed marriage, is in a Catholic church. For serious reasons the bishop may dispense from having the marriage witnessed by a bishop or a parish priest in his parish or by another priest duly dele-

248

gated. In such a case the Catholic seeking such a dispensation from canonical form must still approach the bishop through his parish priest, who may make the request of the bishop stating the *serious* reasons. The Catholic must still promise to have all children baptized and educated only in the Catholic Church. The bishop in granting the special dispensation must be convinced that the arrangement will help to "achieve family harmony or avoid family alienation, or would make possible parental agreement to the marriage." The dispensation cannot be granted simply because the Catholic is weak in character and if there is danger to the faith of the Catholic party as a result. It is not sufficient simply because it is more convenient to be married in the church of the partner.

Various dioceses have special regulations for the preparation for marriage. Some dioceses require a minimum three-month waiting period; others, at least six months. The period is not to be spent simply in waiting, but in prayerful *preparation*, including counseling, special classes, etc. Finally, to receive the Sacrament of Matrimony worthily, one must be in the state of sanctifying grace. It would be sacrilegious to be married in the state of mortal sin. Couples to be married should go to confession shortly before marriage.

While a dispensation may be granted for a mixed marriage, the Church still requires that Catholics make every reasonable effort to marry other Catholics. One should choose a partner who is not merely a nominal "Catholic" but one who regularly participates in the Holy Mass, goes to confession regularly, one who leads a life of prayer and would make a good father/mother to children. Such requires maturity. Unfortunately, many today are attempting marriage at too young an age when they are not sufficiently mature. For this reason premature steady-dating of teenagers should be seriously excluded.

Couples approaching the priest to prepare for marriage should be well informed on the regulations of their diocese, which means approaching the priest from three to six months or more before the intended date of marriage.

So much is marriage ordered toward the procreation and education of children that if a couple got married and intended to obstruct the natural act of marriage in a constant artificial manner to make the conception of children permanently impossible, it would be an invalid marriage. Couples who marry with the intention of spending only their first years practicing artificial contraception are seriously endangering their marriage because they are not getting off to a firm start, by having no firm foundation of love in Christ on which to build. If they intended to begin their marriage with the practice of contraception, that in itself means they are receiving the Sacrament of Marriage sacrilegiously. The reason is that one

249

commits serious sin as soon as the intention is formed, and to receive Matrimony worthily one must be in the state of grace. One who enters marriage with the intention of living in a contraceptive manner is not in the state of grace by that very intention on the day of marriage. A marriage that is not lived in Christ can hardly succeed.

To enter a happy and successful marriage, in addition to the procreation of children, if physically possible, the couple must be disposed to educate the children in the faith. This does not mean simply sending the children to formal religion classes where someone else educates, but the total environment in the home must be conducive to education and formation in Christ. Vatican II stated that the role of parents in the education and formation of children is so indispensable that scarcely anything or anyone can substitute for the parents.

DISCUSSION QUESTIONS

1. How can the Sacrament of the Holy Eucharist be compared with Holy Matrimony?

Both the Holy Eucharist and Holy Matrimony are sacraments of love. In one Jesus Christ gives himself to us in love. In Matrimony husband and wife give themselves to each other in love. Both are special unions in Jesus Christ through grace.

2. What permanency did God attach to marriage from the beginning?

From the beginning of the human race God intended marriage to be a binding contract until death.

3. To what does the Apostle Paul in Ephesians compare the family?

The Apostle Paul in his Letter to the Ephesians compares the family to a little Church, a miniature Mystical Body of Christ. As Jesus Christ is head of the body of the Church so is the husband the head of his wife. The union of Jesus Christ with His Church brings forth new members just as the union of husband and wife in the Sacrament of Matrimony is ordered to bring forth new children in Christ, and all become one in Christ Jesus.

4. What is meant by indissolubility of marriage?

Indissolubility of marriage means that only death can dissolve a true Christian marriage.

5. Does the Church hold to the indissolubility of marriage based on human law alone?

The indissolubility of the marriage bond is based on divine law, not simply the human law. That marriage lasts until death is God's own law.

6. To what is marriage ordered by its very nature?

By its very nature marriage is ordered to the procreation and education of children.

7. What are the four conditions for marriage?

The four conditions for marriage are: 1. For a true marriage opposite sexes are required. 2. The couple entering marriage must intend the union until death of one of the parties. 3. The marriage must exclude all conjugal affections with others. 4. The permanence and exclusiveness must be sealed by a contract.

8. Are the roles of husbands (fathers) and wives (mothers) identical?

God intended the man in a marriage to have a special role and the woman to have another role, and that they complement the roles of each other as both represent God's divine plan to each other and to their children. Each reflects the goodness and powers of God by participation in different but complementary functions.

9. What is meant when it is said that "Love-giving must never be separated from life-giving"?

God did not ordain love-giving to selfish ends but to the generous ends of sharing and self-giving and the multiplication of love in bearing children. The very command of God in creating marriage was "Be fruitful, multiply. . ." (Genesis 1:28).

10. Comment on this statement: "By its words on birth control Vatican II opened the door to dissension regarding Church authority and its teachings on the subject."

Vatican II did not open the door permitting Catholics to dissent from the teaching authority of the Church regarding artificial birth control. On the contrary, Vatican II upheld the teaching authority of the Church. The council in its document on *The Church in the Modern World* (51) explicitly spoke of shameful solutions to population control and added that the faithful "are forbidden to use methods disapproved by the teaching authority of the Church in its interpretation of the divine law."

11. What did Pope Paul VI declare in his encyclical on human life, *Humanae Vitae*?

Pope Paul VI in his encyclical *Humanae Vitae*, facing the problems of modern society, held to the competence of the Church's teaching authority to resolve population problems. He reaffirmed the Church's principles, which must be maintained and held firmly, namely that artificial methods of birth control, including abortion, must never be practiced.

12. Did Jesus Christ give His Church the power to annul a true Christian sacramental marriage?

Jesus Christ did not give His Church the power to annul a true Christian sacramental marriage, but rather said, ". . . From the beginning of creation *God made them male and female. This is why a man must leave father and mother, and the two become one body.* They are no longer two, therefore, but one body. So then, what God has united, man must not divide" (Mark 10:7-9). When a true sacramental marriage has been consummated no power on earth can dissolve it. In some cases the Church declares that there was no true marriage from the beginning.

13. What penalty does the Catholic Church extend to those who have an abortion or aid another in having an abortion?

A Catholic who would have an abortion or aid another in having an abortion is automatically excommunicated from the Church. It would require appeal to the bishop through the local confessor to have such an excommunication lifted when there is true repentance.

14. How does the law of the Church require Catholics to be married?

The law of the Church requires that when either one or both of the people are Catholic they are to have their marriage witnessed by a priest and two other witnesses.

15. If, for a serious reason, a Catholic is granted a dispensation for a mixed marriage, what must the Catholic promise regarding any future children?

A Catholic who has received a dispensation from a bishop, for serious reasons, to enter into a mixed marriage must still promise to have all children, both boys and girls, baptized and educated in the Catholic faith.

16. Comment on this statement: "In the cases of mixed marriage the proper place to be married is in the church of the bride."

The proper place for a Catholic to be married is in the Catholic Church before a priest and at least two other witnesses, not simply in the church of the bride. The bishop may, for very serious reasons, grant a dispensation from canonical form, but not simply for convenience.

17. How long before he hopes to marry should a Catholic approach his/her parish priest?

A Catholic should be informed of the regulations of the diocese about the amount of time he should approach his parish priest before he hopes to marry. It varies from diocese to diocese and can range from three to six months or more.

18. Do parents fulfill their obligation in the religious education of their children when they send them to religion classes?

Parents are the principal educators of their own children and they do not fulfill their serious responsibilities simply by sending their children to formal religion classes. God so intended parents to be primarily responsible for the formation of their own children in the fullness of true faith that scarcely any substitute can supply for them. Teachers in the classroom in formal settings are merely auxiliaries to the parents, who must teach by word and the good example of their daily living of the true faith.

19. A couple plans to marry but intends to practice birth control so that children will always be excluded from their marriage. Comment.

A couple who would enter marriage with the intention of excluding children entirely from their marriage by artificial birth control would not be validly married.

20. Is simply marrying one who calls himself/herself "Catholic" sufficient to guarantee a religiously successful marriage?

A Catholic should seek a Catholic for a partner in marriage who is not simply a nominal "Catholic" but one who sincerely believes and practices what the Church teaches. One's partner should have both spiritual and psychological maturity to make a good husband/father; wife/mother.

CHAPTER 20

Anointing of the Sick and the Four Last Things

The four last things are death, judgment, heaven and hell. Everyone reading these pages will experience at least three of them. Implied in these four last things is the fact that there is no such thing as reincarnation. Immediately after death each person is judged and his/her place in eternity is determined.

Death is the separation of the soul from the body after the cessation of bodily functions. Death ends our human probation, our period of trial or the testing of one's loyalty to God. After death it is no longer possible to gain merit. Death here, of course, refers only to the death of the body, for the soul is immortal. The soul can never die. The Bible does speak of a second death, but it is referring to the souls in hell, where they are separated from God forever (Revelation 20:6).

There are many places in Sacred Scripture which give divine evidence for the immortality of the soul. "Yet God did make man imperishable, he made him in the image of his own nature. . ." (Wisdom 2:23). "In the eyes of the unwise, they did appear to die, their going looked like a disaster, their leaving us, like annihilation, but they are in peace" (Wisdom 3:1-4). The Second Book of Maccabees speaks of "ever-flowing life, by virtue of God's covenant" (7:36). Jesus, in the Sermon on the Mount, said: "Do not be afraid of those who kill the body but cannot kill the soul; fear him rather who can destroy both body and soul in hell" (Matthew 10:28).

To the Good Thief, Jesus said: "Indeed, I promise you, today you will be with me in paradise" (Luke 23:43).

If there were not life after death St. Paul's assertion would not make sense: "Life to me, of course, is Christ, but then death would bring me something more; but then again, if living in this body means doing work which is having good results — I do not know what I should choose. I am caught in this dilemma: I want to be gone and be with Christ, which would be very much the better, but for me to stay alive in this body is a more urgent need for your sake" (Philippians 1:21-23).

Purgatory is not considered one of the last four things, for it will not

253

continue after the General Judgment at the end of the world. Purgatory is the place or condition in which souls of the just after the death of their bodies are perfectly purified before they can enter heaven. Souls are purified in purgatory for two reasons: for unforgiven venial sins on their souls at the moment of death and to make satisfaction for forgiven sins for which one did not make sufficient satisfaction while upon earth.

The sufferings in purgatory are not the same for all souls but are according to each person's degree of sinfulness and amount of satisfaction still needed because of insufficient penance upon earth. The sufferings of the poor souls in purgatory can be lessened both as to duration and intensity through the prayers and good works of the faithful upon earth, especially through the offering of the Sacrifice of the Mass for their repose.

Second Maccabees speaks of the atonement sacrifice made for the dead so that they might be released from their sins. Obviously the belief in life after death and the possibility of purification after death did not arise entirely after the coming of Jesus Christ. Even if some would not consider the books of Maccabees divinely inspired, they cannot be denied as historical books testifying to the ancient practices of praying for the dead. A collection was taken up, "amounting to nearly two thousand drachmae, and sent . . . to Jerusalem to have a sacrifice for sin offered, an altogether fine and noble action, in which he took full account of the resurrection. For if he had not expected the fallen to rise again it would have been superfluous and foolish to pray for the dead. . ." (2 Maccabees 12:43-45).

When Jesus said, as recorded in Matthew 12:32, that whoever speaks blasphemy against the Holy Spirit, it will not be forgiven him either in this world or in the next, our Savior obviously implies that some sins are forgiven in the next world.

The Apostle Paul speaks of being saved as by fire. "That day will begin with fire, and the fire will test the quality of each man's work. If his structure stands up to it, he will get his wages; if it is burned down, he will be the loser, and though he is saved himself, it will be as one who has gone through fire" (1 Corinthians 3:14-15).

It would be impossible to appear before the heavenly throne of God, seeing Him face to face, unless we were in a state of perfection. Few could hope to enter heaven if their salvation depended upon being absolutely purified, perfect, at the moment of death. Ecclesiasticus (Sirach) 5:5 tells us: "Do not be so sure of forgiveness that you add sin to sin." The Catholic Church teaches that even after the forgiveness of sin penance is often needed to make full satisfaction for the offense committed against the justice of God. God in His mercy forgives sin. God in His justice requires satisfaction.

The doctrine of purgatory was held to and practiced in the earliest centuries of Christianity. There was a universal belief in the purification to be undergone in the next world by souls which were holy but not perfectly cleansed. There was the practice of offering prayers and sacrifices, especially the Sacrifice of the Mass, for these souls. The following could be quoted to show that they believed in purgatory: Clement of Alexandria, Origen, St. Ephraem, St. Cyril of Jerusalem, St. Basil, St. Gregory of Nyssa, St. Cyril of Alexandria, St. Cyprian, St. Hilary, St. Ambrose, St. Jerome, etc.

St. Augustine (354-430) distinguished clearly between the damned, in the never-ending fires of hell, and the faithful who die in the state of grace but who still have minor sins or who have not yet perfectly expiated the penalty due to graver sins already forgiven while upon earth. He writes: "Some of the faithful will be saved by a purgatorial fire. . . . In this life do Thou purge me, and make me such that I will have no need of the amending fire that waits for those who will be saved, yet so as by fire."

There is ancient classical pagan literature which admits of the belief by ancient nationalities in a place of purgation. Plato's *Gorgias* and *Phaedo* and Virgil's *Aeneid*, etc., speak of a need for expiation in the next life. This was admitted by the ancient Egyptians, Babylonians, Persians, Chinese, Japanese; even to some extent by the Greeks and Romans.

Our belief in purgatory, however, comes from the constant Tradition of the Church and Sacred Scripture. The *Didache*, an important record of Christian belief, practice and govenment in the first century, tells us to offer prayers ceaselessly to God and to offer the Communion we have received "for those who sleep."

Anointing of the Sick

Our divine and loving Savior, the Good Shepherd, ever solicitous for our salvation, gave His Church a special sacrament for those seriously sick. This sacrament, once called "Extreme Unction," is not a sacrament only for those at the point of death. As soon as any of the faithful, who have reached the age of reason, begin to be in danger of death from sickness or old age, the fitting time to receive this sacrament has arrived.

This Sacrament of the Anointing of the Sick was instituted by Jesus Christ as a sacrament of the New Law to give the sick spiritual aid and strength and to perfect spiritual health. If one is in the state of mortal sin and is able to confess, he or she must receive the Sacrament of Penance before the Anointing of the Sick because the latter is a sacrament of the living, meaning that one must normally be in the state of grace to receive it worthily. In cases where it is physically impossible to confess, this sacrament has the power to remit even serious sin. One who is unconscious and in serious danger of death, who had committed mortal sin since one's last good confession, but who had made at least an imperfect act of contrition with the intention to confess and receive the Sacrament of Penance when one was able, would have mortal sin forgiven through the Anointing of the Sick.

The Apostle James mentions this sacrament. "If one of you is ill, he should send for the elders of the Church, and they must anoint him with oil in the name of the Lord and pray over him. The prayer of faith will save the sick man and the Lord will raise him up again; and if he has committed any sins, he will be forgiven" (James 5:14-16).

This sacrament supernaturalizes the suffering of the person anointed. It elevates this human condition from the mere natural level to the supernatural level, joining it to Jesus Christ whose passion and death made it possible for all human suffering to be meritorious. The actual suffering of the person anointed thus becomes a means of glorifying God and growing in grace. This is a special reason why the anointing of one seriously sick ought not be delayed. In addition to giving the sick person the opportunity of reconciliation with God and His holy Church, the anointing elevates the suffering to a meritorious condition in Jesus Christ. For example, one who is seriously sick from cancer, even though the illness may be protracted for months, ought not wait until death is imminent to receive the anointing. In addition to the risk of dying without the sacrament, one is deprived of the value of supernaturalizing the suffering over the length of days that God gives. The anointing received with good dispositions of heart empowers one in Christ to resignation to the divine will and brings supernatural peace to the heart. This sacrament remits venial sins and at least some of the temporal punishment due to forgiven sin. This sacrament may also be effective in restoring bodily health if it be for the glory of God and the good of the soul.

The rite of administering this sacrament consists essentially in the anointing with oil by a priest on the forehead and the hands, while pronouncing the words: "Through this holy anointing and his most loving mercy, may the Lord assist you by the grace of the Holy Spirit, so that, freed from your sins, he may save you and in his goodness raise you up." The oil used is olive oil which was blessed by a bishop, usually oil that he blessed on Holy Thursday. In case of emergency the priest may give a single anointing on the forehead or any other suitable part of the body.

It is an article of Catholic faith as defined by the Council of Trent and other councils that the Anointing of the Sick is a sacrament instituted by Jesus Christ. In addition to the mention by the Apostle James, the Church further teaches that this sacrament is implied in the reference made in the Gospel where Christ sent out the disciples, who "anointed many sick people with oil and cured them" (Mark 6:13).

Judgment

Ecclesiasticus (Sirach) 7:40 says: "In everything you do, remember your end, and you will never sin." We are on trial upon this earth. The span of our lifetime, here below, is the span of our time of trial. "Since men only die once, and after that comes judgment. . ." (Hebrews 9:27).

Each person will be judged individually immediately after his death, as the soul leaves the body. This is known as the *particular* judgment. At this individual judgment God irrevocably determines a person's reward or punishment for all eternity, depending on his or her cooperation with grace during one's time on earth.

The *general* judgment refers to the universal judgment of the human race at the final resurrection of the dead. The creeds of the Church affirm this belief in saying that Christ now sits at the right hand of God the Father, whence he shall come "to judge the living and the dead." This means He shall judge both the just and the wicked. The general judgment will manifest to the world both the justice and the mercy of God. His justice will be witnessed by all who have ever lived in seeing the condemnation that must be given to unrepentant sinners. God's mercy will be seen in those who are saved. There will be revealed both the moral conduct of people and all the accumulated blessings or injuries that resulted from each person's good or evil deeds.

Heaven

The essential happiness of heaven will consist in the enjoyment of God's beauty, in the vision of God, who is the source and the principle of all goodness and perfection. "And eternal life is this: to know you, the only true God, and Jesus Christ whom you have sent" (John 17:3). "My dear people, we are already the children of God but what we are to be in the future has not yet been revealed; all we know is, that when it is revealed we shall be like him because we shall see him as he really is" (1 John 3:2).

The vision of God which the angels and saints in heaven enjoy is called the Beatific Vision. There will be an intuitive knowledge of God producing heavenly beatitude. The souls of the just "see the divine essence of an intuitive vision and face to face, so that the divine essence is known immediately, showing itself plainly, clearly and openly, and not mediately through any creature" (*Denzinger* 1000-2).

This vision of God, seeing Him "face to face" as Sacred Scripture describes it, is called *vision* in the mind, as analogous to bodily vision. It is called *beatific* because of the happiness produced in man's will and in his entire being. Heaven consists of *"the things that no eye has seen and no ear has heard, things beyond the mind of man, all that God has prepared for those who love him"* (1 Corinthians 2:9). In heaven one shall see God in His own nature and substance which is infinite. "Now we are seeing a dim reflection in a mirror; but then we shall be seeing face to face. The knowledge that I have now is imperfect; but then I shall know as fully as I am known" (1 Corinthians 13:12).

Sharing in the immediate vision of God, the souls of the blessed share in the divine happiness of the Most Blessed Trinity. Heaven is the place and condition of perfect supernatural happiness then. After the essential happiness of the immediate vision and love of God, secondarily the happiness of heaven consists in the knowledge, love and enjoyment of creatures. We shall know and love other souls in heaven, including the angels. Until the final general judgment and resurrection, except for our Lord Jesus Christ and the Blessed Virgin Mary, only the souls of the just are in heaven. At the end of the world there will be a resurrection of bodies, and those in heaven will have their bodies and souls rejoined. These will possess immortality in their risen, glorified bodies, which will share in the glory of their souls which they received from God through Jesus Christ.

In heaven the same infinite God will be seen by all. Yet, not everyone in heaven will have the same degree of glory and happiness. All will be perfectly happy but not equally happy. A simple comparison can be used. Ten glasses with different capacities are filled to the brim with water. All are perfectly full. Each holds a different amount. In heaven all are perfectly happy according to their capacity to be happy, to enjoy the Beatific Vision, which will depend for depth of beatitude on the measure of God's grace in the soul at the moment of death.

Our merits for eternal happiness will depend on the strength of our faith and our response in love while upon earth. The good works of charity done for a supernatural motive; the sacraments received worthily in faith and love; each Sacrifice of the Mass participated in with faith, love and reverence — all will contribute to a higher place in heaven.

Heaven will never cease. It is eternal. Its joys will never stop. Its happiness will be shared with all the angels, saints and those we knew and loved upon earth.

Just as there is a unity in Christ with the faithful upon earth in the Church, so there is a unity and cooperation with those in heaven and in purgatory. They are united as within one Mystical Body of Christ. Sanctifying grace, which is a sharing in the life of God, existing in the souls in purgatory and in the souls in heaven, is the same as that sharing in the life of God that exists in the faithful upon earth. The faithful upon earth, the souls in purgatory and the saints in heaven are thus in communion with one another in Christ.

On earth the faithful profess the same faith within the Catholic Church, obey the same authority of Christ in His Church, and assist each other with their prayers and good works. Members of the Church are in communion with the saints in heaven by honoring them, invoking their prayers and assistance and striving to imitate their virtues. The faithful upon earth do not pray to the saints in the sense that the saints can answer prayers of their own power. It is rather a matter of intercession with God through Jesus Christ, the one essential mediator. All grace, every answer to prayer, comes ultimately from God in, with and through Jesus Christ. The Blessed Virgin, Queen of the Angels and Saints, the souls in purgatory and the saints in heaven intercede for mankind by their merits and prayers.

Hell

Hell is the place and state of eternal punishment. The fallen angels, those who revolted against God, were cast into hell for all eternity. Human beings who die in mortal sin, separated from the love of God, are placed in hell for all eternity. Jesus, in speaking of the Last Judgment, said of those who did not serve Christ in others, " 'Go away from me with your curse upon you, to the eternal fire prepared for the devil and his angels. . . .' And they will go away to eternal punishment, and the virtuous to eternal life" (Matthew 25:41,46). In Matthew 18:8 Jesus spoke of "eternal fire." "And if your hand should cause you to sin, cut it off; it is better for you to enter into life crippled, than to have two hands and go to hell, into the fire that cannot be put out" (Mark 9:43).

Those who would deny the existence of hell are dealing with a denial of the redemption. The gates of heaven were closed with the sin of Adam and Eve. If there were no possibility of eternal damnation, then from what did Jesus Christ save us? The Fourth Lateran Council stated that the wicked will "receive a perpetual punishment with the devil" (*Denzinger* 801). Belief in the existence of hell is consistent with divine justice and human freedom. Those who are lost condemn themselves by refusing to accept God's saving grace.

The Athanasian Creed, written before 428, states: "Whoever wishes to be saved must, above all, keep the Catholic faith; for unless a person keeps this faith whole and entire he will undoubtedly be lost forever. . . . At his coming [Christ's second coming], all men are to arise with their own bodies; and they are to give an account of their lives. Those who have done good deeds will go into eternal life; those who have done evil will go into eternal fire."

It is a matter of Catholic faith *(de fide)* that the souls of those who die in the condition of personal grievous sin enter hell. It also is a matter of faith that the punishment of hell lasts for all eternity. As there is a difference in degree of happiness due to different degrees of merit for those who enter heaven, so the punishment of the damned is proportioned to each one's guilt.

DISCUSSION QUESTIONS

1. Define death.

Death is a separation of the soul from the body after which no merit can be gained.

2. Does the Bible speak of life after death?

Yes, the Bible speaks of life after death, and there are references in both the Old and New Testaments to the immortality of the soul, with references becoming ever more clear as divine revelation increases.

3. What is purgatory?

Purgatory is a place, or state, of temporal cleansing for souls who have died with unforgiven venial sins still on their souls or because they have not made sufficient satisfaction for the temporal punishment attached to forgiven sins. It is a place where one undergoes purification before entrance into heaven.

4. For what reasons do souls go to purgatory?

Souls go to purgatory for two reasons: to make satisfaction to God's justice for unforgiven venial sins and to make satisfaction for the temporal punishment still due on sins which have been forgiven. (See answer to Question 3.)

5. Did belief in life after death and the existence of a place of purgation arise only after the coming of Christ?

The belief in life after death and a place of purification after death existed before the coming of Jesus Christ, as testified to in the Second Book of Maccabees where arrangements are made to offer sacrifice in the temple of Jerusalem for the sins of those slain in battle. The account speaks of resurrection.

6. Does the Bible mention fire in purgatory?

St. Augustine (354-430) spoke of being saved "yet so as by fire" and interpreted 1 Corinthians 3:14-15 as having reference to the cleansing fires of purgatory.

7. What is the difference between God's justice and His mercy?

God's justice demands that satisfaction or reparation be made for every sin committed. God in His mercy forgives us our sins when we repent. His justice still requires satisfaction to repair the harm to the glory of the Holy One.

8. Is there evidence that the early Christians believed in purgatory?

There is evidence that Christians from the very first century believed in purgatory, and this is shown not only in the writings of early Church Fathers but in the ancient catacombs of Rome, where one can still find evidence of prayers for the deceased among the first Christians.

9. On what does the Church base its faith in purgatory?

The Church bases its faith in purgatory on Sacred Scripture and the Tradition of the Church, which has always taught the doctrine and, in practice, prayed for the faithful departed, especially in the Holy Sacrifice of the Mass.

10. When should one receive the Sacrament of the Anointing of the Sick?

One should receive the Sacrament of the Anointing of the Sick as soon as anyone of the faithful who has reached the age of reason begins to be in danger of death from sickness, accident or old age.

11. What does the Anointing of the Sick do for the soul?

Under the proper conditions the Anointing of the Sick may remit even mortal sin from the soul when one cannot confess. It brings spiritual health to the soul, supernaturalizing the sufferings which God has permitted, making them meritorious in Jesus Christ, and removes at least some, if not all, temporal punishment still due to forgiven sins.

12. What does the Anointing of the Sick do for the body?

The Anointing of the Sick when received with great faith and love may, if God wills it for His glory and the salvation of the soul, bring healing to the body.

13. Which apostle clearly mentioned the Anointing of the Sick recorded in the Bible?

The Apostle James (5:14-16) clearly mentioned the Anointing of the Sick.

14. Explain how the anointing supernaturalizes illness.

The Anointing of the Sick supernaturalizes suffering by uniting it to Jesus Christ, who first suffered for our salvation and won redemption for us. We are members of Christ's Mystical Body, the Church, and the sacrament places a sick person in a special way in union with the suffering Christ to draw merits from Christ, who first suffered for us. The sacrament will assist us in performing what St. Paul spoke of when he said, "I am suffering now, and in my own body to do what I can to make up all that has still to be undergone by Christ for the sake of his body, the Church" (Colossians 1:24-25). "Indeed, as the sufferings of Christ overflow to us, so, through Christ, does our consolation overflow" (2 Corinthians 1:5-6). Scripture clearly shows in many places that we can share in Christ's sufferings and that this sacrament elevates the sufferings of sickness, joining them to Jesus Christ.

15. What part of the body does the priest anoint?

In anointing the sick the priest normally anoints the forehead and hands, but if that is impossible he may anoint any suitable part of the body possible.

16. What is the difference between particular and general judgment?

Particular judgment is the individual judgment each one must undergo at the moment of death. It irrevocably determines one's place in eternity. General judgment refers to the universal judgment of the human race at the final resurrection of the dead.

17. What is the essential happiness of heaven?
The essential happiness of heaven consists in the vision of God.

18. Why is the vision of God in heaven called the Beatific Vision?
Seeing God face to face in heaven is called the "Beatific Vision" because *beatific* refers to the happiness produced in man's will and in his entire being, while *vision* refers to the mind of man who sees God who is immaterial and an infinite substance. See, or vision, refers to the knowledge man possesses in heaven, an immediate knowledge of God.

19. What is the secondary happiness of heaven?
The secondary happiness of heaven will consist in the knowledge, love and enjoyment souls have of other creatures, the angels and saints.

20. On what will our degree of happiness in heaven depend?
Our degree of happiness in heaven will depend upon the amount of sanctifying grace in our soul at the moment of death. There are different degrees of grace depending on one's response to faith through works of charity, prayer-life and the sacraments.

21. How is it possible for all in heaven to be perfectly, but not equally, happy?
All souls in heaven are perfectly but not equally happy because those with greater grace have a greater capacity to enter into the beatitude of God's life of happiness. Each soul in heaven will be satisfied fully according to the capacity of which he is capable.

22. What is the Communion of Saints?
The Communion of Saints refers to the union in prayer and grace in Jesus Christ of the faithful still upon earth, the souls in purgatory and the saints in heaven.

23. Does the Bible mention hell as a place of eternal fire?
The Bible quotes Jesus as speaking of "eternal fire" (Matthew 18:8) and of "the fire that cannot be put out" (Mark 9:44).

24. What is the consequence of the denial of the existence of hell?
The consequence of the denial of the existence of hell is denying a dogma of Catholic faith which says that the souls of those who die in the condition of personal grievous sin enter hell. Hell is a place or state of eternal punishment inhabited by those rejected by God because such souls have rejected God's saving grace. In addition to placing oneself in a condition of denying a dogma of faith, one has the consequence of denying the role of Jesus Christ as Redeemer-Savior. If Jesus did not redeem our souls and save us from damnation, then from what did He save us?

CHAPTER 21

Morality
and the Ten Commandments

Neo-Modernists have said: "Law has no place in Christianity." Some claim that Jesus Christ never legislated. St. Paul's words are quoted: "You are living by grace and not by law" (Romans 6:14). They say, "By grace we receive the gift of love which dispenses us from laws and regulations." They quote St. Augustine, who said: "Love and do what you will."

Actually St. Paul's writings in the New Testament are the best evidence that Christianity includes legislation. What St. Paul was fighting was a struggle with legalism. The Jews had developed a system of justification by works involving oppressive directives. Jesus distinguished between law and a spirit of legalism. Jesus defined legalism as subordination of the spirit of the law to its crude letter.

Consider this case. According to the Pharisees a man could pull his ox or donkey out of the ditch into which it may have fallen on the Sabbath, but he could not cure a man of an illness on the Sabbath day. Some interpreted the injunction that the commandments should be before one's eyes at all times in such a manner that they made a little scroll on which the commandments were written and which dangled out in front of them, extending from a headpiece.

It was in the spirit of Jesus Christ that St. Paul was working to get people to look at law. "Does it follow that Law itself is sin?" St. Paul asked, and answered, "Of course not" (Romans 7:7). When St. Paul placed the law and grace in contraposition it was the law of Moses in contrast with its fulfillment in Jesus Christ, in Jesus' law of love and grace. While speaking of the liberating features of grace, St. Paul spoke of himself as "free of the Law myself (though not free from God's law, being under the law of Christ)" (1 Corinthians 9:21).

Morality from the Christian point of view of the Catholic Church is the relation between a human act and the final destiny of a human being. The ultimate end is the possession of God in the Beatific Vision. Since heaven is the ultimate end, a human act is either good or bad according to whether it leads one to or detracts one from his or her heavenly destination. The moral norms of human acts flow necessarily from the nature of God. God has laws determining what is in accordance with the life of grace. Christian morality emphasizes a code of conduct summarized under a sense of personal integrity, social justice and love of neighbor; accountability to God as a loving Father who is also Lord of all.

The Catholic has an obligation to form a *correct* conscience based on the laws of God and the teachings of His Holy Church. It is possible to form our conscience contrary to objective morality because of mistaken judgments. The central factor in the formation of conscience and sound moral judgment should be Christ's role in one's life. (See John 14:6ff, 12:46-50.) To have a correct Catholic conscience, one must listen to the teaching Church, faithfully communicate with the Lord in every phase of one's life, and through personal prayer and participation in the sacramental life and prayer of the Church obtain the strength of grace to live according to one's honestly formed conscience.

"The Church is the indispensable guide to the complete richness of what Jesus teaches. . . . Conscience, though inviolable, is not a law unto itself; it is a practical dictate, not a teacher of doctrine. Doctrine is taught by the Church, whose members have a serious obligation to know what it teaches and to adhere to it loyally" (*National Catechetical Directory*, 190).

What the authentic Christian must realize regarding morality is this: Man's activity is not to be wholly dependent on psychological determinism or on economic, social, cultural and other such conditions. The authority for objective true morality is from above. New morality that is not in harmony with the Gospels and Church teachings is from below. The Church teaches that there are absolutes in morality.

"Christ commissioned his apostles to teach the observance of everything that he had commanded" (cf. Matthew 28:20). Catechesis, therefore, must include not only those things which are to be believed, but also those things which are to be done.

"The moral life of Christians, which is a way of acting that is worthy of a man and an adopted son of God, is a response to the duty of living and growing, under the guidance of the Holy Spirit, in the new life communicated through Jesus Christ.

"The moral life of Christians is guided by the grace and gifts of the Holy Spirit. 'The love of God has been poured out in our hearts through the Holy Spirit who has been given to us' (Romans 5:5).

"The docility with which the Holy Spirit must be obeyed entails a faithful observance of the commandments of God, the laws of the Church and just civil laws.

"Christian freedom still needs to be ruled and directed in the concrete circumstances of human life. Accordingly, the conscience of the faithful, even when informed by the virtue of prudence, must be subject to the magisterium of the Church, whose duty it is to explain the whole moral law authoritatively, in order that it may rightly and correctly express the objective moral order.

"Further, the conscience itself of Christians must be taught that there are norms which are absolute, that is, which bind in every case and on all people. That is why the saints confessed Christ through the practice of heroic virtues; indeed, the martyrs suffered even torture and death rather than deny Christ" (*General Catechetical Directory*, 63).

Examples of absolute norms of morality where such human acts would in all cases and circumstances be seriously sinful: *Adultery*, living intimacy with a married person to whom one is not validly married; *Fornication*, sexual acts between two unmarried persons; *Abortion*, the direct and intentional taking of innocent human life before birth.

In modern times the Church has repeatedly had to defend moral objectivity, which says certain actions are good and others are bad; certain behaviors are virtuous and others sinful in all times and circumstances. Situation ethics, or the new morality, holds that the ultimate standard of human conduct is "not an objective norm found outside of man and independent of his subjective persuasion." These subjective norms of morality of which the Church does not approve hold to an "immediate internal illumination and judgment" of each person for himself. Pope Pius XII already issued an Instruction, *De Ethica Situationis*, stating that such a subjectivist theory "deviates far from the Catholic teaching handed down through the ages" (*Denzinger* 3918).

God makes known through reason and revelation what constitutes a mortal sin, which separates one from His grace. Those who commit adultery, murder, perjury and other such serious crimes with full and deliberate consent estrange themselves from God. It is God who sets down the conditions for estrangement, not men. It is not for humans to decide subjectively whether direct abortion is a mortal sin which deprives them of a sharing in the life of God. Making clever distinctions like, "In doing this act I do not intend to reject God," does not remove us from the reality that such serious crimes do, in fact, estrange us from God's friendship.

The Church's position on mortal sin remains the same. One is guilty of mortal sin when he consents with the fullness of his will to do what he knows is a serious offense against God and the teachings of the Church. A venial sin is committed when the misdeed is not objectively serious and circumstances do not make it serious, or when the matter is serious but full consent was not given by our free will.

Exodus 19 and 20 relate for us the Ten Commandments as given by God. We should remember the words of Jesus Christ whereby His two commandments of love contain all the Ten Commandments: *"You must love the Lord your God with all your heart, with all your soul, and with all your mind.* This is the greatest and the first commandment. The second resembles it: *You must love your neighbor as yourself.* On these two commandments hang the whole Law, and the Prophets also" (Matthew 22:37-40). Notice that the first three of the Ten Commandments concern our direct relationship with Almighty God. The remaining seven concern our relationship to God as we relate with fellow humans.

1. *"I AM THE LORD YOUR GOD. YOU SHALL NOT HAVE OTHER GODS BESIDES ME."*

Our first duty is to adore God as our Supreme Lord and Master. This is the whole purpose of our existence. If we are charitable in a natural way to others but do not have faith in God and believe in Him, it is of no value for eternal life. Adoration is given only to God, not to any angel or saint or fellow creature. Adoration is at once an act of the intellect and the will, recognizing God alone as worthy of supreme honor because He is infinitely perfect, has supreme dominion over all, is our Creator and we have total dependence on Him for everything.

Adoration is given to God by striving to do all things in His presence, by keeping His commandments, by following the teachings of the Church He established in His Son made man, by performing the duties of our state in life, by acts of penance and reparation, by loving our neighbor, by good example, by daily prayer. The highest form of adoration we can give to God is found in the Sacrifice of the Mass, which perpetuates the sacrifice which Jesus Christ offered on the Cross.

Catholics are to give public and official adoration to God only in the Catholic Church, which is the true Church of God with the fullness of Christ's priestly powers to adore God the Father. The Catholic Church forbids its members to engage in indiscriminate worship from one church to another. Only with permission of the local bishop should Catholics join in formal prayer with their separated brethren and only under certain special circumstances. The Catholic Church recognizes that our separated brethren have some Christian truths and the Spirit of Christ can work among them as a means of salvation as they "derive their efficacy from the very fullness of grace and truth entrusted to the Catholic Church.

"Nevertheless, our separated brethren, whether considered as individuals or as communities and Churches, are not blessed with that unity

266

which Jesus Christ wished to bestow on all those to whom he has given new birth into one body, and whom he has quickened to newness of life — that unity which the Holy Scriptures and the ancient Tradition of the Church proclaim. For it is through Christ's Catholic Church alone, which is the universal help towards salvation, that the fullness of the means of salvation can be obtained. It was to the apostolic college alone, of which Peter is the head, that we believe that Our Lord entrusted all the blessings of the New Covenant, in order to establish on earth the one Body of Christ into which all those should be fully incorporated who belong in any way to the people of God. . ." (*Decree on Ecumenism, 3*).

"In certain circumstances, such as in prayer services 'for unity' and during ecumenical gatherings, it is allowable, indeed desirable, that Catholics should join in prayer with their separated brethren. . . .

"Yet worship in common (*communicatio in sacris*) is not to be considered as a means to be used indiscriminately for the restoration of unity among Christians. . ." (*Decree on Ecumenism, 8*).

Catholics may, of course, attend funerals of friends in other communities to show their love. It is obvious to all that they are present for the love of the person deceased, not to take an active part in another form of worship. The same is true of weddings of non-Catholic friends.

To leave the practice of the Catholic Church is a serious sin against the First Commandment. It is a serious sin against the true faith which God has given to a soul. One who gives up or loses the true faith he once had will be judged accordingly, since God as a good Father, once He has given the gift, never takes it back unless the person deliberately disregards it or throws it back in His face. The same would hold for a person who held on to the title "Catholic" but only in a nominal way while deliberately denying essential Catholic doctrines.

To join organizations which are anti-Christian and anti-Catholic is forbidden. Examples: the Communist Party, the Ku Klux Klan. Also forbidden to Catholics are secret societies which have principles at variance with authentic Christian beliefs and practices.

Other things forbidden under the First Commandment are the practice of superstition, palmistry, crystal-gazing, Ouija boards, astrology, spiritism and believing habitually in dreams.

A sacrilege would be the deliberate abuse of a sacred person, place or thing, (priest, church, blessed religious article).

There are some superstitious practices which, while not serious in nature, should be avoided because they are at least venial sins: chain prayers, lucky numbers and emblems. One also must guard against using approved religious articles in a superstitious manner. These articles should be used only as the Church intends them to be used, that is, to lead

267

our hearts and minds to God and to call upon the blessings of the Church.

2. "YOU SHALL NOT TAKE THE NAME OF THE LORD, YOUR GOD, IN VAIN."

To use God's name in vain means to use it flippantly, carelessly, irreverently. Such is contrary to the Second Commandment. To use God's name in cursing or swearing, to use the name of our Savior, Jesus Christ, in any irreverent way is contrary to this commandment. So holy is the name of God that in the Old Testament God's name "Yahweh" could be spoken by no one but the high priest and he could speak it but once a year. The name of God refers to Him whom it represents. To disrespect the name of God is to disrespect the Lord himself.

At the name of Jesus we should bow our heads. The apostles performed miracles through Jesus Christ by the use of His holy name: "In the name of Jesus Christ the Nazarene, walk!" (Acts 3:6).

Blasphemy is speaking against God in a contemptuous, scornful, abusive way. Blasphemy can be committed not only by word but also in thought or deed. One is guilty of blasphemy who seriously ridicules with contempt the saints, sacred objects or persons consecrated to God because God is thus indirectly attacked. Blasphemy is a mortal sin because it is a violation of charity due to God. To sin seriously, the person doing so must realize the contemptuous meaning of what he says or does.

An oath is invoking God's name to bear witness to the truth uttered. A familiar form of oath is, "So help me God." Oaths are to be taken only in very serious matters. Usually they are taken before a priest or judge. Perjury, lying after taking an oath, is seriously sinful.

A vow is a free, deliberate promise made to God to do something which is good. One who violates a promise made under vow is committing a special sin. One may bind himself under vow either in a grave or slight manner according to the intention made. Vows increase the moral value of human acts directed to worship of God and are thus more meritorious than when the same is done without the vow. A person taking a vow surrenders to God the moral freedom of acting otherwise. Vows forestall human weakness. Their purpose is to invoke divine grace to sustain one's resolution. Religious take vows of poverty, chastity and obedience. Vows are so serious that dispensations must be sought from the Church and granted only for very serious reasons.

3. "REMEMBER TO KEEP HOLY THE SABBATH DAY."

Catholics are bound under pain of mortal sin to participate in the Sacrifice of the Mass every Sunday and holy day of obligation. Only a *serious* reason would excuse one. Inconvenience, laziness, company came, being tired, poor clothing, headache, etc., are *not* sufficient excuses.

The Sunday obligation may be fulfilled Saturday evening since, according to the biblical day, the Lord's Day is measured from evening to evening, not from midnight. This means Saturday evening is already counted as the Lord's Day.

Valid excuses for missing Mass on Sundays or holy days would be serious illness; serious work demands, such as jobs at a hospital or nursing home, as a firemen, etc., if every reasonable effort has been made to participate in Mass by finding someone else to substitute for you when you go to Mass. With multiple Masses and different shifts, it should be rare that it would be impossible to get to Mass. People who have seriously sick family members, in danger of death, and desire to be with them in their last hours would be excused from Mass. A blizzard which makes traveling impossible or very dangerous, when distance and conditions make walking impossible, would be validating cause to miss Mass involuntarily.

Parents have a serious obligation to see that all their children who have reached the age of reason (seven years) participate at Mass each Sunday and Holy Day. Parents sin also by causing scandal to their children if they miss deliberately. Also, to deliberately arrive late for Mass is venially sinful if slightly late, and mortally sinful if one misses a major portion of the Mass. The same goes for leaving Mass early without sufficient cause.

Besides the obligation of participating in the Sacrifice of the Mass, God strictly forbids unnecessary manual work on Sundays. One must avoid those activities which would hinder renewal of the soul and body, such as needless work and business activities, or unnecessary shopping.

Recreation, even though strenuous, is not forbidden on Sundays. One may always labor mentally, that is, study or write, which is more of the mind than the body.

Non-Catholics who take Catholic instructions with the intention of joining the Catholic Church should not join the Church if they have no intention of participating in the Sacrifice of the Mass each Sunday and holy day. They should wait until they are attending regularly. Ideally, they should attend Mass during their course of instructions.

The entire day of Sunday is the Lord's Day. There should be a special effort to keep the whole day by a prayerful attitude, by rest, by wholesome recreation. One can engage in other spiritual activities, e.g., spiritual reading, Catholic radio or television programs, charitable acts, such as visiting the sick, those in nursing homes, shut-ins, etc.

The six holy days when U.S. Catholics are bound under pain of mortal sin to participate in the Sacrifice of the Mass are: December 25 (Christmas); January 1 (Solemnity of the Mother of God); Ascension Thursday (40 Days after Easter); August 15 (Assumption of Mary into heaven); November 1 (All Saints); December 8 (Immaculate Conception).

4. "HONOR YOUR FATHER AND YOUR MOTHER."

Some children generally are considered to sin venially by disobedience or disrespect to their parents in small everyday matters. Children advancing into adolescent years, however, may sin seriously by disobeying their parents in company keeping, forbidden activities, keeping late hours and going to places which their parents judge to be seriously harmful.

Just as children have an obligation to obey their parents, parents have a serious obligation to discipline their children. Parents who permit children to keep company with bad companions, date prematurely and steadily so as to endanger their purity, etc., are seriously offending against God by not representing God in their parental authority.

Children have the obligation to obey their parents until they reach an adult age, and the obligation to love and honor their parents binds forever. Children who remain at home after reaching a mature age must still obey their parents in matters of home discipline.

The obligation of parents toward their children includes seeing that children receive solid religious instruction in the Catholic faith and formation in its practice. Parents cannot totally delegate instruction in the faith. The Church teaches that parents are the "primary educators" and scarcely anyone can substitute for them. They must not take for granted that others are teaching their children the basics of the faith, such as the Commandments, the meaning of the sacraments, the fullness of the true Catholic faith. Parents should have discussions with their children to determine that each child is comprehending the basics and striving to live the faith. Simply sending a child to a Catholic school or CCD program does not fulfill parents' obligation to educate their children.

Parents must teach children respect for all lawful civil and Church authorities. This must be done by word and example. Throughout life all must obey the pope as the successor of St. Peter, representative of Jesus Christ upon earth, the visible head of the Church. The bishop is a direct succesor of the apostles. Catholics owe their bishop obedience. He has the same authority given the apostles by Jesus Christ and may make laws and regulations in his diocese to aid us in our search for eternal life. The pastor of the parish represents the bishop, ultimately Christ, in the local parish. Catholics must obey their pastors in matters pertaining to faith and morals unless there is serious reason to believe that an individual priest is misrepresenting the authentic teachings of the Church. Pastors are to be obeyed in matters pertaining to the good order of the parish.

5. "YOU SHALL NOT KILL."

God gives human life and only God can take it away. One must preserve his own life and the lives of others. Nothing can be done to injure oneself or another deliberately. Included under the commandment forbidding murder is anything that leads to killing, namely, anger, hatred or revenge. Murder is always a mortal sin. Anger, hatred and revenge admit of degrees. If serious, these things would be mortal. In self-defense, if absolutely necessary, one could kill an attacker if it is the only way to stop him. By the same principle a country may protect itself in war against an unjust aggressor.

Abortion, the *direct* killing of an unborn baby, is mortally sinful and brings automatic excommunciation to the person having the abortion and to anyone aiding in it. A procedure, rightly called "therapeutic abortion," is sometimes used in which the intention is *not* the direct killing of the child, e.g., if the womb is dangerously diseased and its removal is necessary to save the mother. It is just as lawful in this case to extract the mother's womb as it would be if there were no pregnancy. This is not direct abortion, and such rare surgery is permitted by the principle of double effect. The purpose is to save the mother, not to kill the fetus. In such surgery the evil effect is not intended in itself, but merely allowed as a necessary consequence of the good effect. It is not permitted, however, to deliberately kill the fetus to save the mother. With modern medical developments, such "therapeutic abortions" are becoming more and more rare. In fact, some doctors consider them obsolete. Direct abortion is a serious sin because the intent is to kill innocent life, and that is what happens even though some attempt to deny the reality.

Suicide is the taking of one's own life and is seriously sinful. A person who commits suicide while insane is not responsible for his act. Mercy killing is taking the life of a person who is suffering from sickness. It is murder. Only God can take a human life, and no one may do anything to speed up the death of a patient. To neglect property, machinery, automobiles, etc., in such a way that these become serious hazards to one's own life or that of others is seriously sinful.

It is never permitted to mutilate the human body. Sterilization of either a man or a woman is seriously sinful.

There is just anger. But anger carried beyond reason is sinful. Hatred

271

is the opposite of love. God has commanded that we love everyone, but "liking" is in the emotions. Dislike is not the same as hatred. When temperaments do not blend well, it may be the charitable thing not to associate with a certain person more than necessary. We must manifest charity to those we dislike. Fighting which disrupts peace in the family or community can be mortally sinful, depending upon the degree of its seriousness.

Without a serious reason, man is not permitted to deprive himself of the full use of his intellect and will so that his judgment and actions are impaired. The use of "dope," narcotics or psychedelic drugs, without a doctor's precription, is sinful. While the moderate use of alcohol is not sinful (unless one is under-age and by using it disobeys the law), the use of alcoholic beverages to the degree of deliberate drunkenness is seriously sinful. Alcoholism has brought untold suffering, not only to the one who drinks excessively, but often to one's spouse and the entire family. One who cannot control alcohol before marriage is destined not to make a good husband or wife. "You know perfectly well that people who do wrong will not inherit the kingdom of God: people of immoral lives, idolaters, adulterers, catamites, sodomites, thieves, usurers, drunkards, slanderers and swindlers will never inherit the kingdom of God" (1 Corinthians 6:9-10). One who deliberately becomes intoxicated assumes responsiblity for whatever immorality he/she may be guilty of in such a state.

Scandal is murder of the soul. Parents and any others who by word or deed are the cause of leading others into sin are guilty not only of their own sins but of those sins which they cause others to commit. "But anyone who is an obstacle [scandal] to bring down one of these little ones who have faith in me would be better drowned in the depths of the sea with a great millstone around his neck. Alas for the world that there should be such obstacles! Obstacles indeed there must be, but alas for the man who provides them!" (Matthew 18:6-7).

6. "YOU SHALL NOT COMMIT ADULTERY."
9. "YOU SHALL NOT COVET YOUR NEIGHBOR'S WIFE."

The Sixth and Ninth Commandments are studied together because the Sixth concerns unchaste actions while the Ninth concerns unchaste thoughts and desires.

It is thought that as a result of original sin, the greatest disharmony caused in man's nature was the disturbance of his sexual powers, insofar as man finds them the most difficult to keep in balance as God intended when He created the first man and woman. Sex as created by God is good in itself. It is the abuse of sex that makes it sinful. Chastity is the Christian virtue whereby a person regulates the sexual passions according to God's laws and right reason. Only a truly married husband and wife have the right to use sex, and it must be, exclusively, only with each other. Husbands and wives must always use their sexual powers in the natural way as God intended and without any artificial contraceptives. "In vitro" fertilization, which results in a so-called "test-tube" baby is condemned by the Catholic Church as unnatural. The end never justifies the means.

We live in a society that is experiencing a sexual revolution. It is a sex-saturated society that takes sex out of the sanctity of matrimony and makes it a cheap and dirty thing, a thing of mere animal pleasure. The deliberate use of sex outside of God's plan, whether alone or with another, is mortally sinful. "Nobody who actually indulges in fornication or impurity or promiscuity — which is worshipping a false god — can inherit anything of the kingdom of God" (Ephesians 5:5). How far our society is from the Christian mandate: "Among you there must be not even a mention of fornication or impurity in any of its forms, or promiscuity: this would hardly become the saints!" (Ephesians 5:3).

Adultery (sexual intercourse of a married person with someone other than rightful spouse) is mortally sinful. Fornication (sexual intercourse between two unmarried persons) is mortally sinful. Masturbation (the deliberate use of sex by solitary acts while fully awake) is seriously sinful.

Sometimes young couples mistakenly think that as long as they do not go "all the way" they have avoided serious sin. That is not true. Impure touching, impure actions of various kinds, passionate embracing and kissing among the unmarried are seriously sinful. When the things are done deliberately to arouse sexual passion among unmarried people, there can be no doubt of serious sin. Couples who date and strive to be pure, but realize they unintentionally are falling into a serious temptation because of circumstances, have a grave obligation to remove themselves from the place and circumstances and be a help to one another to remain pure. Unnecessary occasions of sin must be avoided. Suggestive dancing and immodest dress must be avoided. Also, impure talk and dirty stories with the intention to develop impure thoughts in others are often serious occasions of sin, and one who does these things can thus be responsible for many serious sins.

Good Christians must avoid all unnecessary occasions of sin. Occasions of sin can be persons, places or things that may lead us into sin. Unchaste entertainment of any kind — movies, television, songs — must be avoided.

To lead a life of purity one should pray daily, receiving the sacraments frequently and worthily. One should not fear confessing such sins committed in moments of weakness. To conceal serious sins in the confessional can eventually result in the total loss of faith. To develop the virtue of purity, one should develop a strong personal devotion to the Blessed Virgin Mary. It has been said by saints that more souls go to hell because of sins against purity (sins of the flesh) than for any other reason.

7. "YOU SHALL NOT STEAL."
10. "YOU SHALL NOT COVET ANYTHING THAT BELONGS TO YOUR NEIGHBOR."

The Catholic Church holds to the right to private property to lead a good Christian life and to raise a family in reasonable comfort. God has ordained two of His commandments to protect this right to ownership of property. The Seventh Commandment deals with the actual taking of anything that does not rightfully belong to us. Coveting refers to the strong desire to possess material things. It implies that the desire is inordinate.

A person who covets or is avaricious will be tempted to steal if he does not learn to suppress such desires, put his trust in God to provide essentials and not be inordinately attached to worldly goods which are not necessary. This spirit of covetousness is manifested in buying beyond one's means and in buying what one really does not need. Living beyond one's means can destroy peace in the home. It can eventually lead to stealing. Running up a charge account and then not paying one's bills is the same as stealing.

The gravity of the sin of stealing depends upon circumstances, e.g., the amount stolen and the harm wrought on the party who is the victim. Generally, a small amount is considered a venial sin. A large amount is mortal. Children should be strictly dealt with, even in very small matters, so that they learn respect for the property of others. One who steals a small amount with the intention to gradually accumulate a large amount is guilty of serious sin.

One who has stolen and who repents must make restitution as soon as reasonably possible if he wishes to be forgiven. Restitution can be made secretly. To confess that one has stolen a large amount with no intention of making restitution will not bring forgiveness because repentance is lacking. One would, in that case, fail to promise to make right the injustice.

To be deceptive in selling goods is the same as stealing. To make something seem to be worth much more than it actually is, is not only lying, but stealing. "Your legal verdicts, your measures — length, weight and capacity — must all be just. Your scales and weights must be just, a just ephah [bushel] and a just hin [six-quart measure]" (Leviticus 19:35-36).

274

Both the employer and the employee must be just to each other. The employer must pay a living wage, enabling a man to support his family. Working conditions and decent hours must all be considered. At the same time the worker must do a day's work for a day's pay and be concerned about the problems of his employer. To waste the time and the commodities of the employer is the same as stealing.

Obtaining money under false pretenses, such as begging for money while pretending one is sick or needy, is the same as stealing. To damage another's property deliberately, including public property, requires restitution. It is a sin against the rights of others when judges, political officials, policemen, or any other public servants are influenced or bribed not to enforce justice.

While it is true that one is permitted to possess property that does not belong to him when the circumstances are so dire that it is needed to protect or preserve one's life, provided it causes no great harm to others, yet, in our country this rule can scarcely be applied because there are so many charitable agencies available.

Gambling is not a sin in itself. Excessive gambling, i.e., gambling away what is needed for one's own support or the support of others, is seriously sinful. Gambling also becomes a sin if, as a result, personal honesty is lost.

8. "YOU SHALL NOT BEAR FALSE WITNESS AGAINST YOUR NEIGHBOR."

The ability to speak is, in itself, a sign that we are made in the image and likeness of Almighty God. Speech is a sign of intelligence. The highest faculties of the human soul are the intellect and will by which a man knows and loves. Speech expresses acts of the soul which is an image of God who is infinitely knowing and loving. Such power distinguishes man from the mere beast. Such powers of the soul, expressed in an external way by the use of the tongue, ought not be abused. In Sacred Scripture God the Son is called the "Word." Jesus, the Word, is the image of the Father, and Christians are destined to become more and more like Christ.

Most sins are committed by the use of the tongue in some way. There is the lie, the insult, swearing, cursing, gossip. "The only man who could reach perfection would be someone who never said anything wrong — he would be able to control every part of himself. Once we put a bit into the horse's mouth, to make it do what we want, we have the whole animal under our control. Or think of ships: no matter how big they are, even if a gale is driving them, the man at the helm can steer them anywhere he likes by controlling a tiny rudder. So is the tongue only a tiny part of the body, but it can proudly claim that it does great things. Think how small a flame can set fire to a huge forest; the tongue is a flame like that. Among all the parts of the body, the tongue is a whole wicked world in itself: it infects the whole body; catching fire itself from hell, it sets fire to the whole wheel of creation. Wild animals and birds, reptiles and fish can all be tamed by man, and often are; but nobody can tame the tongue — it is a pest that will not keep still, full of deadly poison. We use it to bless the Lord and Father, but we also use it to curse men who are made in God's image: the blessing and the curse come out of the same mouth" (James 3:2-10).

A lie is speaking contrary to what one knows is the truth. The gravity of a lie depends upon the harm done. If the consequence of a lie leads to serious injustice to others, the sin is mortal. Slight harmful consequences of a lie would be venial. There is no such thing as a "white lie." There may be times when mental reservation is used, for instance, when one has information which he is not permitted to share lest it break professional secrecy and/or bring great harm to another. Such may often be the case with a priest, a lawyer or anyone who counsels individuals who confide to them. If there is information one is not permitted to share, he can simply say, "I don't know." He is not lying. He is simply not sharing knowledge which he is forbidden to share. Mental reservation may not be used for selfish reasons or when it is knowledge one is required to share for the common good. A priest, of course, under no circumstances can share knowledge from the confessional.

Lies lead to many other sins — discord, hatred, even stealing — because they represent a dishonest spirit. One is not permitted to reveal the hidden faults of another on the ground that it is the truth. Gossip can be mortally sinful when it leads to the destruction of another's reputation. Both calumny and detraction are sinful. These are sins against justice, and restitution must be made. One must try to repair the harm done to another's good name. He must also make up for any foreseen temporal loss, such as the loss of employment or of customers.

Rash judgment is forming an unquestioning conviction about another's conduct without adequate grounds for judgment. The sinfulness lies in the hasty imprudence with which the critical appraisal was made and in the loss of reputation that a person suffers in the eyes of the one who so judges. Couples can bring grave damage to their marriage by such suspicion toward each other.

Insult is the dishonoring of another by contemptuous words or actions. The seriousness of the sin will depend upon the foreseen consequences. To reveal secrets is to sin against justice and charity. There is hidden knowledge which is not to be revealed and, to do so is to break a trust. The same is true of reading letters or materials which one knows are considered private. How serious a sin results from revealing secrets or unjustly obtaining secret knowledge depends upon circumstances, especially the damage which results.

It is important that each one disciplines his curiosity and trains his tongue. Without such a mastery, one will fall into many other kinds of sin. "The only man who could reach perfection would be someone who never said anything wrong — he would be able to control every part of himself" (James 3:2).

DISCUSSION QUESTIONS

1. Does Christianity include legislation? Explain your answer.
Christianity does include legislation, the first being the law of love of God, and then love of neighbor for the love of God. These laws of love lead one to keep the Ten Commandments.

2. How did Jesus explain legalism?
Jesus defined legalism as the subordination of the spirit of the law to its crude letter.

3. Did the Apostle Paul mean to do away with all legislation in Christianity? Explain.
The Apostle Paul specifically stated that he was not doing away with law. He placed the law and grace in contraposition, that is, the law of Moses with the liberating grace of Jesus Christ. He was talking of the superiority of the law of love in Christ which Jesus has merited for us. Jesus came not to destroy but to fulfill.

4. What is the ultimate end of morality from the viewpoint of authentic Christianity?
The ultimate end of morality is the glory of God and for Christians to get to heaven.

5. What determines the moral norms of human conduct for the authentic Christian?
The moral norms of human conduct for the authentic Christian are determined, not by public polls or man's opinions, but by the very nature of God and His revelation.

6. Is a Catholic free to form any kind of conscience?
A Catholic is free to form any kind of conscience only in the sense that God does not force our love. If he wants to be an authentic sincere Catholic, however, his conscience must be formed correctly according to the teachings of the Church, aided in his personal life by grace through prayer and the sacraments.

7. What is objective morality?
Objective morality means the conformity of human acts with the moral stan-

dards determined by God himself, in His revelation, in His very nature. It is opposed to determining morality merely subjectively, according to human opinions or wrong judgments which are made.

8. Explain: There are absolutes in morality.

"Absolutes in morality" means that there are certain human acts which in all circumstances, without exception, are either sinful or virtuous. For instance, adultery, fornication, abortion and perjury are always sinful; truthfulness and charity always virtuous.

9. Give at least three examples of absolute norms of morality.

See answer to Question 8.

10. Why does the Church condemn situation ethics or mere subjective norms of morality?

Situation ethics or mere subjective norms of morality are condemned by the Catholic Church because they let man and his opinion, not God, determine morality and deny absolutes, but would have morality be determined by feelings.

11. Who determines what acts will separate man from union with God?

God makes known through reason and revelation what constitutes a mortal sin which separates man from grace. We need the Church for this as it speaks for God in Christ Jesus.

12. When is one guilty of mortal sin in breaking one of the Commandments?

One is guilty of mortal sin when he/she consents with full will to do what one knows is a serious offense against God or the teachings of His Church.

13. What is the difference between the first three Commandments and the other seven?

The first three Commandments concern our relationship with God. The other seven refer to our relationship with God as we relate to our fellow humans.

14. Define adoration.

Adoration is directed only to God as the Supreme Being and it recognizes God as Creator in whom we are totally dependent. It is the submission of ourselves before our Creator who is perfect. The highest form of worship is the Sacrifice of the Mass.

15. What did the Second Vatican Council say about indiscriminate worship?

The Second Vatican Council said that worship in common is not to be used indiscriminately. It requires the permission of the bishop, which is given only in special circumstances. (Catholics are to worship on Sundays and holy days only in the Catholic Church at the Sacrifice of the Mass.)

16. Can one be saved who has been baptized and educated in the Catholic faith and, after once having believed in the fullness of true faith, loses it?

God, who has given the gift of the fullness of true faith to a Catholic by having him both baptized and educated and formed in the true faith, will not take that gift back from a person. If one loses it, he loses it of his own fault. If one knows the

Catholic faith is the true faith but gives it up, he cannot be saved if he dies unrepentant.

17. Name at least three kinds of sin against the Second Commandment of God.

Sins against the Second Commandment: to use God's name irreerently; to blaspheme, speaking against God in a contemptuous, scornful way; to commit perjury after an oath which invoked God as witness.

18. What obligation do Catholics have regarding Mass on Sundays and holy days?

Catholics are obligated under pain of mortal sin to participate in the Sacrifice of the Mass every Sunday and Holy Day of Obligation.

19. Name some excusing causes when one could miss Mass on a Sunday or a holy day without committing a sin.

Circumstances which would excuse one from the obligation of Mass would be: serious illness, serious necessary work when it is impossible to get a substitute, severe weather which would endanger life or health if one attempted to travel to Mass.

20. What does the Second Commandment bind on Sunday in addition to participation in the Sacrifice of the Mass?

In addition to participation in the Sacrifice of the Mass, the obligation to avoid unnecessary manual labor is seriously binding.

21. Name the six holy days of obligation.

The six holy days of obligation: Christmas (Dec. 25), Solemnity of the Mother of God (Jan. 1), Ascension Thursday (40 days after Easter), Assumption of the Blessed Virgin Mary (Aug. 15), All Saints Day (Nov. 1), Immaculate Conception (Dec. 8).

22. What kind of sin does a teenager commit who, contrary to serious parental orders, keeps late hours or engages in steady dating, or goes with forbidden companions?

A teenager who disobeys his parents in matters which the parents consider serious, like late hours, bad company, steady dating, etc., is sinning seriously against parental authority.

23. Does a parent fulfill his obligation as primary religious educator of his children if he sends children to a Catholic school or to religion classes without attention to what the children are taught, how they are taught, or whether the child is comprehending?

A parent as primary religious educator of his children does not fulfill his obligation by merely delegating teaching responsibilities to others. He must keep himself informed as to whether his child is taught correctly. The parent himself should discuss the faith with his child, determine if the child is growing in knowledge of the faith. The parents by good and personal exhortation must lead the child to be formed in the practice of the faith.

24. Name some of the sins which lead to murder.

Some sins which can lead eventually to murder are: anger, hatred, revenge.

25. What special penalty is there for Catholics who have an abortion or aid in one?
Catholics who have an abortion or aid another in having an abortion are automatically excommunicated from the Church.

26. What does the Catholic Church say about "in vitro" fertilization?
"In vitro" fertilization is condemned by the Catholic Church as being against nature as ordained by Almighty God. The baby itself is not the sin but the manner of fertilization is.

27. Besides artificial birth control for married couples, name at least three types of serious sins against human sexuality.
Besides artificial birth control, other serious sins against human sexuality are adultery, fornication and masturbation.

28. What use of the sexual powers is permitted to unmarried couples who are dating?
Unmarried couples who are dating have no right whatsoever to deliberately arouse their sexual passions or to express such passions in relationship to each other. The use of sexual powers before marriage is mortally sinful. They have a serious obligation to keep their sexual passions under control.

29. John Jones steals $500. He is sorry and goes to confession. What more is expected of him?
He must be willing to make restitution, i.e., give back what he has stolen.

30. Mary Smith has a habit of buying beyond her means. She runs up a large charge account which she never intends to pay. Explain the morality of her actions.
To run up a charge account with no intention of ever paying one's bills is the same as stealing.

31. Comment on this statement: "It is always permitted to tell the truth about others."
It is not permitted to tell the truth about another if it will seriously ruin that person's reputation or bring harm to the person in any way.

32. If one has seriously harmed another's reputation by gossip, or has caused another to lose his job by revealing secret knowledge, what obligation does one have besides confessing such a sin?
Besides confessing serious sins of gossip, or of having revealed secret knowledge, one must do all he can to make restitution by attempting to restore the person's good name and to undo whatever other harm was caused.

CHAPTER 22

Prayer and Mysticism

If one were to use the shortest explanation of prayer, it would be "loving God who is all Good." Traditionally prayer has been defined as the lifting of the mind and heart to God. Prayer is the result of knowing God by faith and responding to this knowledge by loving the all-good Creator who is our heavenly Father. Prayer is the willing response to God's presence which is all about us.

There are four chief purposes of prayer: 1. *Adoration*. This is a response to the greatness of God and one's total dependence upon Him. 2. *Thanksgiving*. This is a response of gratitude to God for His benefits both spiritual and material. Everything comes from God, natural and supernatural benefits, and in prayer God expects us to thank Him. 3. *Reparation*. This includes sorrow for sins committed and begging God's mercy. It is also called satisfaction as it is offered to repair the divine justice and glory we have insulted and harmed externally by our sins. 4. *Petition*. We ask God for all the things we need, natural needs in this world as well as graces needed.

To pray, one needs faith. Faith is the assent of the mind to God's revelations. Supernatural faith is not simply an activity of the intellect. It requires divine grace, either actual or sanctifying or both. One cannot give himself the gift of supernatural faith. It is infused by God, normally at Baptism, as a seed which must be nourished to sprout and to grow. Faith is performed under the influence of the will which requires the help of grace. One can reject the gift of faith. One can grow in the intensity of faith. A life of prayer and good works performed for a supernatural motive, the love of God and fellowman in Christ, is an exercise of faith. Explicit acts of faith should be made during times of temptation. That is to say, we should pray in times of temptation. "Pray not to be put to the test" (Luke 22:40). A simple act of faith is: "My God, I believe in you and all that your Church teaches, because you have revealed it and your word is true. Amen."

If a person does not nourish his faith with constant prayer the faith can weaken and be lost; "pray continually and never lose heart" (Luke 18:1). God gives faith as a gift and expects it to be used. If we pray in a spirit of adoration, thanksgiving, reparation or petition, we are exercising the supernatural virtue of faith. An example in Scripture testifying that no one can pray without help from above is found in 1 Corinthians 12:3. "No one can say, 'Jesus is Lord' unless he is under the influence of the Holy Spirit."

There are different degrees of faith. Some have a stronger faith than others. This may be due to a greater gift of God or to a greater correspondence with the gift of faith God has given. "There is a variety of gifts but always the same Spirit; there are all sorts of service to be done, but always the same Lord. . . . One may have the gift of preaching with wisdom given him by the Spirit . . . and another the gift of faith given by the same Spirit. . ." (1 Corinthians 12:4, 5, 9).

The act of hope is also a form of prayer for it is an exercise of the infused theological virtue, received at baptism, together with sanctifying grace and it has the possession of God as its primary object. Hope belongs to the will and empowers a person to desire eternal life, which means, ultimately the heavenly vision of God. Hope gives one confidence of receiving the grace necessary for salvation. By hope we have trust in God to forgive us our sins, grant us grace and final perseverance and thus lead us to eternal life in heaven. A short form of the prayer of hope is: "O my God, relying on your infinite goodness and promises, I hope to obtain pardon of my sins, the help of your grace and life everlasting. Amen." God commands acts of hope to lead us to salvation.

The act of charity is the infused supernatural virtue by which one loves God above all things for His own sake and to love others for the sake of God. It is a theological virtue based on divine faith, that is, belief in God's revealed truth. Supernatural charity cannot be acquired by human effort alone. It is given only with divine grace. Therefore, since charity and sanctifying grace must always coexist, one cannot be in the human soul without the other. Charity is frequently identified with the state of grace. To lose charity is to lose sanctifying grace. One may lose sanctifying grace, however, without losing faith and hope. One needs faith and hope, and thereby must respond to actual grace calling one back to the Father's love, to be restored to sanctifying grace and reactivate supernatural charity in the soul. "No one can come to me unless he is drawn by the Father who sent me" (John 6:44).

One who falls into mortal sin, thus losing the supernatural virtue of charity and sanctifying grace, may think he still loves God. In faith and hope he still looks to God with affection. While having faith and hope his love can be only a natural love. His good works are not rooted in God, in divine charity. Therefore good works are not supernaturally meritorious unless performed while in the state of grace.

It is the divine will that we obtain many of the things we need only by asking God. "Ask, and it will be given to you; search, and you will find; knock, and the door will be opened to you. For the one who asks always receives; the one who searches always finds; the one who knocks will always have the door opened to him. Is there a man among you who would hand his son a stone when he asked for bread? Or would hand him a snake when he asked for a fish? If you, then, who are evil, know how to give your children what is good, how much more will your Father in heaven give good things to those who ask him!" (Matthew 7:7-11).

In the above words we are assured by Jesus Christ that no prayer goes unanswered. God is a good Father. He will give us only what is good for us. If what we request could bring harm to body or soul, affect our eternal salvation and the glory we owe God, it would not be granted. Still, God always answers prayers, and often He gives more and better things than those which we request. If we obtained everything as and when we desire it, we could destroy our very selves. Suffering is not evil in itself. Jesus suffered in the garden, His sweat becoming as blood trickling down upon the ground. It was the will of the Father that Jesus die for the redemption of the world. Being a man in all things except sin, Jesus prayed: "My Father . . . if it is possible, let this cup pass me by. Nevertheless, let it be as you, not I, would have it" (Matthew 26:39). He submitted His human will to the divine will and thus brought infinite glory to God from human nature and won redemption for the world.

St. Luke tells us how the prayer, "If you are willing, take this cup away from me" (22:42), was, nonetheless, answered by His Father. The evangelist adds immediately after this prayer of Jesus: "Then an angel appeared to him, coming from heaven to give him strength. In his anguish he prayed even more earnestly" (Luke 22:43). Something better was given to Jesus who expressed His human desire while submitting it to the divine will. Humanly, He was given strength by the angel to bear His suffering. In a divine way He won glory for himself unto His Father and merited the same for His brothers unto the end of time, if they will but request that same glory and respond to the Father drawing them. Jesus showed us the correct way to make a prayer of petition.

The desire on God's part to receive *thanksgiving* from His people was expressed by Jesus when on the way to Jerusalem 10 lepers came to meet Him. They called to Him, "Jesus! Master! Take pity on us." Jesus had them go show themselves to the priests, "Now as they were going away they were cleansed. Finding himself cured, one of them turned back praising God at the top of his voice and threw himself at the feet of Jesus and thanked him. The man was a Samaritan. This made Jesus say, 'Were not all ten made clean? The other nine, where are they? It seems that no one has come back to give praise to God, except this foreigner.' And he said to the man, 'Stand up and go on your way. Your faith has saved you' '' (Luke 17:11-19).

In the very act of instituting the Holy Eucharist, Jesus was mindful of the human need in relationship with God to render thanks. "Then he took some bread, and when he had given thanks, broke it and gave it to them, saying, 'This is my body. . .'" (Luke 22:19). Jesus, having become a man in all things except sin, had the human need to pray as men must pray, in petition, thanksgiving, adoration and, of course, He rendered infinite reparation for us all by His death on the Cross.

The entire life of our divine Lord Jesus Christ was one of prayer. At times He prayed formally. "Now it was about this time that he went out into the hills to pray; and he spent the whole night in prayer to God" (Luke 6:11-13). "He took Peter and John and James and went up the mountain to pray. As he prayed, the aspect of his face was changed and his clothing became brilliant as lightning. . ." (Luke 9:28-30). "His reputation continued to grow, and large crowds would gather to hear him and to have their sickness cured, but he would always go off to some place where he could be alone and pray" (Luke 5:15-16). Jesus prayed before choosing His 12 apostles. He prayed before performing miracles. John, in his 17th chapter, recorded the long priestly prayer of Jesus Christ, as He prayed for unity among His followers.

Jesus adored His Father perfectly in His death on the Cross, recognizing the supreme dominion of God over His human nature, which He was giving up in sacrifice and doing so willingly. At the Last Supper Jesus made it possible for mankind to perpetuate that act of perfect adoration given on the Cross: ". . . for this is my blood, the blood of the covenant, which is to be poured out for many for the forgiveness of sins" (Matthew 26:28).

The adoration we owe God is possible through the adoration we give Jesus Christ who is present in the Blessed Sacrament. As explained in an earlier chapter, the Mass itself gives infinite adoration as it perpetuates the Sacrifice of Calvary. At the same time, the Blessed Sacrament, preserved in the tabernacles of our churches and occasionally exposed in the sacred monstrance for Benediction, deserves the same adoration due God the Father, for here is present the incarnate Son of God in the Holy Eucharist, the one essential Mediator between God and man. In adoring Jesus in the Blessed Sacrament, we adore God the Father, in fact, the entire Blessed Trinity. "Philip said, 'Lord, let us see the Father and then we shall be satisfied.' 'Have I been with you all this time, Philip,' said Jesus to him, 'and you still do not know me? To have seen me is to have seen the Father' '' (John 14:8-9).

Prayer of reparation or satisfaction is found to perfection in the Sac-

284

rifice of the Mass, which perpetuates Calvary's infinite act of reparation. But prayers of expiation for wrongdoing can be any of our own choosing offered to God to repair for sins committed against Him. The penance imposed by a priest before giving sacramental absolution has this effect. Any prayers said begging God's mercy and forgiveness have the function of satisfaction if offered in sincere faith and trust.

When asked, "Lord, teach us to pray," Jesus responded by teaching them the Lord's Prayer (Matthew 6:9-13; Luke 11:2-4). The "Our Father" or Lord's Prayer is called the perfect prayer, not because it has infinite power of adoration as does the Sacrifice of the Mass, but because its seven petitions are a synthesis of the faith. It has a balanced structure in an expression of the true hierarchy of values dealing first with the things of God and then the needs of man. (The longer ending familiar to Protestants was originally a liturgical ending not taught by Christ.)

While prayer is proper at all times and in all places, there are certain places where God dwells in a special way and bestows His grace more abundantly. God dwells in heaven in a special way but also on earth, as in the soul in grace. In our Catholic churches, where the Most Blessed Sacrament of the Altar is reserved in our tabernacles, there is a special place to pray and give adoration to God.

There are various kinds of prayer. But as one advances in the spiritual life, there are different degrees of intensity of prayer-life in one's union with God. The *prayer of quiet* is an internal peaceful repose wherein the soul is captivated by the presence of God. The mind, enlightened by divine grace, is permeated with a spiritual delight affecting one's entire person.

The *prayer of simplicity* is a simple loving thought of God. The person focuses on one or more of God's attributes or some Christian mystery. Rather than reasoning discursively, a person experiencing simple prayer rests lovingly under the operation of the Holy Spirit. Joy fills the heart as in love one relishes divine realities.

The *prayer of union* comes when the soul is conscious of an intimate union with God. The person experiences God's presence within the soul by grace while the interior faculties are suspended. The soul is wholly absorbed in God and without distractions. A great peace and joy floods the soul, and no effort is required as the soul ardently desires to glorify God and be detached from created things while being submissive to the will of God and filled with love for neighbor.

Mental prayer is an internal act of the mind and of the affections. It may be either simple meditation or contemplation. As *meditation*, mental prayer is a loving reflective consideration of religious truths or mysteries of faith. As *contemplation*, mental prayer is a loving considera-

285

tion which is immediately perceptive of truths or mysteries of faith which the mind admires. The memory, intellect and will are all used in mental prayer. Memory recalls matter for meditation or contemplation (or a spiritual reading book is used to aid the memory). The intellect considers the meaning and implications for practice. The will expresses sentiments of faith, trust and love. A good resolution follows all this.

Mental prayer is divided into three stages. According to Sts. Teresa of Avila and John of the Cross, there is first the *purgative way*, where the soul's main concern is awareness of its sins, sorrow for the past and the desire to make reparation for the offenses against God. In the *illuminative way* the soul has an enlightenment of the mind in the ways of God and a clear understanding of His will for one's state in life. There is, finally, the *unitive way*, in which the soul has arrived at a rather habitual awareness of God's presence and a disposition of conformity of the human will to the will of God.

A person may shift back and forth between these three stages of mental prayer. No sincere Christian should think that advancements in prayer are meant only for priests or Religious or very select souls. All men, regardless of their state in life, are called by God to holiness. It is possible for every Christian who takes his faith seriously to advance beyond the mere recitation of memorized prayer-formulae. St. Francis de Sales said that if one is saying vocal prayers and one's heart feels drawn to mental prayer, he ought not to resist it. The knowledge of our holy Catholic faith ought to form the basis of our prayer life. To love, one must first know. For that reason we have placed our chapter on prayer near the end of this volume. Hopefully, the spirit of prayer has permeated the study of all these pages.

St. John Vianney, the patron of parish priests, said that the more we pray, the more we desire to pray. St. Teresa of Avila said that the only way to find God is to pray. Prayer is necessary for salvation. It is seriously sinful to give up prayer entirely for great lengths of time. Readers would do well to consider again the chapter on the angels who lead us to God. If we are open to the good angels, they will lead us to faith, to trust, to love, to adoration of the all-good God. To exercise the theological virtues is to pray.

Everyone should have a *spiritual program*. Just as we must organize our lives in natural matters if we are to be successful in this world, so, in that which concerns our eternal salvation and the glory of God, we ought to be organized with a spiritual program. A suggested balanced spiritual program follows:

1. Sign of the Cross — first act of each day.
2. Morning Prayers — include the Morning Offering.

3. Angelus — Noon and about 6 p.m. (or with family meals).

4. Liturgy — Holy Communion at least each Sunday and frequent confession (at least monthly).

5. Daily Rosary — while meditating on the Joyful, Sorrowful or Glorious Mysteries.

6. Aspirations — short prayers throughout the day.

7. Visits to the Most Blessed Sacrament (at least once per week).

8. Spiritual Reading — 15 to 20 minutes daily.

9. Evening Prayers — with examination of conscience.

10. Lay Apostolate — practical works for the good of others.

St. Augustine summarized prayer in this manner: "Place yourself at the foot of the cross, prostrate yourself before that God who became man and died for you and then think on anything you wish, since all will be prayer. Whether you adore God, or admire him, whether you praise him, love him, or thank him, rejoice with him: all will be prayer, and worship of him." Padre Pio said that we should set aside a definite time and place for prayer and persist in our efforts and not give in to ourselves until the assigned time is up.

In praying we ought to seek the God of consolations and not the consolations of God. Great saints, such as St. Teresa of Avila, were known to spend many years in spiritual dryness, getting little or no personal consolation from their prayers. When we pray, even when consolations are lacking, we exercise our will in pure love of God and not for self-satisfaction. St. Teresa said: "There is but one road which reaches God, and that is prayer; if anyone shows you another, you are being deceived."

The story is told in the life of St. John Vianney that he noticed an old man in his parish who would come to the parish church every day and sit before the tabernacle for two hours. One day Father Vianney approached the old man and inquired what he prayed about each day: "What do you say to God when you pray?" The old man answered: "I don't say anything. I just look at God and He looks at me."

Mysticism is a very special gift of God given to select souls. It is a supernatural state of the soul in which God is known and loved in a way that would be impossible through human efforts alone. There is an immediate, personal experience of God of great intensity and kind. It is the result of a totally unmerited grace which God gives.

Christian mysticism is not to be confused with non-Christian mysticism of the Oriental world. There are natural explanations for Eastern practices of learning how to rest, breathe, relax and achieve a certain supposed union with the deity. In authentic Christian mysticism the soul recognizes that the reality to which it penetrates simply transcends the soul and the things of this world. There is no confusion between the soul and God but a profound humility before the infinite majesty of God. For the Christian mystic, all union between the soul and God is a moral union of love, doing God's will even at great sacrifice to self. There is no question of losing one's being in God, that is, of having one's personality destroyed and absorbed into the divine. The Christian becomes a more perfect copy of Jesus Christ but without losing his personal identity.

The Christian mystic frequently achieves union of soul with God in deep contemplation when there is a deep awareness of the divine presence — the indwelling of the Most Blessed Trinity in the soul of grace. There are a variety of grades, or levels, of mystical union which different souls have experienced, as testified to in the lives of many of the saints. Extraordinary phenomena have been recorded in the lives of certain persons who have reached one of the higher forms of mental prayer.

When a person claims to have mystical experiences in the form of apparitions which involve messages for others, the Church is most cautious lest it be the result of self-suggestion, illusions or hallucinations. Before the Church grants permission for such messages to be proclaimed as worthy of human faith, the Church's policy is to require proof. If there seems to be grounds for credibility, a commission may be appointed by the bishop of the diocese where the phenomena are reported. Sometimes years of serious investigation are required before a decision is reached. Even then, when the Church approves of such apparitions or messages, it is only because there is a harmony with the Gospel and the teachings of the Church, reaffirming what is already the faith of the Church.

Examples of devotions in the Church which have received emphasis in modern times, because of the stimuli of approved apparitions, are those of the Sacred Heart of Jesus and the Immaculate Heart of Mary.

The devotion to the Sacred Heart of Jesus is the subjective response of the faithful to the objective revelation of the love of Jesus Christ for mankind. His love is both human (in His created human nature) and divine (in His eternal person as Son of God). The physical heart of Jesus represents the human and divine love of Jesus Christ. The Sacred Heart devotion is an outgrowth of devotion to the sacred humanity of Jesus Christ, to His role as mediator. It is also a modern development of the New Testament presentation of Jesus Christ as the Good Shepherd.

Over the centuries there has been a succession of mystics who have contributed to the Sacred Heart devotion, and the Church has defended it as valid, since the human nature of Jesus Christ forms one person with the divine nature; that is, with the second person of the Most Blessed Trinity. Some of the better known mystics contributing to this devotion were: St. Bernard of Clairvaux (c. 1090-1153); St. Bonaventure (c. 1217-74); St. Mechtilde (c. 1209-c. 1282); St. Gertrude (c. 1256-1302; St. Frances of

Rome (c. 1384-1440); St. Francis de Sales (1567-1622); St. John Eudes (1601-1680).

Most notable in giving widespread devotion to the Sacred Heart of Jesus was St. Margaret Mary Alacoque (1647-1690), who received many revelations from the Divine Lord while in prayer before the Most Blessed Sacrament. Her spiritual advisor was Blessed Claude de la Colombiere (1641-1682), who was a Jesuit. Consequently the Society of Jesus promoted the devotion to the Sacred Heart of Jesus through the Apostleship of Prayer.

Pope Pius XII wrote a magnificent encyclical on the Sacred Heart, *Haurietis Aquas*. The physical heart of Jesus Christ is a symbol of a threefold love: 1. The love with which Jesus loves His eternal Father and all mankind; therefore it is a symbol of the divine love He shares with the Father and the Holy Spirit which the Word made flesh manifests in His weak, created body. 2. The burning love which was infused into His soul, enriching His human will, enlightening and governing His acts by the most perfect knowledge, knowledge received from the Beatific Vision as well as that directly infused. 3. The Sacred Heart is a symbol of sensible love, since the body of Jesus Christ possesses the full powers of feeling and perception to the most perfect human degree possible.

The Church has approved the observance of *First Fridays* as a result of the apparitions to St. Margaret Mary Alacoque. Our Lord said to her: "I promise in the excess of the mercy of my Heart, that its all powerful love will grant to all those who receive Communion on the first Friday of every month for nine consecutive months the grace of final repentance, that they shall not die under my displeasure, and without their sacraments, that my Heart shall be their secure refuge at that last hour." (This is interpreted as meaning such persons who need the sacraments to be restored to grace before death would be given that opportunity.) Holy Communions received on First Fridays are to be offered in reparation to the Sacred Heart of Jesus, especially for sins committed against Him in the Most Blessed Sacrament.

Among others, St. Anthony Mary Claret (1807-1870) spread devotion to the Immaculate Heart of Mary. This saint wrote: "For myself, I say this to you: The man who burns with the fire of divine love is a son of the Immaculate Heart of Mary, and wherever he goes, he enkindles that flame; he desires and works with all his strength to inflame all men with the fire of God's love. Nothing deters him; he rejoices in poverty; he labors strenuously; he welcomes hardships; he laughs off false accusations; he rejoices in anguish. He thinks only of how he might follow Jesus Christ and imitate him by his prayers, his labors, his sufferings, and by caring always and only for the glory of God and the salvation of souls."

The physical heart of the Blessed Virgin Mary is a sign and symbol of her compassion and sinlessness, and her great love for God, her Incarnate Son and for all her spiritual children, since she is Mother of the Church. Devotion to the Immaculate Heart of Mary means living the Christ-life as Mary did. It consists in living the beatitudes as Mary did. One who is devoted to the Immaculate Heart of Mary works to follow the example of the perfect Woman of Faith who loved better than all. Mary pondered the Word of God in her heart. She conceived the Word of God in her Immaculate Heart before she did in her womb. Having a perfect faith upon earth, Mary responded with a perfect love. In heaven she intercedes for us in her Immaculate Heart with the Father, through her Son's Heart in the unity of the Holy Spirit, whose spouse she is.

Devotion to the Immaculate Heart gained worldwide prominence through the apparitions at Fatima in 1917 and their subsequent approval by the Holy See, with each succeeding pope having a strong devotion to Our Lady of Fatima. At Fatima Our Lady said that God wants devotion to her Immaculate Heart established in the world. Understanding the times, and understanding what is meant by the Immaculate Heart, one can more readily see the importance of such heavenly intervention to bring mankind to the Gospels. Pope Pius XII described Fatima as "a reaffirmation of the Gospels."

As a result of the Fatima apparitions, *First Saturday* devotions have become widespread among many devout Catholics. Our Lady spoke these words to Sister Lucia: "My daughter, look at my Heart surrounded with the thorns with which ungrateful men pierce it at every moment by their blasphemies and ingratitude. You, at least, try to console me, and say that I promise to assist at the hour of death with all the graces necessary for salvation all those who, on the first Saturday of five consecutive months, go to Confession and receive Holy Communion, recite five decades of the Rosary and keep me company for a quarter of an hour while meditating on the mysteries of the Rosary, with the intention of making reparation to me."

While the Church offers such approved apparitions as worthy of human belief, yet it does not command that they be accepted as part of divine Catholic faith. The investigations, however, have been thorough, the apparitions and messages judged authentic. It would seem foolish in the light of evidence not to accept them. What must be accepted on divine faith are divine revelations contained in the Scriptures and the defined doctrines of Catholic faith. We must pray to be saved. It is human to develop devotions to express subjectively the faith and love in human hearts. The Church guides its children in giving approval to certain devotions which are in harmony with the dogmas of faith and the Scriptures.

290

One can well conclude that the Sacred Heart of Jesus is a perfect example of prayer on the part of the God-Man. The Immaculate Heart of Mary is an example of perfect prayer from a human heart which was not divine in her person as was Jesus Christ's, Mary being entirely a created human person. Mary's Immaculate Heart is the perfect model through the faith she lived on earth, the response she gave in love and the intercession she continues in heaven as mediatrix of all graces. These two inseparable Hearts show us the way to prayerful love.

DISCUSSION QUESTIONS

1. Briefly state the four purposes of prayer.
The four purposes of prayer are: adoration, thanksgiving, reparation and petition.

2. Explain what is meant by the supernatural virtue of faith.
The supernatural virtue of faith is a power infused into the soul by God at Baptism. By the virtue of faith we are empowered to believe with the assent of the mind to what God has revealed and His Church teaches.

3. Explain what is meant by the supernatural virtue of hope.
The supernatural virtue of hope also is infused into the soul at Baptism. It belongs to the will and empowers a person to desire eternal life and to trust that God in His infinite goodness will keep His promises to bring us to everlasting life.

4. Explain what is meant by the supernatural virtue of charity.
The supernatural virtue of charity is also one of the theological virtues, together with faith and hope, which is infused into the soul at Baptism. It empowers the soul to love God above all things for His own sake and love others for the sake of God. It exists only with sanctifying grace and cannot be acquired by human effort alone.

5. Which of the supernatural virtues is lost by mortal sin?
The supernatural virtue of charity is always lost by mortal sin as it coexists in the soul together with sanctifying grace, which is the sharing in the life of God, and this grace is lost with mortal sin.

6. Can all prayers of petition really be answered when men often do not get what they ask for?
All prayers of sincerity of heart are answered, but not always in the way we ask them. God will answer our prayers only if they be asked in such a way as to contribute to His glory and our salvation. If they cannot be answered in this way, God will answer them in another way of more value than the intention for which we prayed.

7. How did Jesus show us the correct way to prayerfully petition God as He prayed in the garden during His agony?
In the Garden of Olives Jesus prayed in a human way but added that He sub-

jected His human will to the divine will. He expressed His human desire not to have to undergo suffering but immediately added that if that were not possible He would accept the divine will for the glory of the Father.

8. How was Jesus' prayer during the agony in the garden answered?

Jesus' prayer in the garden was not answered as His human will first desired, but His prayer was, nonetheless, answered by God the Father, who sent an angel to give Him human strength to endure His sufferings, which were necessary for the salvation of the world.

9. Give an example from the life of Jesus Christ to show that God desires gratitude from men.

An example from the life of Jesus Christ which indicates that God desires gratitude, that is, the prayer of thanksgiving, from men, was when He cured 10 lepers and asked why only one bothered to return to give thanks.

10. Give examples of special times when Jesus prayed for special intentions.

Jesus' entire life was one of prayer, but special times directed exclusively to formal prayer were when He was about to choose the 12 apostles, before performing miracles, and especially before entering His great sufferings of Holy Week at the Last Supper. At times He withdrew from the crowds and went into the hills to spend the whole night in prayer.

11. When are the prayers of adoration and reparation offered in an infinitely pleasing way?

Infinite adoration and reparation were given to God the Father by Jesus Christ on the Cross. Jesus perpetuates the same at every Sacrifice of the Mass.

12. If the "Our Father" is a perfect prayer, how can the Sacrifice of the Mass exceed it in value?

The "Our Father" is a perfect prayer in the sense that it has a perfect balanced structure in an expression of the true hierarchy of values dealing first with the things of God and then the needs of man. The Mass is not simply balanced in containing all the purposes of prayer and hierarchy of values but is infinite inasmuch as it perpetuates the infinite act of redemption which Christ rendered in His sacrificial death on the Cross.

13. What is mental prayer?

Mental prayer is an internal act of the mind and of the affections. It may be in the form of meditation, that is, a discursive or reflective consideration of religious truths or mysteries of faith. It may also be contemplation, a loving consideration which immediately perceives truths or mysteries of faith to which the mind adheres and which it admires.

14. Are most people called only to vocal prayer?

All people are called to vocal prayer, but not only vocal prayer. Unfortunately, some may never rise above the level of vocal prayer if they do not put the effort into developing mental prayer.

15. Why is it important to have a spiritual program?

It is important to have a spiritual program in order to have our spiritual lives organized. Our spirituality involves our eternal salvation and that of others. Eternal life is worth more than the effort it takes to attain it.

16. Briefly explain Christian mysticism.

Christian mysticism involves achieving union of the soul with God in deep contemplation when there is a profound awareness of the Divine Presence and the indwelling of the Most Blessed Trinity in the soul by grace.

17. Why is the Church cautious about reports of apparitions or messages from heaven?

The Church is cautious about **reported** apparitions and messages from heaven because most are the result of self-suggestion, illusions and hallucinations, however sincere the persons reporting the experiences may be. At times, though, such as at Lourdes and Fatima, reported apparitions and messages prove to be authentic after careful investigation by the Church.

18. Give examples of Catholic devotions which are approved and popularized as the result of private revelations.

Besides Fatima (1917) and Lourdes (1858), approval has been given to Our Lady of Guadalupe in Mexico City (1531), where God's Mother left the imprint of her image on the tilma, or cactus clothing, of Juan Diego; the miraculous medal as given by Our Lady to St. Catherine Laboure in 1830; Our Lady's appearance at Knock in Ireland (1879), where she appeared together with St. Joseph and St. John the Evangelist, vested as a bishop, holding a book in his right hand, raised as if he were preaching, and to the apostle's left an altar on which stood a cross and a young lamb. There have been other approved apparitions, but these are among the better known.

19. Explain the meaning of the Sacred Heart devotion.

The Sacred Heart devotion has reference to the love Jesus Christ has for mankind both in a human way and in a divine way. The physical heart represents the human and divine love of Jesus Christ. It is a reminder of the love of God poured out for us by His death on the Cross. Wounded by the sins of men, yet He calls for our love out of His infinite merciful love.

20. Explain the meaning of the Immaculate Heart devotion.

The Immaculate Heart devotion presents to us the Blessed Virgin Mary as the perfect model of faith in her life upon earth and her perfect response in love, not only upon earth but as her perfect love continues in intercession in heaven. Her Immaculate Heart presents to us the manner of living the Christian life to perfection.

21. What is the First Friday devotion?

The First Friday devotion refers to receiving Holy Communion in reparation for the sins committed against the Heart of Jesus, especially for sins of sacrilege against Our Lord in the Most Blessed Sacrament. According to St. Margaret Mary, those who receive Communion of reparation on the First Fridays of nine consecutive months will receive the grace of dying in the state of grace.

22. What is the First Saturday devotion?

First Saturday devotion is directed to reparation to the Immaculate Heart of Mary on five consecutive First Saturdays. It consists of praying five decades of the Rosary; meditation on the Mysteries of the Rosary for at least 15 minutes; and both Confession and Communion of Reparation. It also carries the promise of dying in God's favor. It is directed, too, to obtaining peace for the Church and for the world.

CHAPTER 23

Living a Catholic Life

We must live the Catholic Faith. Knowledge of it is not sufficient. There must be a response in love. "It is not those who say to me, 'Lord, Lord,' who will enter the kingdom of heaven, but the person who does the will of my Father in heaven" (Matthew 7:21-22). Jesus said that a wise person not only listens to His words but "acts on them" (Matthew 7:24). In fact, to have knowledge of the true faith, yet not live it, is to place ourselves in great spiritual jeopardy. "If I had not come, if I had not spoken to them, they would have been blameless; but as it is they have no excuse for their sin" (John 15:22).

The Christian life really covers the whole spectrum of our faith put into practice. The authentic Catholic life is faith bearing fruit in love of God and neighbor. A living faith requires good works.

One of the practical implementations of Catholic principles into daily living is seen in the use of sacramentals.[1] Sacramentals were instituted by the Church, rather than by Jesus Christ himself. While they imitate the sacraments, their spiritual influences come from the merits of the faithful. The efficacy of sacramentals depends on the power of the prayers of the Church in blessing them and on the devotion of the person who uses them. The variety of the sacramentals is vast, involving almost every occasion and place where faith and love penetrate into daily Christian living. While the seven sacraments are essential to living an authentic Catholic life, sacramentals are aids to spiritualizing various aspects of daily life.

Included among sacramentals are the Stations of the Cross, the Rosary, the crucifix, holy water, blessed medals, blessed candles, prayer books, incense, blessed ashes, scapulars, statues and pictures. These blessed religious articles serve to uplift one's mind to God, to things holy, to the intercession of the persons represented. Holy water when used to bless oneself, calls down the blessing which the Church through its priest

---

[1]Sacramentals are not to be confused with the seven sacraments which were instituted by Jesus Christ directly and contain the power of Jesus Christ within themselves. The sacraments confer the grace they signify.

placed upon the water for those who use it. It serves as a reminder of one's baptism. The Sacrament of Baptism admits one to membership in the Church. It is fitting then that the *sacramental* of holy water is commonly used at the entrances to our church buildings to call to mind one's baptism.

Candles call to mind the presence of Jesus Christ, the Light of the World. Wherever the Blessed Sacrament is contained in the tabernacle, the sanctuary lamp burns in honor of the Real Presence of Jesus Christ. Lighted candles burn on the altar during Mass as well. Candles are also used as votive candles burned before some statue or shrine to give honor to Our Lord, Our Lady, or one of the saints. They burn to represent one's continuous prayer and act of love ascending toward heaven.

Prayer books contain devotional prayers for private use or for communal use by members of a religious community, confraternity or any family. Prayer books are useful for thanksgiving after Holy Communion and Mass as well as a preparation for the same. They also frequently contain an examination of conscience before confession and proper prayer before and after receiving the Sacrament of Reconciliation (Penance). Popular prayer books contain litanies to the Sacred Heart of Jesus, to the Blessed Virgin Mary, to St. Joseph, the saints and angels, etc.[2] It is spiritually profitable for the faithful to own and keep one or more prayer books for daily use.

Priests are obliged to say the *Divine Office* fully each day. It is also known as *The Liturgy of the Hours*, and since the *Divine Office* is now available in the vernacular, many of the laity as well as Religious pray the Office each day. It consists of the group of psalms, hymns, prayers, biblical and spiritual readings formulated by the Church to be said at stated times every day. The *Divine Office* has its origin in apostolic times when it consisted entirely of biblical psalms and scriptural readings. The Office follows the liturgical cycle of the Church year, e.g., Christmas, Lent, Easter, etc.

The Sacramentary (sometimes called the Missal) is the large book which the priest uses in offering the Sacrifice of the Mass. The faithful may obtain small books or missalettes with the same ritual and prayers in order to assist at Mass. The Church encourages active participation of the faithful in the divine liturgy, and such small missals are frequently a great help.

---

[2]A litany is a form of prayer consisting of a series of petitions led by a person to which people respond with a fixed prayer, e.g., "have mercy on us" or "pray for us." The author of this volume, *The Catholic Faith,* has several prayer books available from the publisher, notably, *A Catholic Prayer Book* and *A Prayer Book for Young Catholics.*

Incense is aromatic gum or resin in the form of powder or grains which when burned give off a fragrant smoke. The burning represents zeal; the fragrance signifies virtue; the rising smoke represents human prayer ascending to the throne of God. Incense is used at more solemn celebrations of the Mass, at the Benediction of the Blessed Sacrament and whenever our divine eucharistic Lord is exposed in a monstrance for public adoration.

Blessed ashes are used on Ash Wednesday to introduce Lent and are a reminder of the Jews and early Christians who performed penance in sackcloth and ashes. They remind us that man was originally made of dust and shall return to dust. The reception of ashes is an outward manifestation of one's intention to enter into the holy season of Lent, 40 days of special penance.

Penance should not be restricted to the 40 days of Lent. In fact, every Friday is a day of penance in the week, as Lent is a season of penance in the year.

In 1966 the National Conference of Catholic Bishops of the United States issued a *Pastoral Statement on Penitential Observance for the Liturgical Year*. They spoke as follows:

". . . We hope that the observance of Lent as the principal season of penance in the Christian year will be intensified. This is the more desirable because of new insights into the central place in Christian faith of those Easter mysteries for the understanding and enjoyment of which Lent is the ancient penitential preparation.

"Wherefore, we ask, urgently and prayerfully, that we, as people of God, make of the entire Lenten season a period of special penitential observance. Following the instructions of the Holy See, we declare that the obligation both to fast and to abstain from meat, an obligation observed under a more strict formality by our fathers in the faith, still binds on Ash Wednesday and Good Friday. No Catholic Christian will lightly excuse himself from so hallowed an obligation on the Wednesday which solemnly opens the Lenten season and on that Friday called 'Good' because on that day Christ suffered in the flesh and died for our sins.

"In keeping with the letter and spirit of Pope Paul's constitution 'Poenitemini,' we preserve for our dioceses the tradition of abstinence from meat on each of the Fridays of Lent, confident that no Catholic Christian will lightly hold himself excused from this penitential practice.

"For all other weekdays of Lent, we strongly recommend participation in daily Mass and a self-imposed observance of fasting. In the light of grave human needs which weigh on the Christian conscience in all seasons, we urge, particularly during Lent, generosity to local, national and world programs of sharing of all things needed to translate our duty to penance into a means of implementing the right of the poor to their part in our abundance. We also recommend spiritual studies, beginning with the Scriptures as well as the traditional Lenten Devotions (sermons, Stations of the Cross and the Rosary) and all the self-denial summed up in the Christian concept of 'mortification.'

"Let us witness to our love and imitation of Christ by special solicitude for the sick, the poor, the underprivileged, the imprisoned, the bedridden, the discouraged, the stranger, the lonely, and persons of other color, nationalities or backgrounds than our own. A catalogue of not merely suggested but required good works under these headings is provided by Our Blessed Lord himself in His description of the Last Judgment (Matthew 25:34-40). This salutary word of the Lord is necessary for all the year, but should be heeded with double care during Lent. . . .

". . . The Catholic bishops of the United States, far from downgrading the traditional penitential observance of Friday, and motivated precisely by the desire to give the spirit of penance greater vitality, especially on Fridays, the day that Jesus died, urge our Catholic people, henceforth, to be guided by the following norms:

"1. Friday itself remains a special day of penitential observance throughout the year, a time when those who seek perfection will be mindful of their personal sins and the sins of mankind which they are called upon to help expiate in union with Christ Crucified.

"2. Friday should be in each week something of what Lent is in the entire year. For this reason we urge all to prepare for that weekly Easter that comes with each Sunday by freely making of every Friday a day of self-denial and mortification in prayerful remembrance of the passion of Jesus Christ.

"3. Among the works of voluntary self-denial and personal penance which we especially commend to our people for the future observance of Friday, even though we hereby terminate the traditional law of abstinence binding under pain of sin, as the sole prescribed means of observing Friday, we give first place to abstinence from flesh meat. We do so in the hope that the Catholic community will ordinarily continue to abstain from meat by free choice as formerly we did in obedience to Church law. Our expectation is based on the following considerations:

"a. We shall thus freely and out of love for Christ Crucified show our solidarity with the generations of believers to whom this practice frequently became, especially in times of persecution and of great poverty, no mean evidence of fidelity to Christ and His Church.

"b. We shall thus also remind ourselves that as Christians, although immersed in the world and sharing its life, we must preserve a saving and necessary difference from the spirit of the world. Our deliberate, person-

298

al abstinence from meat, more especially because no longer required by law, will be an outward sign of inward spiritual values that we cherish. . . .

"In summary, let it not be said that by this action, implementing the spirit of renewal coming out of the Council, we have abolished Friday, repudiated the holy traditions of our fathers, or diminished the insistence of the Church on the fact of sin and the need for penance. Rather, let it be proved by the spirit in which we enter upon prayer and penance, not excluding fast and abstinence freely chosen, that these present decisions and recommendations of this Conference of Bishops will herald a new birth of loving faith and more profound penitential conversion, by both of which we become one with Christ, mature sons of God and servants of God's people."

What is to be noted in the bishops' remarks implementing the council and the pope's Constitution on Penance is that the call is for a more intensified life of penance, especially during Lent and the Fridays of the year, not less. While other forms of penance were permitted on the Fridays outside Lent, Friday may not be ignored as a day of penance, and the bishops continued to recommend abstinence from meat as having "first place." If abstinence from meat were not chosen on the Fridays outside of Lent, other forms of penance were to be practiced, but emphasis was on penance on *all* Fridays. The traditional law of abstinence, with its *serious* implications, held for the Fridays of Lent and for Ash Wednesday. Fasting was not excluded during Lent, simply the old legal aspects as regards fasting. Scripture recommends fasting as a form of penance. The bishops reminded Catholics of the "Church's constant recognition that all the faithful are required by divine law to do penance." Also, "as from the fact of sin we Christians can claim no exception, so from the obligation to penance we can seek no exemption."

Penance is the virtue or disposition of heart whereby a person repents of his own sins and is converted to God. *Reparation* is the act or fact of making amends or satisfaction. Reparation is an effort to restore things to their normal conditions as they were before an offense was committed. With respect to God, therefore, reparation means making up with acts of love for the failure in love through sin. It means restoring what was unjustly taken from God, namely, the glory, the adoration, that He deserves to receive in love from His children. Reparation can be made, not simply for one's own sins, but for the sins of others, indeed, for the sins of the world.

The greatest act of reparation is the Sacrifice of the Mass. Participating in Mass, not simply to fulfill an obligation on Sundays and holy days, but to make reparation for the injury done to God who loves us so much, is the most excellent form of reparation. This implies that our Holy Communions may be received in reparation for the sins committed against God, against His Mother, the angels and saints and our fellow-man. The doctrine of the Mystical Body of Christ reminds us why we may make reparation for the sins of others and thus draw from the spiritual treasury for others. While the Mass is the supreme form of reparation, since it perpetuates Calvary's sacrifice, anything we do that is not sin may be offered to God in reparatory love.

There is a *spiritual treasury of merits* which has been built up by Jesus Christ and the superabundant merits of the Blessed Virgin Mary and the saints. Whereas the merits of Jesus Christ are in themselves infinite, there are certain souls whose holy lives and whose acts of penance and reparation were more than sufficient for themselves. The Blessed Mother of God, of course, had no need of reparation for herself, being perfectly sinless. Great saints have lived the Christ-life so perfectly that they acquired from Christ superabundant merits which are applicable to other members of the Mystical Body.

Our prayers, good works, acts of reparation can benefit others. The Church, which has the keys of the kingdom of heaven, as given to St. Peter and his successors, can draw from the treasury of merits for its members. This the Church does in the case of granting indulgences.

"The taking away of the temporal punishment due to sins when their guilt has already been forgiven has been called specifically 'indulgence.'

"In fact, in granting indulgences, the Church . . . intervenes with its authority to dispense to the faithful, provided they have the right dispositions, the treasury of satisfaction which Christ and the saints won for the remission of temporal punishment" (Pope Paul VI, *Apostolic Constitution on the Revision of Indulgences*).

The very word indulgence comes from *indulgentia.* In the historical context of the Church's development of indulgences, the word meant *forbearance.* This forbearance means kindness in not exacting the full measure of what is due to God from the sinner, as with the man in the Gospel who was forgiven the heavy debt with the implicit understanding that he would remit the lesser amount that another man owed him. Likewise, we must understand indulgences as a work of reparation whereby the Church calls upon and draws from the spiritual resources (treasury of merits) of the whole Church.

The Church in granting an indulgence is drawing, then, not simply from the spiritual resources of the individual who has sinned and needs to make reparation, but from the entire Mystical Body. This, as already mentioned, means drawing from the treasury built up, essentially by Jesus Christ, but also from the superabundant merits of Mary and the saints whose prayers, good works, acts of penance and reparation more then compensated for themselves. In gaining an indulgence, the faithful, repentant of their sins, in addition to the remission of temporal punishment which their action merits, receive an equal remission through the intervention of the Church.

Gaining an indulgence otherwise has an effect on the soul similar to the purpose for which the priest gives a penance when one goes to confession. The sin is forgiven by the mercy of God but due to God's justice we must make satisfaction even for sin already forgiven. By the granting of indulgences the Church determines specific types of penances in the way of special prayers or good works we may do which have a special efficacy for the soul in making satisfaction to God.

To be capable of gaining an indulgence for oneself, one must be baptized, a member of the Church, in the state of grace at least at the completion of the prescribed works, and a subject of the one granting the indulgence. One must have at least a general intention to gain indulgences and perform the enjoined works at the time and in the manner prescribed. All indulgences, whether partial or plenary, can be applied to the faithful departed.

The Church designates indulgences only as plenary and partial. A former designation of years or days (which was commonly misunderstood as to meaning) has been done away with. A *plenary* indulgence remits temporal punishment entirely. A *partial* indulgence remits part of the temporal punishment due to forgiven sin. A plenary indulgence can be acquired only once in the course of a day.

According to Pope Paul VI January 1, 1967: "To acquire a plenary indulgence it is necessary to perform the work to which the indulgence is attached and to fulfill the following three conditions: sacramental confession, eucharistic Communion, and prayer for the intention of the Sovereign Pontiff. It is further required that all attachment to sin, even venial sin, be absent" (*Enchiridion of Indulgences*, 26).

Examples of practices, under the proper conditions, for the gaining of a *plenary* indulgence are: the pious exercise of the *Way of the Cross*; visiting devoutly the parochial church on the titular feasts; reciting the Rosary in a church or public oratory or in a family group. (The vocal recitation of the Rosary must be accompanied by pious meditation on the mysteries.)

Examples of practices by which the faithful may gain a *partial* indulgence: any invocation that complements any action by which the faithful raise their heart and mind with humble confidence to God in performing their duties or bearing the trials of life. Examples of invocations joined to such offerings (although they may come spontaneously from one's own disposition): May Jesus Christ be praised (or some similar customary Christian greeting) — Lord, I believe in you — I adore you — I place my trust in you — I love you — All for you, most Sacred Heart of Jesus — Thanks be to God — May God be blessed — Your kingdom come — Your will be done — As the Lord wills — My Jesus, mercy — Christ conquers! Christ reigns! Christ commands! — Most Sacred Heart of Jesus, have mercy on us — My God and my all — My Lord and my God — Jesus, Mary, Joseph — My Mother, my confidence — May the Most Blessed Sacrament be praised and adored everywhere — O Mary conceived without sin, pray for us who have recourse to you — Pray for us, O Holy Mother of God, that we may be made worthy of the promises of Christ, etc.

The Catholic Church, having keys to the spiritual treasury of Jesus Christ, in granting indulgences, places greater value on the action (*opus operantis*) of the faithful than on works of piety (*opus operatum*). The desire of the Church in granting indulgences is to move the faithful to live holier and more useful lives, thus healing "the dichotomy between the faith which many profess and the practice of their daily lives . . . by gathering their humane, domestic, professional, social and technical enterprises into one vital synthesis with religious values, under whose supreme direction all things are harmonized unto God's glory" (*Pastoral Constitution on the Church in the Modern World*, n. 43).

The Church desires Catholics, in striving to gain indulgences, not to look to the Church as some automatic dispenser of privileges but rather to lead the faithful to an authentic Christian way of living while cultivating the spirit of prayer and penance and to practice the theological virtues of faith, hope and charity.

In his apostolic constitution on indulgences, Pope Paul VI wrote as follows: "The doctrine of purgatory clearly demonstrates that even when the guilt of sin has been taken away, punishment for it or the consequences of it may remain to be expiated or cleansed. They often are. In fact, in purgatory the souls of those 'who died in the charity of God and truly repentant, but who had not made satisfaction with adequate penance for their sins and omissions,' are cleansed after death with punishments designed to purge away their debt. All this is gathered also from the prayers of the liturgy Christian people, admitted to holy communion, have addressed to God since very ancient times: 'May we who are justly punished for our sins be freed through your mercy and for the glory of your name.'

"All men who walk this earth commit at least venial and so-called daily sins (see James 3:2). All, therefore, need God's mercy to set them free from sin's penal consequences. . . (n. 3).

". . . The conviction was present in the Church that the pastors of the Lord's flock could set the individual free from the vestiges of sin by applying to him the merits of Christ and of the saints: In the course of the centuries and under the influence of the Holy Spirit's continuous inspiration of the People of God, this conviction led to the practice of indulgences. It was a progression in the Church's doctrine and discipline rather than a change. From the roots of Revelation something had grown up, a new privilege which was for the benefit of the faithful and the whole Church" (n. 7).

The previous chapter explained the importance of prayer and the practice of a rule of life, a balanced spiritual program. In addition to daily exercises of prayer in one's regular spiritual program, it is good occasionally to make retreats, days of recollection and spiritual renewal. Any balanced spiritual program must include regular Sunday Mass as well as holy days as a minimum and frequent participation in the sacraments of Confession and Holy Communion. It should be noted that what is required as a minimum is not considered a Christian ideal.

The Church lists certain specific duties expected of Catholic Christians which traditionally have been mentioned as the Precepts of the Church. Listed below are the duties outlined by the National Conference of Catholic Bishops.[3]

1. To keep holy the day of the Lord's Resurrection: to worship God by participating in Mass every Sunday and holy day of obligation:* to avoid those activities that would hinder renewal of soul and body, e.g., needless work and business activities, unnecessary shopping, etc.

2. To lead a sacramental life: to receive Holy Communion frequently and the Sacrament of Penance regularly:
— minimally, to receive the Sacrament of Penance at least once a year (annual confession is obligatory only if serious sin is involved);*
— minimally, to receive Holy Communion at least once a year, between the First Sunday of Lent and Trinity Sunday.*

3. To study Catholic teaching in preparation for the Sacrament of Confirmation, to be confirmed, and then to continue to study and advance the cause of Christ.

4. To observe the marriage laws of the Church:* to give religious training

---

[3]The seven points are taken from *Basic Teachings For Catholic Religious Education*, January 11, 1973.
*The traditional Precepts of the Church.

(by example and word) to one's children; to use parish schools and religious education programs.

5. To strengthen and support the Church:* one's own parish community and parish priests; the worldwide Church and the Holy Father.

6. To do penance, including abstaining from meat and fasting from food on the appointed days.*

7. To join the missionary spirit and apostolate of the Church.

DISCUSSION QUESTIONS

1. What are sacramentals?
Sacramentals are blessed objects or actions which the Church uses in imitation of the seven sacraments which were instituted by Jesus Christ. The Church itself instituted sacramentals, which have their efficacy from the prayers of the Church and the merits of the faithful. The sacramentals, therefore, do not have power within themselves.

2. Explain the Church's use of holy water.
Holy water is a sacramental of the Church, and those who use it call down upon themselves the prayers of the Church which were used in blessing it. Holy water is also a reminder of one's baptism and can serve as a renewal of one's baptismal promises.

3. What is the meaning of blessed ashes?
Blessed ashes are used on Ash Wednesday after the practice of ancient Jews and early Christians, symbolizing penance for one's sins. By receiving ashes publicly one gives public testimony of his intention to enter into 40 days of penance. It is also a reminder that our stay on earth is temporary, that we are on pilgrimage to heaven.

4. In their 1966 Pastoral on Penitential Observance, which gave new emphasis to penance after the Second Vatican Council, did the U.S. bishops call for less penance?
Neither the Holy See nor the American bishops called for less penance as a result of the Second Vatican Council. The Church's effort has been to purify and spiritualize the intentions of the faithful in performing penance in sorrow for sins and from love of God rather then simply for the purpose of obeying laws which bind one seriously. The bishops asked for intensified penance on Fridays and during Lent.

5. When are Catholics seriously required to abstain from meat and to fast?
Catholics are seriously required to abstain from meat on Ash Wednesday and the Fridays of Lent. This law obliges beginning at the age of 14. Fast laws, mean-

*The traditional Precepts of the Church.

ing one full meal and two lighter meals only, bind seriously on Ash Wednesday and Good Friday. The fast laws begin at the age of 21.

6. What did the bishops call for regarding the Fridays outside of Lent?

The Church sets aside every Friday of the year as a special day of penance, although it does not require abstinence from meat as the sole means of doing penance. The Church asks that we give "first place" to voluntary abstinence from meat on the Fridays of the entire year. Other forms of penance are also proper according to what is real penance for each individual.

7. Can some persons be entirely dispensed from all forms of penance?

No one can be entirely excluded from the divine law requiring penance, since all men are sinners.

8. What is reparation?

Reparation is the act or fact of making amends to God for sins committed against Him. Reparation repairs, that is, makes satisfaction to God for sins against His glory and the love and adoration which He deserves from His children. Sin is an insult to God. Reparation is an apology, as acts of love are performed to God's justice, repairing the harm done to His glory.

9. What is the greatest act of reparation one can offer to Almighty God?

The greatest possible act of reparation is the Sacrifice of the Mass, because its value is infinite since it perpetuates the Sacrifice of the Cross. While other acts of reparation are proper, especially as offered in union with the Holy Sacrifice of the Mass being offered throughout the world, the Mass is the perfect act of reparation in which we can join.

10. Explain the meaning of the spiritual treasury of merits.

The **treasury of merits** refers to the superabundance of merits earned by Jesus Christ and the saints, from which the Church can draw in granting indulgences. This **treasury of merits**, because there is a Communion of Saints, makes it possible for the faithful to do good works of spiritual benefit to others.

11. Define indulgences.

Indulgences are the remission of temporal punishment due to sins already forgiven through the intervention of the Church, to whom Jesus gave the power of the keys of heaven. It lessens in part or entirely removes the punishment we would otherwise have to endure in purgatory.

12. Explain how the effect of indulgences is similar to that of the penance given by the priest when one goes to confession.

The penance the priest gives us in confession has the same effect that the granting of indulgences has, the remission of temporal punishment due to forgiven sin.

13. Rather than viewing indulgences as simply privileges, what view does the Church desire that Catholics hold?

In striving to gain the indulgences, the Church desires that the faithful be led to a more authentic Christian way of living, while cultivating the spirit of prayer and penance, and the virtues of faith, hope and charity.

14. Does the value of the indulgences which the Church grants come from the efficacy alone of the faith and prescribed good work of the individual striving to gain indulgences?

The Church in granting indulgences is drawing not simply from the spiritual resources of the individual who has sinned and needs to make reparation, but from the merits of the good works of the entire Mystical Body. It is a practical application of the doctrine of the Communion of Saints whereby the faithful on earth, the souls in purgatory and the saints in heaven can help one another. All indulgences can be applied to the faithful departed. The faithful, who, repentant of their sins, perform an action to which a partial indulgence is attached, receive, in addition to the remission of temporal punishment which their action merits, an equal remission through the intervention of the Church.

15. What is the difference between partial and plenary indulgences?

A partial indulgence remits part of the temporal punishment due to forgiven sin while a plenary indulgence remits all.

16. What are the six traditional precepts of the Church binding upon Catholics?

The six traditional precepts of the Church binding upon Catholics are:

(1) To participate in the Sacrifice of the Mass on all Sundays holy days of obligation.
(2) To fast and abstain on the days appointed.
(3) To confess our sins at least once a year.
(4) To receive Holy Communion during the Eastertime (between the first Sunday of Lent and Trinity Sunday).
(5) To contribute to the support of the Church.
(6) To observe the laws of the Church concerning marriage.

CHAPTER 24

Becoming a Catholic

"Becoming a Catholic" could apply to those outside full union with the Catholic Church. The term also could apply to those already in some way identified with the Church but who are in need of growing more deeply into the faith and its practices. Not every practice of Catholics is essential to the faith, as we saw in the previous chapter. The Church has a multitude of sacramentals and devotions. Not all will appeal to everyone, nor are all desirable for each person. It would be as impossible as it would be imprudent to attempt practicing every devotion recognized by the Church as in harmony with the faith.

There are beliefs and practices, however, which are essential for anyone who desires to be an authentic Catholic. Catholics must accept all the dogmas of Catholic faith, that is, all formally revealed truths promulgated as such by the Church. They are revealed either in Sacred Scripture or Tradition. The dogmas of faith are revealed either *explicitly* — the Incarnation, that is God the Son or the Word made flesh — or *implicitly* — the dogmas of the Assumption and the Immaculate Conception.

In becoming a Catholic one must profess the faith which the Catholic, Apostolic Church teaches. One must believe that the Catholic Church is the one true Church, which Jesus Christ founded on earth and to which one must submit with all his heart. One must believe in those truths contained in the Apostles' Creed. Also, one must believe that seven sacraments were instituted by Jesus Christ for the salvation of mankind; namely, Baptism, Confirmation, Holy Eucharist, Penance, Anointing of the Sick, Holy Orders and Matrimony.

In making a profession of Catholic faith, one must believe that the pope, the bishop of Rome, is the vicar of Jesus Christ on earth; that he is the supreme visible head of the Church while Jesus Christ is the invisible head, and that the pope teaches infallibly in matters of faith and morals what we must believe and do to be saved.

One must believe everything that the holy, catholic, apostolic Church defines and declares we must believe. One must accept all the ecumenical councils of the Catholic Church. One must reject every error and schism that the Church rejects.

Having taken a course of Catholic instructions, to become a Catholic one must have faith that the Holy Eucharist is both *Sacrifice*, perpetuating the Sacrifice of the Cross in the Holy Mass, and *Sacrament*, containing the Body, Blood, Soul and Divinity of Jesus Christ. One must believe that the priest, through the Sacrament of Holy Orders, has the power to forgive sins. One must intend to participate in Mass each Sunday and holy day if possible, and intend to receive the sacraments of the Church worthily.

One is not ready to become a Catholic until he believes all that the Church believes and teaches. To deliberately reject what one knows is a dogma of Catholic faith is to place oneself outside the Catholic Church, or, if one has not yet joined, such rejection will keep one from honestly making a profession of Catholic faith.

Jesus did not command the apostles to teach part of what He had taught them, but *all*. He did not give His Church some of the authority He had received, with each one being free to pick and choose what to believe and what to do. Jesus rather gave His Church *full authority*. "All authority in heaven and on earth has been given to me. Go, therefore, make disciples of all the nations; baptize them in the name of the Father and of the Son and of the Holy Spirit, and teach them to observe all the commands I gave you. And know that I am with you always; yes, to the end of time" (Matthew 28:18-20).

The Church is identified with Jesus Christ as His Mystical Body. In placing oneself under the authority of the Catholic Church, therefore, one is placing oneself under the authority of Jesus Christ. To embrace the Church is to embrace Jesus Christ in the fullness of true faith. One who joins the Catholic Church, having been previously nourished in some other Christian community, rejects nothing that is good and true of the faith he possessed before. All is kept. In the Catholic Church, however, one comes to the *fullness* of true faith, with the fullness of the authority and powers of Jesus Christ as given to His Church, which Scripture calls repeatedly, "the body of Christ." If one possessed a beautiful bud of Christian faith before discovering Catholicism, he now discovers that that bud has come into full bloom.

While it is true that not all Catholics understand or live their faith fully, and membership in the Catholic Church is not assurance of automatic salvation since one must live the faith, responding in supernatural love, yet, the fullness of true faith is in the Catholic Church which Jesus Christ himself founded. He promised that the gates of hell would never prevail against it. While some who call themselves "Catholic" may obscure the true face of Catholicism, they cannot destroy the reality which Jesus himself promised to keep in the truth through the Holy Spirit unto the end of time. One who knows that the Catholic Church is the ancient Church which Jesus Christ founded, and that it possesses the fullness of true faith, has a serious obligation in conscience to join it and to live its teachings.

When there is still a reasonable doubt of a previous valid baptism, after a diligent investigation, one seeking membership in the Catholic Church is to be baptized conditionally. If validity of baptism in another community is certain, one makes a profession of faith according to the following rite of reception.

Priest: Name_____, *you have asked to be received into full communion with the Catholic Church. You have made your decision after careful thought and prayer under the guidance of the Holy Spirit. Now come forward with your sponsor and profess the Catholic faith in the presence of this community. This is the faith in which, for the first time, you will be one with us at the eucharistic table of the Lord Jesus, the sign of the Church's unity.*

The one to be received then recites the *Nicene Creed* with all present. It is the same creed which is recited at Mass each Sunday. The person being received into the Church then adds:

I believe and profess all that the Holy Catholic Church believes, teaches, and proclaims to be revealed by God.

The priest then lays his right hand upon the head of the one to be received and says:

Name_____ *the Lord receives you into the Catholic Church. His love has led you here so that, in the unity of the Holy Spirit, you may have full communion with us in the faith that you have professed in the presence of his family.*

If the person is to be confirmed,[1] the sponsor places his right hand upon the shoulder of the candidate. The priest dips his right thumb into the sacred chrism, makes the sign of the cross on the forehead of the one to be confirmed saying:

Be sealed with the gift of the Holy Spirit.

---

[1]If the one received into the Catholic Church has never been baptized and is baptized absolutely there is no need to make a confession before the Sacrament of Confirmation and First Holy Communion. However, if there is conditional baptism or only a profession of Catholic faith, the person must make a confession and receive absolution before receiving any of the sacraments in the Catholic Church.

*   *   *

PRAYERS TO BE MEMORIZED

The Sign of the Cross

In the name of the Father, and of the Son, and of the Holy Spirit. Amen.

The Lord's Prayer

Our Father, Who art in heaven, hallowed be Thy name, Thy kingdom come, Thy will be done on earth as it is in heaven. Give us this day our daily bread and forgive us our trespasses as we forgive those who trespass against us, and lead us not into temptation. But deliver us from evil. Amen.

The Hail Mary

Hail Mary, full of grace! The Lord is with thee: blessed art thou among women, and blessed is the fruit of thy womb, Jesus.
Holy Mary, Mother of God, pray for us sinners, now and at the hour of our death. Amen.

Glory Be

Glory be to the Father, and to the Son, and to the Holy Spirit. As it was in the beginning, is now, and ever shall be, world without end. Amen.

The Act of Contrition

O my God, I am heartily sorry for having offended You, and I detest all my sins, because of Your just punishments, but most of all because they offend You, my God, Who art all-good and deserving of all my love. I firmly resolve, with the help of Your grace, to sin no more and to avoid the near occasions of sin.

*   *   *

OTHER CATHOLIC PRAYERS

The Act of Faith

O My God, I firmly believe that You are one God in three Divine Persons, Father, Son and Holy Spirit; I believe that Your Divine Son became man and died for our sins, and that He will come to judge the living and the dead. I believe these and all the truths which the Holy Catholic Church teaches because You have revealed them, Who can neither deceive nor be deceived.

The Act of Hope

O My God, relying on Your infinite goodness and promises, I hope to obtain pardon of my sins, the help of Your grace, and life everlasting, through the merits of Jesus Christ, my Lord and Redeemer.

The Act of Love

O My God, I love You above all things, with my whole heart and soul, because You are all-good and worthy of all love. I love my neighbor as myself for the love of You, I forgive all who have injured me, and ask pardon of all whom I have injured.

The Apostles' Creed

I believe in God, the Father Almighty, Creator of heaven and earth; and in Jesus Christ, His only Son, our Lord; Who was conceived by the Holy Spirit, born of the Virgin Mary, suffered under Pontius Pilate, was crucified, died, and was buried. He descended into hell; the third day He arose again from the dead; He ascended into heaven, sits at the right hand of God, the Father Almighty; from thence He shall come to judge the living and the dead. I believe in the Holy Spirit, the Holy Catholic Church, the communion of saints, the forgiveness of sins, the resurrection of the body, and life everlasting. Amen.

The Confiteor

I confess to Almighty God, and to you my brothers and sisters, that I have sinned through my own fault, in my thoughts and in my words, in what I have done and in what I have failed to do. And I ask blessed Mary, ever virgin, all the angels and saints, and you my brothers and sisters, to pray for me to the Lord our God. May Almighty God have mercy on us, and forgive us our sins, and bring us to live everlasting. Amen.

The Hail Holy Queen

Hail Holy Queen, Mother of Mercy, our life, our sweetness and our hope! To you do we cry, poor banished children of Eve; to you do we send up our sighs, mourning and weeping in this valley of tears! Turn, then, most gracious Advocate, your eyes of mercy toward us, and after this, our exile, show unto us the blessed fruit of your womb, Jesus. O clement, O loving, O sweet Virgin Mary!

The Memorare

Remember, O most gracious Virgin Mary, that never was it known that anyone who fled to your protection, implored your help and sought your intercession was left unaided. Inspired by this confidence, I fly to you, O Virgin of virgins, my Mother. To you I come; before you I stand, sinful and sorrowful. O Mother of the Word Incarnate, despise not my petitions, but in your mercy hear and answer me. Amen.

The Grace before Meals

Bless us, O Lord, and these Thy gifts, which we are about to receive from Thy bounty, through Christ, Our Lord. Amen.

The Grace after Meals

We give Thee thanks, O Lord, for all Thy gifts which we have received from Thy bounty through Christ, Our Lord. Amen.

Morning Offering

O Jesus, through the Immaculate Heart of Mary, I offer You my prayers, works, joys, and sufferings of this day in union with the holy sacrifice of the Mass throughout the world. I offer them for all the intentions of Your Sacred Heart: the salvation of souls, reparation for sin, the reunion of all Christians; I offer them for the intentions of our bishops, and of all members of the apostleship of prayer, and in particular for those recommended by our holy father this month.

The Angelus

℣. The angel of the Lord declared unto Mary.
℞. And she conceived of the Holy Spirit. Hail Mary, etc.
℣. Behold the handmaid of the Lord.
℞. Be it done unto me according to thy word. Hail Mary, etc.
℣. And the Word was made flesh.
℞. And dwelt among us. Hail Mary, etc.
℣. Pray for us, O holy Mother of God.
℞. That we may be made worthy of the promises of Christ.
Let us pray:
Pour forth, we beseech Thee, O Lord, Thy grace into our hearts, that we to whom the incarnation of Christ, Thy Son, was made known by the message of an angel, may by His passion and cross be brought to the glory of His resurrection, through the same Christ our Lord. Amen.

Prayer to the Holy Spirit

Come, Holy Spirit, fill the hearts of Thy faithful and enkindle in them the fire of Thy love.

V. Send forth Thy Spirit and they shall be created.

R. And Thou shalt renew the face of the earth.

Let us pray:

O God, who didst instruct the hearts of the faithful by the light of the Holy Spirit, grant us in the same Spirit to be truly wise, and ever to rejoice in His consolation. Through Christ our Lord. Amen.

HOW TO SAY THE ROSARY

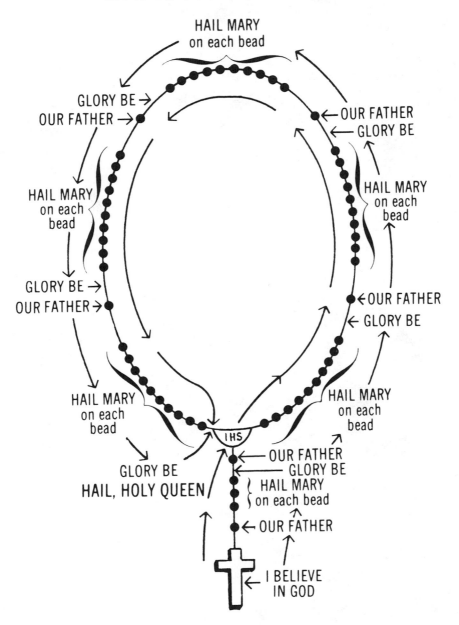

HAIL MARY
on each bead

GLORY BE →
OUR FATHER →

OUR FATHER ←
GLORY BE ←

HAIL MARY
on each
bead

HAIL MARY
on each
bead

GLORY BE →
OUR FATHER →

OUR FATHER ←
GLORY BE ←

HAIL MARY
on each
bead

HAIL MARY
on each
bead

IHS

OUR FATHER ←
GLORY BE ←
HAIL MARY
on each bead

GLORY BE
HAIL, HOLY QUEEN

OUR FATHER ←

I BELIEVE
IN GOD

About the Author

A pastor for 29 years in various parishes in South Dakota, Father Robert Joseph Fox is a columnist for the *National Catholic Register* and writes regularly for *Twin Circle*.

He has produced the television series "Sharing the Faith" (which inspired the writing of this book) for the Eternal Word Network.

Father Fox is founder-director of the Sons of the Immaculate Heart of Mary, a community dedicated to the formation of priests. National chaplain for the youth division of the World Apostolate of Fatima, he leads youth pilgrimages to Europe each summer.

Author of numerous articles in *Our Sunday Visitor*, *The Priest* and *Homiletic and Pastoral Review*, Father Fox has written some 20 books, including *Rediscovering Fatima* and *Charity, Morality, Sex and Young People*, as well as several popular prayer books.